Discourse and Power

Discourse and Power

Teun A. van Dijk

First published 2008 by
PALGRAVE MACMILLAN

Palgrave Macmillan in the UK is an imprint of Macmillan Publishers Limited, registered in England, company number 785998, of Houndmills, Basingstoke, Hampshire RG21 6XS.

Palgrave Macmillan in the US is a division of St Martin's Press LLC, 175 Fifth Avenue, New York, NY 10010.

Palgrave Macmillan is the global academic imprint of the above companies and has companies and representatives throughout the world.

Palgrave® and Macmillan® are registered trademarks in the United States, the United Kingdom, Europe and other countries.

ISBN-13: 978–0–230–57408–3 hardback
ISBN-10: 0–230–57408–4   hardback
ISBN-13: 978–0–230–57409–0 paperback
ISBN-10: 0–230–57409–2   paperback

This book is printed on paper suitable for recycling and made from fully managed and sustained forest sources. Logging, pulping and manufacturing processes are expected to conform to the environmental regulations of the country of origin.

A catalogue record for this book is available from the British Library.

A catalog record for this book is available from the Library of Congress.

Printed and bound in Great Britain by
CPI Antony Rowe, Chippenham and Eastbourne

Contents

Acknowledgements

The author and publisher wish to thank the following for permission to use copyright material:

John Benjamins Publishing Company, for 'Political Discourse and Political Cognition', in *Politics as Text and Talk: Analytical Approaches to Political Discourse*, ed. P. A. Chilton and C. Schäffner, pp. 204–36 (2002), and 'War Rhetoric of a Little Ally: Political Implicatures of Aznar's Legitimization of the War in Iraq', in *Journal of Language and Politics*, 4(1), pp. 65–92 (2005);

Cengage Learning Services Ltd, for 'Discourse, Power and Access', in *Texts and Practices: Readings in Critical Discourse Analysis*, ed. C. R. Caldas-Coulthard and M. Coulthard, pp. 84–104 (1996);

Sage Publications, Inc., for 'Discourse and the Denial of Racism', in *Discourse & Society*, 3, pp. 87–118 (1992), 'Discourse and Manipulation', in *Discourse & Society*, 17(2), pp. 359–83 (2006), and 'Structures of Discourse and Structures of Power', in *Communication Yearbook 12*, ed. J. A. Anderson, pp. 18–59 (1989);

Wiley-Blackwell Publishing Ltd, for 'Critical Discourse Analysis', in *Handbook of Discourse Analysis*, ed. D. Schiffrin, D. Tannen and H. Hamilton, pp. 352–71 (2001), and 'Discourse and Racism', in *The Blackwell Companion to Racial and Ethnic Studies*, ed. D. Goldberg and J. Solomis, pp. 145–59.

Every effort has been made to trace the copyright holders but, if any have been inadvertently overlooked, the author and publisher will be pleased to make the necessary arrangements at the first opportunity.

I am indebted to Carmen Rosa-Caldas, Michelle Lazar and Theo van Leeuwen for their critical reading, corrections and suggestions for Chapter 1.

Preface

This book is about two fundamental phenomena in society: *discourse* and *power*. These are also two of the basic notions of Critical Discourse Studies (CDS), an academic movement that has quickly spread in linguistics and the social sciences since its first book publication in 1979, namely, *Language and Control* by Roger Fowler, Bob Hodge, Gunther Kress and Tony Trew, a team that advocated what they called 'critical linguistics'. Similar movements have inspired other disciplines, such as psychology, sociology and anthropology, all fundamentally interested in how power and especially power abuse are *reproduced* in society. Similarly, discourse analysts in the humanities and social sciences have specifically been interested in how *discourse* is involved in this process. They have shown that many forms of social inequality, such as those based on gender, class and race, are construed, perpetuated and legitimated by text and talk, and especially by the forms of public discourse controlled by the *symbolic elites*: politicians, journalists, scholars, writers and bureaucrats.

The chapters in this book examine these forms of the discursive reproduction of elite power more closely. They focus not just on power in society, more generally, but rather on power *abuse*, that is on *domination*, and more specifically, on the *illegitimate* uses of group and elite power that leads to social *inequality* and *injustice*.

Together with my other work, such as my research on ideology, context and knowledge, this study of power and domination is intended as a contribution to Critical Discourse Studies and its conceptual foundations as a movement. CDS scholars have formulated many different aims over the last 30 years, but generally agree on the goal to study how power abuse is being reproduced by discourse. However, as soon as we focus on notions such as 'abuse', we then need to reflect on such fundamental concepts as 'legitimacy' as a criterion for the very enterprise of doing critical research in the first place: if we have the pretension to criticize dominant elite discourse and its authors and organizations, we need to be quite clear why and how such discourse is illegitimate, why and how it violates fundamental norms and values of society.

Besides more general and conceptual discussions, the chapters in this book also report on concrete research results. As has been the case for my other books in CDS, several of these chapters deal with the fundamental social problem of *racism* – one of the most serious forms of social domination and inequality in 'western' societies. There are many personal, social and political reasons for this choice. But perhaps the major one is that few social problems of European and Europeanized societies have been as consistently ignored, mitigated and denied as racism. Indeed, as I have also shown in other work, there is no property more characteristic of elite racism than its denial. As all readers of this book can easily verify in their own daily lives, this means that in *our* parliamentary debates, in *our* mass media, in *our* textbooks or in *our* social sciences, there is today enormous interest in immigrants and minorities – often emphasizing the problems *they* have or cause – but comparatively little interest for and analysis of the problems *we* cause with our racism. One of the major aims of this book is to further document that thesis, a thesis very well known among ethnic minorities or immigrants themselves, by whom 'white' racism, discrimination and prejudice are consistently mentioned as one of the major problems they face in their everyday lives. So, we'll examine news in the press, parliamentary debates, textbooks as well as everyday conversations inspired by such elite discourses, in order to detect how racism is discursively construed, confirmed and propagated in western societies.

As Fowler and his team in 1979 already showed, the crucial theoretical notion of power and domination is 'control'. Applied to discourse this means that we must ask who has access to the fundamental power resource of public discourse, who has access to political discourse, to media discourse, educational discourse and scholarly discourse. Who is able to control production of such discourse, as is the case for press conferences and press releases and other ways of influencing journalists and media? Because once you control part of the production of public discourse, you also control part of its contents, and hence, indirectly, the public mind – maybe not exactly what people will think, but at least what they will think *about*. What we find is that while 'white' elites control such public discourses and their production, ethnic minorities and immigrants have virtually no access and hence their views and opinions seldom reach the press and public opinion. They are mostly only talked *about*, and usually negatively, as is also the case for poor people, or any other outgroup or part of the world. We have seen that the same is true for political discourse, textbooks and scholarship. Hence, power is related to control, and control of discourse means preferential access to its production and hence to its contents and style, and finally to the public mind.

Besides mass media discourse, the chapters of this book will focus especially on political discourse. I shall do so more concretely through an analysis of racist political discourse, but also in more general terms, for instance by exploring another dimension of my research, namely *social cognition*. With others I argue that racism is not prejudice of individual bigots but socially shared cognitive representations of groups, that is, attitudes and ideologies, and that these are the basis of racist social practices such as biased discourse and other forms of discrimination.

I show that Critical Discourse Studies should be practised within a multidisciplinary perspective that combines (at least) the following three dimensions: Discourse, Cognition and Society – and when possible also a Historical and a Cultural dimension, which I shall not deal with here, however. It is demonstrated that the reproduction of political power, political systems and political groups needs various genres of political discourse, and that such discourse again needs to be produced and understood in terms of various kinds of political cognition, such as ideologies. More generally, it is being repeated here, as well as elsewhere in my work, that cognition is the interface between discourse and society. We do not understand how social situations or social structures impinge on text and talk if we do not understand how people understand and represent such social conditions in terms of special mental models: context models. The same is true for the 'effects' of discourse on people – an influence that must be described in terms of people's mental representations (for a detailed statement of my theory of context models, see my two new multidisciplinary books on context, *Context and Discourse* and *Society and Discourse: How Social Contexts Influence Text and Talk* (2008).

Besides the empirical studies on racism, this book at the same time develops and applies new theory on the relations between discourse, cognition and society. The relations between power and discourse can only be fully understood when they are being articulated in such a broader multidisciplinary framework. I emphasize this point, because both in Critical Discourse Studies, as well as in the social sciences more generally today, a 'cognitive' dimension is not very popular.

Finally, many of the notions dealt with here, such as power, access, context and cognition, are finally applied in critical studies of parliamentary discourse about Iraq – one of the most pervasive topics of public debate of recent years. Such a study also gives rise to the examination of another major notion of CDS, namely *manipulation*. Again, what is involved here are powerful groups and organizations and the ways they control public discourse, especially that of public policy and the media, and the mind of the citizens. After such a more theoretical analysis of manipulation, I show how Tony Blair manipulates the British Parliament into accepting his motion to go to war in Iraq.

Similarly, I show how José María Aznar, in the Spanish Cortes, defends his policy to support President George W. Bush and the US-led invasion of Iraq. Going beyond the usual analysis of political discourse in terms of preferred topics, style, rhetoric or argumentation, I focus on how such discourse has an important, less obvious property, namely that of *political implicatures*, that is, implications derived not so much from discourse itself, but based on the (usually implicit) contexts as the participants construct and understand them. Similarly, such a 'contextual' analysis is able to focus also on other aspects that are not always manifest in discourse: *lies*. Through an analysis of the contextual management of knowledge, we'll see that such a study is able to contribute to our insights into political discourse in general, and into the parliamentary debates about Iraq in particular.

Through these theoretical analyses of some of the basic notions of the social sciences in general, and of CDS in particular, as well as through the case studies in which these notions are applied, I hope these chapters will contribute to the advancement of critical scholarship in general.

Except for the Introduction and the last chapter, the chapters in this book have appeared before in several journals and books. However, in order to have them together as one coherent statement about the foundations of CDS, I thought it would be useful to collect this work in one volume, especially also for those who do not have easy access to journal articles. In order to maintain the original versions of the articles, any changes have been limited to the correction of typographical errors and minor stylistic changes. There will inevitably be some overlap of theory fragments between chapters, although these will always been formulated in a different way. The advantage of having the complete articles here is that they can be read individually and in any order.

The book can be used in classes in many of the social sciences, such as linguistics, discourse analysis, political science, sociology, ethnic studies, communication and social psychology.

As usual, although I develop rather complex theoretical frameworks, I have done my best to do so in an accessible style, so that the book can be read by students of all the humanities and the social sciences. As shown above, access is fundamental, especially in scholarship, and even more so in CDS, so that we should be very much aware that our writings, even on complex social issues, are always as accessible as possible for as many people as possible.

This book will also appear in a Spanish version (to be published by

Gedisa, Barcelona), a Portuguese version (to be published by Contexto, São Paulo), and an Arabic version (in preparation).

As always, the readers are welcome to send their comments and criticism to me by e-mail (vandijk@disourses.org) and are invited to visit my website for many other resources, papers, bibliographies and a list of my other publications (www.discourses.org).

Barcelona   Teun A. van Dijk

1

Introduction: Discourse and Domination

If we define Critical Discourse Studies (CDS) as a scholarly movement specifically interested in theory formation and critical analysis of the discursive reproduction of power abuse and social inequality, a detailed examination of the concept of power is a central task of CDS. Yet, as is the case for many fundamental notions of the social sciences, the notion of power is as complex as it is fuzzy. Not surprisingly, a vast number of books and articles have been dedicated to the analysis of this central concept in many disciplines. It is therefore imperative that I focus on those dimensions of power that are directly relevant to the study of language use, discourse and communication.

However, my object of study, namely the 'discursive reproduction of power abuse and social inequality', is hardly an unproblematic notion itself, and hence also in need of detailed theoretical analysis. For example, how do a specific intonation, a pronoun, a headline, a topic, a lexical item, a metaphor, a colour or a camera angle, among a host of other semiotic properties of discourse, relate to something as abstract and general as power relations in society? That is, we somehow need to relate typical micro-level properties of text, talk, interaction and semiotic practices to typical macro-level aspects of society such as groups or organizations and their relationships of domination.

Moreover, CDS is not merely interested in any kind of power but it specifically focuses on *abuse* of power, in other words, on forms of domination that result in social inequality and injustice. Such a normative notion (abuse is *bad*) requires analysis in terms of other normative notions and criteria of the social sciences, such as legitimacy, which in turn presuppose an applied ethics and moral philosophy. Thus, in this book I often deal with the discursive reproduction of racism, and a critical analysis of such discursive

1

practices presupposes that, at least from *my* point of view, racism is wrong because racist practices are inconsistent with norms of social equality.

The general aim of CDS to study discursive power abuse also involves differential access to social power, and I shall therefore pay special attention below to different kinds of access to public discourse as one of the resources of social power.

In other words, we see that many CDS concepts need to be formulated in terms of very fundamental notions of the social sciences. In this book, I try to contribute to this debate about the foundations of CDS by developing theoretical notions and applying these to concrete examples of critical analysis. In this Introduction, I present these different contributions within a coherent theoretical framework.

Critical Discourse Studies

Before presenting the theoretical framework for the study of the discursive reproduction of power abuse, I first need to make the case for the critical study of discourse in more general terms.

Although the label *Critical Discourse Analysis* (*CDA*) has now generally been adopted, I would like to propose to change it to *Critical Discourse Studies* (*CDS*) for a number of obvious reasons. The main reason is that CDS is *not*, as is very often assumed, especially in the social sciences, a *method* of discourse *analysis*. There is no such method. CDS uses any method that is relevant to the aims of its research projects and such methods are largely those used in discourse studies generally.

Indeed, and for the same reason, *discourse analysis* itself is not a *method* but rather a domain of scholarly practice, a cross-discipline distributed over all the humanities and social sciences. For the same reason, I prefer to use the label *Discourse Studies* (*DS*) for that discipline.

Methods of (Critical) Discourse Studies

Both within Discourse Studies generally, and within CDS in particular, we find the usual interplay of theory, methods of observation, description or analysis, and their applications. So, there is no more 'a' (one) discourse analysis, as a method, than there is a social analysis or a cognitive analysis. Both DS and CDS have many different methods of study, depending on the aims of the investigation, the nature of the data studied, the interests and the qualifications of the researcher and other parameters of the research context. Thus, in both fields we may find such ways of studying the structures and strategies of text and talk as:

- grammatical (phonological, syntactic, lexical, semantic) analysis;
- pragmatic analysis of speech acts and communicative acts;
- rhetorical analysis;
- stylistics;
- the analysis of specific (genre, etc.) structures: stories, news reports, parliamentary debates, lectures, advertisements, etc.;
- conversation analysis of talk in interaction;
- semiotic analysis of sounds, images and other multimodal properties of discourse and interaction.

These different types of analysis (observation, description, etc.) may combine and overlap in many ways, so that an investigation may focus on the semantics of narrative, the rhetoric of political discourse, the pragmatics of conversation, or the semiotics of style. Within each type of research there are again many alternatives (sometimes also described as 'methods' or 'approaches'), such as formal analysis or functional analysis, which themselves may be quite different in the many theories, schools or 'sects' in each scholarly discipline. Most of the time such analyses will be qualitative descriptions of the details of discourse structure but depending on the data such descriptions may be quantified, as is increasingly the case in corpus linguistics, which provides new methods for CDS research.

Despite all these differences, we may nevertheless call these approaches *ways* of doing discourse *analysis* or *description*. Although it is not so common to speak of 'methods' in this case, in the traditional sense, there is no serious problem in describing these 'ways of analysis' in terms of 'methods'.

Besides these different analytical approaches, research in discourse studies has recourse to the usual methods of the social sciences, such as:

- participant observation;
- ethnographic methods;
- experiments.

Discourse is not only analysed as an autonomous 'verbal' object but also as situated interaction, as a social practice, or as a type of communication in a social, cultural, historical or political situation. Instead of analysing a conversation among neighbours, we may, for example, have to do fieldwork in a neighbourhood, observe how people talk in cafés or other public places, and describe many other relevant aspects of these communicative events, such as temporal or spatial settings, special circumstances, the participants and their communicative and social roles and the various other activities being accomplished at the same time.

Whereas these different forms of observation and analysis are quite typical of the social sciences, many types of psychology may engage in controlled laboratory or field experiments in order to test specific hypotheses. There is a vast amount of research on the many mental parameters that influence discourse production and comprehension, and often we are only able to know what these are, and how they operate, by examining in an experiment how special experimental conditions (circumstances, data, tasks, etc.) have special consequences for the way we talk or understand discourse.

In sum, both discourse studies and critical discourse studies make use of a vast amount of methods of observation, analysis and other strategies to collect, examine or evaluate data, to test hypotheses, to develop theory and to acquire knowledge.

Special analytical focus in CDS

It is important to notice, however, that despite this methodological pluralism there are preferences and tendencies, given the special focus in CDS on aspects of power abuse and hence more generally on the social conditions and consequences of text and talk. First of all, CDS research generally prefers methods that in no way infringe upon the rights of the people it studies, and that are consistent with the interests of the social groups in whose interests it engages in research in the first place. In other words, CDS methods are chosen so as to contribute to the social empowerment of dominated groups, especially in the domain of discourse and communication.

Secondly, CDS methods specifically focus on the complex relations between social structure and discourse structure, and how discourse structures may vary or be influenced by social structure. For instance, certain syntactic structures of sentences are obligatory (such as articles preceding nouns in English), independent of the social situation of discourse, and hence will not directly vary as a function of the power of the speaker. Whether you are on the Left or on the Right, the grammar of the language is the same for everyone. In other words, power abuse can only manifest itself in language use where there is the possibility of variation or choice, such as calling the same person a terrorist or a freedom fighter, depending on your position and ideology. Similarly, news reports in the press always have headlines, whether or not they play a role in the reproduction of ethnic prejudices. So, it is rather the form and meaning of a headline than the structural property of a headline itself that may be related to the social situation. Although such a perspective is generally correct, there are cases where structures of domination not only influence options or variations of language use or discourse, but whole semiotic or discursive systems, genres and other social practices.

We may conclude that CDS will generally focus on those systems and structures of talk or text that may depend on or vary as a function of relevant social conditions of language use, or that may contribute to specific social consequences of discourse, such as influencing the social beliefs and actions of the recipients. More specifically, CDS prefers to focus on those properties of discourse that are most typically associated with the expression, confirmation, reproduction or challenge of the social power of the speaker(s) or writer(s) as members of dominant groups.

Such properties may range from special intonation or visual and auditory properties (colour, typography, image configurations, music), to syntactic structures (such as actives and passives), lexical selection, the semantics of presuppositions or person descriptions, rhetorical figures or argumentative structures, on the one hand, to the selection of specific speech acts, politeness moves or conversational strategies, on the other hand.

Racist discourse, and more generally ideological discourse of ingroup members, for instance, typically emphasize, in many discursive ways, the positive characteristics of Our own group and its members, and the (purported) negative characteristics of Others, the Outgroup. Authors may do so by selecting special topics, the size or the colour of headlines, the use of photographs or cartoons, by gestures or by choosing special lexical items or metaphors, by arguments (and fallacies), storytelling, and so on. We see that one general strategy involved in the discursive reproduction of (for instance, racist or sexist) domination, namely ingroup–outgroup polarization (ingroup praise vs. outgroup derogation) may be realized in many ways and at many levels of discourse.

In such an analysis, polarized discourse structures play a crucial role in the expression, construction, confirmation and hence the reproduction of social inequality. Note though that such a relation between discourse structures and social structures is not a simple correlational or causal relationship. Rather, we have to take into consideration a very complex sociocognitive process, involving for instance the mental models or other cognitive representations of the participants. We also have to take into account how these are influenced by discourse structures, on the one hand, and influence interaction (and hence future discourse), on the other hand.

General aims of CDS

Despite the large diversity of methods being used in CDS, it has some quite general aims most scholars in the field agree on. I already formulated one of these aims above, namely *the study of the discursive reproduction of power abuse*. In other words, CDS is specifically interested in the (critical) study of social issues, problems, social inequality, domination and related phenomena, in general, and the role of discourse, language use or communication in such phenomena, in particular. We may call this the special *domain* of CDS: specific social phenomena, specific problems and specific themes of research.

However, this is not all. The notion 'critical' also needs to be made more explicit. Studying social issues or problems is a normal task of the social sciences, but such mainstream studies are not inherently 'critical'. In other words, there is in CDS a normative aspect involved, a perspective, an attitude, a special way of doing socially relevant research.

It is not easy to define the precise properties of such a critical perspective or attitude, and the following is neither fully explicit nor exhaustive. Discourse Studies more specifically may be defined as 'critical' if they satisfy one or several of the following criteria, where 'domination' means 'abuse of social power by a social group':

- relations of domination are studied primarily from the perspective of, and in the interest of the dominated group;
- the experiences of (members of) dominated groups are also used as evidence to evaluate dominant discourse;
- it can be shown that the discursive actions of the dominant group are illegitimate;
- viable alternatives to the dominant discourses can be formulated that are consistent with the interests of the dominated groups.

These points clearly imply that scholars in CDS are not 'neutral', but commit themselves to an engagement in favour of dominated groups in society. They take position, and do so explicitly. Whereas much 'neutral' social research may well have an implicit social, political or ideological position (or, indeed, deny taking such a position, which obviously is also taking position), scholars in CDS recognize and reflect about their own research commitments and position in society. They are not only scientifically aware of their choice of topics and priorities of research, theories, methods or data, but also sociopolitically so. They do not merely study social problems or forms of inequality because these are 'interesting' things to study, but explicitly also with the aim of contributing to specific social change in favour of the dominated groups. They self-critically examine whether the results of their research might benefit the dominant position of powerful groups in society. In addition to taking the perspective of dominated groups, CDS scholars may also attempt to influence and cooperate with crucial 'change agents' or 'dissidents' of dominant groups.

There has been a great deal of debate about whether sociopolitically committed scholarly research is at all 'scientific'. Accusations of 'bias' against critical research are routine occurrences, and themselves in need of critical analysis – if only because *not* committing oneself politically is also a political choice. However, as critical scholars we should take all serious criticism seriously. It is crucial to emphasize that a critical and socially committed perspective does not imply less rigorous research. None of what has just been described about critical research in the social sciences implies that the theories and methods of CDS should be less scientific.

On the contrary, CDS scholars are aware that discourse studies of social problems that may effectively benefit dominated groups and that may contribute to the abandonment or change of illegitimate discursive practices of the symbolic elites usually require research programmes, theories and methods that are complex and multidisciplinary. It is one thing to formally study, for instance, pronouns, argumentation structures or the moves of conversational interaction, and quite another to do so, equally rigorously, as part of a much more complex research programme that shows how such structures may contribute to the reproduction of racism or sexism in society.

As we have seen above, this will often mean relating discourse structures to cognitive structures on the one hand and social structures on the other. This requires multidisciplinary theories and methods.

In other words, CDS specifically deals with complex social problems, for which it needs to apply or to develop complex theories and methods from several disciplines, and at the same time, it must satisfy the social criteria mentioned above – such as being relevant for dominated groups. This means that, on the whole, the criteria for CDS research are often more demanding than those for other forms of discourse studies.

Notice also that we are *not* saying that all discourse studies should be *critical* studies, only that critical studies are not less scientific because they are critical. Critical studies should be theoretically and methodologically adequate because otherwise they would be unable to contribute to their sociopolitical goals. In sum, bad discourse analysis, also in CDS, does not meet the very high criteria of CDS, namely to be able to contribute to social change.

CDS scholars may well engage in theory development that as yet does not have direct applications, but that may contribute to improve the foundations of CDS research. If CDS scholars are especially interested in the general topic of the discursive reproduction of power abuse in society, they may have to examine, also in more general terms, the relation between discourse and power, or what makes power abuse illegitimate.

It should also be stressed here that despite its general aims and principles of critical social research, CDS is not a homogeneous movement – as is true for any social movement. Thus, I have chosen to focus CDS on power abuse, that is, on domination, and on its consequences: social inequality, and how these are reproduced by discourse. However, one may opt for a broader aim, and include the study of power and the relations between power and discourse, more generally – as is also the case in many chapters in this book. Similarly, we may also count as one of the aims of CDS the study of the relations between discourse and society. No doubt a study of the relations between discourse and power, or between discourse and society more generally, are at the basis of CDS, and presupposed by its more specific research projects. However, I prefer to formulate more specific aims for CDS, because otherwise CDS would collapse with or even include sociolinguistics, the sociology of language, linguistic anthropology, political science and related (sub)disciplines, with which CDS is obviously related. The reason for my decision to focus on the normative notions of power *abuse* and *social inequality* resides in the rationale of *critical* research. Such research critically analyses what according to specific social norms and values is *wrong, illegitimate, misguided* or *bad*. We do not pretend to be able to study all social and political relations of power in society, but focus on illegitimate power and want to know how and why such power, and specifically its discursive dimension, is illegitimate. We want to examine the many ways in which discourse may be abused, for instance by a systematic study of (and distinction between) discursive manipulation, misinformation, lies, slurs, propaganda and other forms of discourse that are aimed at illegitimately managing the minds and controlling the actions of people with respect to the reproduction of power. I shall summarize this complex aim with the two notions of *discourse* and *domination*. This is already a vast task, a task which I hold to be the core task of CDS. As we shall see below and in the rest of this book, this means that we need to borrow or develop theoretical instruments of a more general nature, such as those of power, social structure, social groups, ideology, context and other general notions involved in the study of discursive domination.

Discourse and the Reproduction of Social Power

It is within such a broader perspective of the aims and foundations of Critical Discourse Studies that I examine the complex relations between discourse and power.

Although there are many concepts of power in philosophy and the social sciences, in this book I essentially define *social* power in terms of *control*, that is, of control of one group over other groups and their members. Traditionally, control is defined as control over the actions of others. If such control is also in the interest of those who exercise such power, and against the interest of those who are controlled, we may speak of power *abuse*. If the actions involved are communicative actions, that is, discourse, we more specifically deal with control over the discourse of others, which is one of the obvious ways discourse and power are related: people are no longer free to speak or write when, where, to whom, about what or how they want, but are partly or wholly controlled by powerful others, such as the state, the police, the mass media or a business corporation interested in suppressing the freedom of (typically critical) text and talk. Or conversely, they must speak or write as they are told to do.

Such control is pervasive in society. Few people have the total freedom to say and write what they want, where and when they want and to whom they want. There are social constraints of laws (e.g., against slander or racist propaganda) or of norms of appropriateness. And most people have jobs in which they are required to produce specific kinds of talk or text. In that respect, discourse control seems to be the rule, rather than the exception. To investigate the abuse of such discourse control, thus, we need to formulate specific conditions, such as specific violations of human or social rights, to be discussed below.

Control does not only apply to discourse as social practice, but also to the minds of those who are being controlled, that is, their knowledge, opinions, attitudes, ideologies as well as other personal or social representations. In general, mind control is indirect, an intended but only possible or probable consequence of discourse. Those who control discourse may indirectly control the minds of people. And since people's actions are controlled by their minds (knowledge, attitudes, ideologies, norms, values), mind control also means indirect action control. Such controlled action may again be discursive, so that powerful discourse may, indirectly, influence other discourses that may be in the interest of those in power. With this summary we account for the fundamental process of the reproduction of power through discourse. Let me examine this process somewhat closer.

Context control: access

If discourse controls minds, and minds control action, it is crucial for those in power to control discourse in the first place. How do they do so? If communicative events not only consist of 'verbal' text and talk but also of a context that influences discourse, then the first step of discourse control is to control its contexts. For instance, powerful elites or organizations may decide who may participate in some communicative event, when, where and with what goals.

This means that we need to examine in detail the ways *access* to discourse is being regulated by those in power, as it is typically the case for one of the most influential forms of public discourse, namely that of the mass media: who has access to the (production of) news or programmes, and who controls such access? Who is capable of organizing press conferences that will be attended by many journalists? Whose press releases are being read and used? Who is being interviewed and cited? Whose actions are defined as news? Whose opinion articles or letters to the editor are being published? Who may participate in a television show? And more generally: whose definition of the social or political situation is accepted and taken seriously?

In all these cases we are talking about *active* access, that is, participation in control of the contents and forms of the media, and not about the more or less 'passive' access of consumers (even when these consumers may actively resist media messages through dispreferred interpretations). Also, it should be emphasized that enhanced, global access to powerful media may mean the obliteration of small, alternative media that have fewer financial and technological resources. In other words, the very notion of access needs to be further analysed because it has many dimensions. In this book, I shall only deal with access as a form of active contribution to, or participation in, the production of public discourse – for instance the ways organizations or citizens have access to journalists and are able to influence media coverage.

Discourse control

Once it is established how such parameters of the context and the production of discourse are controlled, we may investigate how structures of discourse itself are being controlled: *What* (from global topics to local meanings) can or should be said, and *How* this can or should be formulated (with which words, more or less detailed, precise, in which sentence form, in which order, more or less foregrounded, etc.)? And which speech acts or other communicative acts must or may be accomplished by such discourse meanings and forms, and how are such acts organized in social interaction?

Mind control

For each phase of the reproduction process we need detailed and sophisticated social, cognitive and discursive analysis. Many of the relationships just mentioned are as yet barely understood. We are beginning to understand how discourse is being understood, but much less about how such understanding leads to various forms of 'changes of mind': learning, persuasion, manipulation or indoctrination. 'Mind control' involves much more than just understanding text or talk, but also personal and social knowledge, previous experiences, personal opinions and social attitudes, ideologies and norms or values, among other factors that play a role in changing one's mind.

Once we have insight into such complex cognitive representations and processes, we might be able to show, for instance, how racist reporting about immigrants can lead to the formation or confirmation of prejudices and stereotypes, which in turn can lead to – or be controlled by the formation of – racist ideologies, which themselves can be used to produce new racist text or talk in other contexts, which finally can contribute to the discursive reproduction of racism. We understand much of this today in very general terms but, again, the details of such processes of discursive influences on the minds or people are barely understood.

The study of media influence in terms of 'mind control' should take place within a broader sociocognitive framework that relates the complex structures of today's (new) media landscape to the uses of these media, and finally the many complex ways such uses may influence the minds of people. True, 'mass' media have given way to an enormous diversity of alternative media, special 'niche' media, and especially the vast possibilities of internet, cell phones and their more individual uses of news, entertainment and other 'content'. Readers and viewers may have become more critical and independent. Yet, it remains to be seen, and needs much more critical analysis, whether such diversity of technologies, media, messages and opinions also means that citizens are better informed and able to resist the sophisticated manipulation by messages that seemingly address them more personally – but that might well implement dominant ideologies that have not changed much. The illusion of freedom and diversity may be one of the best ways to produce the ideological hegemony that will be in the interest of the dominant powers in society, not least of the companies that produce the very technologies and media contents that produce such an illusion.

Discourse Analysis as Social Analysis

Similar theoretical and empirical problems characterize the definition of powerful groups or organizations; in other words, the very origin of the cycle of the discursive reproduction of power. What characteristics do groups of people need to have in order to be described as powerful? This may intuitively be clear for governments, parliaments, state agencies, the police, the mass media, the military and big business corporations, and it may be for some professionals such as doctors or professors, or some social roles, such as parents. But although this may be the case for the mass media as organizations and enterprises, does this also imply that individual reporters are powerful? Most of them will probably deny such an assertion, even if they do realize that they have the power to influence the minds of hundreds of thousands, if not millions. Power in this sense should not be defined as the power of a person, but rather as that of a social position and as being organized as a constituent part of the power of an organization. Therefore, we need to engage in much more sophisticated social analysis so as to pinpoint who controls public discourse, and how.

Similar examples may be given for another major field of 'symbolic power', namely education. We know that teachers and textbooks influence the minds of students, and we can hardly deny that we expect them to do so if we want our children to *learn* something. But it is very difficult to distinguish between learning that really serves the students in their present and future lives, on the one hand, and the indoctrination of ideologies of powerful groups or organizations in society, or the prevention of students developing their critical potential, on the other hand. Still, one would hardly focus on and blame one teacher or one prejudiced passage in a textbook because the form of influence may be much more diffuse, complex, global, contradictory, systematic and barely noticed by all involved: indeed, from the Ministry of Education issuing a curriculum, from the authors, teams and publishers who produce textbooks or the teacher committees that approve them, finally to the teachers that teach them, all may be convinced that what these textbooks teach is good for the kids.

These examples may be multiplied for all domains of society, that is, for politics, the law, health care, the bureaucracies and state agencies and corporate business, and from top to bottom, from the leading elites to those who execute the policies, the guidelines and the plans decided above.

Again: power and access

In sum, when we 'do' discourse analysis as social analysis we become involved in vastly complex structures of organization, control and power, of which public texts and talk may only be one of many other social practices to be scrutinized. Moreover, such a critical study of complex and powerful organizations has its own methodological problems, for instance serious limitations of access. For instance, we can critically analyse a public news report or an editorial, a textbook or classroom interaction, the propaganda of a party, or the advertising of a company, but seldom have access to the kind of discursive interaction at the top: the cabinet meeting, the editorial meeting at a newspaper, the meetings of the top of a political party or the deliberations at the board of a business company.

In the practice of fieldwork, the general rule is that the higher up and more influential the discourses, the less they are public and the less they accessible for critical scrutiny – sometimes so by law, as is the case for cabinet meetings.

For instance, in my own field of research on racism and the press, as far as I know, no researcher has ever been able to get access to editorial meetings of a newspaper. And everyone who has done fieldwork knows that interviewing the elites is always vastly more difficult than getting to talk to ordinary people in their own environment – people who are often happy to talk, because usually no one asks their opinion or about their experiences in the first place.

This is why we do have public data about the racism of political debates, news reports, textbooks or party programmes, but not about how cabinet ministers, party leaders, editors, board members or high- placed bureaucrats speak and write, internally, about immigrants and minorities.

Power as control over public discourse

In this book, I show how critical social analysis is closely intertwined with contextual discourse analysis. Traditionally, the social power of groups (classes, organizations) was defined in terms of their preferential access to, or control over, specific material resources, such as capital or land, to symbolic resources such as knowledge, education or fame, or to physical force.

Many forms of contemporary power, however, should be defined as *symbolic* power, that is, in terms of the *preferential access to, or control over, public discourse*, following the logic of reproduction sketched above. Control of public discourse is control of the mind of the public, and hence, indirectly, control of what the public wants and does. One needs no coercion if one can persuade, seduce, indoctrinate or manipulate people.

In these terms, then, the symbolic elites today, such as politicians, journalists, writers, professors, teachers, lawyers, bureaucrats and all others who have special access to public discourse, or the business managers who indirectly control such access, for instance as owners of mass media empires, are those who should be defined as powerful by such a criterion.

Symbolic power may be derived from other kinds of power. Thus, politicians have access to public discourse because of their political power, and professors because of their knowledge resources. If power is defined in terms of the control of (the members of) one group over others, then such forms of political, academic or corporate power really become effective if they provide special access to the means of discourse production, and hence to the management of the minds of the public.

Whereas classically power was defined in terms of class and the control over the material means of production, today such power has largely been replaced by the control of the minds of the masses, and such control requires the control over public discourse in all its semiotic dimensions.

We should therefore go beyond the (usually correct, but too simple) slogans of the popular critical literature about the power of politics or the media in terms of 'mind managers' and examine in close detail what exactly this means: how specific groups in society are able to control the definition (that is, mental models) of, and the emotions about, public events, general sociocultural knowledge and common sense, attitudes about controversial issues or, most fundamentally, the basic ideologies, norms and values that organize and control such social representations of the public at large.

Re-analysing hegemony

We see how closely social analysis is related to discourse analysis and how in various ways such a relationship also requires cognitive analysis. We see how the classical notion of hegemony, as defined by Gramsci in his *Prison Notebooks*, is given substance by a much more explicit analysis of the processes involved, namely how ideologies are reproduced and how people may act, out of their own free will, in the best interest of those in power.

This account of the discursive and cognitive means of the reproduction of social power in society obviously should also go beyond the usual macro-level analyses of sociology or political economy. Politics and the media undoubtedly mutually influence and control each other, both being in turn controlled by fundamental business interests, the market and what is financially 'viable'. Such macro analyses may be further refined by an analysis of the relations and forms of control of classes, groups or organizations.

The micro analysis of power

Discourse analysts, however, tend to study these general relationships at a more local and micro level, such as the daily interaction routines in which politicians and journalists are involved, how press releases are manufactured and distributed, how press conferences are conducted, how critical questions of journalists are strategically answered, and so on.

If those in power need to control their image in the mass media so as to garner support and influence public moods and minds, then they need to control the discursive and interactional details of the *production* of public discourse – such as the timing, the detailed contents and style of a press release, a business report or advertisement or the conversations and interviews with journalists. Through a detailed analysis of such organizational discursive practices – aimed at controlling the production of public discourse – we are able to show how social macro structures are related to the structures of public discourse, and finally how these may influence the minds of the public at large.

It should be stressed that such social processes of reproduction are not deterministic. For example, despite many forms of influence by the state or by powerful organizations, newspapers as organizations and journalists as individuals may resist (up to a point) such pressure and formulate news according to their own perspective and interests.

The same is true for the audience of news organizations. Of course, people are influenced by the news they read or see, if only in order to acquire and update knowledge about the world. But their comprehension of the news and the way they change their opinions or attitudes depends on their own earlier attitudes or ideologies (shared with other group members) as well as on their personal experiences. It is this personal interpretation of the news, this mental model of events, which is the basis of specific personal action of individuals.

In other words, the link between macro structures of societal power, on the one hand, and individual agency, on the other, is very complex and indirect, for the discursive reproduction of power we are examining here.

Discourse, cognition and society . . .

The brief analysis of the discursive reproduction of power given above establishes fundamental relationships of a triangle of concepts that organize most of my research, also in other publications: discourse, cognition and society. In my view, any kind of CDS needs to pay attention to all three dimensions, even when, occasionally, we may want to focus on one or two of them. The general tendency in critical research is to *directly* link society – and especially power and domination – with discourse, social practices or other phenomena we study.

According to my theoretical framework, such a direct link does not exist: there is no direct influence of social structure on text or talk. Rather, social structures are observed, experienced, interpreted and represented by social members, for instance as part of their everyday interaction or communication. It is this (subjective) representation, these mental models of specific events, this knowledge, these attitudes and ideologies that finally influence people's discourse and other social practices. In other words, personal and social cognition always mediates between society or social situations and discourse. Hence, in CDS we need to study social problems in terms of the discourse–cognition–society triangle. None of its three dimensions can be really understood without the other.

. . . and history and culture

That these three dimensions are necessary does not mean that they are sufficient. There are at least two more dimensions that are fundamental in CDS research: *history* and *culture* – although I take these both as part of the social dimension. That is, most of the issues dealt with in this chapter and this book, such as racism, the mass media, politics or education, have an important historical dimension whose analysis will contribute to our more complete understanding of contemporary social problems. Racism is not an invention of today but has a history of centuries. On the other hand, there are also vast social changes of the last decades, such as those of class, gender and ethnicity, and many contemporary societies in Europe, North America and Australia have undergone sometimes dramatic changes when compared to how they were only 50 years ago. CDS should examine these changes, also in the discursive reproduction of power, and on the other hand show whether and how fundamental power relations may precisely not have changed.

Finally, the same is true for culture. All we have said here also should be qualified culturally. Discourses and the ways they reproduce power are different in different cultures, and so are the social structures and the social cognitions that are involved in such a reproduction process. Due to increasing globalization, some discourse genres may have become quite uniform, as is the case for much international news and even some forms of entertainment. Yet, also the members of different cultures may understand and use such discourses in different ways, consistent with their own culturally shared knowledge and attitudes. The same is true for the production of discourse and its social conditions, which also may be different in different societies and cultures. This means that also CDS should always make sure it examines the discursive reproduction of power against the cultural background of the participants – and increasingly how discourse is being influenced by the cross-cultural experiences of many contemporary societies.

From Power to Power Abuse: Domination

It is a common misunderstanding that power is inherently 'bad' and that the analysis of discourse and power is by definition 'critical' analysis. This is, however, a rather limited conception of power and of CDS. Power obviously and trivially can be used for many neutral or positive ends, as when parents and teachers educate children, the media inform us, politicians govern us, the police protect us and doctors cure us – each with their own special resources.

This is not merely a disclaimer to introduce a limiting '*but . . .*'. On the contrary, society would not function if there was no order, no control, no checks and balances, without the many legitimate relationships of power. In that sense, much social analysis involves analysis of power and related notions.

CDS presupposes insight into social structures in general and into power relations in particular. Only then are we able to examine power *abuse*, how such abuse may hurt people and how social inequality may be produced and reproduced in everyday life. Only then are we able to understand how power is unequally distributed in society.

The illegitimate uses of power

CDS is interested in the critical analysis of power abuse of politicians rather than in their legitimate exercise of power, in how the media misinforms rather than informs them, or in how professionals and scholars abuse their knowledge to harass students, clients or other citizens rather than to educate or cure them. I call such forms of power abuse *domination*, a notion that implies the negative dimension of 'abuse' and also the dimension of inequities, injustice and inequality, that is, all forms of *illegitimate* actions and situations.

Domination covers equally the various kinds of *communicative power abuse* that are of special interest to critical discourse analysts, such as manipulation, indoctrination, or disinformation. Other, non-discursive, examples of domination readily come to mind, and everyday experiences, stories and news reports are full of them: sexual harassment of women by men, parental violence, political corruption, harassment and violence by the police, terrorism and counter-terrorism, wars, and so on. I just mention these to emphasize that CDS is able to study only a small (but important) part of all forms of domination and inequality.

In order to contribute to a well-founded practice of critical discourse study, we therefore should be much more explicit about the definition of abuse. How do we distinguish between the *use* and the *abuse* of language, discourse or communication, of news and argumentation, of parliamentary debates and laws, of scholarly studies or of professional reports, among a vast number of other genres and communicative practices?

Thus, we may expect the mass media to inform us about civil unrest, but when exactly does such 'information' about 'riots' slip into prejudiced text about black youths or the Third World, or class ideologies about the poor? Or when does a research project about immigration or the everyday lives of minorities lapse into confirming stereotypes, e.g., about drug abuse or violence, and ignore the ways these minorities are daily discriminated against by the authorities, the police and the symbolic elites?

In sum, the study of the obvious ways discourse is being abused, as in explicit racist propaganda or pseudo-science, needs to be complemented by much more subtle analyses of everyday practices in which 'good' and 'bad' may go together in text and talk.

So when exactly do we start to speak of 'abuse' when describing such everyday discursive practices? We have begun to describe such abuse in terms of legitimacy: abuse of power is *illegitimate* use of power. Such an analysis soon leads us to the foundations of social and political analysis. Power abuse, thus, means the violation of fundamental norms and values in the interest of those in power and against the interests of others. Power abuse means the violation of the social and civil rights of people. In the area of discourse and communication, this may mean the right to be (well) taught and educated, to be well informed, and so on.

The normative notion of legitimacy is, however, very complex, and its adequate analysis relevant for the very foundations of CDS. If we want to analyse and criticize domination, and if domination is defined as illegitimate, we need to be very explicit about the norms, criteria or standards of legitimacy. Crucially, then, the question is: who defines what is legitimate in the first place? A well-known answer in liberal democracies is that such is the task of democratically elected representatives, such as those of a parliament, a city council, etc. However, we know from history that there have been many racist, sexist and classist laws and regulations so that laws, as such, do not guarantee legitimacy as soon as we apply other norms and criteria. This is even the case for the formulation of international human rights – which we also know to have changed historically. In other words, as is the case for all our norms, values and knowledge, the standards of legitimacy are relative and change historically and vary cross-culturally – even when we claim each time that they are 'universal'.

If we have legitimate power use and illegitimate power abuse, we must accept that we may also have legitimate forms of inequality that are produced by them. This is not only the case in the obvious differences of political power but also wherever else power resources are not distributed equally – beginning with the material ones, such as money. Relevant for us is that this is also true for non-material, symbolic resources of power, such as knowledge and the access to public discourse. We thus find 'normal' inequalities as the differences of power between professors and students, professionals and their clients, experts and lay persons or journalists and their audience. The crucial question in CDS is therefore which of such power differences are legitimate by today's standards of justice and equity, or on the basis of international human rights, and which represent cases of illegitimate power abuse. When are the power resources of the journalist, such as special knowledge and information as well as direct access to the mass media, used legitimately, e.g., to inform the citizens, and when is such power abused of to misinform, to manipulate or harm citizens.

We see that much of the definition of the (il)legitimacy of text and talk is framed in terms of the negative *mental consequences* of discursive domination – disinformation, manipulation, stereotypes and prejudices, lack of knowledge and indoctrination – and how these may mean or lead to social inequality, for example, because such mental consequences in turn can influence (illegitimate) social interaction, such as discrimination.

Although we can accept the general definition of discursive domination in terms of its negative social consequences for the recipients, specifying the precise norms and values that make such negative consequences explicit is very hard and of course depends on one's perspective.

It is not difficult to formulate why racist reporting is 'bad', for instance because it helps form and confirm racist stereotypes and ideologies, which in turn are the basis of racist discrimination – which by definition is against the best interests of those who are discriminated against and violates their fundamental rights. This is also why racist reporting or political propaganda is prohibited by law in many countries.

An example: racist reporting

But what if a newspaper covers, for instance, looting by black youth during a 'riot', as we have seen on several occasions in the UK or the USA, and as I analysed in my book *Racism and the Press*? Obviously, covering criminal actions of members of minority groups is, as such, not racist nor otherwise an infringement of their civil rights, even when such 'negative' reporting may confirm ethnic prejudices among many white people. So, one needs to engage in a detailed analysis of text and context in order to be justified to conclude that such reporting is racist. For instance, such coverage becomes more or less racist if the following conditions hold:

- if only the negative actions of black youths are represented, and not those of other youths or, indeed, of the police;
- if the negative actions of black youths are emphasized (by hyperboles, metaphors) and those of the police de-emphasized (e.g., by euphemisms);
- if the actions are specifically framed in 'ethnic' or 'racial' terms, instead of actions of, say, youths, or poor people, men or another, more relevant category;
- if riots, looting or violence are focused on as events without social causes, for instance as a consequence of frequent police harassment, or within a broader pattern of poverty and discrimination;
- if the newspapers systematically engage in this kind of racist coverage, and hence seem to have a policy of negative reporting about minorities;

- if only or predominantly 'white' sources are used that tend to blame black youth and exonerate the police.

We see that the norms that are violated here are not controversial. On the contrary, they are part and parcel of the professional norms of adequate reporting which require balanced representations of events, explaining them in terms of social causes and contexts, and a watchdog function against abuse of power of agencies or forces of the state. Journalists know and should know the possible consequences of racist reporting about minority communities and hence should be very careful to respect the general norms of professional reporting. They need not close their eyes to minority misdeeds, nor apply self-censorship, but only apply their own professional norms consequently when covering the Others.

Legitimate partiality

Even the example of racist reporting of 'riots' is still relatively straightforward because we can apply general norms and values of professional reporting to evaluate such reporting critically. However, there are many other examples of more or less 'bad' or partisan reporting that do not violate existing norms, and that do not have negative social consequences, for instance when a leftist newspaper highlights the positive qualities of a leftist candidate in elections and the negative qualities of the right-wing candidate. Such obvious bias may be motivated when most of the press is conservative and represents left-wing candidates (more) negatively.

Similarly, the press may want to represent negatively politicians that are corrupt, industries that pollute or discriminate, and so on, and such coverage may be 'biased' against such parties, but obviously the consequences are no doubt for the public good.

Thus, we can conclude that for each discursive practice we need to examine carefully the specific context, norms and values that define adequate practice. However, as a general rule of thumb, we can speak of illegitimate use of discursive power, that is, of domination, if such discourse or its possible consequences systematically violate the human or civil rights of people. More specifically, such is the case if such discourse promotes forms of social inequality, as when it is favouring the interests of dominant groups, and against the best interests of non-dominant groups, precisely because the latter do not have the same access to public discourse.

For each discourse genre or discursive practice, we then need to specify its particulars. We have given the example of news in the press, but of course we need to develop such criteria for all types of public discourse, such as parliamentary debates, political propaganda, advertising, corporate discourses, textbooks and classroom interaction, legal discourse, scientific discourse, or bureaucratic discourse.

The counter-argument: The inability to control the consequences

Another complication in such a theory of discursive domination is that it is not just formulated in terms of discourse structures, that is, structures that authors can (more or less) control, and hence for which they are (more or less) accountable, especially also in terms of the (mental) consequences of such structures. Politicians and journalists routinely defend themselves against accusations of prejudiced talk or text by saying that they have no control over how people read, understand or interpret their discourses.

Such a defence is not entirely without ground, because there is no causal relation between discourse and its interpretation: we know from the psychology of discourse comprehension that discourses themselves are only one factor in a complex set of conditions that influence understanding and interpretation, such as the context of reading, the given knowledge and ideologies of the readers, their personal biography and current experiences, their current intentions and goals, their current role and status, and so on.

Yet, despite such individual and contextual variations, this does not mean that discourses themselves are irrelevant in the processes of social influence. There is general insight into the ways knowledge, prejudice and ideologies are acquired, also through discourse. Hence, especially, professional authors and organizations should have insight into the possible or likely consequences of their discourses on the social representations of the recipients.

There is little doubt, for instance, that repeated emphasis and focus on the deviant or criminal characteristics of minorities creates and confirms *socially shared* racist attitudes in society, and not just the opinions of some bigoted individuals.

There is also little doubt that most of our ideologies are formed discursively. In this sense, then, the lack of direct control of the minds of recipients is no excuse for discursive malpractice, given professional knowledge about the likely tendencies of the overall influence of such practices on the minds and actions of recipients. Indeed, the same elite groups and organizations perfectly well know what effects their 'information', their advertising and their propaganda have on the public – otherwise they would not engage in public communication in the first place.

The Practical Relevance of Critical Discourse Studies

What has been said above applies primarily to CDS research. Such research, we hope, produces useful insights into how discourse plays a role in the reproduction of domination and how such power abuse leads to social inequality. Crucial though for CDS is that such insights also should have practical relevance for dominated groups. Although there have been many examples of practical 'applications' of CDS research, this dimension of CDS is most in need of further development and self-critical analysis. So let me briefly formulate some of the options.

Mediation and consultancy

If a politician, journalist or professor claims not to know (or have known) the possibly negative social consequences of their discourses, there is obviously a mediating role for critical discourse analysts. They can show, in detail, how topics, headlines and leads of news discourse, or abstracts and conclusions of scholarly articles, or slogans in political discourse can be used and abused to 'define the situation', that is, how these discourse structures may be used to build the upper level (macro) structures of mental models of events. As critical analysts, we can show how specific lexical items or metaphors are used to construe the details of events or the characteristics of people in such mental models – or indeed how mental models tend to be generalized to prejudices or other commonly held social attitudes.

CDS can and should intervene in the discursive education of professionals, so as to show how the public discourses of the elites may influence the minds of the citizens, and how such influence plays a role in the reproduction of social structure. To be aware of the consequences of one's discourse (and of any public action) is one of the conditions of accountability, as is also the case for our knowledge about the effects of chemical products on the environment. In such a case the excuse 'We didn't know!' (or the German variant, used as an excuse after World War II: *Wir haben es nicht gewusst!*) is no longer valid, as is also the case for the critical evaluation of polluting practices.

Teaching, obviously

Teaching CDS is also relevant for citizens more generally because they can learn to be more aware of the goals of the discursive elites and how public discourses may misinform, manipulate or otherwise harm them. That is, the main social and practical goal of CDS is to develop strategies of discursive dissent and resistance.

Professional advice, codes of conduct

In order to be able to reach such goals, we need to investigate in detail which discourse properties, which discourse genres, and in what communicative contexts, are likely to have which sociocognitive consequences on the formation of knowledge, attitudes and ideologies. Such investigation requires the cooperation of discourse analysts with linguists, psychologists and social scientists, each examining some of the components of the complex discursively based reproduction process of social inequality.

Although teaching CDS is crucial as a form of resistance against discursive domination, it is not sufficient. Few newspapers have changed their practices of racist reporting as a consequence of CDS analyses. The same is true for most critical studies. Yet, as we have seen for the successes of the feminist and ecological movements, resistance may have effects even on the most powerful.

The long road traditionally has been the one through the institutions, that is, by educating journalists and other professionals with the basic results of our insights. That is, in the university our aims are clear: to teach students how to critically analyse text and talk, how to teach that to others and how to develop new theories to improve such analyses.

More direct forms of resistance that have been successful in other domains may also be effective for CDS, for instance in the area of racist or sexist reporting or by providing critical expert testimony to international bodies who do have at least some power, such as the United Nations or the Council of Europe – both have repeatedly taken action against racism.

For instance, if we are able to show how such racism is reproduced by the mass media, we may at the same time formulate concrete recommendations which may take the form of voluntary professional codes, as they exist in many areas. Such codes can formulate criteria for the diversity of newsrooms, news gathering, news topics and news sources, among other recommendations – that is, the enforcement of general professional norms and values. They can explicitly suggest the elimination of all irrelevant references to the ethnic background of news actors, especially in negative (crime, etc.) news. The same is true, and has been suggested, for the coverage of the Third World or of Islam – in the same way that has repeatedly been proposed for the media coverage of gender.

Racism is bad for business

Besides teaching, research and political action involving influential international organizations, another important strategy of CDS resistance affects the core of neoliberal ideologies and practices: profits. We should argue and show that racist or sexist discourse, or a lack of diversity in general, is bad for business. In the increasingly multicultural society of the USA, Europe or Australia, in which many non-European people have become citizens and consumers, it is obviously hardly wise to antagonize these potential customers by racist policies, reporting, teaching, or other discursive practices. If such citizens have the choice between a racist and a non-racist newspaper or TV programme, school or business, we can imagine what most of them will choose, especially if they themselves have become explicitly aware of racism.

Diversity in the newsroom may not be enough. Minority journalists, if recruited at all, are selected for the similarity of their values with those of the owner or chief editor of newspapers, or because such journalists soon adapt to their colleagues in order to maintain their job or liveable working conditions. In that case, it is the diversity of the buyers of newspapers that is a very powerful incentive to change editorial policies. More generally, businesses will tend to discriminate less when their management understands that both for in recruitment of qualified personnel as well as in satisfying their clients, such racism is bad for business.

Alliances and cooperation

CDS research is especially efficient through its strategic alliances with those organizations, NGOs, minority groups or institutions that are engaged in the struggle against all forms of social inequality in general, and against discursive discrimination in particular, such as racism, sexism and classism in politics, the media, education and research. This may not be the whole field of operation of CDS, but large enough for a vast amount of research projects and forms of cooperation and social action.

What to Do?

Summarizing, the practical relevance of CDS can be found especially in the critical education of students as future professionals, in its role in preparing expertise for powerful international organizations as well as for grass-roots organizations, and by showing to corporate enterprises that any form of discursive discrimination ultimately will be bad for business.

CDS scholars can critically analyse textbooks and propose new ones to publishers and education authorities. They can offer to teach courses of non-racist news writing to journalists. They can intervene in work-shops on non-racist interaction with clients in many businesses. And so on and so on.

It should finally be repeated again that such important practical goals of CDS can only be realized if based on a vast amount of detailed research into the crucial discursive practices in society, and especially in politics, the media, education and research, that is, on the symbolic or discursive elites and their daily practices and products. The articles collected in this book are intended as contributions to that collective research effort.

2

Structures of Discourse and Structures of Power*

This chapter examines some of the relationships between discourse and social power. After a brief theoretical analysis of these relationships, we review some of the recent work in this new areas of research. Although we draw upon studies of power in several disciplines, our major perspective is found in the ways power is enacted, expressed, described, concealed, or legitimated by text and talk in the social context. We pay special attention to the role of ideology but, unlike most studies in sociology and political science, we formulate this ideological link in terms of a theory of social cognition. This formulation enables us to build the indispensable theoretical bridge between societal power of classes, groups, or institutions at the macro level of analysis and the enactment of power in interaction and discourse at the social micro level. Thus our review of other work in this field focuses on the impact of specific power structures on various discourse genres and their characteristic structures.

The discourse analytical theory that forms the background of this study presupposes, but also extends, my earlier work on discourse (e.g., van Dijk, 1977, 1980, 1981; van Dijk and Kintsch, 1983), as well as other approaches of current discourse analysis (see the contributions in van Dijk, 1985a). That is, continuing my recent work on news discourse, and on racism in discourse which will briefly be reviewed here, this chapter shows a more social approach to discourse, and bears witness to a more general development towards a critical study of text and talk in the social context.

* For critical remarks and suggestions on the first version of this chapter, I am indebted to James Anderson, Charles Berger, Norman Fairclough, Cheris Kramarae and Ruth Wodak.

Our discourse analytical framework and the obvious space limitations of a single chapter impose a number of restrictions. First, we presuppose but do not discuss or review current work on the more general relationships between power and language which has been the focus of several recent studies (Kramarae, Schulz and O'Barr, 1984; Mey, 1985). Our discussion focuses on discourse as a specific 'textual' form of language use in the social context and only some of the sociolinguistic work that deals with the role of dominance or power in language variation and style (Scherer and Giles, 1979). Second, we must ignore much of the related field of the study of power in interpersonal communication, a field that has been aptly reviewed already by Berger (1985) (see also Seibold, Cantrill and Meyers, 1985) as we are interested in social or societal power rather than in personal power. Third, we must regrettably limit ourselves to the role of power in 'western' cultures. Therefore, we neglect the insights into the role of power in other cultures obtained in some work in the ethnography of speaking (Bauman and Scherzer, 1974; Saville-Troike, 1982), or in the current work on intercultural communication. Fourth, feminist studies on male dominance and power in language have already been discussed (see the extensive bibliography of Kramarae, Thorne and Henley, 1983), therefore, we limit ourselves to a brief review of research focusing on gender power and discourse. To further constrain the size of our review, few references will be made to the many interesting studies on the relationships between language, discourse, power and ideology in several European and Latin American countries.

The Analysis of Power

The analysis of power in several disciplines has created an extensive literature. Some recent work includes studies by Dahl (1957, 1961), Debnam (1984), Galbraith (1985), Lukes (1974, 1986), Milliband (1983), Mills (1956), Therborn (1980), White (1976) and Wrong (1979), among many others. Most of this work is carried out within the boundaries of sociology and political science. It cannot be our task in this chapter to review or summarize this rich tradition. Therefore, we select a number of major properties of social power and reconstruct those within our own theoretical framework. It should be understood, however, that in our opinion the complex notion of power cannot simply be accounted for in a single definition. A full-fledged, interdisciplinary theory is necessary to capture its most important implications and applications. The properties of power that are relevant for our discussion may be summarized as follows:

1   Social power is a property of the relationship between groups, classes or other social formations, or between persons as social members. Although we may speak of personal forms of power, this individual power is less relevant for our systematic account of the role of power in discourse as social interaction.

2   At an elementary but fundamental level of analysis, social power relationships are characteristically manifested in interaction. Thus we say that group A (or its members) has power over group B (or its members) when the real or potential actions of A exercise social control over B. Since the notion of action itself involves the notion of (cognitive) control by agents, the social control over B by the actions of A induces a limitation of the self-control of B. In other words, the exercise of power by A results in the limitation of B's social freedom of action.

3   Except in the case of bodily force, power of A over B's actual or possible actions presupposes that A must have control over the cognitive conditions of actions of B, such as desires, wishes, plans and beliefs. For whatever reasons, B may accept or agree to do as A wishes, or to follow the law, rules, or consensus to act in agreement with (the interests of) A. In other words, social power is usually indirect and operates through the 'minds' of people, for instance by managing the necessary information or opinions they need to plan and execute their actions. Most forms of social power in our society imply this kind of 'mental control', typically exercised through persuasion or other forms of discursive communication, or resulting from fear of sanctions by A in case of non-compliance by B with A's wishes. It is at this point that our analysis of the role of discourse in the exercise, maintenance or legitimation of power becomes relevant. Note, however, that this 'mental mediation' of power also leaves room for variable degrees of freedom and resistance of those who are subjected to the exercise of power.

4   A's power needs a basis, that is, resources that socially enable the exercise of power, or the application of sanctions in case of non-compliance. These resources usually consist of socially valued but unequally distributed attributes or possessions, such as wealth, position, rank, status, authority, knowledge, expertise, or privileges, or even mere membership in a dominant or majority group.

Power is a form of social control if its basis consists of socially relevant resources. Generally, power is intentionally or unwittingly exercised by A in order to maintain or enlarge this power basis of A, or to prevent B from acquiring it. In other words, the exercise of power by A is usually in A's interest.

5   Crucial in the exercise or the maintenance of power is the fact that for A to exert mental control over B, B must know about A's wishes, wants, preferences, or intentions. Apart from direct communication, for instance in speech acts such as commands, request, or threats, this knowledge may be inferred from cultural beliefs, norms, or values; through a shared (or contested) consensus within an ideological framework; or from the observation and interpretation of A's social actions.

6   Total social control in contemporary western societies is further limited by the field and the scope of power of power agents. That is, power agents may be powerful in only one social domain – politics, the economy, or education – or in specific social situations, as in the classroom or in court. Similarly, the scope of their actions may be limited to a few people or extend to a whole class or group of people or to specific actions. And finally, the powerful may be assigned special responsibilities in their exercise of power. Besides this form of power distribution, which also involves various forms of power sharing, there is the important dimension of resistance: dominated groups and their members are seldom completely powerless. Under specific socioeconomic, historical, or cultural conditions, such groups may engage in various forms of resistance, that is, in the enactment of counter-power, which in turn may make the powerful less powerful, or even vulnerable, typically so in revolutions. Therefore, the enactment of power is not simply a form of action, but a form of social interaction.

7   The exercise and maintenance of social power presupposes an ideological framework. This framework, which consists of socially shared, interest-related fundamental cognitions of a group and its members, is mainly acquired, confirmed, or changed through communication and discourse.

8   It should be repeated that power must be analysed in relation to various forms of counter-power or resistance by dominated

groups (or by action groups that represent such groups), which also is a condition for the analysis of social and historical challenge and change.

Discourse Control and the Modes of Discursive Reproduction

One important condition for the exercise of social control through discourse is the control of discourse and discourse production itself. Therefore, the central questions are: Who can say or write what to whom in what situations? Who has access to the various forms or genres of discourse or to the means of its reproduction? The less powerful people are, the less they have access to various forms of text or talk. Ultimately, the powerless have literally 'nothing to say', nobody to talk to, or must remain silent when more powerful people are speaking, as is the case for children, prisoners, defendants, and (in some cultures, including some-times our own) women. In everyday life, most people have active access as speakers only to conversation with family members, friends, or colleagues on the job. Occasionally, in more formal dialogues, they may speak to institutional representatives, or with job superiors, but in that case they have a more passive and reactive role. At the police station, in the courtroom, at the welfare agency, in the classroom or in other insti-tutions of the social bureaucracy, they are expected to speak, or to give information, only when requested or ordered to do so. For most formal, public or printed discourse types (including those of the mass media) the less powerful are usually only recipients.

More powerful groups and their members control or have access to an increasingly wide and varied range of discourse roles, genres, occasions and styles. They control formal dialogues with subordinates, chair meet-ings, issue commands or laws, write (or have written) many types of reports, books, instructions, stories or various mass media discourses. They are not only active speakers in most situations, but they may take the initiative in verbal encounters or public discourses, set the 'tone' or style of text or talk, determine its topics and decide who will be partic-ipant or recipient of their discourses. It is important to stress that power not only shows 'in' or 'through' discourse but is relevant as a societal force 'behind' discourse. At this point, the relation between discourse and power is close, and a rather direct manifestation of the power of class, group, or institution, and of the relative position or status of their members (Bernstein, 1971–5; Mueller, 1973; Schatzman and Strauss, 1972).

Power is directly exercised and expressed through differential access to various genres, contents and styles of discourse. This control may be analysed more systematically in terms of the forms of (re)production of discourse, namely, those of material production, articulation, distribution and influence. Thus mass media organizations and their (often international) corporate owners control both the financial and the technological production conditions of discourse, for instance those of the newspaper, television, printing business, as well as the telecommunication and computer industries (Becker, Hedebro, and Paldán, 1986; Mattelart, 1979; Schiller, 1973). Through selective investments, budget control, hiring (and firing), and sometimes through direct editorial influence or directives, they may also partly control the contents or at least the latitude of consensus and dissent of most forms of public discourse. For the privately operated media that depend on advertising, this indirect control may also be exercised by large corporate clients and even by prominent (mostly institutional) news actors that regularly supply information on which the media depend. These same power groups also control the various modes of distribution, especially of mass media discourse, and therefore also partly control the modes of influence of public text and talk.

The production mode of articulation is controlled by what may be called the 'symbolic elites', such as journalists, writers, artists, directors, academics and other groups that exercise power on the basis of 'symbolic capital' (Bourdieu, 1977, 1984; Bourdieu and Passeron, 1977). They have relative freedom, and hence relative power, in deciding about the discourse genres within their domain of power and determine topics, style or presentation of discourse. This symbolic power is not limited to articulation per se but also extends to the mode of influence: they may set the agendas of public discussion, influence topical relevance, manage the amount and type of information, especially who is being publicly portrayed and in what way. They are the manufacturers of public knowledge, beliefs, attitudes, norms, values, morals and ideologies. Hence their symbolic power is also a form of ideological power. Despite the problems with the notion of 'elite' (Domhoff and Ballard, 1968), we maintain this term to denote an extended concept (contrasted with Mills, 1956, for example) involving exclusive social control by a small group. That is, we claim that besides the political, military and economic elites, the symbolic elites play an essential role in the ideological supporting framework for the exercise or maintenance of power in our modern, information and communication societies.

Because, however, most of these elites are managed by the state or private corporations, they too have constraints on their freedom of articulation that emerge in various properties of their discourse. The voice of the elite is often the voice of the corporate or institutional master. The interests and ideologies of the elites are usually not fundamentally different from those who pay or support them. Only a few groups (e.g., novelists and some academics) have the potential to exercise counter-power, which still must be expressed within the constraints of publication. The dependence of the elite is typically ideologically concealed by various professional norms, values or codes, for instance, by the widespread belief in 'freedom of expression' in the mass media (Altheide, 1985; Boyd-Barrett and Braham, 1987; Davis and Walton, 1983; Downing, 1980; Fishman, 1980; Gans, 1979; Golding and Murdock, 1979; Hall, Hobson, Lowe and Willis, 1980).

Strategies of Cognitive Control and Ideological Production

If most forms of discursive power in our society are of the persuasive type as claimed earlier, then, despite the essential and often ultimate control of the modes of production and distribution (especially for mass-mediated discourse), the decisive influence on the 'minds' of the people is symbolically rather than economically controlled. Similarly, recognizing the control expressed over the less powerful in the socioeconomic domain (money, jobs, welfare), a major component in the exercise and maintenance of power is ideological, and is based on various types of acceptance, negotiation, and challenge, and consensus. It is, therefore, crucial to analyse the strategic role of discourse and its agents (speakers, writers, editors and so on) in the reproduction of this form of sociocultural hegemony. Given that the symbolic elites have major control over this mode of influence through the genres, topics, argumentation, style, rhetoric or presentation of public text and talk, their symbolic power is considerable, albeit exercised within a set of constraints.

A New Approach to Ideology

Because the notion of ideology is crucial for our argument about the role of discourse in the enactment or legitimation of power, it deserves a few remarks, although it is impossible even to summarize the classical proposals and the current discussions on the subject (see Abercrombie, Hill and Turner, 1980; Barrett, Corrigan, Kuhn and Wollf, 1979; Brown, 1973; Centre for Contemporary Cultural Studies [CCCS], 1978; Donald and Hall, 1986; Kinloch, 1981; Manning, 1980). Despite the variety of approaches to the concept of ideology, it is generally assumed that the term refers to group or class 'consciousness', whether or not explicitly elaborated in an ideological system, which underlies the socioeconomic, political and cultural practices of group members in such a way that their (group or class) interests are (in principle, optimally) realized. Both the ideology itself and the ideological practices derived from it are often acquired, enacted or organized through various institutions, such as the state, the media, education or the church, as well as in informal institutions such as the family. Classical Marxist analyses suggest, more specifically, that the dominant ideology in a given period is usually the ideology of those who control the means of ideological reproduction, namely, the ruling class. This may imply that certain dominated groups or classes may develop biased conceptions of their socioeconomic position ('false consciousness'), which in turn may lead them to act against their own basic interests. Conversely, the dominant groups or classes tend to conceal their ideology (and hence their interests), and will aim to get their ideology generally accepted as a 'general' or 'natural' system of values, norms and goals. In that case, ideological reproduction assumes the nature of consensus formation, and the power derived from it takes on a hegemonic form.

Ignoring many details and complexities, our analysis of ideology takes a somewhat different and more specific direction than traditionally crafted (see also van Dijk, 1998). Although there are undeniably social practices and institutions that play an important role in the expression, enactment or reproduction of ideology, we first assume that ideology 'itself' is not the same as these practices and institutions. Rather, we assume that ideology is a form of social cognition, shared by the members of a group, class, or other social formation (see, for example, Fiske and Taylor, 1984, for a more general introduction to the study of social cognition). This assumption does not mean that ideology is simply a set of beliefs or attitudes. Their sociocognitive nature is more elemental. An ideology according to this analysis is a complex cognitive framework that controls the formation, transformation and application of other social cognitions, such as knowledge, opinions and attitudes, and social representations, including social prejudices. This ideological framework itself consists of socially relevant norms, values, goals and principles, which are selected, combined and applied in such a way that they favour perception, interpretation and action in social practices that are in the overall interest of the group. In this way, an ideology assigns coherence among social attitudes which in turn codetermine social practices. It should be stressed that ideological social cognitions are not systems of individual beliefs or opinions, but essentially those of members of social formations or institutions. Similarly, according to this analysis, we do not use terms such as 'false' in order to denote specific 'biased' ideologies. Ideologies (including scientific ones) embody an interest-dependent (re)construction of social reality. (One appropriate criterion for the evaluation of such a construction would be its relevance or effectiveness for the social practices of social formations and their members in the realization of their goals or interests.)

The acquisition of an ideology, however, is not just guided by the 'objective interests' of each group or class, although on many occasions, and historically, these interests may eventually override other conditions of ideological (re)production. Therefore, discourse and communication, we suggested, play a central role in the (trans)formation of ideology. In that perspective, it is indeed crucial to examine who, using what processes, controls the means or institutions of ideological (re)production, such as the media or education. Although the formation of the fundamental sociocognitive framework of ideology is a very complex process, it at least needs a basis of (true or false) beliefs. This chapter tries to show that discourse, and in particular discourse of powerful institutions and groups, is the essential social practice that mediates and manages these beliefs (Roloff and Berger, 1982). Contrary to most approaches to ideology in the social and political sciences, we aim at a more systematic sociocognitive analysis of ideological frameworks, and of the processes involved in their (trans)formation and application. This goal means that ideologies need to be spelled out in detail, and that it should be shown how such group cognitions influence social constructions of reality, social practices and hence, the (trans)formation of societal structures. Similarly, we need an explicit analysis of the structures, strategies and processes of discourse and its specific role in the reproduction of ideologies. In other words, much classical work on ideology derives from typical macroanalyses of society to the neglect of the actual structures and processes at the micro level of the operation of ideology. This global and superficial approach also prevents the establishment of the link between societal or group ideologies (and the power structures they determine, conceal or legitimate) with concrete social practices of intra- or inter-group interaction, including the precise role of discourse in ideological (trans)formations.

Discourse and Ideological Reproduction

To form and change their minds, people make use of a multitude of discourses, including interpersonal ones, and of the information derived from them. Note, however, that the complexity of text processing and of attitude formation, of course, does not allow immediate transformations of public beliefs and opinions, let alone of highly organized attitudes and ideologies (Petty and Cacioppo, 1981; Roloff and Miller, 1980; van Dijk and Kintsch, 1983). And yet, it is the symbolic elite and its discourses that control the types of discourses, the topics, the types and the amount of information, the selection or censoring of arguments and the nature of rhetorical operations. These conditions essentially determine the contents and the organization of public knowledge, the hierarchies of beliefs and the pervasiveness of the consensus, which in turn are potent factors in the formation and the reproduction of opinions, attitudes, and ideologies (Burton and Carlen, 1979).

In the news media, this strategic control of knowledge is exercised through restricted topic selection, and more generally by specific reconstructions of social and political realities (Hall et al., 1980; Tuchman, 1978; van Dijk, 1987b, 1987c). This process is itself governed by a system of news values and professional ideologies about news and newsworthiness which happen to favour attention to and the interests of various elite actors, persons, groups, classes, institutions, nations or world regions (Galtung and Ruge, 1965). Preferential access and coverage (whether positive or negative) of news actors is one factor in the mass-mediated reproduction of social power (Brown, Bybee, Wearden and Murdock, 1982). The same is true in education, where the curriculum, textbooks, educational materials and lessons are also governed by educational objectives, subjects, topics and learning strategies that mostly happen to be consistent with the values or interests of the various power elite groups (Apple, 1979; Lorimer, 1984; Young, 1971). Therefore, we see that the symbolic elites that control the style and content of media and educational discourse are also those that have partial control of the mode of influence, and hence of ideological reproduction in society.

The symbolic elites, we suggested, are not independent of other, mostly economic and political, power groups (Bagdikian, 1983). There may be conflict and contradiction between the interests and, therefore, the ideologies of these respective power groups. These other power groups not only have direct or indirect means to control symbolic production, they have their own strategies for the manufacture of opinion. For the media, these strategies consist in the institutional or organizational supply of (favourable) information in press releases, press conferences, interviews, leaks or other forms of preferred access to newsmakers. Journalistic routines are such that these preformulations are more likely to be reproduced than other forms of source discourse (Collins et al., 1986; Gans, 1979; Tuchman, 1978; van Dijk, 1987b).

In education, the overall constraint of avoiding 'controversial' issues censors most radical social and political views that are inconsistent with dominant sociopolitical ideologies. More concretely, state organizations or corporations may supply free educational materials, advertise in educational journals and have other ways to influence teachers and textbook content (Domhoff, 1983).

Similarly, the power elites also have the access to measures that control dissent and resistance, for example, through selective hiring and funding, by subtle or more overt censorship, through defamation campaigns and other means of silencing 'radicals' and their media (Domhoff, 1983; Downing, 1984; Gamble, 1986). Thus in many western countries it is sufficient to be branded as a 'communist', or as an opponent of our type of 'freedom', or of similar dominant values, in order to be disqualified as a serious formulator of counter-ideologies. This is a potent strategy to keep the symbolic elite itself under control, both internally and externally. In other words, there is a broad array of economic, cultural and symbolic strategies through which the various power groups may concurrently, though sometimes not without mutual conflict and contradiction, manage knowledge and information, convey dominant goals and values and thereby provide the building blocks of dominant ideologies. The consensus-shaping power of these ideologies provides the conditions that make a 'conspiracy' of these power groups unnecessary.

The Analysis of Power and Discourse

Within this very general framework of social power and the control of discourse, we may now focus more specifically on the many ways discourse is related to this form of social control.

Discourse genres and power

We begin our analysis with a typology of the ways power is enacted by discourse as a form of social interaction:

1   Direct control of action is achieved through discourses that have directive pragmatic function (elocutionary force), such as commands, threats, laws, regulations, instructions and more indirectly by recommendations and advice. Speakers often have an institutional role, and their discourses are often backed by institutional power. Compliance in this case is often obtained by legal or other institutional sanctions.

2   Persuasive discourse types, such as advertisements and propaganda, also aim at influencing future actions of recipients. Their power is based on economic, financial, or, in general, corporate or institutional resources, and exercised through access to the mass media and to widespread public attention. Compliance in this case is manufactured by rhetorical means, for example, by repetition and argumentation, but of course backed up by the usual mechanisms of market control.

3   Beyond these prescriptive discourse forms, future actions may also be influenced by descriptions of future or possible events, actions or situations; for instance, in predictions, plans, scenarios, programmes and warnings, sometimes combined with different forms of advice. The power groups involved here are usually professionals ('experts'), and their power basis often the control of knowledge and technology (Pettigrew, 1972). The rhetorical means often consist of argumentation and the description of undesired alternative courses of action. More implicitly, scholarly reports about social or economic developments may thus influence future action.

4   Various types of sometimes widespread and, hence, possibly influential narrative, such as novels or movies, may describe the (un)desirability of future actions, and may have recourse to a rhetoric of dramatic or emotional appeals, or to various forms of topical or stylistic originality. The power groups involved here form what we call the symbolic elites. A specific case of this class of discourse is news reports in the media which not only describe current events and their possible consequences but which essentially portray the actions, and represent the opinions of, the political, economic, military and social power elites. It is mainly in this way that the consensual basis of power is manufactured, and through it the general public gets to know who has power and what the powerful want. This is a crucial condition for the development of the supporting ideological framework of power but also for various forms of resistance ('know thine enemies').

This first typology shows that the discursive enactment of power is mostly persuasive. Powerful groups or institutions only rarely have to prescribe what the less powerful should do, although ultimately such directives may be decisive in controlling others, as is especially the case in state control. Rather, they argue by providing economic, political, social or moral reasons and by managing the control of relevant information. In this way, communication may be biased through selective release of information that is favourable to the power elites, or by constraining information that is unfavourable to them. The realization of these goals may be facilitated by various rhetorical or artistic means.

Levels of discourse and power

A second dimension goes beyond this simple typology of discourse genres and their contributions to social control. It features the various levels of discourse that may specifically enact, manifest, express, describe, signal, conceal or legitimate power relations between discourse participants or the groups they belong to.

Thus as we have seen earlier, power may first be enacted at the pragmatic level through limited access, or by the control of speech acts, such as commands, formal accusations, indictments, acquittals, or other institutional speech acts. Second, in conversational interaction, one partner may control or dominate turn allocation, self-presentation strategies and the control of any other level of spontaneous talk or formal dialogue. Third, selection of discourse type or genre may be controlled by more powerful speakers, for instance in the classroom, courtroom, or within the corporation: Sometimes stories of personal experiences are allowed, but more often than not, they tend to be censored in favour of the controlled discourse genres of the business at hand, for instance interrogations. Fourth, outside of everyday conversation, topics are mostly controlled by the rules of the communicative situation, but their initiation, change, or variation are usually controlled or evaluated by the more powerful speaker. The same is true for style and rhetoric.

Dimensions of Power

The analysis of power structures allows us to list other relevant categories, namely, those dimensions of power that may have an impact on discourse and its structures: the various institutions of power, the internal power structures of these institutions, power relations between different social groups and the scope or domain of the exercise of power by (members of) these institutions or groups. Without a further analysis of these structures and dimensions of social power, we simply argue here that they are also manifested in the various structures of 'powerful' text and talk.

In this list we first find the major power institutions, such as the government, parliament, state agencies, the judiciary, the military, big corporations, the political parties, the media, the unions, the churches and the institutions of education. Each of these institutions may be associated with its specific discourse genres, communicative events, topics, styles and rhetorics. Second, there is the usual hierarchy of position, rank or status within these institutions and these imply different speech acts, genres or styles, for example, those signalling authority and command.

Third, parallel and sometimes combined with the institutions, we have group power relations, such as those between the rich and the poor, men and women, adults and children, white and black, nationals and foreigners, the highly educated and those who have little education, heterosexuals and homosexuals, believers and non-believers, the moderates and the radicals, the healthy and the sick, the famous and the unknown, and generally those between Us and Them. Both within institutional and in everyday, informal interaction, these power relations may be structurally enacted by the members of the respective dominant groups. As is the case for institutional members, members of dominant groups may derive their individually exercised power from the overall power of the group they belong to. The effect on discourse in these cases will be especially obvious in the unbalanced control of dialogue, turn-taking, speech acts, topic choice and style.

Fourth, the enactment of power may be analysed as to its domain of action or scope and type of influence. Some institutions or their leading members may accomplish discursive acts that affect whole nations, states, cities, or large organizations, or they may affect life and death, health, personal freedom, employment, education, or the private lives of other people, whereas other institutions or their members have a less broad and a less serious impact on other people.

Finally, we may distinguish between the various kinds of legitimacy for these forms of social control, which may vary between total control imposed or maintained by force (as in a dictatorship, and in some domains also in a democratic system of government), on the one hand, and partial control sanctioned by an elite, by a majority or, on the other hand, by a more or less general consensus. These (gradual) differences reflect the possible sanctions of the powerful, as well as the acceptance or resistance of those subjected to the enactment of power.

These differences in the modes of legitimation are also manifest in different genres, topics and styles of discourse. Discussion, argumentation and debate, for example, are not characteristic of dictatorial discourse. Hence the importance of the amount and nature of discursive legitimation in these different sorts of power systems. It may be expected that each political system, viewed as an institutionalization of power, for instance by the state, is associated with its own characteristic orders or modes of discourse. Since the principles (norms, rules, values, goals) of legitimacy are embedded in an ideology, the processes of legitimation will also appear as discursive processes.

Different Approaches

With these various dimensions of power in mind, we should be able to make the next step and establish systematic links between these dimensions and the various structural dimensions of discourse. However, this may be done in different ways and from different, complementary perspectives. Thus the social scientist may start with an analysis of the dimensions of social power just mentioned and then examine through what discourses or discursive properties these power structures are expressed, enacted or legitimated. This (macro) approach favours a more general and integrated analysis of various discourse genres and properties related to a class, institution or group (for instance, the discourse of the legal system, or the patriarchal power of men over women). On the other hand, the sociolinguist will usually start with an analysis of specific properties of language use or discourse, and try to show how these may vary, or depend on, different social positions, relations or dimensions, for example those of class, gender, ethnic group, or situation. This perspective will usually pay more detailed attention to linguistic properties of text and talk, and take a more general view of the various social 'circumstances' of such properties.

We opt for an approach that combines the advantages of these two alternatives, namely the analysis of discursive (sub)genres and communicative events in social situations (Brown and Fraser, 1979). Such a 'situation analysis' requires an integration of both discourse analysis and social analysis. Through an interdisciplinary study of everyday conversations, classroom dialogues, job interviews, service encounters, doctors' consultations, court trials, boardroom meetings, parliamentary debates, news reporting, advertising, or lawmaking, among many other communicative events, we are able to assess both the relevant discourse structures and the relevant structures of dominance and control in the social context. That is, understanding these communicative genres requires an analysis of participant representation, interactional strategies, turn allocation, topic and code selection, stylistic registers, rhetorical operations, and also an analysis of the roles, relations, rules, norms or other social constraints that govern the interaction of participants as social group members. In this way, we capture both the properties and processes of text and talk, and the micromechanisms of social interaction and societal structure. Also, this level and scope of analysis allows a sociocognitive assessment of knowledge, opinions, attitudes, ideologies and other social representations that exercise the cognitive control of acting agents in such situations. Finally, these social microstructures (e.g., the lesson) may in turn be related (e.g., by comparison or generalization) to relevant social macrostructures, such as institutions (e.g., the school, the education system, and their ideologies) and overall social relations (e.g., the dominance of whites over blacks) (Knorr-Cetina and Cicourel, 1981).

Power in Discourse: A Review

In the previous sections, I have given a brief theoretical analysis of the notion of power and its links with discourse and communication. We have witnessed how the powerful have recourse to many strategies that allow them to control the material and symbolic production of text and talk and, therefore, part of the cognitive processes that underlie the cognitive management and the manufacturing of consent from the less powerful. On several occasions, this discussion has mentioned some properties of discourse that are specifically affected by this process of (re)productive control, for instance, conversational turn-taking, topics and style. In the remainder of this chapter, we analyse in more detail how power is actually expressed, signalled, reproduced or legitimated in various structures of text and talk. Whereas the previous sections focused on various social strategies of discourse and communication control, we will now systematically examine the discursive strategies that implement such (inter)actions, and briefly review empirical studies that show power 'at work' in text and talk. We will organize our discussion around a few selected discourse types, namely, subgenres or communicative events, that also embody typical social relations, including specific power relations. In this discussion, a reinterpretation of research will sometimes be necessary, for instance, when the notion of power is not used as such. We begin with various sorts of spoken, dialogical discourse, and then discuss written types of text. We will focus on social power and disregard types of individual power, influence, or status in interpersonal communication (see Berger, 1985 for a review of this work, and Brooke and Ng, 1986, and Falbo and Peplau, 1980, for empirical studies on interpersonal influence).

Conversation

Although the analysis of conversation generally presupposes that speakers have equal social roles (Sacks, Schegloff and Jefferson, 1974; Atkinson and Heritage, 1984; McLaughlin, 1984), it is obvious that group and institutional membership of speakers, and in general social inequality, introduce differences in control over the ongoing dialogue. These differences appear, for instance, in talk between men and women, adults and children, whites and blacks, the rich and the poor, or between the more or less educated. It is assumed that such control by the more powerful speaker may extend to turn allocation or appropriation, speech act choice, topic selection and change, and style. The enactment of this control, however, need not be static, but may be dynamically negotiated or challenged by the less powerful speakers. In other words, talk is continuously contextualized by signalling various conditions or constraints of the social situation in general, and by the social relationships between the speech participants in particular. And although it makes sense to make a distinction between everyday, personal, or informal talk, on the one hand, and, on the other hand, formal, institutional discourse, it should be stressed that informal or private discourse may be imbued with formal and institutional constraints. Conversely, institutional discourse also may be informal and an everyday accomplishment among other social practices.

Conversation between parents and children

One of the more obvious power differences in many cultures is that between parents and children. Although there is important cultural variation (Snow and Ferguson, 1977), and differences between fathers and mothers (Gleason and Geif, 1986), parental control is generally enacted in parent–child talk in many ways: 'The low status of children in stratified societies can keep them silent, forbid them to initiate or discuss certain topics, prevent them from interrupting, or require them to use a special deferential variety of speech' (Ervin-Tripp and Strage, 1985, p. 68).

As these and other authors show in detail, parents may also control child behaviour more directly, for example, through scolding, threatening, directing, or correcting children in talk. More indirect forms of action control in parent–child talk may take the form of advice, requests, or inducement through promises. These differences in parental control in talk have often been related to class differences (Cook-Gumperz, 1973). Relevant to our discussion of social power, social representations of power are acquired and displayed rather early, as through different forms of discursive politeness and deference, or through verbal power play and ritual (Bavelas, Rogers and Millar, 1985; Ervin-Tripp, O'Connor and Rosenberg, 1984; Labov, 1972; Lein and Brenneis, 1978).

Conversation between women and men

The power differences between women and men and their manifestation in language have received extensive attention, especially during the last decade, and by feminist researchers (Eakins and Eakins, 1978; Kramarae, 1980, 1983; Spender, 1980; Thorne and Henley, 1975; Thorne, Kramarae and Henley, 1983, who provide an extensive bibliography). Therefore, we mention only a few general conclusions of this important work, which in many respects has become paradigmatic for the analysis of power in language and communication, and focus on the more recent studies of gender power in discourse (for a brief review, see West and Zimmerman, 1985).

Although differences may sometimes be subtle and dependent on situation (Leet-Pellegrini, 1980), and on social position (Werner, 1983), it has been found that women generally 'do more work' than men do in conversation, by giving more topical support, by showing more interest, or by withdrawing in situations of conflict (Falbo and Peplau, 1980; Fishman, 1983). Several studies document that men tend to interrupt women more often, especially at irregular turn transition places (Eakins and Eakins, 1978; Natale, Entin and Jaffe, 1979; West and Zimmerman, 1983).

Some of the studies collected by Trömel-Plötz (1984) show that male dominance is not restricted to informal situations, such as the home, but also appears in public contexts, such as television talk shows, which are moderated mostly by men (see also Owsley and Scotton, 1984). For instance, women tend to get the floor less often than men do, and men talk longer, more often, and use long, complicated sentences and various types of pseudostructuring of conversational contributions.

Gender differences in talk may also be studied in a more general perspective as instances of 'powerful' and 'powerless' speech, which may be found in other social situations (Bradac and Street, 1986; Erickson, Lind, Johnson and O'Barr, 1978), to which we turn next.

Racist talk

What is true for the subordination of women in talk also holds for discourse addressed to, or about, blacks and other minority groups in many western countries (Smitherman-Donaldson and van Dijk, 1987). White group power may also be exercised through verbal abuse and derogation of minority group members (Allport, 1954). Although there are many historical and literary sources that document the pervasiveness of racial slurs, there are few systematic studies of their usage and functions. Kennedy (1959) provides a brief list of 'etiquette rules' for the ways blacks and whites should address each other in the period of Jim Crow racism in the United States. One of these rules was that blacks should never be addressed as 'Mr.', 'Mrs.', 'Sir', or 'Ma'am', but by first names only, whereas whites always must be addressed in the polite form. Although the last decades have seen much of this verbally expressed racism mitigated because of changing official norms and laws, racial slurs still exist in everyday white talk. Verbal derogation of blacks, as well as of Chinese, Italian, Mexican, or Puerto Rican Americans, is common in the United States, and of Turkish, Moroccan, South Asians, Caribbean, and other minorities or immigrants in Western Europe (Helmreich, 1984).

Ethnic conflict may also be manifested in different speech styles that lead to misunderstanding and stereotyping (Kochman, 1981). Within a German project on language acquisition by immigrant workers, attention was paid to the ways these 'Gastarbeiter' were addressed in terms of a perceived, simplified 'foreigner German' (Dittmar and von Stutterheim, 1985; Klein and Dittmar, 1979). Often, such talk by itself may signal superiority of the speakers and their group. This is an interesting specific case of the functions of linguistic accommodation and conflict in interethnic communication (Giles and Powesland, 1975; Giles and Smith, 1979; Gumperz, 1982a, 1982b).

Much recent research on prejudice and racism suggests that, even if racist opinions, talk and action have become more indirect and subtle in certain contexts, basic attitudes may not have changed very much (Barker, 1981; Dovidio and Gaertner, 1986; Essed, 1984). Greenberg, Kirkland and Pyszczynski (1987) show that the use of racial slurs by experimental confederates against black subjects may activate such basic attitudes among white subjects and result in more negative evaluations of these black subjects. Among the conservative elites, racist discourse has taken a more 'cultural' orientation during the last decade. Such discourse emphasizes assumed cultural differences between ingroups and outgroups, and sometimes subtly advocates nationalist cultural autonomy of the dominant white group (Seidel, 1987a, 1987b).

In my own work on the expression of ethnic opinions and prejudice in everyday talk, such explicit racial slurs appear to be rare, both in the

Netherlands and in California (van Dijk, 1984a, 1987a). However, the informal interviews on which my research is based are typically examples of talk with relative strangers (university students), and, therefore, such talk is likely to be heavily monitored by official norms of non-discrimination. In fact, white people routinely express their knowledge of such norms, and elaborately affirm that whatever they may say about 'foreigners' they do not mean to be racist.

Therefore, the overall strategy of talk about minorities is twofold. On the one hand, many white people express negative experiences and opinions about ethnic minority groups. On the other hand, however, this negative 'other-presentation' is systematically balanced by positive self-presentation, namely, as tolerant, non-racist, understanding citizens. This overall strategy is implemented by many local strategies and tactics, such as apparent denials and concessions ('I have nothing against them, but . . .' 'There are also good ones among them, but . . .' and so on), contrasts that emphasize group differences, competition, generally the us/them opposition ('We work hard, and they don't have to do anything'), and transfer ('I don't mind, but other people in the country, city, street, or department do'). Besides such semantic and rhetorical strategies of positive self-presentation, negative other-presentation is mainly implemented by argumentation and concrete storytelling. Stories are based on one's own personal experiences, and, therefore, 'true' and good 'evidence' for negative conclusions. Most of these stories feature events and actions of minority groups that are perceived to violate dominant (white) norms, values, goals and interests, but which also happen to substantiate current stereotypes and prejudices. Often, the news media are used to legitimate such stories and opinions, for instance by referring to minority crime 'about which you read in the paper every day'. More subtly, conversational properties such as hesitations, repairs, and corrections provide insight into the underlying cognitive processes and monitoring in such talk. Lexical choice and the use of identifying pronouns and demonstratives also suggest social distance: 'them', 'those people', 'those Turks (Mexicans, and so on)'. In this way, everyday talk among white majority group members reproduces such prejudices within the ingroup, while at the same time verbally confirming group membership, and group goals and norms, which in turn are relevant in the maintenance of white group power.

Institutional dialogue

Dialogues with and within institutions or organizations are forms of institutional interaction and, therefore, also enact, display, signal, or legitimate a multitude of power relations (Pettigrew, 1973; Pfeffer, 1981). Participants in such interactions may follow context dependent rules and norms of interaction, but may also negotiate different roles or positions, including those of status, hierarchy, or expertise. Another difference with everyday, informal conversation is that institutional members are mostly professionals, experts 'at work' (see also Coleman, 1984, 1985b). Let us examine some of the more prominent subgenres of institutional dialogue.

Job interviews

Ragan (1983) showed that in job interviews power differences manifest themselves in what she calls 'aligning actions', such as accounts, metatalk, side sequences, digressions, or qualifiers. Interviewers more often had recourse to strategies that control conversational pace and progress, such as formulations, metatalk and metacommunicative digressions. Applicants, on the contrary, are more often engaged in justifying or explaining their behaviour, for instance through accounts, qualifiers and 'you knows', even when these were unnecessary. This study complements earlier social psychological work on the (power) effect of language attitudes in job interviews which shows that otherwise identical applicants may be discriminated against because of their foreign accent, for instance, by getting lower evaluations for higher-level jobs and higher evaluations for lower-level jobs (Kalin and Rayko, 1980).

In a series of experimental studies, Bradac and associates examined the role of powerful and powerless styles in job interviews (Bradac and Mulac, 1984). As in early studies of women's language, hesitations, and tag questions were found to characterize the powerless style (see also Bradac and Street, 1986). We shall see that similar results have been found in styles of courtroom talk.

Doctor–patient discourse

Doctor–patient discourse is just one specific example of medical discourse in general (Fisher and Todd, 1983, 1986; Freeman and Heller, 1987), which has often been criticized for a variety of reasons, including the abuse of power by medical practitioners. Edelman (1974), in a critical article, shows how the language of people in the helping professions, typically in psychiatry, in many ways conceals the real nature of their intentions and actions which are geared toward the control of patients.

In this way, direct power may be masked by the discourse of 'helping', in which patients who have good reasons to be angry may be categorized as 'aggressive'. Such patients will be put in what is euphemistically called a 'quiet room' instead of 'solitary confinement'. Similarly, the use of such terms as 'predelinquent' may mean that professionals get carte blanche in the 'treatment' of (mostly powerless, e.g., young, poor) people who have shown no sign of deviance. Professional power here combines with the power of class and age. Indeed, as we shall see next, power seldom comes alone: institutional power is frequently enacted at the same time as group power derived from gender, class, race, age, subculture, or nationality (see also Sabsay and Platt, 1985).

West (1984) shows that the inherent social asymmetry in doctor–patient relationships is also displayed in their conversations and that gender and race play a role here: male doctors interrupt patients (especially black patients) much more often than the reverse, without any medical function or relevance; on the contrary, these interruptions make them miss important information. Female doctors, however, are interrupted more often by their (male) patients. Generally, in doctor–patient talk there is an imbalance in information exchange: doctors initiate most questions and patients stutter when asking their few questions, with the exception of a specific type of conditional query. West concludes that, 'Quantitative and qualitative evidence suggests that physicians stand in nearly godlike relation to their patients – as entities "not to be questioned"' (West, 1984, p. 51). Formal expressions are used to address the doctor, whereas doctors tend to use the first names of patients, especially when the patients are black. Fisher and Todd (1983) also find an interaction between medical and gender power. They showed that female patients are subject to 'friendly persuasion' by (male) practitioners to use birth control pills, while being kept uninformed about the pills' possible negative effects or about alternative forms of birth control.

In a critical analysis of clinical interviews, Mishler (1984) found discursive evidence for the domination of what he calls the 'biomedical voice' of doctors, and concludes: 'Typically, the voice of the lifeworld was suppressed and patients' efforts to provide accounts of their problems within the context of their lifeworld situations were disrupted and fragmented' (p. 190). Treichler et al. (1984) argue that the physician's focus on biomedical aspects hinders the full expression of the patient's concerns. Thus concerns readily expressed to a medical student were not included in the physician's medical records. Doctors are found to use irony in showing dismissal of the patient's complaints. Finally, just as for job interviews, social psychological work on language attitudes shows that doctors may evaluate their patients differently depending upon whether or not they have a dialect or sociolect accent (Fielding and Evered, 1980).

What has been found for general practitioners may be expected to be true for other medical professionals. Coleman and Burton (1985) studied control in dentist–patient consultations in Great Britain, and found that dentists control both verbal and non-verbal activity: dentists talk 71 per cent and patients 26 per cent of the time (assistants 3 per cent). Dentists have more turns, and longer turns (4.6 versus 2.1 seconds). Obviously, control in this case takes a very literal form: patients usually have their mouths open so are prevented from speaking in such a situation, and, therefore, have little opportunity to speak. Compliance with dentists' power may also depend on fear of pain. Thus the authors found that dentists regularly respond to patients' reports by making no acknowledgement, by minimizing them as irrelevant, or by dismissing them as incorrect. As is the case for most professional forms of power, the major resource of dentist dominance is expertise (see also Candlin, Burton and Coleman, 1980). As noted earlier, power may derive from institutional organization and routinization. Medical power is a characteristic example. The results of the studies just reviewed should also be interpreted in that perspective. Thus Strong (1979) specifies some other factors that limit the freedom of patients in consultation discourse: doctors use technical language (see also Coleman, 1985a); there are few doctors and many patients; doctors are organized and patients are usually not; doctors have high status; in some countries, there are no or few (affordable) alternatives for the public health service provided by doctors and, therefore, little medical competition and reduced possibilities for second opinions. We see that the local enactment and organization of power in doctor–patient talk is intricately interwoven with more general social and institutional forms of control.

These findings are also relevant in counselling or admission interviews, in which professionals act as gatekeepers of institutions and may exert relevant group power on the differential conversational treatment of minority clients or candidates (Erickson and Shultz, 1982; Mehan, 1986). Similarly, in classroom talk, teachers may be expected to exercise control over students through a series of strategies: they decide about discourse type, they initiate and evaluate topics and question–answer sequences, they monitor student speech style and generally control both the written and spoken discourses of the students. Unfortunately, although there is much work on classroom dialogues (Sinclair and Brazil, 1982; Stoll, 1983; Wilkinson, 1982), little specific attention is paid to these routine enactments of institutional power.

Discourse in court

More than in most other institutional contexts, the enactment of power in court is systematically governed by explicitly formulated rules and procedures of dialogical interaction between the judge, the prosecution, defence counsel and the defendant. Much work has been done on court-room dialogues in the tradition of conversational analysis but, again, little attention has been paid to such social dimensions as power, control, or dominance (Atkinson and Drew, 1979). The stylistic power of highly technical jargon shared by the participating legal representatives may be internally balanced among these professionals, but ultimately further subordinates the defendant. The combined powers of indictment by the prosecution, judicial courtroom control and final judgement may be expected to show in what court officials say and imply dominance towards the defendant, towards witnesses and even towards the defence counsel. Conversely, whatever defendants in their inherent position of subordination may say, it 'may be used against them', which places a special burden on their talk.

In court, the distribution of speaking turns and speech acts is strictly regulated. Unlike most other situations of dialogical interaction, defendants have the obligation to talk when requested to do so and to answer questions with specific statements, such as simply 'yes' or 'no' (Walker, 1982). Refusal to talk or to answer questions may be sanctioned as contempt of court. Harris (1984) examined how questions in court are used to control defendants or witnesses and found that question syntax appeared to be important for what will count as an appropriate response. He also found that information control is exercised by questioning sequences, rather than by long accounts, which also firmly establish the control of the questioner. Most questions are for yes/no questions that restrict possible answers because they contain already completed propositions. Thus questioning rules and strategies, as well as legal power, together regulate the choice of a restricted set of speech acts: most questions ask for information or make accusations (see also Mead, 1985; Shuy, 1986). Obviously, these discursive methods of control in the courtroom may vary according to the procedures of direct or cross-examination (see also Adelswärd et al., 1987).

Besides turn-taking, sequencing, speech acts and topic control, style may be an important feature of self-presentation and persuasion of defendants and witnesses, although these may not always be preserved in courtroom transcripts (Walker, 1986; see also Parkinson, Geisler and Pelias, 1983). These strategies of interaction and impression formation in court were examined by Erickson, Lind, Johnson and O'Barr (1978) in their influential study of powerful and powerless styles. These authors found that powerless style can be characterized by the frequent use of intensifiers, hedges, hesitation forms and questioning intonation, whereas powerful style is marked by less frequent use of these features. Experiments suggest that powerful style results in greater attraction to the witness, independent of sex of witness or subject, but that powerful style leads to enhanced perceived credibility only when witness and subject are of the same sex (see also Bradac, Hemphill and Tardy, 1981). In a later experimental study, these authors show that the evaluation of the defendants or witnesses may also depend on whether the defence counsel relinquishes control by letting them tell their own stories (Lind and O'Barr, 1979).

As in all cases already discussed, factors of class, gender and race play a role, and may possibly reinforce or mitigate the subordination of the defendant. Thus Wodak (1984, 1985) shows that middle-class defendants are better able to build a positive image in court proceedings. They know the strategies of courtroom interactions, tell coherent stories and mention plausible facts. Working-class defendants, however, appear to perform less successfully on these crucial tasks. Such class differences also appear in the way the judge addresses the defendant, for instance through forms of politeness, patience, understanding and showing interest in the occupation of professional, middle-class defendants. On the other hand, Maynard (1985), in a study of plea bargaining, suggests that the discursive characterization of defendants in terms of specific categories (old, woman, minority) may sometimes be taken as arguments to dismiss a case. That is, unlike cases of discrimination, age, class, or race may sometimes be used to reduce the responsibility of the defendant. Maynard claims that knowledge of the social interaction (of justice) is needed to make conclusions about discrimination, and that general assumptions about unfair treatment of the less powerful in court may not always be warranted.

Whereas the enactment and reproduction of legal power surfaces most concretely in courtroom interaction, it also characterizes other types of legal and bureaucratic discourse, such as laws, contracts, regulations and many other texts. Besides the power embodied in their pragmatic functions of legal directives, such texts also indirectly manifest power by their exclusive 'legalese'. This archaic lexical, syntactic and rhetorical style not only symbolizes and reproduces a legal tradition, thus facilitating communication among legal professionals, but obviously excludes lay persons from effective understanding, communication, and, hence, resistance (Charrow, 1982; Di Pietro, 1982; Danet, 1980, 1984; Radtke, 1981).

Organizational discourse

Discourse in business organizations has, unfortunately, led to fewer studies of details of dialogical interaction. Especially in 'vertical' communication between bosses and their subordinates, such talk is obviously an enactment and expression of hierarchical power (McPhee and Tompkins, 1985). In their review of organizational communication, Blair, Roberts and McKechnie (1985) found that managers spend 78 per cent of their time in verbal communication; when leaders dominate leader–subordinate communications, subordinates react by deferring; and there is more self-disclosure upward than downward in the organization. Focusing more on the content of such talk, Riley (1983) found in an analysis of interviews that power in organizations is expressed through signification, legitimation and domination. Verbal symbols, such as (military) metaphors, myths, jokes and legends, dominate the discussions, whereas game metaphors provide legitimation by expressing possible sanctions.

Power differentials in business may be expected to show in different forms of politeness, deference and, hence, in forms of address (Brown and Levinson, 1978). Slobin, Miller, and Porter (1972) studied forms of address in business corporations and found that the first name is used primarily when subordinates are addressed by their superiors. Conversely, title and last name are used when talking to higher management, who communicate among themselves mostly on a first-name basis. These different forms of address appear to be more or less independent of age differences. The authors not only found, expectedly, more self-disclosure among fellow workers, but found non–reciprocal self-disclosure to immediate superiors (even when no first names are used). These results confirm the rules established by Brown and his associates (Brown and Gilman, 1960; Brown and Ford, 1972): the greater the status difference, the greater the tendency towards non-reciprocal address. However, unlike the findings by Brown et al., subordinates show more self-disclosure to bosses than the reverse. That is, the use of first names in business contexts is not always associated with greater familiarity, and vice versa.

Whereas organizational hierarchy and power may be directly enacted in commands, orders, instructions, or other directives, power may also be expressed by representation. Members in the organization may be expected to talk about daily events, and thus try to make sense of their lives. Such experiences are typically expressed in narrative. In one of the few studies of its kind, Kelly (1985) analysed scripts and schemata of stories told by people at different levels of 'high-tech' organizations. He found that many of these stories focused on the boss and, whether positive or negative, they emphasized the power structure and at the same time legitimated it.

Political discourse

Since the rhetorical treatises of classical Greece and Rome, political discourse – and its persuasive power – have received much attention as a special object of study (Chaffee, 1975; Nimmo and Sanders, 1981; Seidel, 1985). Unlike most other discourse forms, political discourse may be relevant for all citizens. Its power derives both from this scope and from its various degrees of legitimacy. Few forms of oral discourse are as well known, routinely quoted, or distributed as widely through the mass media as that of top politicians, such as the president or prime minister. Especially in the United States, speeches and media perform-ances of the president are both a prominent social or political event, and a preferred object of study (Hart, 1984; Lindegren-Lerman, 1983). This dominant presence in, and preferential access to, the media may be interpreted as a manifestation of political power.

In light of what we just assumed, we may expect many studies to deal with political discourse. This is indeed the case, but many of these stud-ies focus on what is commonly called 'political language', which mostly means specific lexical style (see Bergsdorf, 1983; Edelman, 1964; Guespin, 1976; Hudson, 1978; Shapiro, 1984). Thus ideologies have been studied through analysis of preferential use of specific words or concepts, typically so for extremist politicians of the Left or the Right (fascist or communist language). It is interesting, however, to go beyond the study of single words and look into other discourse structures, of which some are even less in the control of the speaker, and therefore often more revealing of attitudes and ideologies (see also Guespin, 1976; Pêcheux, 1975). Although only indirectly interested in the analysis of power, Atkinson (1984) investigated various properties of political oratory, such as the management of applause by political speakers, and the careful preparation of such performance by experts (for instance by taking speech lessons). Against the background of my remarks on gender and especially racial power, it is interesting to note that Atkinson found that applause is particularly likely after passages in which different outgroups are negatively discussed.

Institutional texts

Whatever the power of directors, top politicians, corporate boards, professors, judges, or doctors in face-to-face discourse, their real power seems to have formal consequences only when somehow 'fixed' in writing or print. Therefore, many types of formal dialogues, such as meetings, interviews, or debates, have a written counterpart in the form of minutes, protocols, or other official transcripts that define the 'record' of the encounter, and are often the institutional or legal basis for any further action or decision-making.

Institutional dialogues are often accompanied by various types of text, which function as guidelines or reference for the accomplishment of the spoken discourse. Thus most formal meetings involve a written agenda as well as various kinds of documents. Courtroom dialogue is related to many written texts, such as law texts, a formal indictment, written statements, witness reports and a final judgement. Even in oral consultation, doctors may sometimes have recourse to medical handbooks and make notes, and the encounter is often closed after writing out a prescription or a referral to a specialist. Records in medical organizations play a vital role. School or university lessons are unthinkable without textbooks or a host of other written (or to be written) materials. In other words, most formal business, even when accomplished orally, requires written texts as its basis or its consequence. Thus texts are literally the consolidation of communicative power in most institutional contexts.

Written discourse is, for the most part, explicitly programmed or planned and, therefore, better controlled. In complex ways, this property has implications for the exercise of power. Whereas less monitored, face-to-face encounters allow the exercise of illegitimate dominance, for instance against women or ethnic minorities in service encounters, job interviews or counselling discourse, written discourse is, in principle, often public, and therefore its writers may be held accountable. This publicness may imply that in texts, power may need to be enacted and formulated in more indirect, veiled, formalized ways, especially when such power is not legally or organizationally established. Another factor that makes the exercise of power through written communication less direct is that often authors of institutional texts are not identical with the public speakers, senders, or sources of such discourse. Public discourse, therefore, is often a form of collective, institutional discourse, as is the power it enacts.

Media discourse: news reports and news production

There can be little doubt that of all forms of printed text, those of the

mass media are most pervasive, if not most influential, when judged by the power criteria of recipient scope. Besides the spoken and visual discourses of television, newspaper texts play a vital role in public communication. Contrary to popular and scholarly beliefs, news in the press is usually better recalled than is television news (Robinson and Levy, 1986), and is perceived to be qualitatively superior (Bruhn Jensen, 1986), which may enhance its persuasive influence and therefore its power.

We have seen that many power holders (as well as their talk) get routine coverage by the news media, and thus their power may be further confirmed and legitimated. Even when the power of the media is a form of mediating power, it has its own autonomous role in the production and reproducton of social power structures. Through selective source use, news beat routines, and story topic selection, the news media decide which news actors are being publicly represented, what is being said about them, and, especially, how it is said. Much recent work on news production has shown that these processes are not arbitrary and not simply determined by intuitive, journalistic notions of interestingness. Journalists learn how to portray the power of others and at the same time learn how to contribute to the power of their own organization, for example, by making it independent of other organizations (Turow, 1983). Newsworthiness is based on ideological and professional criteria that grant preferential media access to elite persons, organizations and nations, thereby recognizing and legitimating their power (Galtung and Ruge, 1965; Gans, 1979). Similarly, the routine organization of news production favours news gathering in the institutional contexts that guarantee a constant source of news stories, such as the major political bodies of the state, the police, the courts, and the big corporations (Fishman, 1980; Tuchman, 1978). In sum, the corporate embedding of most western media, especially newspapers, as well as the routine organization of news production, the reliance on readily available and credible sources and the general professional and ideological aspects of newsworthiness, all concur in social cognitions and text production that favour stories about the most powerful people, groups, or institutions in society (van Dijk, 1987b). In this way, instead of simply being a mouthpiece of the elite, the media also show that they are an inherent part of the societal power structure, of which they manage the symbolic dimension.

Such power is, of course, locally embodied and exercised by media professionals. The question then arises: how do journalists reproduce or challenge the ideologies they are confronted with? Critical media schol- ars have emphasized that, because of their socialization and class membership, journalists tend to reproduce the dominant ideologies of the elite (Hall et al., 1980). It has also been argued, however, that journalists are critical of dominant politics and business, and do not always share the ideologies of these elites (see a review of this position in Altheide, 1985). Despite these contradictions, we may assume with the critical theorists that media practices usually remain within the boundaries of a flexible, but dominant, consensus, even when there is room for occasional dissent and criticism. Fundamental norms, values and power arrangements are seldom explicitly challenged in the dominant news media. In fact, this latitude of dissent is itself organized and controlled. Opposition, also by the media, is limited by the boundaries set by the powerful institutions, and may thus also become routinized.

One important aspect of the process of power (re)production is how journalists acquire the professional and ideological frameworks that guide their daily practice. Turow (1983) examined the processes whereby journalists learn how to portray institutional power. He argues that the media, just like other organizations, want to reduce their dependence on other organizations. They cope with environmental risks through routines. Journalists, writers and directors must produce creative products, but these must be successful. This happens, for example, through formulas, both in fiction (plots, characters and settings) and in news reports. This analysis from an organizational point of view partly agrees with the microsociological analysis of news production routines studied by Tuchman (1978).

In a series of discourse analytical case studies of news in the press, I examined how subordinate social groups are represented in news reports (van Dijk, 1987c; see also van Dijk, 1985b). Minorities, refugees, squatters, and Third World countries and peoples appear to be represented in ways that are often rather similar, that is, in contrast with the portrayal of powerful groups and nations. The general conclusion of these studies is that these and other outgroups (a) tend to have less access to the dominant mass media, (b) are used less as credible and routine sources, (c) are described stereotypically if not negatively, primarily as a 'problem', if not as a burden or even as a threat to our valued resources, (d) are assumed to be 'deficient' or 'backward' in many ways, as compared to our norms, goals, expertise, or culture, and, therefore, (e) need our (altruistic) help, understanding, or support, assuming they adapt to our social and political norms and ideology. These general implications may be inferred from the analysis of news production routines, amount, size, and prominence of presentation, dominant topics, as well as style of news reporting (see also Cohen and Young, 1981, for studies with similar conclusions).

Within the framework of the New International Information Order debate, I examined the international coverage of a characteristic media event – the assassination of President-Elect Bechir Gemayel of Lebanon in September 1982 (van Dijk, 1984b, 1987c). In addition to the usual content analytical study of this coverage in newspapers (from some hundred countries), I performed a more qualitative analysis of news discourse. It may be expected that political, ideological, cultural, or regional differences influence the perception, interpretation and description of this event which was taking place in the confused and controversial Middle East conflict. I found that although there may have been differences of size, and especially of editorial commentary, the news reports themselves were surprisingly similar as to their schematic, conventional format, and as to their topical contents. An unexpected, major difference was found between First World and Third World newspapers as to their use of their own correspondents: Most Third World newspapers relied on the western news agencies. My interpretation of these findings was that, on the one hand, there may be historical and professional conditions that impose an internationally pervasive news schema for the press reproduction of news events, but that, on the other hand, western dominance and power, in many complex ways, was an explanation of the pervasiveness of 'western' formats in reporting. Time constraints, lack of money and correspondents, western-influenced professional socialization and other factors will favour more or less the same type of stories in western and non-western countries. Stories from and about Third World countries are most likely to be either written by western journalists or adapted to international (i.e., western) agency formats in order to reach and be used by these agencies and their (rich) western clients.

These conclusions partly confirm some of the critiques levelled by many Third World countries against the information hegemony of European and US media organizations (Mankekar, 1978; UNESCO, 1980; see also the discussions in Richstad and Anderson, 1981, and in Atwood, Bullion and Murphy, 1982). As may be expected, western news media and politicians have forcefully rejected these allegations, and usually ignore results from scholarly research that support them (Fascell, 1979). For my study of power and discourse, it is interesting to witness that such rejections are typically framed in terms of 'attack on the freedom of the press'. My analysis of power suggests that in such cases the notion of 'freedom' may often simply be translated as (our) 'power' or 'control'. Knowledge acquisition and opinion formation about most events in the world appears to be largely based on news discourse in the press and on television, which is shared daily by millions of others. Probably no other discourse type is so pervasive and so shared and read by so many people at more or less the same time. Its power potential, therefore, is enormous, and close scrutiny of the schemata, topics and style of news reports is therefore crucial to our understanding of the exercise of political, economic, social and cultural power, and of the communication and acquisition of the ideologies that support it.

This potential does not mean that media power can simply be understood in terms of simplistic, direct 'effects'. Depending on socioeconomic and sociocultural differences, people obviously interpret, represent and evaluate news reports and news events quite differently and, hence, form different opinions, attitudes and ideologies. Although in some specific cases, direct forms of influence indeed do exist, especially when there are no other information sources and when no counter-information is available or relevant, we should see the power of news media discourse in more structural terms. Structural influence implies the development of a socially shared, selective knowledge basis, goals, norms, values and the interpretation frameworks based on them. Media power thus implies the exclusion of alternative sources, alternative information and other relevancies in the description of world events. Governments and/or media corporations may effectively control the publication or broadcasting of such alternative 'voices', and therefore limit the information freedom of citizens, for instance by prohibiting, harassing, or marginalizing the 'radical' media (Downing, 1984).

Another feature that has often been found to characterize western news discourse is the ethnocentric, stereotypical portrayal of Third World nations and peoples. Although not all news about the Third World is of the 'coups and earthquakes' brand (Rosenblum, 1981; Schramm and Atwood, 1981), it certainly focuses on only a few types of events and actors, which are generally stereotypical if not negative: poverty, lack of (our type of) democracy, dictatorship, violence and civil war, and technological and cultural 'backwardness' (see Said, 1981, for the currently highly relevant coverage of Islam). Downing (1980) found that Third World leaders are often portrayed in a condescending way, and seldom are allowed to speak for themselves.

The same is true for ethnic and racial minorities and their representation in western countries and their media. Hartmann and Husband (1974), in their classic study of racism and the press, concluded from a content analysis of the British press that (Third World) immigrants tend to be portrayed primarily as 'problem people', as people who threaten our valued resources (space, housing, work, education), if not simply as welfare cheats or criminals. I found similar evidence in our qualitative studies of the Dutch press (van Dijk, 1983, 1987c). Ethnic minority groups in the Netherlands (immigrant workers from Mediterranean countries, and people from former colonies, such as Indonesia and Surinam) do not have routine access to news beats or the newspaper columns, and are seldom employed by the media. If they are portrayed at all, the topics tend to be stereotypical or negative, focusing on immigration difficulties and illegality, emphasizing perceived cultural differences and the problems entailed by them, language and educational problems, their competition for housing and employment, and their illegal or criminal activities, centred around dominant notions such as aggression, violence, and drug abuse (see also Hall et al., 1978). These ethnocentric, if not prejudiced and racist, portrayals can be found at all levels of textual organization, including headlining, the relevant hierarchy of news reports, and in style and rhetoric. Note that these expressions of group power may be very subtle and indirect in the quality press and on television. Overt racial abuse is exceptional. Rather, 'ethnic' properties and situations are described in a manner that may be used by readers as components or arguments in the development of ethnic prejudice. These results show agreement with the general conclusions found in most other studies of racism in the media in other western countries (Ebel and Fiala, 1983; Hartmann and Husband, 1974; Merten, 1986; Troyna, 1981; Wilson and Gutiérrez, 1985; see also the papers in Smitherman-Donaldson and van Dijk, 1987).

A characteristic feature of the syntactic style of reporting about outgroups of various kinds appears in several studies of the expression of semantic and social roles. Fowler et al. (1979) studied the news coverage in the British press of racial disturbances in London. They found that the ideology of newspapers showed in the ways the participants of varying power were represented in sentential syntax, namely, as active agents, placed in first subject position, or in later positions in passive sentences, or as implied, but absent actors. They found that when the authorities are associated with negative acts, they tend to be placed in later positions, or simply left out of the sentence. Conversely, minorities, who are usually in later, dependent syntactic positions, typically occupy first-subject positions as soon as they are negative actors (see also Fowler, 1985; Kress, 1985; Kress and Hodge, 1979). In this way, the negative characteristics of ingroups or elites may be downgraded and those of outgroups emphasized. This action is in agreement with current social psychological theories of prejudice and intergroup perception (Hamilton, 1981; Tajfel, 1981; van Dijk, 1987a).

I reached the same conclusions in an analysis of the headlines in news reports about ethnic groups in the Dutch press (van Dijk, 1987e), as well as in my study of refugee immigration to the Netherlands (van Dijk, 1987c). Ingroup perspective, ethnocentrism and group power consequently also influence the syntactic formulation of underlying semantic representations. Further, Downing (1980) shows that such biased representations hold for minorities in western countries and for peoples in Third World countries alike. Sykes (1985, 1987) arrives at similar conclusions in her study of official British (welfare) discourse about ethnic minorities: syntactic structures of sentences suggest the passiveness and dependence of black youth and downgrades their own active initiative.

The importance of these various studies of racism in the mass media is that they show an interesting interaction between group power and organizational power. White journalists (also mostly male) write both as professional representatives of media institutions and, at the same time, as members of the dominant, white, western group. This position shapes their social cognitions and, therefore, their processing of information about outgroups. Social position and social cognition allow them to exercise their power by writing, and continuing to write, despite many protests and studies, in a stereotypical or even negative way about relatively powerless ethnic or racial minority groups. Typically, they may do so unwittingly and will mostly forcefully reject the conclusion, made by ethnic groups and black or white researchers, that such reporting is ethnocentric, if not racist.

The effectiveness of media power also shows in the sources people use for their knowledge and attitude formation about ethnic groups (Hartmann and Husband, 1974). In the interviews we collected in Amsterdam about white people's experiences with and opinions about their 'foreign' neighbours, it appears that they often refer to the newspaper to warrant prejudices about ethnic groups (van Dijk, 1987a). Stereotypical media topics also appear to be dominant topics in everyday talk. Even when the media are ambiguous in their various discourses, the information they communicate may, nevertheless, be used to develop and confirm extant racist attitudes. The same is more generally true of racist discourse by other powerful groups or elites, for instance in the polity (Reeves, 1983).

Similar conclusions hold for the representation in the media of the working class, of women (especially feminists), of youth, demonstrators, squatters, punks and all social groups that tend to be discriminated against, marginalized, subordinated, or stereotyped but that also engage in various forms of resistance that may be seen as a bid for counter-power (see Cohen and Young, 1981; Halloran, Elliott and Murdock, 1970; Tuchman, Daniels and Benet, 1978; van Dijk, 1987c).

In a series of studies of television news about industrial conflicts in Great Britain, the Glasgow University Media Group (1976, 1980, 1982) concludes that the presentation of the major participants in these conflicts tends to be subtly in favour of employers and, therefore, negative for strikers. This bias is manufactured through time and type of interviews: employers tend to be interviewed in quiet contexts and in dominant positions, for instance in their offices, whereas strikers – if interviewed at all – are asked questions in the disturbing noise of the picket line. Camera angles and position, and the topical association by citizens of strikes with trouble, also reveal the anti-strike perspective of the media. Lexical choice represents strikers as demanding, whereas government or employers are represented more positively as making offers or otherwise as being in control. Workers are not said to 'offer' their labour under specified conditions. These and many other features of news production, source contact, interviewing, presentation, quotation, dominant topics, associations and style, subtly convey the social and ideological positions involved, including those of the media themselves.

What holds for news also holds for other media discourse, such as advertising. Here, corporations and advertising agencies combine powers in the production of persuasive discourse for public consumption. Unlike corporate representations in news reports, their public display in advertising, and hence their possible influence, is bought. The power of resistance by the public may be reduced by many tactical means (Percy and Rossiter, 1980). Like news reports, however, advertisements tend to reproduce social power structures and stereotypes, for instance of women or blacks (Culley and Bennett, 1976; Dyer, 1982; Greenberg and Mazingo, 1976; Goffman, 1979; King and Stott, 1977; Manstead and McCullogh, 1981; Tuchman, Daniels and Bent, 1978; Wilson and Gutiérrez, 1985). In this framework, Goffman (1979) speaks of the 'ritualization of subordination'. Advertisements attract public attention while at the same time controlling exposure and opinion and concealing corporate power through complex strategies of incompleteness, novelty, ambiguity, repetition and positive self-presentation (Davis and Walton, 1983; Packard, 1957; Tolmach Lakoff, 1981).

Textbooks

Like the mass media, educational discourse derives its power from its enormous scope. Unlike most other types of texts, textbooks are obligatory reading for many people, which is a second major condition of their power. Together with instructional dialogues, textbooks are used extensively by all citizens during their formal education. The knowledge and attitudes expressed and conveyed by such learning materials, again, reflect a dominant consensus, if not the interests of the most powerful groups and institutions of societies. Because textbooks and the educational programmes they are intended to realize should, in principle, serve public interests, they are seldom allowed to be 'controversial'. In other words, alternative, critical, radical voices are usually censored or mitigated (McHoul, 1986).

Many studies have shown that most textbooks reproduce a nationalistic, ethnocentric, or racist view of the world – of other peoples as well as of ethnic minority groups (Ferro, 1981; Klein, 1986; Milner, 1983; Preiswerk, 1980; van Dijk, 1987d). The observations are familiar from our news media analysis: underrepresentation, voicelessness and stereotyping. Minority groups and their history and culture tend to be ignored, and a few stereotypical cultural differences are emphasized and often negatively contrasted with properties of the 'own' group, nation, or culture. Although cultural differentiation and pride may be a feature of all or most groups, cultures, or countries, western or white dominance is shown through special attention to 'our' superior technology, culture and political system. Third World countries and (black) minorities may thus be portrayed as 'backward' compared to 'our' position and development, if not as 'primitive', 'lazy', and 'stupid'. At the same time, the dominant white group or the western world has its 'burden' to 'help these people', through aid, welfare, or technological advice. Although there are variations among textbooks (and in some countries these properties of books for children seem to change slowly), these messages dominate the history, geography, social science, or language textbooks in many countries of the western world (and Japan). Again, opposition, for example by teachers, requires extensive knowledge of, and access to, other sources of information, and the (usually restricted) freedom to deviate from established curricula and traditions. Thus, together with the media, textbooks and other educational materials form the core of both symbolic power and the textual reproduction and legitimation of power in society (Bourdieu, 1984; Bourdieu and Passeron, 1977).

Conclusions

In this chapter, we have examined some of the relationships between social power and discourse. We started from a general analysis of social power in terms of group-based or institutional control over actions and cognitions of other people and groups, usually in the interest of the powerful. Generally, an increase in power diminishes freedom for those who are subjected to this power. This interaction may be restricted to a specific social domain, and also affect the power holder. At the same time, the exercise of power may lead to resistence and the exercise of counter-power. Social power was further analysed in terms of its institutional or group basis, its domain, scope and legitimation. Personal power, which is not analysed in this chapter, may sometimes emphasize, but also counter, these forms of social power. Indeed, some women may dominate their husbands, some students their teachers and some children their parents; and conversely, not all doctors or men are medical or male chauvinists. Despite these personal differences, we focused on more general, structural properties of power relations and discourse in society.

Text and talk appear to play a crucial role in the exercise of power. Thus discourse may directly and coercively enact power, through directive speech acts, and through text types such as laws, regulations, or instructions. Power may also be manifested more indirectly in discourse, as representation in the form of an expression, description, or legitimation of powerful actors or their actions and ideologies. Discursive power is often directly or indirectly persuasive and, therefore, features reasons, arguments, promises, examples, or other rhetorical means that enhance the probability that recipients build the desired mental representations. One crucial strategy in the concealment of power is to persuade the powerless that wanted actions are in their own interest.

Discursive power also involves the control over discourse itself: who is speaking in what contexts; who has access to various types and means of communication; and which recipients can be reached? We found that there is a direct correlation between the scope of discourse and the scope of power: the powerless generally may have control only in everyday conversation, and are merely passive recipients of official and media discourse. The powerful have recourse to a large variety of dialogical, and especially printed, formal forms of text and talk, and, in principle, can reach large groups of people. Thus the powerful control discourse through control of its material production, its formulation and its distribution. Crucial in the exercise of power, then, is the control of the formation of social cognitions through the subtle management of knowledge and beliefs, the preformulation of beliefs, or the censorship of counter-ideologies. These representations form the essential cognitive link between social power itself and the production and understanding of discourse and its social functions in the enactment of power.

Against this more general background of the analysis of the links between power and discourse, our more concrete discourse analysis focused on the central micro-units of power and discourse, namely, communicative events, such as everyday conversations, courtroom trials, or classroom talk. In a review of some recent work, we thus examined how power is expressed, described, displayed, or legitimated in various genres of text and talk, and at various levels of analysis, such as speech acts, turn-taking, topic selection, style and rhetoric. Special attention was paid to the various ways institutional power is enacted by professionals and experts over their clients, and to the ways women and minority groups are subjected to power strategies, both in institutional dialogue and in media texts, such as news reports, textbooks and advertising. It was found that in this way, communicative events may be structured by several dimensions of power at the same time, not only those of the institution but those of gender, race and class.

Our theoretical analysis and our review show that, whether in its direct or in its indirect forms, power is both enacted and reproduced in and by discourse. Without communication – text and talk – power in society can hardly be exercised and legitimated. Power presupposes knowledge, beliefs and ideologies to sustain and reproduce it. Discourse structurally shows and communicates these crucial conditions of reproduction for all societal levels, dimensions and contexts. This chapter has presented an outline of these processes. Much further theoretical and empirical work will be necessary to fill in the many details of this discursive enactment and reproduction of power.

3

Discourse, Power and Access

Dimensions of Dominance

One of the crucial tasks of Critical Discourse Analysis (CDA) is to account for the relationships between discourse and social power. More specifically, such an analysis should describe and explain how power abuse is enacted, reproduced or legitimized by the text and talk of dominant groups or institutions. Within the framework of such an account of discursively mediated dominance and inequality this chapter focuses on an important dimension of such dominance, that is, patterns of *access* to discourse.

A critical analysis of properties of access to public discourse and communication presupposes insight into more general political, sociocultural and economic aspects of dominance. This chapter merely gives a succinct summary of this broader conceptual framework. Leaving aside a detailed discussion of numerous philosophical and theoretical complexities, the major presuppositions of this framework are, for example, the following (see, e.g., Clegg, 1989; Lukes, 1974, 1986; Wrong, 1979):

1   Power is a property of relations between social groups, institutions or organizations. Hence, only *social power*, and not individual power, is considered here.
2   Social power is defined in terms of the *control* exercized by one group or organization (or its 'members') over the *actions* and/or the *minds* of (the members of) another group, thus limiting the freedom of action of the others, or influencing their knowledge, attitudes or ideologies.
3   Power of a specific group or institution may be 'distributed', and may be restricted to a specific social *domain* or *scope*, such as that of politics, the media, law and order, education or corporate business, thus resulting in different 'centres' of power and elite groups that control such centres.

4   *Dominance* is here understood as a form of social power *abuse*, that is, as a legally or morally illegitimate exercise of control over others in one's own interests, often resulting in social inequality.

5   Power is *based* on privileged access to valued social resources, such as wealth, jobs, status, or indeed, a preferential access to public discourse and communication.

6   Social power and dominance are often *organized* and *institutionalized*, so as to allow more effective control, and to enable routine forms of power reproduction.

7   Dominance is seldom absolute; it is often *gradual*, and may be met by more or less *resistance* or counter-power by dominated groups.

For the discussion in this chapter, it is important to stress one element in these short definitions of power and dominance, that is, the relevance of the *cognitive* dimension of control. Power abuse not only involves the abuse of force, for example in police aggression against black youths, and may result not merely in limiting the freedom of action of a specific group, but also and more crucially may affect the *minds* of people. That is, through special access to, and control over the means of public discourse and communication, dominant groups or institutions may influence the structures of text and talk in such a way that, as a result, the knowledge, attitudes, norms, values and ideologies of recipients are – more or less indirectly affected – in the interest of the dominant group. Much 'modern' power in democratic societies is persuasive and manipulative rather than coercive (using of force), or incentive, such as the explicit issuing of commands, orders, threats or economic sanctions. Obviously, discourse plays a crucial role in thus 'manufacturing the consent' of others (Herman and Chomsky, 1988). It is therefore an important task of CDA to also study the precise cognitive structures and strategies involved in these processes affecting the *social cognitions* of groups (for details on social cognition, see e.g., Fiske and Taylor, 1991). Generally speaking, what is involved here is the manipulation of *mental models* of social events through the use of specific discourse structures, such as thematic structures, headlines, style, rhetorical figures, semantic strategies, and so on (for details, see van Dijk and Kintsch, 1983; van Dijk, 1990). Unless the readers or listeners have access to alternative information, or mental resources to oppose such persuasive messages, the result of such manipulation may be the formation of *preferred models* of specific situations (e.g., of a 'race riot'), which may in turn be generalized to more general, preferred knowledge, attitudes or ideologies (e.g., about blacks, or about youths).

do meijer
do fund agencies

Discourse and Access

One major element in the discursive reproduction of power and dominance is the very access to discourse and communicative events. In this
respect, discourse is similar to other valued social resources that form the
basis of power and to which there is unequally distributed access. For
instance, not everyone has equal access to the media or to medical, legal,
political, bureaucratic or scholarly text and talk. That is, we need to
explore the implications of the complex question *Who may speak or write
to whom, about what, when, and in what context,* or *Who may participate in
such communicative events in various recipient roles,* for instance as addressees,
audience, bystanders and overhearers. Access may even be analysed in
terms of the topics or referents of discourse, that is, who is written or
spoken about. We may assume, as for other social resources, that *more*
access according to these several participant roles, corresponds with *more*
social power. In other words, measures of discourse access may be rather
faithful indicators of the power of social groups and their members.

Patterns and strategies of discursive access may be spelled out for
virtually all social domains, institutions, professions, situations and genres.
Thus, in the *political* realm, only ministers have active access to Cabinet
meetings, and only parliamentarians to parliamentary debates. Secretaries
or clerks may have passive access to Cabinet meetings, that is, only in
their roles as people who take notes or carry out orders; they speak only
when invited to do so. In public sessions of parliaments, members of the
public may have passive access, but only as listeners (or rather, as 'overhearers'). Similar patterns of access exist also in *business corporations,* for
board meetings or in boss–employee interaction.

In *education,* teachers usually control communicative events, distribute
speaking turns, and otherwise have special access to, and hence control
over, educational discourse. On the other hand, students have in principle access to talk in classrooms only when talked to and invited to speak.
In some cases, also in other domains, such limited access may be voluntary, in others it may be obligatory, for example, when students must
answer exam questions, when citizens are ordered to speak in hearings,
defendants in police interrogations or when in court. Similarly, in *medical*
encounters, doctors may control many parts of the conversations with
their clients, such as the setting (time, place and circumstances, e.g., after
'appointment' only), topics (medical problems only) and style.

Most obvious and consequential are the patterns of access to the mass
media: who has preferential access to journalists, who will be interviewed,
quoted and described in news reports, and whose opinions will thus be

able to influence the public? That is, through access to the mass media, dominant groups also may have access to, and hence partial control over, the public at large. Except for letters to the editor, the public generally has passive media access only as readers or viewers.

Finally, in everyday *conversations*, there may be culturally different patterns of access based on age, gender, class, education or other criteria that define dominance and discrimination: women may have less access than men, blacks less than whites, young people less than adults.

Thus, for each social domain, profession, organization or situation, we may sketch a discursive and communicative *schema of conditions and strategies of access* for the various social groups involved: indeed, who may say/write what, how, to whom in what circumstances?

Analysing Patterns of Access

The examples informally discussed show different patterns of access, depending on various social or institutional roles, gender, age, position, context or topicality. In order to examine such conditions and strategies of access more explicitly, a number of analytical distinctions need to be made. Although it is a relevant concept in the study of discourse and power, 'access' is a rather vague notion, and therefore needs further specification. It may involve the way people take the initiative for communicative events, the modalities of their participation, as well as the ways they control the various other properties of discourse, such as turn-taking, sequencing, topics, or even the ways they are being represented, as referents or topics, in discourse. Let us briefly discuss some of these dimensions of access.

Planning

Planning of discourse access already begins with taking the initiative, the preparation or the *planning* of a communicative event. Thus a chairperson may 'call' a meeting, a judge may issue a warrant to appear in court and a professor may decide to hold an exam. Such plans will usually imply decisions about the setting (time, place) and an 'agenda' for talk, as well as the participants being invited or ordered to appear. For medical or educational encounters, patients or students may take the initiative, but doctors and professors usually decide about the setting. Such is also the case for most service encounters, such as with bureaucratic agencies. In media encounters, the relative position and power of news actors and journalists usually determines who may access whom: who has access to a press conference or who 'gives' an interview.

Setting

There are many elements of the setting of communicative events that may be controlled by different participants. First of all, who is allowed or obliged to participate, and in what role, may be decided by the chairperson or by other powerful participants who control the interaction. We have already seen that time, place and circumstances of text and talk may similarly be controlled by powerful actors. Also other circumstances, such as distance, positioning and the presence of 'props of power' (the bench and the robes of a judge, the uniform of police officers, or the 'head' of the table for chairs), may involve differential patterns of access for different participants.

Controlling communicative events

The crucial form of access consists of the power to control various dimensions of speech and talk itself: which mode of communication may/must be used (spoken, written), which language may/must be used by whom (dominant or standard language, a dialect, etc.), which genres of discourse are allowed, which types of speech acts, or who may begin or interrupt turns at talk or discursive sequences. Besides these overall constraints, participants may have differential access to topics, style or rhetoric. Thus, defendants in court may be required to speak the standard language, to answer questions only (and only when required to speak), to speak only about the topic being discussed, and using a polite, deferential style. Similar constraints may exist for subordinates in business companies or students in school. That is, virtually all levels and dimensions of text and talk may have obligatory, optional or preferential access for different participants, for example, as a function of their institutional or social power. Or rather, such power and dominance may be enacted, confirmed and reproduced by such differential patterns of access to various forms of discourse in different social situations. Thus, having access to the speech act of a command presupposes as well as enacts and confirms the social power of the speaker.

Scope and audience control

For dialogues such as formal meetings, sessions or debates, initiators or participants may allow or require specific participants to be present (or absent), or to allow or require these others to listen and/or to speak. Beyond the control of content or style, thus, speakers may also control audiences. That is, discourse access, especially in public forms of discourse, also and most crucially implies audience access. At public meetings or through the mass media, discourses and their speakers or authors may thus have a greater or lesser power scope. Full access to a major newspaper or television network thus also implies access to a large audience: obviously, access to the *New York Times* or CBS signals more power than access to a local newspaper or local radio station. The same is true for writers, teachers, professors or politicians and the relative sizes of their audiences.

Although the scope of access, in terms of the size of the audience of one's discourse, is an important criterion of power, control is much more effective if the minds of the audience can also be successfully 'accessed'.

When speakers are able to influence the mental models, knowledge, attitudes and eventually even the ideologies of recipients, they may indirectly control their future actions. That is, mentally mediated control of the actions of others is the ultimate form of power, especially when the audience is hardly aware of such control, as is the case in manipulation. Indeed, most forms of discursive and communicative access we discussed above, such as control of setting, interaction, topic or style, will be geared towards the control of the minds of participants, recipients or the audience at large, in such a way that the resulting mental changes are those preferred by those in power, and generally in their interest.

Synthesizing criteria of access

After this discussion of the various types of access, we are now able to spell out – for each type of discourse or communicative event, and for each social group or institution – the various access patterns that establish one of the relationships between discourse and social power. For a court trial, for instance, we might specify the following schema of access, in terms of who control(s) what aspect of such a trial, as informally discussed above (the schema is not complete; for conversational details, see e.g., Atkinson and Drew, 1979; for style, see Erickson et al., 1978; O'Barr, 1982; for access to specific genes, Wodak, 1985; note also that all variation and control is limited by the overall sociocultural constraints of the legal context and the speech situation).

    Initiative: judge
    Setting (time, place, participants): judge, prosecutor, barristers
    Communicative event
    Participants: judge (e.g., judge may exclude prosecution witnesses)

Turn allocation and distribution: judge
Sequencing (e.g., opening and closing the session): judge
Speech acts:
  Verdict, sentencing, commands, requests, questions, assertions: judge
  Verdict: jury (e.g., in British and US legal systems)
  Indictment, accusations, questions, assertions: prosecutor
  Defence, requests, questions, assertions: defence counsel
  Assertions (as answers to questions): defendant, witnesses
Topic(s): judge, prosecutor, defence counsel
Style: judge
Recording: clerks
Audience/scope: immediate: usually small; mass mediated: large.
Result: possibly serious for defendant (loss of money, freedom, or life).

Conversely, we may examine the power of social groups or professions, such as judges, by analysing their range and patterns of access (as judges), and we see that they control most properties of the court trial. However, since (important) trials are often routinely covered by the media, judges also have relatively easy media access as described above, although such access is not total: judges may not control what exactly is written or said about them (Anderson et al., 1988; Chibnall, 1977; Graber, 1980; Hariman, 1990). Although the normal access range and scope of judges is only the legal domain, that is legal discourse in general (e.g., when writing a verdict), and trials in particular, judges may also have access to education and research when giving lectures or writing textbooks, or to politics or finance when they are appointed as members of committees or boards because of their legal expertise or influence. In sum, judges appear to have a medium range of access, corresponding to their relative power. However, since they are, in principle, the only ones who decide about freedom or even about life and death, the consequences of their otherwise moderate power may be tremendous. This is, of course, especially the case for judges of courts of appeal and Supreme Courts, which may even have the last word in deciding on major socio-political issues affecting a whole nation, such as abortion or civil rights. That is, beyond the scope and the range of their discourse access, the power of judges should especially also be measured by the personal, social and political consequences of such access. Indeed, in the legal domain, their discourse may be law.

Similar analyses may be made, each for their own domain of power, for more or less powerful presidents, Cabinet ministers, members of parliament or congress, popes and priests, chief executive officers, professors, newspaper editors or union leaders, among others, but also, at lower levels of the power hierarchy, for 'ordinary' citizens, bureaucrats, police officers, teachers or shopkeepers. It is our contention that there should generally be a rather close interdependence between power (and hence access to valued social resources), on the one hand, and access to – control over – the conditions, structural properties and consequences of discourse, on the other hand. In other words, if discourse access is a measure of power, Critical Discourse Analysis becomes an important diagnostic tool for the assessment of social and political dominance.

Discourse, Power and Racism

To further illustrate the analysis of discursive social power and access patterns presented above, let us finally examine in somewhat more detail some of the ways social power is being enacted, legitimized and repro-duced in one major domain of dominance, that by white (European) groups over ethnic or racial minorities, refugees or other immigrants.

Empirical data that form the backdrop of this discussion are derived from our extensive research project on discourse and racism, carried out at the University of Amsterdam since 1980 (van Dijk, 1984a, 1987a, 1991, 1993a). The various discourses studied for this project were every-day conversations, high school textbooks, news reports in the press, parliamentary debates, scientific discourse, and corporate discourse among others.

The aim of our discussion here is only to show how ethnic-racial dominance, or racism, is also reproduced through differential patterns of discourse access for majority and minority groups, and not only because of differential access to residence, jobs, housing, education or welfare. This dominance may take two forms: the discursive reproduction of ethnic prejudice and racism within the dominant white group itself, on the one hand, and forms of everyday racism in talk between majority and minor-ity members (e.g., slurs, impoliteness, unfounded accusations), on the other hand (Essed, 1991).

One strategy of such dominant discourse is to persuasively define the ethnic status quo as 'natural', 'just', 'inevitable' or even as 'democratic', for instance through denials of discrimination or racism, or by de-racializing inequality through redefinitions in terms of class, cultural difference or the special (unique, temporary) consequences of immigrant status. The persuasive or manipulatory success of such dominant discourse is partly due to the patterns of access of such text and talk. That is, most power elites are themselves white, and their power implies preferential access to the means of mass communication, political decision-making discourse, the discourses of the bureaucracy and the legal system. That is, relative to minority groups, dominance is duplicated: it is the white group as a whole that has special privileges and access to social resources, including the symbolic resources of communication, whereas the white power elites additionally control the white group at large by their persuasive influence on the mental conditions (stereotypes, prejudices, ideologies) of the discriminatory practices of white group members.

The opposite is true for ethnic minority groups, whose subordination is further exacerbated by their (generally) lower class position. That is, their lack of access is not merely defined in terms of racial or ethnic exclusion but also by their class-dependent lack of access to good education, status, employment or capital, shared with poor whites. The exclusion and marginalization that result from limited socioeconomic and symbolic (discursive, communicative) access hardly need to be spelled out (for details, see Essed, 1991; Jaynes and Williams, 1989). Thus, minorities or immigrants generally have less or no access to the following crucial communicative contexts, as analysed above:

- government and legislative discourses of decision-making, information, persuasion and legitimation, especially at the national state levels;
- bureaucratic discourses of higher level policy-making and policy implementation;
- mass media discourse of major news media;
- scholarly or scientific discourse;
- corporate discourse.

Politics

Especially in Europe, virtually no minority group members are members of national governments, and only very few are members of the legislature (for the UK, see Solomos, 1989). In some countries, such as the Netherlands, some minorities that do not have Dutch nationality, but have been residents for five years, have active and passive access to local elections, and thus have a (minimal) voice in city councils, a small 'privilege' fiercely opposed in, say, France and Germany. Due to the size of ethnic minority groups in the USA, there is at least some political representation of minorities and hence access to political decision-making, especially at the local level, for example in cities with a large minority population (Ben-Tovim et al., 1986; Jaynes and Williams, 1989; Marable,

1985). Since most 'ethnic' policies, however, are national or federal, minorities are more or less effectively excluded from more influential text and talk about their own position. On the other hand, minorities are frequent topics of political talk and text, but this form of passive access is hardly controlled by them: they have virtually no influence on this 'representation' in political discourse (van Dijk, 1993a).

Media

The access of minorities to the mass media is a critical condition for their participation in the public definition of their situation. Despite the generally liberal self-definitions of many journalists, lack of media access by minorities is one of the most conspicuous properties of the symbolic dominance of white elites (Hujanen, 1984; Mazingo, 1988; Minority Participation in the Media, 1983; Wilson and Gutiérrez, 1985). In Europe, there are virtually no minority journalists, least of all in controlling editorial positions. Major quality newspapers may have just one or two token minorities, often in non-tenured contract or freelance positions. Even in the USA, 51 per cent of the newspapers have no minority journalists, and promotions to higher positions are notoriously problematic. Television has limited access only for some (very 'moderate') visible token minorities. As a result, the newsroom staff are virtually wholly white and this will of course have serious consequences for news production, writing style, source access and general perspective of news discourse or television programmes (Hartmann and Husband, 1974; Martindale, 1986; Smitherman-Donaldson and van Dijk, 1988; van Dijk, 1991).

Moreover, due to their limited social and economic power, minority groups and organizations also lack the usual forms of organized media access, such as press conferences, press releases and public relations departments (Fedler, 1973). Conversely, most white journalists are known to routinely prefer (white) institutional sources (Tuchman, 1978), and generally find minorities less credible, especially when these are providing critical opinions about dominant white elites. Communication problems and differences of style between white journalists and minority sources may further limit minority access to the media (Kochman, 1981).

Differential access of majority elites and minorities to the media predictably results in differential access to the structures of news reports as well. Selection and prominence of news *issues* and *topics* are those stereotypical and negative ones preferred by the white political, corporate, social or scholarly elites and their institutions. Thus, the frequent issue of immigration will be primarily defined as an invasion and as essentially problematic, and seldom as a welcome contribution to the economy or the culture of the country. Crime, drugs, violence and cultural deviance are other preferred issues of 'ethnic' news coverage. Conversely, due to limited minority access to the definition of the situation, issues and topics that are directly relevant for minorities are less covered or made less prominent. This is the case for issues such as discrimination, racism, police brutality, shortage of jobs, miserable working conditions, the failures of minority education, and so on, especially when the white elites are to blame for the situation. On the other hand, the actions of white elites that are defined as 'positive' for minorities are usually covered prominently. As in the coverage of North–South relations, 'our' helping 'them' is a very newsworthy topic. Thus, news topic selection and prominence is a direct function of the differential access, interests and perspectives of majority and minority news actors.

Similarly, lack of access to journalists also predicts that minority speakers will be less *quoted* than white majority speakers, as is indeed the case (van Dijk, 1991). If they are quoted at all, then either moderate spokespersons will be quoted who share the opinions or perspective of the majority, or radicals or extremists will be quoted in order to facilitate ridicule or attack (Downing, 1980). Minorities are especially quoted on 'soft' and less 'risky' topics, such as religion, the arts, folklore, or culture more generally (Hartmann and Husband, 1974; Johnson, 1987; van Dijk, 1991). Also, unlike majority group speakers, minorities are seldom allowed to speak alone. Their accusations of the host society and its elites, when quoted at all, *never* go unchallenged.

Similar observations may be made for all properties and levels of news reports. *Headline* content and syntactic structure systematically favour 'us' and problematize 'them', as is also the case for lexical *style* (e.g., 'riots' instead of 'disturbances'), *rhetoric*, disclaimers and other strategic semantic *moves* ('We have nothing against Turks, but . . .'; 'We are a tolerant society, but . . .'), as well as other discursive properties. Thus, on the whole, 'their' negative actions are made more prominent (e.g., by topicalization, first-page coverage, headlining, rhetorical emphasis), whereas 'our' negative actions are de-emphasized by denials, euphemism, mitigation or other strategies for avoiding negative self-presentation (van Dijk, 1991, 1992). Because of a lack of alternative information sources about ethnic relations, the effects of such daily reporting of the models and attitudes of many white readers are predictable: widespread prejudice and xenophobia. Thus, minorities and their representatives have little access to the general public, unless by protests and disruptive behaviour that will precisely be defined as a confirmation of prevailing stereotypes and prejudices.

Academia

Rather similar remarks may be made about patterns of access to educational and scholarly discourse (for details, see van Dijk, 1993a). Minorities, especially in Europe, generally have little access to universities, and even less to the active control of scholarly discourse, even in 'ethnic' studies about them. In the Netherlands, for instance, more than 95 per cent of all 'ethnic' research is carried out by white Dutch researchers, and even more is under white Dutch supervision. Ethnic studies departments, if any, are usually largely white. The topics of such 'ethnic' research are surprisingly similar to those in the mass media: cultural difference and deviance, crime, educational problems, etc. With the usual delays, high school textbooks typically reproduce prevailing scholarly stereotypes about minorities. Not surprisingly, the media will in turn pay special attention to those research results that nicely fit the prevailing stereotypes, such as about youth gangs, drugs, crime or the cultural problems of young immigrant women.

Critical issues, such as discrimination and especially racism, are as little studied as they are covered in the press. Moreover, the few studies of these issues tend to be ignored, denied, marginalized and attacked as 'unscientific' or 'political' scholarship (Essed, 1987).

Thus, ethnic groups, and even their scholarly elites, have virtually no access to, let alone control over, the ways the ethnic situation is defined in the social sciences. Since much of this research is also used as a source for national policies (and for media accounts), we see how dominant white elites jointly collude in preventing access to the hegemonic basis of power, that of knowledge and beliefs and the manufacture of the consensus. It needs no further argument that curricula, scholarly journals, conferences and other vehicles of scholarly discourse are also usually dominated by white scholars, except for small 'niches' of 'black' journals that have virtually no influence on the scholarly establishment in the social sciences as a whole. The hype, especially in the USA, about what is defined as 'political correctness' in academia reflects an overreaction of dominant white elites against minor and local cultural shifts and minority resistance, rather than a fundamental change in prevailing academic discourse and access patterns (Aufderheide, 1992; Berman, 1992).

Business

Corporate discourse is usually less public, and hence only indirectly involved in manufacturing consent. However, it is ultimately vastly influential through its consequences for the socioeconomic implications of the ethnic status quo. If corporate discourse explains high minority unemployment especially in terms that blame the victim (language deficiencies, lack of skills, lower education, failing work ethos, etc.), this discourse will also have easy access to the press and to political decision-making (Fernandez, 1981; Jenkins, 1986; van Dijk, 1993a). Managerial talk about affirmative action and other forms of social responsibility may be associated with many negative properties, such as loss of competition, social unfairness and so on. Also this feature of prominent corporate discourse, especially in Europe, will indirectly become public, for instance through politicians or journalists repeating or emphasizing this point of view.

Few minority group members have leading managerial positions and, when they do, they make sure not to speak too radically about the claims or complaints of their own group, unless they want to lose their jobs. Thus, minorities have very little influence on dominant corporate discourse. That is, they are unable to successfully challenge the ideologies that underlie discrimination and marginalization of minorities in employment, business and finance in the first place. On the contrary, blaming the victim is a major strategy of white elite dominance, also in corporate discourse: charges of discrimination will be reversed by accusing minorities (especially blacks) of causing their own predicament, as noted above.

Some Examples

After the more theoretical analysis of the relations between discourse, power and access, and the review of access patterns for discourse on ethnic relations, let us finally discuss some concrete examples. These will be taken from the coverage of ethnic affairs in the British press during the first six months of 1989. Many reports during these months dealt with the Salman Rushdie affair, and – as usual in the press – with 'illegal' immigration.

Example 1

Thus *The Sun* begins one of its articles (23 January 1989) on immigration as follows:

GET LOST, SPONGERS

By Victor Chapple

A BLITZ on illegal immigration is being launched by the Government. The number of staff dealing with foreign spongers will be more than DOUBLED and TOUGH new curbs are planned against bogus overseas students. Key targets will be phoney colleges which enrol youngsters, but provide no courses. When immigration officers raided one in East London last year, they found that 990 of the 1000 'students' had no right to be in Britain. Home secretary Douglas Hurd is considering law changes to stop foreign visitors switching to student status while here.

The huge (23 x 3 cm) banner headline of this article represents the evaluative comment of the *Sun* on the plan of the government. The same is true for the use of 'bogus' and 'phoney', when describing students and colleges. These evaluative terms are not likely to be those used by the British government or Home Secretary Mr Douglas Hurd. It is at this point that the power, the autonomy and hence the responsibility of the newspaper are obvious: they could hardly blame the 'politicians' for the racist language they use to influence the readers. In terms of our analysis of patterns of access, the style of reporting is accessible only to the reporter (Victor Chapple) or the editors of the *Sun*, and so is the persuasive effect such negative other-presentation may have on the minds of the readers. The direct contribution to the confirmation of well-known ethnic prejudices in the UK, that is, of immigrants as 'spongers', is thus within the scope of the responsibility of the tabloid.

At the same time, however, we need to emphasize the 'collusion' between the press elites on the one hand and the political elites on the other. After all, the policies and political actions written *about* are those of the British authorities: they will do anything to reduce what they define as 'illegal' immigration. The tabloid does not merely report such actions, however, but supports them, and even fabricates their reasons (students will be expelled because they are 'spongers'). Thus, in many ways, the right-wing press supports conservative immigration policies, while at the same time framing them in a popular rhetorical style ('get lost', 'spongers', 'phoney', etc.) that makes such policies seem to respond to popular demand and resentment against immigration, thereby legitimizing them.

Besides the direct access of the newsmakers to the style (size, lexicalization, etc.) of the headlines and the style of the rest of the article, we also witness some degree of access of a prominent politician, that of the Home Secretary, whose picture is reproduced, whose actions are covered (positively) and whose future policies are mentioned. In the rest of the article, not quoted here, about a Sri Lankan refugee, Mr Viraj Mendis (described as an 'activist') – who had sought refuge in a church but was arrested in a police raid and expelled after many years of residence in the UK – Douglas Hurd is also quoted, as is a Tory Member of Parliament (MP), both protesting against the action of churches in hiding refugees. The churches have no access to the press here: no spokespersons are quoted. Viraj Mendis, in a separate small article, is quoted as wanting to 'expose the racism of the British government', and a picture of him is also shown. However, the framing of *his* words is dramatically different from that of Hurd. He is portrayed, in the text, as 'sip[ping] mineral water in an exclusive club in Colombo', which implies that someone who is in such a situation can hardly be a serious refugee, and hence not a credible speaker. The very fact that he accuses the British government of racism is so preposterous for the *Sun* that such an accusation hardly needs further discrediting of Mendis, as the tabloid had done during the whole Mendis affair (for a more detailed analysis of right-wing reporting in the UK on the Viraj Mendis case, see van Dijk, 1993b).

In sum, we find several modes of access here. First, access of media elites: tabloid reporters and editors themselves, who chose the topic as being newsworthy, and control its style and rhetoric, layout, photos, and who thus also have direct and persuasive access to the 'minds' of the readers.

Second, access of political elites: Mr Hurd as main actor has access to the topic, the quotations and the visual images of a tabloid read by about five million British readers.

Third, access of other politicians: access of a Tory MP, supporting Mr Hurd (or rather being critical of him for not having acted fast enough) and hence also sustaining the negative evaluation of the *Sun*.

Fourth, access of a refugee: passive access of Viraj Mendis to a secondary topic of this article (and to the main topic of a related short story), to quotation and photographs, but embedded in a negative framework so as to invalidate his credibility.

Example 2

The next example is also taken from *The Sun*, and was published a few days later (2 February 1989):

BRITAIN INVADED BY AN ARMY OF ILLEGALS
SUN News Special
By John Kay and Alison Bowyer

Britain is being swamped by a tide of alleged immigrants so desperate for a job that they will work for a pittance in our restaurants, cafes and nightclubs.

Immigration officers are being overwhelmed with work. Last year, 2,191 'illegals' were being nabbed and sent back home. But there are tens of thousands more, slaving behind bars, cleaning hotel rooms and working in kitchens. . . . Illegals sneak in by:

- **DECEIVING** immigration officers when they are quizzed at airports.
- **DISAPPEARING** after their entry visas run out.
- **FORGING** work permits and other documents.
- **RUNNING** away from immigrant detention centres.

We again find the familiar picture of a huge banner headline, featuring three major negative expressions, usually associated with immigrants and refugees: 'Invaded', 'army', and 'illegals'. This style of describing undocumented immigrants is fully under the control (and access) of the *Sun* journalists, with the probable consequences for the access to the public mind, as described above. Note the special semantic implications and associations of the use of 'invasion' and 'army' which explicitly relates immigration with violence and threats to 'Britain': Immigration is War.

Since this is a 'News Special', the responsibility seems to be even more that of the tabloid: they do not report a news event, such as a political action, as is the case in the previous example, but they bring a 'report' based on their own journalistic 'investigations'. The 'facts' thus constructed by the tabloid are as familiar as their metaphorical style, by which refugees and other immigrants are routinely compared to a 'tide' that 'swamps' the country. The term 'swamped' is familiar. It was also used by Margaret Thatcher before she was elected prime minister, when she said that she feared that Britain would be 'rather swamped' by people of an alien culture. Hence, the metaphors, though under full access and control of the journalists, are as such hardly new, and belong to the stock-in-trade of racist conservatives speaking about immigration. Obviously, as is the case with the use of 'invaded' and 'army', being 'swamped' by a 'tide' of 'illegals' is just as threatening for the (white) British population, which is the primary audience for such style. The rest of the article shows the same style, for example when the police actions are called a 'battle to hunt down the furtive workforce'. This is indeed what it is: a war to keep Britain white.

Immigration officers also have (passive, topical) access to this article, and are duly pitied as being 'overwhelmed' by the task. No harsh word will be found in the *Sun* about the ways that immigration officers accomplish their task of 'tracking' down 'illegals'. Note though that there seems to be a suggestion of commiseration with the immigrants as well, as may be inferred from the use of 'working for a pittance' and 'slaving'. At the same time, the style of the rest of the article does not seem to confirm this journalistic mood in favour of the immigrants. Rather 'working for a pittance' also implies that since immigrants will do any job for any wage, they compete with white British workers. Thus, such a representation supports the familiar racist conclusion: 'They take away our jobs!' Indeed, nowhere is it stressed in the article that most white British no longer want such work.

The next fragment, emphasized by bold capitals and attention-seeking 'bullets', summarizes the various forms of deviance, violation and crime attributed to immigrants: they are liars and frauds. The rest of the article is similar (they do not pay taxes, etc.), but also focuses on the businesses that are being 'raided' by the police. However, the focus of illegality is not on employers, businesses and all those others who exploit immigrants and pay sub-standard wages. Indeed, the headline of the article is *not* BRITAIN THREATENED BY A GANG OF IMMIGRANT-EXPLOITING BUSINESSES. Even the use of the passive voice in the syntax of the sentences hides those who do illegal hiring: 'They [immigration officials] ended up taking away THIRTEEN Nigerians, all employed illegally', of which the last clause hides the agent of illegal hiring. As for the relations of power and access involved, we first of all find the reporters (and possi- bly the editors) of the *Sun* again responsible for the selection of the topic of this 'special report', for its style and the focus on certain dimensions (immigrants as threat and criminals) and not on others (employers engag- ing in illegal hiring and exploiting minorities). That is, the media elites have exclusive and active access to, and control over, a large part of this text, and such is also their responsibility in manipulating the minds of the readers: the 'facts' of immigration are not to be blamed (as the reporters would undoubtedly say), but the journalistic ways of fabricating, representing and persuasively formulating such 'facts'. At the same time, other news actors are involved and have various measures of access. Positively represented, as could be expected, are the immigration officers (in ethnic reporting in the right-wing press, the officers of law and order are always presented posi- tively, as the guardians of Britain, who valiantly struggle in the racial war). One of them is also introduced in a later quote which tells the readers that he doesn't know how many illegals there are (apparently, the *Sun* does know) but that the officials are stepping up 'their efforts to track them down'. Employers, we have seen, are stylistically absent: their businesses may be raided, but they are literally out of the picture; only 'illegal' (that is immigrants, not managers) are found there. Yet, at the end, and in a small separate article, some bosses may talk; however, they affirm that they hire only legal immigrants (from the EU), a claim that is not presented as at all doubtful by the *Sun*. Not a single negative word about employers is found in this article, despite the fact that the 'illegal' immigrants are working for a pittance. On the contrary, they are represented as victims, who are some-times 'tricked by false credentials'.

In sum, also throughout this special report, 'we' or 'our' people (offi-cials, business, Britain), are consequently represented in a positive way, and 'they' in a very negative way, as an invading army or as a swamping tide, people who, in the *Sun*'s words, must be 'nabbed' and 'carted off' by the immigration officials.

We see that patterns of access (who is written about, who is allowed to speak, who may address whom, and who may use what style, etc.) are closely related to modes of self- and other-presentation in public discourse on ethnic affairs. Access to the press, through access to the jour-nalists, also presupposes group membership: those who belong will have more access, especially the elites, but at the same time they will also be represented more positively. The inverse is true for 'them'. Indeed, not a single 'illegal immigrant' is quoted in this 'special report': their views, experiences, backgrounds are irrelevant. With a foreign army, that is, the enemy, one does not talk: one 'hunts them down'.

Other Examples

Many similar examples may be given: in the tabloid press most reporting has the same overall structures and strategies of access to selection, topi-cality, style and quotation, along the familiar US–THEM schema of racist representations. For the right-wing tabloids, this also means that 'them' (immigrants) are associated with 'them' of the 'loony left', another famil-iar target of tabloid attacks, as in the first of the following banner head-lines and text fragments:

> **LEFTIES HAND £20,000 TO ILLEGAL IMMIGRANT**
> (*Sun*, 6 February 1989)
> **BE BRITISH, HURD TELLS IMMIGRANTS**
> **A DIRECT warning to Britain's 750,000 Moslems will be issued by Home Secretary Douglas Hurd today.**

He will tell them they must learn to live with British laws and customs – particularly for the sake of their children. The alternative would be growing public
anger and resentment and renewed social conflict. (*Daily Mail*, 24 February 1989)

NO RACIALISM IN TORY PARTY, SAYS THATCHER (*Daily Telegraph*,
23 June 1989)

Thus, immigrants and the left share the familiar accusations of 'fraud'
exposed by the tabloids, as in the first headline. Indeed, 'ratepayers'
money', as is often stressed, is thus presented as 'squandered' by loony left
councils or programmes, a topic obviously popular with many tabloid
readers.

In the second example, Home Secretary Hurd, responsible for immigration and ethnic relations, appears again, this time with a full account
of a speech he *will* give (some news is not about the past, but about the
near future), and which is worth an immense headline in 3 cm high capitals. That is, after the Rushdie affair, Muslims have become fair game both
for paternalistic, if not threatening, political action, as well as for the press
(and not only the right-wing tabloids), which associates *all* Muslims with
the radical fundamentalists among them. If cultural autonomy was occasionally an official policy of western governments, the words now being
spoken by Hurd and emphasized by the *Mail* leave no doubt about the
real, assimilationist goals of ethnic relation policies: adapt to us, or get out.
Worse, as is the case in much tabloid reporting and editorials, as soon as
immigrants or minorities are represented as violating the law (as in 'riots')
or trespassing the norms of cultural adaptation, popular 'resentment' (or
even the fascists) is made to appear as a threat. Ironically, if not cynically,
we need to realize that this resentment is created and fed by the tabloids
themselves. Similarly, the threat of 'racial conflict' is not attributed to
white racists but to immigrants themselves, a familiar move of strategic
reversal in the attribution of responsibilities.

The third example speaks for itself. As prime minister, Margaret
Thatcher obviously had most privileged access to the media, thus being
allowed to define the ethnic situation, and thus, of course, to deny racism
(while at the same time using the familiar conservative mitigation, 'racial-
izing'). Notice, that if (well-founded) accusations of racism are reported
at all, the conservative press will routinely use the distance- or doubt-
implying term 'claim' (for details, see van Dijk, 1991). Not so when
Thatcher 'flatly denies', during a parliamentary debate, that there is no
racism in the Conservative party, a claim met with derision from the
Labour benches, here represented, however, as less credible than

Thatcher. Indeed, the denial of racism is one of the hallmarks of elite racism (see van Dijk, 1993c).

Again we find the familiar patterns of access: Hurd, as a conservative politician, and by castigating Muslims, has ample access to the tabloid, its topic selection, its headline, and quote, and so has Thatcher. The immigrants and Muslims have passive access (as topics), but *they* do not control their representation, and their spokespersons are not quoted, unless it is a radical fundamentalist who will gladly oblige by confirming the prejudices of the reporter about the threat posed by Muslims and Arabs.

Conclusions

The conclusions of this chapter are brief. Within the framework of a critical analysis of discourses, the study of the reproduction of power and dominance through discourse is a primary objective. One element in this reproduction process is the structures and strategies of 'access': who controls the preparation, the participants, the goals, the language, the genre, the speech acts, the topics, the schemata (e.g., headlines, quotes), the style and the rhetoric, among other text features, of communicative events. That is, who can/may/must say what, to whom, how, in what circumstances and with what effects on the recipients?

Among the resources that form the power base of dominant groups, the preferential access to public discourse is an increasingly important asset because it allows access to the control mechanisms of the public mind. In modern societies, discourse access is a primary condition for the manufacture of consent and therefore the most effective way to exercise power and dominance.

Our brief analysis of some examples from the British press shows how the tabloids, conservative politicians and the forces of law and order have preferential access to the public definition of immigration and minorities, as well as to their derogation as criminals, frauds, invading armies and radical assassins, among many other other-descriptions of 'them', while at the same time presenting 'us' as tolerant, tough and valiant, if not as victims. That is, the power of preferential access to the media is intimately related to the power of dominant groups to define the ethnic situation, and to contribute to the reproduction of racism, that is, the power of the white group.

4

Critical Discourse Analysis

Introduction: What is Critical Discourse Analysis?

Critical discourse analysis (CDA) is a type of discourse analytical research that primarily studies the way social power abuse, dominance and inequality are enacted, reproduced and resisted by text and talk in the social and political context. With such dissident research, critical discourse analysts take explicit position, and thus want to understand, expose and ultimately resist social inequality.

Some of the tenets of CDA can already be found in the critical theory of the Frankfurt School before the Second World War (Agger, 1992b; Rasmussen, 1996). Its current focus on language and discourse was initiated with the 'critical linguistics' that emerged (mostly in the UK and Australia) at the end of the 1970s (Fowler et al., 1979; see also Mey, 1985). CDA has also counterparts in 'critical' developments in sociolinguistics, psychology and the social sciences, some already dating back to the early 1970s (Birnbaum, 1971; Calhoun, 1995; Fay, 1987; Fox and Prilleltensky, 1997; Hymes, 1972; Ibañez and Íñiguez, 1997; Singh, 1996; Thomas, 1993; Turkel, 1996; Wodak, 1996). As is the case in these neighbouring disciplines, CDA may be seen as a reaction against the dominant formal (often 'asocial' or 'uncritical') paradigms of the 1960s and 1970s.

CDA is not so much a direction, school, or specialization next to the many other 'approaches' in discourse studies. Rather, it aims to offer a different 'mode' or 'perspective' of theorizing, analysis and application throughout the whole field. We may find a more or less critical perspective in such diverse areas as pragmatics, conversation analysis, narrative analysis, rhetoric, stylistics, sociolinguistics, ethnography, or media analysis, among others.

Crucial for critical discourse analysts is the explicit awareness of their role in society. Continuing a tradition that rejects the possibility of a 'value-free' science, they argue that science, and especially scholarly discourse, is inherently part of and influenced by social structure and produced in social interaction. Instead of denying or ignoring such a relation between scholarship and society, they plead that such relations be studied and accounted for in their own right, and that scholarly practices be based on such insights. Theory formation, description and explanation, also in discourse analysis, are sociopolitically 'situated', whether we like it or not. Reflection on the role of scholars in society and the polity thus becomes an inherent part of the discourse analytical enterprise. This may mean, among other things, that discourse analysts conduct research in solidarity and cooperation with dominated groups.

Critical research on discourse needs to satisfy a number of requirements in order to effectively realize its aims:

- as is often the case for more marginal research traditions, CDA research has to be 'better' than other research in order to be accepted;
- it focuses primarily on *social problems* and political issues, rather than on current paradigms and fashions;
- empirically adequate critical analysis of social problems is usually *multidisciplinary*;
- rather than merely *describe* discourse structures, it tries to explain them in terms of properties of social interaction and especially social structure;
- more specifically, CDA focuses on the ways discourse structures enact, confirm, legitimate, reproduce, or challenge relations of *power* and *dominance* in society.

Fairclough and Wodak (1997: 271–80) summarize the main tenets of CDA as follows:

1   CDA addresses social problems.
2   Power relations are discursive.
3   Discourse constitutes society and culture.
4   Discourse does ideological work.
5   Discourse is historical.
6   The link between text and society is mediated.
7   Discourse analysis is interpretative and explanatory.
8   Discourse is a form of social action.

Whereas some of these tenets have also been discussed above, others need a more systematic theoretical analysis, of which we shall present some fragments here as a more or less general basis for the main principles of CDA (for details about these aims of critical discourse and language studies, see, e.g., Caldas-Coulthard and Coulthard, 1996; Fairclough, 1992a, 1995a; Fairclough and Wodak, 1997; Fowler et al., 1979; van Dijk, 1993b).

Conceptual and Theoretical Frameworks

Since CDA is not a specific direction of research, it does not have a unitary theoretical framework. Within the aims mentioned above, there are many types of CDA, and these may be theoretically and analytically quite diverse. Critical analysis of conversation is very different from an analysis of news reports in the press or of lessons and teaching at school. Yet, given the common perspective and the general aims of CDA, we may also find overall conceptual and theoretical frameworks that are closely related. As suggested, most kinds of CDA will ask questions about the way specific discourse structures are deployed in the reproduction of social dominance, whether they are part of a conversation or a news report or other genres and contexts. Thus, the typical vocabulary of many scholars in CDA will feature such notions as 'power', 'dominance', 'hegemony', 'ideology', 'class', 'gender', 'race', 'discrimination', 'interests', 'reproduction', 'institutions', 'social structure' and 'social order', besides the more familiar discourse analytical notions.[1]

In this section, I focus on a number of basic concepts themselves, and thus devise a theoretical framework that critically relates discourse, cognition and society.

Macro vs. micro

Language use, discourse, verbal interaction and communication belong to the micro level of the social order. Power, dominance, and inequality between social groups are typically terms that belong to a macro level of analysis. This means that CDA has to theoretically bridge the well-known 'gap' between micro and macro approaches, which is of course a distinction that is a sociological construct in its own right (Alexander et al., 1987; Knorr-Cetina and Cicourel, 1981). In everyday interaction and experience, the macro and micro level (and intermediary 'mesolevels') form one unified whole. For instance, a racist speech in parliament is a discourse at the micro level of social interaction in the specific situation of a debate but at the same time may enact or be a constituent part of legislation or the reproduction of racism at the macro level.

There are several ways to analyse and bridge these levels, and thus to arrive at a unified critical analysis:

1   *Members–groups*: Language users engage in discourse as members of (several) social groups, organizations, or institutions; and conversely, groups thus may act 'by' their members.
2   *Actions–process*: Social acts of individual actors are thus constituent parts of group actions and social processes, such as legislation, newsmaking, or the reproduction of racism.
3   *Context–social structure*: Situations of discursive interaction are similarly part or constitutive of social structure; for example, a press conference may be a typical practice of organizations and media institutions. That is, 'local' and more 'global' contexts are closely related, and both exercise constraints on discourse.
4   *Personal and social cognition*: Language users as social actors have both personal and social cognition: personal memories, knowledge and opinions, as well as those shared with members of the group or culture as a whole. Both types of cognition influence interaction and discourse of individual members, whereas shared 'social representations' govern the collective actions of a group.

Power as control

A central notion in most critical work on discourse is that of power, and more specifically the *social power* of groups or institutions. Summarizing a complex philosophical and social analysis, we will define social power in terms of *control*. Thus, groups have (more or less) power if they are able to (more or less) control the acts and minds of (members of) other groups. This ability presupposes a *power base* of privileged access to scarce social resources, such as force, money, status, fame, knowledge, information, 'culture', or indeed various forms of public discourse and communication (of the vast literature on power, see, e.g., Lukes, 1986; Wrong, 1979).

Different *types of power* may be distinguished according to the various resources employed to exercise such power: the coercive power of the military and of violent men will rather be based on force, the rich will have power because of their money, whereas the more or less persuasive power of parents, professors, or journalists may be based on knowledge, information, or authority. Note also that power is seldom absolute. Groups may more or less control other groups, or only control them in specific situations or social domains. Moreover, dominated groups may more or less resist, accept, condone, comply with, or legitimate such power, and even find it 'natural'.

The power of dominant groups may be integrated in laws, rules, norms, habits, and even a quite general consensus, and thus take the form of what Gramsci called 'hegemony' (Gramsci, 1971). Class domination, sexism and racism are characteristic examples of such hegemony. Note also that power is not always exercised in obviously abusive acts of dominant group members, but may be enacted in the myriad of taken-for-granted actions of everyday life, as is typically the case in the many forms of everyday sexism or racism (Essed, 1991). Similarly, not all members of a powerful group are always more powerful than all members of dominated groups: power is only defined here for groups as a whole.

For our analysis of the relations between discourse and power, thus, we first find that access to specific forms of discourse, e.g., those of politics, the media, or science, is itself a power resource. Secondly, as suggested earlier, action is controlled by our minds. So, if we are able to influence people's minds, e.g., their knowledge or opinions, we indirectly may control (some of) their actions, as we know from persuasion and manipulation.

Closing the discourse–power circle, finally, this means that those groups who control most influential discourse also have more chances to control the minds and actions of others.

Simplifying these very intricate relationships even further for this chapter, we can split up the issue of discursive power into two basic questions for CDA research:

1 How do (more) powerful groups control public discourse?
2 How does such discourse control mind and action of (less) powerful groups, and what are the social consequences of such control, such as social inequality?

I address each question below.[2]

Control of public discourse

We have seen that among many other resources that define the power base of a group or institution, *access to* or *control over* public discourse and communication is an important 'symbolic' resource, as is the case for knowledge and information (van Dijk, 1996). Most people have active control only over everyday talk with family members, friends, or colleagues, and passive control over, e.g., media usage. In many situations, ordinary people are more or less passive targets of text or talk, e.g., of their bosses or teachers, or of the authorities, such as police officers, judges, welfare bureaucrats, or tax inspectors, who may simply tell them what (not) to believe or what to do.

On the other hand, members of more powerful social groups and institutions, and especially their leaders (the elites), have more or less exclusive access to, and control over, one or more types of public discourse. Thus, professors control scholarly discourse, teachers educational discourse, journalists media discourse, lawyers legal discourse, and politicians policy and other public political discourse. Those who have more control over more – and more influential – discourse (and more discourse properties) are by that definition also more powerful. In other words, we here propose a discursive definition (as well as a practical diagnostic) of one of the crucial constituents of social power.

These notions of discourse access and control are very general, and it is one of the tasks of CDA to spell out these forms of power. Thus, if discourse is defined in terms of complex communicative events, access and control may be defined both for the context and for the *structures of text and talk themselves.*

Context is defined as the mentally represented structure of those properties of the social situation that are relevant for the production or comprehension of discourse (Duranti and Goodwin, 1992; van Dijk, 1999). It consists of such categories as the overall definition of the situation, setting (time, place), ongoing actions (including discourses and discourse genres), participants in various communicative, social, or institutional roles, as well as their mental representations: goals, knowledge, opinions, attitudes and ideologies. Controlling context involves control over one or more of these categories, e.g., determining the definition of the communicative situation, deciding on time and place of the communicative event, or on which participants may or must be present, and in which roles, or what knowledge or opinions they should (not) have, and which social actions may or must be accomplished by discourse.

Also crucial in the enactment or exercise of group power is control not only over content, but over the structures of text and talk. Relating text and context, thus, we already saw that (members of) powerful groups may decide on the (possible) discourse *genre(s)* or *speech acts* of an occasion. A teacher or judge may require a direct answer from a student or suspect, respectively, and not a personal story or an argument (Wodak, 1984a). More critically, we may examine how powerful speakers may abuse their power in such situations, e.g., when police officers use force to get a confession from a suspect (Linell and Jonsson, 1991), or when male editors exclude women from writing economic news (van Zoonen, 1994).

Similarly, genres typically have conventional *schemas* consisting of various *categories*. Access to some of these may be prohibited or obligatory, e.g., some greetings in a conversation may only be used by speakers of a specific social group, rank, age, or gender (Irvine, 1974).

Also vital for all discourse and communication is who controls the *topics* (semantic macrostructures) and topic change, as when editors decide what news topics will be covered (Gans, 1979; van Dijk, 1988a, 1988b), professors decide what topics will be dealt with in class, or men control topics and topic change in conversations with women (Palmer, 1989; Fishman, 1983; Leet-Pellegrini, 1980; Lindegren-Lerman, 1983).

Although most discourse control is contextual or global, even local details of *meaning, form*, or *style* may be controlled, e.g., the details of an answer in class or court, or choice of lexical items or jargon in courtrooms, classrooms or newsrooms (Martín Rojo, 1994). In many situations, volume may be controlled and speakers ordered to 'keep their voice down', or to 'keep quiet', women may be 'silenced' in many ways (Houston and Kramarae, 1991), and in some cultures one needs to 'mumble' as a form of respect (Albert, 1972). The public use of specific words may be banned as subversive in a dictatorship, and discursive challenges to culturally dominant groups (e.g., white, western males) by their multicultural opponents may be ridiculed in the media as 'politically correct' (Williams, 1995). And finally, action and interaction dimensions of discourse may be controlled by prescribing or proscribing specific speech acts, and by selectively distributing or interrupting turns (see also Diamond, 1996). In sum, virtually all levels and structures of context, text and talk can in principle be more or less controlled by powerful speakers, and such power may be abused at the expense of other participants. It should, however, be stressed that talk and text do not always and directly enact or embody the overall power relations between groups: it is always the context that may interfere with, reinforce, or otherwise transform such relationships.

Mind control

If controlling discourse is a first major form of power, controlling people's minds is the other fundamental way to reproduce dominance and hegemony.[3] Within a CDA framework, 'mind control' involves even more than just acquiring beliefs about the world through discourse and communication. Suggested below are ways that power and dominance are involved in mind control.

First, recipients tend to accept beliefs, knowledge and opinions (unless they are inconsistent with their personal beliefs and experiences) through discourse from what they see as authoritative, trustworthy, or credible sources, such as scholars, experts, professionals, or reliable media (Nesler et al., 1993). Second, in some situations participants are obliged to be recipients of discourse, e.g., in education and in many job situations. Lessons, learning materials, job instructions and other discourse types in such cases may need to be attended to, interpreted and learned as intended by institutional or organizational authors (Giroux, 1981). Third, in many situations there are no public discourses or media that may provide information from which alternative beliefs may be derived (Downing, 1984). Fourth, and closely related to the previous points, recipients may not have the knowledge and beliefs needed to challenge the discourses or information they are exposed to (Wodak, 1987).

Whereas these conditions of mind control are largely *contextual* (they say something about the participants of a communicative event), other conditions are *discursive*, that is, a function of the structures and strategies of text or talk itself. In other words, given a specific context, certain meanings and forms of discourse have more influence on people's minds than others, as the very notion of 'persuasion' and a tradition of 2000 years of rhetoric may show.[4]

Once we have elementary insight into some of the structures of the mind, and what it means to control it, the crucial question is how discourse and its structures are able to exercise such control. As suggested above, such discursive influence may be due to *context* as well as to the *structures of text and talk themselves*.

Contextually based control derives from the fact that people understand and represent not only text and talk, but also the whole communicative situation. Thus, CDA typically studies how context features (such as the properties of language users of powerful groups) influence the ways members of dominated groups define the communicative situation in 'preferred context models' (Martín Rojo and van Dijk, 1997).

CDA also focuses on how *discourse structures* influence mental representations. At the *global* level of discourse, *topics* may influence what people see as the most important information of text or talk, and thus correspond to the top levels of their mental models. For example, expressing such a topic in a headline in news may powerfully influence how an event is defined in terms of a 'preferred' mental model (e.g., when crime committed by minorities is typically topicalized and headlined in the press: Duin et al., 1988; van Dijk, 1991). Similarly, argumentation may be persuasive because of the social opinions that are 'hidden' in its implicit premises and thus taken for granted by the recipients, e.g., immigration may thus be restricted if it is presupposed in a parliamentary debate that all refugees are 'illegal' (see the contributions in Wodak and van Dijk, 2000) Likewise, at the *local level*, in order to understand discourse meaning and coherence, people may need models featuring beliefs that remain implicit (presupposed) in discourse. Thus, a typical feature of manipulation is to communicate beliefs implicitly, that is, without actually asserting them, and with less chance that they will be challenged.

These few examples show how various types of discourse structure may influence the formation and change of mental models and social representations. If dominant groups, and especially their elites, largely control public discourse and its structures, they thus also have more control over the minds of the public at large. However, such control has its limits. The complexity of comprehension, and the formation and change of beliefs, is such that one cannot always predict which features of a specific text or talk will have which effects on the minds of specific recipients.

These brief remarks have provided us with a very general picture of how discourse is involved in dominance (power abuse) and in the production and reproduction of social inequality. It is the aim of CDA to examine these relationships in more detail. In the next section, we review several areas of CDA research in which these relationships are investigated.[5]

Research in Critical Discourse Analysis

Although most discourse studies dealing with any aspect of power, domination, and social inequality have not been explicitly conducted under the label of CDA, we shall nevertheless refer to some of these studies below.

Gender inequality

One vast field of critical research on discourse and language that thus far has not been carried out within a CDA perspective is that of gender. In many ways, feminist work has become paradigmatic for much discourse analysis, especially since much of this work explicitly deals with social inequality and domination. We will not review it here; see Kendall and Tannen, this volume; also the books authored and edited by, e.g., Cameron (1990, 1992); Kotthoff and Wodak (1997); Seidel (1988);

Thorne et al. (1983); Wodak (1997); for discussion and comparison with an approach that emphasizes cultural differences rather than power differences and inequality, see, e.g., Tannen (1994b); see also Tannen (1994) for an analysis of gender differences at work, in which many of the properties of discursive dominance are dealt with.

Media discourse

The undeniable power of the media has inspired many critical studies in many disciplines: linguistics, semiotics, pragmatics and discourse studies. Traditional, often content analytical approaches in critical media studies have revealed biased, stereotypical, sexist or racist images in texts, illustrations and photos. Early studies of media language similarly focused on easily observable surface structures, such as the biased or partisan use of words in the description of Us and Them (and Our/Their actions and characteristics), especially along sociopolitical lines in the representation of communists. The critical tone was set by a series of 'Bad News' studies by the Glasgow University Media Group (1976, 1980, 1982, 1985, 1993) on features of TV reporting, such as in the coverage of various issues (e.g., industrial disputes (strikes), the Falklands (Malvinas) war, the media coverage of AIDS).

Perhaps best known outside of discourse studies is the media research carried out by Stuart Hall and his associates within the framework of the cultural studies paradigm. (See, e.g., Hall et al., 1980; for introduction to the critical work of cultural studies, see Agger, 1992a; see also Collins et al., 1986; for earlier critical approaches to the analysis of media images, see also Davis and Walton, 1983; and for a later CDA approach to media studies that is related to the critical approach of cultural studies, see Fairclough 1995b).

An early collection of work of Roger Fowler and his associates (Fowler et al., 1979) also focused on the media. As with many other English and Australian studies in this paradigm, the theoretical framework of Halliday's functional-systemic grammar is used in a study of the 'transitivity' of syntactic patterns of sentences. The point of such research is that events and actions may be described with syntactic variations that are a function of the underlying involvement of actors (e.g., their agency, responsibility and perspective). Thus, in an analysis of the media accounts of the 'riots' during a minority festival, the responsibility of the authorities and especially of the police in such violence may be systematically de-emphasized by defocusing, e.g., by passive constructions and nominalizations; that is, by leaving agency and responsibility implicit. Fowler's later critical studies of the media continue this tradition, but also pay tribute to the British cultural studies paradigm that defines news not as a reflection of reality, but as a product shaped by political, economic and cultural forces (Fowler, 1991). More than in much other critical work on the media, he also focuses on the linguistic 'tools' for such a critical study, such as the analysis of transitivity in syntax, lexical structure, modality and speech acts. Similarly, van Dijk (1988b) applies a theory of news discourse (van Dijk, 1988a) in critical studies of international news, racism in the press and the coverage of squatters in Amsterdam.

Political discourse

Given the role of political discourse in the enactment, reproduction, and legitimization of power and domination, we may also expect many critical discourse studies of political text and talk. So far most of this work has been carried out by linguists and discourse analysts because political science is among the few social disciplines in which discourse analysis has remained virtually unknown, although there is some influence of 'postmodern' approaches to discourse (Derian and Shapiro, 1989; Fox and Miller, 1995) and many studies of political communication and rhetoric overlap with a discourse analytical approach (Nimmo and Sanders, 1981). Still closer to discourse analysis is the current approach to 'frames' (conceptual structures or sets of beliefs that organize political thought, policies and discourse) in the analysis of political text and talk (Gamson, 1992).

In linguistics, pragmatics and discourse studies, political discourse has received attention outside the more theoretical mainstream. Seminal work comes from Paul Chilton; see, e.g., his collection on the language of the nuclear arms debate (Chilton, 1985), as well as later work on contemporary nukespeak (Chilton, 1988) and metaphor (Chilton, 1996; Chilton and Lakoff, 1995).

Although studies of political discourse in English are internationally best known because of the hegemony of English, much work has been done (often earlier, and often more systematic and explicit) in German, Spanish and French. This work is too extensive to even begin to review here beyond naming a few influential studies.

Germany has a long tradition of political discourse analysis, both (then) in the West (e.g., about Bonn's politicians by Zimmermann, 1969), as well as in the former East (e.g., the semiotic-materialist theory of Klaus, 1971) (see also the introduction by Bachem, 1979). This tradition in Germany witnessed a study of the language of war and peace

(Pasierbsky, 1983) and of speech acts in political discourse (Holly, 1990). There is also a strong tradition of studying fascist language and discourse (e.g., the lexicon, propaganda, media and language politics; Ehlich, 1989). In France, the study of political language has a respectable tradition in linguistics and discourse analysis, also because the barrier between (mostly structuralist) linguistic theory and text analysis was never very pronounced. Discourse studies are often corpus-based and there has been a strong tendency towards formal, quantitative and automatic (content) analysis of such big datasets, often combined with critical ideological analysis (Pêcheux, 1969, 1982; Guespin, 1976). The emphasis on auto-mated analysis usually implies a focus on (easily quantifiable) lexical analyses.

Critical political discourse studies in Spain and especially also in Latin America has been very productive. Famous is the early critical semiotic (anti-colonialist) study of Donald Duck by Dorfman and Mattelart (1972) in Chile. Lavandera et al. (1986, 1987) in Argentina take an influential sociolinguistic approach to political discourse, e.g., its typology of authoritarian discourse. Work of this group has been continued and organized in a more explicit CDA framework especially by Pardo (see, e.g., her work on legal discourse; Pardo, 1996). In Mexico, a detailed ethnographic discourse analysis of local authority and decision-making was carried out by Sierra (1992). Among the many other critical studies in Latin America, we should mention the extensive work of Teresa Carbó on parliamentary discourse in Mexico, focusing especially on the way delegates speak about native Americans (Carbó, 1995), with a study in English on interruptions in these debates (Carbó, 1992).

Ethnocentrism, anti-semitism, nationalism and racism

The study of the role of discourse in the enactment and reproduction of ethnic and 'racial' inequality has slowly emerged in CDA. Traditionally, such work focused on ethnocentric and racist representations in the mass media, literature and film (Hartmann and Husband, 1974; UNESCO, 1977; Wilson and Gutierrez, 1985; van Dijk, 1991; Dines and Humez, 1995). Such representations continue centuries-old dominant images of the Other in the discourses of European travellers, explorers, merchants, soldiers, philosophers and historians, among other forms of elite discourse (Barker, 1978; Lauren, 1988). Fluctuating between the emphasis on exotic difference, on the one hand, and supremacist derogation stressing the Other's intellectual, moral and biological inferiority, on the other hand, such discourses also influenced public opinion and led to broadly shared social representations. It is the continuity of this sociocultural tradition of negative images about the Other that also partly explains the persistence of dominant patterns of representation in contemporary discourse, media and film (Shohat and Stam, 1994).

Later discourse studies have gone beyond the more traditional, content analytical analysis of 'images' of the Others, and probed more deeply into the linguistic, semiotic and other discursive properties of text and talk to and about minorities, immigrants and Other peoples. Besides the mass media, advertising, film and textbooks, which were (and still are) the genres most commonly studied, this newer work also focuses on political discourse, scholarly discourse, everyday conversations, service encounters, talk shows and a host of other genres.

Many studies on ethnic and racial inequality reveal a remarkable similarity among the stereotypes, prejudices and other forms of verbal derogation across discourse types, media and national boundaries. For example, in a vast research programme carried out at the University of Amsterdam since the early 1980s, we examined how Surinamese, Turks, and Moroccans, and ethnic relations generally, are represented in conversation, everyday stories, news reports, textbooks, parliamentary debates, corporate discourse and scholarly text and talk (van Dijk, 1984a, 1987a, 1987b, 1991, 1993a). Besides stereotypical topics of difference, deviation and threat, story structures, conversational features (such as hesitations and repairs in mentioning Others), semantic moves such as disclaimers ('We have nothing against blacks, but . . .', etc.), lexical description of Others, and a host of other discourse features also were studied. The aim of these projects was to show how discourse expresses and reproduces underlying social representations of Others in the social and political context. Ter Wal (1997) applies this framework in a detailed study of the ways Italian political and media discourse gradually changed, from an anti-racist commitment and benign representation of the '*extracommunitari*' (non-Europeans) to a more stereotypical and negative portrayal of immigrants in terms of crime, deviance and threat.

The major point of our work is that racism (including anti-semitism, xenophobia and related forms of resentment against 'racially' or ethnically defined Others) is a complex system of social and political inequality that is also reproduced by discourse in general, and by elite discourses in particular.

Instead of further elaborating the complex details of the theoretical relationships between discourse and racism, we shall refer to a book that may be taken as a prototype of conservative elite discourse on 'race' today, namely, *The End of Racism* by Dinesh D'Souza (1995). This text embodies many of the dominant ideologies in the USA, especially on the right, and it specifically targets one minority group in the USA: African Americans. Space prohibits detailed analysis of this 700-page book (but see van Dijk, 1998a). Here we can merely summarize how the CDA of D'Souza's *The End of Racism* shows what kind of discursive structures, strategies and moves are deployed in exercising the power of the dominant (white, western, male) group, and how readers are manipulated to form or confirm the social representations that are consistent with a conservative, supremacist ideology.

The overall strategy of D'Souza's *The End of Racism* is the combined implementation, at all levels of the text, of the positive presentation of the ingroup and the negative presentation of the outgroup. In D'Souza's book, the principal rhetorical means are those of hyperbole and metaphor, viz., the exaggerated representation of social problems in terms of illness ('pathologies', 'virus'), and the emphasis on the contrast between the Civilized and the Barbarians. Semantically and lexically, the Others are thus associated not simply with difference, but rather with deviance ('illegitimacy') and threat (violence, attacks). Argumentative assertions of the depravity of black culture are combined with denials of white deficiencies (racism), with rhetorical mitigation and euphemization of its crimes (colonialism, slavery), and with semantic reversals of blame (blaming the victim). Social conflict is thus cognitively represented and enhanced by polarization, and discursively sustained and reproduced by derogating, demonizing and excluding the Others from the community of Us, the Civilized.

From Group Domination to Professional and Institutional Power

We have reviewed in this section critical studies of the role of discourse in the (re)production inequality. Such studies characteristically exemplify the CDA perspective on power abuse and dominance by specific social groups.[6] Many other studies, whether under the CDA banner or not, also critically examine various genres of institutional and professional discourse, e.g., text and talk in the courtroom (Danet, 1984; O'Barr et al., 1978; Bradac et al., 1981; Lakoff, 1990; Ng and Bradac, 1993; Lakoff, 1990; Wodak, 1984a; Pardo, 1996; Shuy, 1992; Wodak, 1984a), bureaucratic discourse (Burton and Carlen, 1979; Radtke, 1981), medical discourse (Davis, 1988; Fisher, 1995; Fisher and Todd, 1986; Mishler, 1984; West, 1984; Wodak, 1996), educational and scholarly discourse (Aronowitz, 1988; Apple, 1979; Bourdieu, 1984, 1989; Bernstein, 1975,

1990; Bourdieu et al., 1994; Giroux, 1981; Willis, 1977; Atkinson et al., 1995; Coulthard, 1994; Duszak, 1997; Fisher and Todd, 1986; Mercer, 1995; Wodak, 1996; Bergvall and Remlinger, 1996; Ferree and Hall, 1996; Jaworski, 1983; Leimdorfer, 1992; Osler, 1994; Said, 1979; Smith, 1991; van Dijk, 1987, 1993a), and corporate discourse (Mumby, 1988; Boden, 1994a; Drew and Heritage, 1992; Ehlich, 1995; Mumby, 1988, 1993; Mumby and Clair, 1997), among many other sets of *genres*. In all these cases, power and dominance are associated with specific social domains (politics, media, law, education, science, etc.), their professional elites and institutions, and the rules and routines that form the background of the everyday discursive reproduction of power in such domains and institutions. The victims or targets of such power are usually the public or citizens at large, the 'masses', clients, subjects, the audience, students and other groups that are dependent on institutional and organizational power.

Conclusion

We have seen in this chapter that critical discourse analyses deal with the relationship between discourse and power. We have also sketched the complex theoretical framework needed to analyse discourse and power, and provided a glimpse of the many ways in which power and domination are reproduced by text and talk.

Yet several methodological and theoretical gaps remain. First, the cognitive interface between discourse structures and those of the local and global social context is seldom made explicit, and appears usually only in terms of the notions of knowledge and ideology (van Dijk, 1998). Thus, despite a large number of empirical studies on discourse and power, the details of the multidisciplinary *theory* of CDA that should relate discourse and action with cognition and society are still on the agenda. Second, there is still a gap between more linguistically oriented studies of text and talk and the various approaches in the social sciences. The first often ignores concepts and theories in sociology and political science on power abuse and inequality, whereas the second seldom engage in detailed discourse analysis. Integration of various approaches is therefore very important to arrive at a satisfactory form of multidisciplinary CDA.

Notes

I am indebted to Ruth Wodak for her comments on an earlier version of this chapter, and to Laura Pardo for further information about CDA research in Latin America.

1   It comes as no surprise, then, that CDA research will often refer to the lead-
    ing social philosophers and social scientists of our time when theorizing
    these and other fundamental notions. Thus, reference to the leading scholars
    of the Frankfurt School and to contemporary work by Habermas (for
    instance, on legitimation and his last 'discourse' approach to norms and
    democracy) is, of course, common in critical analysis. Similarly, many critical
    studies will refer to Foucault when dealing with notions such as power,
    domination and discipline or the more philosophical notion of 'orders of
    discourse'. More recently, the many studies on language, culture and society
    by Bourdieu have become increasingly influential; for instance, his notion of
    'habitus'. From another sociological perspective, Giddens' structuration
    theory is now occasionally mentioned. It should be borne in mind that,
    although several of these social philosophers and sociologists make extensive
    use of the notions of language and discourse, they seldom engage in explicit,
    systematic discourse analysis. Indeed, the last thing critical discourse scholars
    should do is to uncritically adopt philosophical or sociological ideas about
    language and discourse that are obviously uninformed by advances in
    contemporary linguistics and discourse analysis. Rather, the work referred to
    here is mainly relevant for the use of fundamental concepts about the social
    order and hence for the metatheory of CDA.

2   Space limitations prevent discussion of a third issue: how dominated groups
    discursively challenge or resist the control of powerful groups.

3   Note that 'mind control' is merely a handy phrase to summarize a very
    complex process. Cognitive psychology and mass communication research
    have shown that influencing the mind is not as straightforward a process as
    simplistic ideas about mind control might suggest (Britton and Graesser,
    1996; Glasser and Salmon, 1995; Klapper, 1960; van Dijk and Kintsch, 1983).
    Recipients may vary in their interpretation and uses of text and talk, also as
    a function of class, gender, or culture (Liebes and Katz, 1990). Likewise, recip-
    ients seldom passively accept the intended opinions of specific discourses.
    However, we should not forget that most of our beliefs about the world are
    acquired through discourse.

4   In order to analyse the complex processes involved in how discourse may
    control people's minds, we would need to spell out the detailed mental repre-
    sentations and cognitive operations studied in cognitive science. Since even
    an adequate summary is beyond the scope of this chapter, we will only briefly
    introduce a few notions that are necessary to understand the processes of
    discursive mind control (for details, see, e.g., Graesser and Bower, 1990; van
    Dijk and Kintsch, 1983; van Oostendorp and Zwaan, 1994; Weaver et al.,
    1995).

5   Note that the picture just sketched is very schematic and general. The rela-
    tions between the social power of groups and institutions, on the one hand,
    and discourse on the other, as well as between discourse and cognition, and
    cognition and society, are vastly more complex. There are many contradic-

tions. There is not always a clear picture of one dominant group (or class or institution) oppressing another one, controlling all public discourse, and such discourse directly controlling the mind of the dominated. There are many forms of collusion, consensus, legitimation, and even 'joint production' of forms of inequality. Members of dominant groups may become dissidents and side with dominated groups, and vice versa. Opponent discourses may be adopted by dominant groups, whether strategically to neutralize them or simply because dominant power and ideologies may change, as is for instance quite obvious in ecological discourse and ideology.

6 Unfortunately, the study of the discursive reproduction of class has been rather neglected in this perspective; for a related approach, though, see Willis (1977).

5

Discourse and Racism

Introduction

For most people, and probably also for many readers of this chapter, the notion of racism is not primarily associated with that of discourse. More obvious associations would be discrimination, prejudice, slavery, or apartheid, among many other concepts related to ethnic or 'racial' domination and inequality dealt with elsewhere in this book.

And yet, although discourse may seem just 'words' (and therefore cannot break your bones, as do sticks and stones), text and talk play a vital role in the reproduction of contemporary racism.

This is especially true for the most damaging forms of contemporary racism, namely, those of the elites. Political, bureaucratic, corporate, media, educational and scholarly elites control the most crucial dimensions and decisions of the everyday lives of immigrants and minorities: entry, residence, work, housing, education, welfare, health care, knowledge, information and culture. They do so largely by speaking or writing, for instance; in cabinet meetings and parliamentary debates, in job interviews, news reports, advertising, lessons, textbooks, scholarly articles, movies or talk shows, among many other forms of elite discourse.

That is, as is true also for other social practices directed against minorities, discourse may first of all be a form of verbal discrimination. Elite discourse may thus constitute an important elite form of racism: similarly, the (re)production of ethnic prejudices that underlie such verbal and other social practices largely takes place through text, talk and communication.

In sum, especially in contemporary information societies, discourse lies at the heart of racism. This chapter explains how and why this is so.

Racism

To understand in some detail how discourse may contribute to racism, we first need to summarize our theory of racism. Whereas racism is often reduced to racist ideology, it is here understood as a complex societal system of ethnically or 'racially' based domination and its resulting inequality (for detail, see van Dijk, 1993a).

The system of racism consists of a social and a cognitive subsystem. The social subsystem is constituted by social practices of discrimination at the local (micro) level, and relationships of power abuse by dominant groups, organizations and institutions at a global (macro) level of analysis (most classical analyses of racism focus on this level of analysis; see, e.g., Dovidio and Gaertner, 1986; Essed, 1991; Katz and Taylor, 1988; Wellman, 1993; Omi and Winant, 1994).

As suggested above, discourse may be an influential type of discriminatory practice. And the symbolic elites, that is, those elites who literally have everything 'to say' in society, as well as their institutions and organizations, are an example of groups involved in power abuse or domination.

The second subsystem of racism is cognitive. Whereas the discriminatory practices of members of dominant groups and institutions form the visible and tangible manifestations of everyday racism, such practices also have a mental basis consisting of biased models of ethnic events and interactions, which in turn are rooted in racist prejudices and ideologies (van Dijk, 1984a, 1987a, 1998). This does not mean that discriminatory practices are always intentional, but only that they presuppose socially shared and negatively oriented mental representations of Us about Them. Most psychological studies of 'prejudice' deal with this aspect of racism, though seldom in those terms, that is, in terms of their role in the *social* system of racism. Prejudice is mostly studied as a characteristic of individuals (Brown, 1995; Dovidio and Gaertner, 1986; Sniderman et al., 1993; Zanna and Olson, 1994).

Discourse also plays a fundamental role for this cognitive dimension of racism. Ethnic prejudices and ideologies are not innate, and do not develop spontaneously in ethnic interaction. They are acquired and learned, and this usually happens through communication, that is, through text and talk. And vice versa, such racist mental representations are typically expressed, formulated, defended and legitimated in discourse and may thus be reproduced and shared within the dominant group. It is essentially in this way that racism is 'learned' in society.

Discourse

Definition

Without knowledge of racism, we do not know how discourse is involved in its daily reproduction. The same is true for our knowledge about discourse. This notion has become so popular that it has lost much of its specificity. 'Discourse' is here understood to mean only a specific communicative event, in general, and a written or oral form of verbal interaction or language use, in particular. Sometimes 'discourse' is used in a more generic sense to denote a type of discourse, a collection of discourses, or a class of discourse genres, for instance, when we speak of 'medical discourse', 'political discourse', or indeed of 'racist discourse'. (For an introduction to contemporary discourse analysis, see the chapters in van Dijk, 1997a.)

Although it is often used in that way, we do *not* understand by discourse a philosophy, ideology, social movement, or social system, as in phrases such as 'the discourse of liberalism' or 'the discourse of modernity', unless we actually refer to collections of talk or text.

In the broader, 'semiotic' sense, discourses may also feature non-verbal expressions such as drawings, pictures, gestures, face-work, and so on. However, for brevity's sake, these will be ignored here, although it should be obvious that racist messages may also be conveyed by photos, movies, derogatory gestures or other non-verbal acts.

Structural analysis

Discourses have many different structures, which also may be analysed in many different ways depending on general approaches (linguistic, pragmatic, semiotic, rhetorical, interactional, etc.) or the kind of genres analysed, such as conversation, news reports, poetry, or advertisements. It will be assumed here that both written/printed text and oral talk may thus be analysed at various levels or along several dimensions. Each of these may be involved directly or indirectly in discriminatory interaction against minority group members or biased discourse about them, for instance, as follows:

- *Non-verbal structures*: a racist picture; a derogatory gesture; a headline size or page layout that emphasizes negative meanings about 'Them';
- *Sounds*: an insolent intonation; speaking (too) loudly;
- *Syntax*: (de-)emphasizing responsibility for action, for instance by active vs. passive sentences;

- *Lexicon*: selection of words that may be more or less negative about Them, or positive about Us (e.g., 'terrorist' vs. 'freedom fighter');
- *Local (sentence) meaning*: for instance, being vague or indirect about Our racism, and detailed and precise about Their crimes or misbehaviour;
- *Global discourse meaning (topics)*: selecting or emphasizing positive topics (like aid and tolerance) for Us, and negative ones (such as crime, deviance, or violence) for Them;
- *Schemata (conventional forms of global discourse organization)*: presence or absence of standard schematic categories – such as a resolution in a narrative schema, or a conclusion in an argument schema – in order to emphasize Our Good things and Their Bad things;
- *Rhetorical devices*: metaphor, metonymy, hyperbole, euphemism, irony, etc. – again to focus attention on positive/negative information about Us/Them;
- *Speech acts*: e.g., accusations to derogate Them, or defences to legitimate Our discrimination;
- *Interaction*: interrupting turns of Others, closing meetings before Others can speak, disagreeing with Others, or non-responding to questions, among many other forms of direct interactional discrimination.

Although not yet very detailed, nor very sophisticated, this brief list of levels and some structures of discourse gives a first impression of how discourse and its various structures may link up with some aspects of racism. Note also that the examples given show the kind of group polarization we also know from underlying prejudices, namely, the overall tendency of ingroup favouritism or positive self-presentation, on the one hand, and outgroup derogation or negative other-presentation, on the other.

In other words, with the many subtle structures of meanings, form and action, racist discourse generally emphasizes Our good things and Their bad things, and de-emphasizes (mitigates, hides) Our bad things and Their good things. This general 'ideological' square not only applies to racist domination but in general to ingroup-outgroup polarization in social practices, discourse and thought.

The Cognitive Interface

An adequate theory of racism is non-reductive in the sense that it does not limit racism to just ideology or just 'visible' forms of discriminatory practices. The same is true for the way discourse is involved in racism. This is especially the case for 'meanings' of discourse, and hence also for beliefs, that is, for cognition. Discourses are not only forms of interaction or social practices, but also express and convey meanings, and may thus influence our beliefs about immigrants or minorities.

The point of the analysis of discourse structures above, thus, is not only to examine the detailed features of one type of discriminatory social practice, but especially also to gain deeper insight in the way discourses express and manage our minds. It is especially this discourse–cognition interface that explains how ethnic prejudices and ideologies are expressed, conveyed, shared and reproduced in society. For instance, a passive sentence may obscure responsible agency in the mental models we form about a racist event, a special type of metaphor (such as in 'an invasion of refugees') may enhance the negative opinion we have about Others, and a euphemism such as 'popular resentment' may mitigate the negative self-image an expression such as 'racism' might suggest. In this and many other ways, thus, the discourse structures mentioned above may influence the specific mental models we have about ethnic events, or the more general social representations (attitudes, ideologies) we have about ourselves and Others. And once such mental representations have been influenced in the way intended by racist discourse, they may also be used to engage in other racist practices. It is in this way that the circle of racism and its reproduction is closed.

The Social Context: the Elites

Research suggests that the discursive reproduction of racism in society is not evenly distributed over all members of the dominant majority. Apart from analysing their structures and cognitive underpinnings, it is therefore essential to examine some properties of the social context of discourse, such as who its speakers and writers are. We repeatedly suggest in this chapter that the elites play a special role in this reproduction process (for details, see van Dijk, 1993a). This is not because the elites are generally more racist than the non-elites, but especially because of their special access to, and control over, the most influential forms of public discourse, namely, that of the mass media, politics, education, research and the bureaucracies. Our definition of these elites is thus not in terms of material resources that are the basis of power, such as wealth, nor merely in terms of their societal positions of leadership, but rather in terms of the symbolic resources that define symbolic 'capital', and in particular their preferential access to public discourse. The elites, defined in this way, are literally the group(s) in society who have 'most to say', and thus also have preferential 'access to the minds' of the public at large. As the ideological leaders of society, they establish common values, aims, and concerns; they formulate common sense as well as the consensus, both as individuals and as leaders of the dominant institutions of society.

This is also true for the exercise of 'ethnic' power – in which the dominant majority needs guidance in its relationships to minorities or immigrants. Given our analysis of the role of the 'symbolic' elites in contemporary society, we conclude that they also have a special role in the reproduction of the system of racism that maintains the dominant white group in power. This means that an analysis of elite discourse offers a particularly relevant perspective on the way racism is reproduced in society.

At the same time, however, further sociological and political analysis is necessary to examine in more detail how the symbolic elites relate to the population at large, including incorporating and translating popular confusion or resentment into the forms of dominant racist discourse they deem to be most relevant to maintain their own power and status. For instance, critique of unemployment and urban decay against the (political) elites may thus be deflected by blaming them on the immigrants. More extremist forms of popular racism, whether or not organized in political parties, may then be publicly denounced so as to protect one's own non-racist face and to propagate more 'moderate' forms of racism in mainstream parties. It is not surprising therefore that racist parties are 'useful idiots' and, with reference to democratic values, seldom prohibited. The various social and political processes may easily be detected in an analysis of elite discourses in contemporary societies.

Of course, this special perspective on the role of the elites in the reproduction of racism, based on the simple argument that they control public discourse, also explains the role of small groups of elites in the non-dominant forms of *anti-racism*. If it is generally true that the leaders are responsible and need to give a good example, this conclusion also implies that anti-racist policies and change should not so much focus on the population at large, but on those who claim to need it less: the elites. If the most influential forms of racism are at the top, it is also there where change has to begin.

The Role of Context

Current discourse analysis emphasizes the fundamental role of context for the understanding of the role of text and talk in society. As will also appear several times below, dominant discourses do not merely exercise their influence out of context. When defining discourse as communicative events, we also need to take into account, for example, the overall social domains in which they are used (politics, media, education); the global social actions being accomplished by them (legislation, education); the local actions they enact; the current setting of time, place and circumstances; the participants involved, as well as their many social and communicative roles and (e.g., ethnic) group membership; and not least the beliefs and goals of these participants. These and other properties of the social situation of the communicative event will influence virtually all properties of text and talk, especially those properties that can vary, such as their style: how things are said. That is, similar prejudices may be formulated in very different ways depending on these and other context structures – for example, in government discourse or parliamentary debates, quality – broadsheet or tabloid, on the Left or on the Right, and so on. In other words, the large variety of racist discourses in society not only reflect variable underlying social representations, but especially also adapt to different contexts of production: who says what, where, when, and with what goals. A theory of context also explains in part why, despite the dominant ethnic consensus, not all talk on minorities will be the same.

Conversation

After the more theoretical introduction about the way discourse is involved in racism and its reproduction, we now proceed to some examples of the various genres whose role in racism has been studied.

A genre is a *type* of discursive social practice, usually defined by specific discourse structures and context structures as spelled out above. For instance, a parliamentary debate is a discourse genre defined by a specific style, specific forms of verbal interaction (talk) under special contextual constraints of time and controlled speaker change, in the domain of politics, in the institution of parliament, as part of the overall act of legislation, engaged in by speakers who are MPs, representative of their constituencies as well as members of political parties, with the aim (for instance) to defend or oppose bills, with formal styles of address and argumentative structures supporting a political point of view . . . and this is merely a short summary of such a definition of a genre, which usually needs both textual and contextual specification.

Thus, in the same way, everyday conversation is a genre, probably the most elementary and widespread genre of human interaction and discourse, typically defined by lacking the various institutional constraints mentioned above for parliamentary debates. Indeed, we virtually all have access to conversations, whereas only MPs have access to parliamentary debates. Much of what we learn about the world is derived from such everyday conversations with family members, friends and colleagues. The same is true for ethnic prejudices and ideologies.

Study of conversations of white people in the Netherlands and California about immigrants (van Dijk, 1984a, 1987a) shows a number of interesting characteristics. Casually asked about their neighbourhood, many speakers spontaneously begin to speak about 'those foreigners', often negatively (see also the following studies of racist conversations: Jäger, 1992; Wetherell and Potter, 1992; Wodak et al., 1990).

Whereas everyday conversations are often about other people, and anything may come up in such talk, *topics* about minorities or immigrants are often limited to a few topic types, namely, the increasingly negative topic classes of difference, deviance and threat. Thus, ethnic outgroups are first of all talked about in terms of how they look and act differently from us – different habits, language, religion, or values. Such talk may still be neutral in the sense that such differences need not be negatively evaluated; indeed, differences may even be discussed in a 'positive' way as being interesting, exotic and culturally enriching. More often than not, however, different characteristics will be negatively framed when compared to those of the ingroup. Next, Others may be talked about even more negatively in terms of deviance, that is, of breaking our norms and values, in Europe typically so in negative remarks about Islam, or the way Arab men treat women. Finally, immigrants or minorities may be talked about even more negatively, in terms of a threat, for instance, in stories about aggression or crime or presented as taking away our jobs, housing, or space, or (especially in elite discourse) when seen as threatening 'our' dominant culture.

Whereas topics are meanings that characterize whole conversations or large parts of them, a more local semantic analysis of everyday talk about minorities or immigrants reveals other interesting features. One of the best known are *disclaimers*, that is, semantic moves with a positive part about Us, and a negative part about Them, such as:

- *apparent denial*: We have nothing against blacks, but . . .
- *apparent concession*: Some of them are smart, but in general . . .
- *apparent empathy*: Of course refugees have had problems, but . . .
- *apparent ignorance*: I don't know, but . . .
- *apparent excuses*: Sorry, but . . .

- *reversal (blaming the victim)*: Not they, but we are the real victims . . .
- *transfer*: I don't mind, but my clients . . .

We see that these local moves instantiate within one sentence the overall (global) strategies of positive self-presentation (ingroup favouritism) and negative other-presentation (outgroup derogation). Note that some disclaimers are called 'apparent' here, because the first, positive part primarily seems to function as a form of face-keeping and impression management: the rest of the text or fragment will focus on the negative characteristics of the Others, thus contradicting the first 'positive' part.

In the same way, we may examine several other dimensions of every-day talk about minorities. Thus it was found that in *narrative structures* of everyday negative stories about immigrants, often the resolution category was lacking. This may be interpreted as a structural device that enhances precisely the negative aspects of the complication category of a story: stories that have (positive) resolutions of problems or conflicts are less efficient as complaint stories about Others.

Similarly, stories also often have the role of premises that present the undeniable 'facts' of personal experience in *argumentations* that lead to negative conclusions about minorities. It need hardly be stressed that such argumentations are replete with fallacies. Thus negative statements about the Others will typically be supported by the authority move that says that people 'saw it on TV'. In the same way as prejudices are stereo-typical negative social representations, arguments themselves may be stereotypical and conventional. Thus, refugees will typically be described as a 'financial burden' for Our society, who would be taken better care of 'in their own region', dissuaded from coming because they may 'suffer from popular resentment' here, or recommended to stay in their own country in order to 'help build it up'.

Finally, even at the surface levels of actual talk management, for instance, in turn – taking, fluency and so forth, we may witness that white speakers appear to show insecurity or uneasiness, for example, by the extra use of hesitations, pauses and repairs when they have to name or identify minorities.

As we have stressed before, these and other properties of discourse about Others have interactional-social conditions, functions and conse-quences, as well as cognitive ones. Thus, outgroup derogation is itself a social, discriminatory practice, but at the same time its discursive mani-festations express underlying prejudices, which may in turn contribute to the formation or confirmation of such prejudices with the recipients.

News Reports

Everyday conversations are the natural locus of everyday popular racism. Because they do not have active control over public elite discourse, ordinary people often have no more 'to say' or 'to do' against the Others than talking negatively to Them, and about Them. Of course, ethnic stereotypes and prejudices, just like rumours, may spread fast in such a way.

As suggested, however, much everyday talk about minorities is inspired by the mass media. Speakers routinely refer to television or the newspaper as their source (and authority) of knowledge or opinions about ethnic minorities. This is especially the case for those topics that cannot be observed directly in everyday interaction, even in ethnically mixed countries or cities. Immigration is a prominent example in which most citizens depend on the mass media, which in turn depend on politicians, bureaucrats, the police, or state agencies. Of course, in cities, regions, or countries with few minorities, virtually all beliefs about the Others come from mass media discourse, literature, textbooks, studies, or other forms of elite discourse. In other words, not only for ordinary citizens but also for the elites themselves, the mass media are today the primary source of 'ethnic' knowledge and opinion in society.

It is not surprising therefore that the representation of minorities in the media such as television, newspapers, and movies has been extensively investigated (Dates and Barlow, 1990; Jäger and Link, 1993; Hartmann and Husband, 1974; van Dijk, 1991). Much earlier work is content-analytical, that is, quantitative research into observable features of text or talk, such as how often members of a specific ethnic group are portrayed in the news or advertising and in what roles. These studies offer some general insight but do not tell us in detail *how* exactly the media portray minorities or ethnic relations. Sophisticated discourse analysis is able to provide such a study, and also is able actually to explain why media discourses have the structures they have, and how these affect the minds of the recipients. It is only in such a way that we get insight into the fundamental role of the media in the reproduction of racism.

If we focus more specifically on the media genre that is at the basis of most beliefs about minorities, namely the news, we may proceed in a way that is similar to that presented above for conversations. That is, we examine each of the levels identified above, and search for structures or strategies that seem typical for media portrayals of the Others.

News reports in the press, for instance, have a conventional schematic structure consisting of such categories as summary (headline + lead), main events, background (previous events, context, history), comments and evaluation. Thus, we may focus on *headlines* and see whether these typical summaries of news reports are different for minorities than when they are about dominant group members. Following the general ideological square introduced above, we may for instance assume that headlines in the news tend to emphasize the negative characteristics of minorities. Much research has shown that this is indeed the case. In a Dutch study, for instance, we found that of 1,500 headlines on ethnic issues, not a single one was positive when it involved minorities as active, responsible agents, whereas such is much more normal when one of Us is the semantic agent in a headline. Also the syntax of headlines may thus be biased in favour of the ingroup, for instance when passive constructions diminish their responsibility for negative actions.

Headlines summarize the most important information of a news report, and hence also express its main topic. Further analysis of these overall meanings of discourse confirms what we already found in everyday conversations, which apparently seem to follow the media in that respect (and vice versa, the media in a sense also reflect commonsense beliefs), namely, that *topics* can be classified as being about difference, deviance and threat. If we list the most important topics in 'ethnic' news in different western countries, or countries where Europeans are dominant, we always come up with a standard list of preferred topics, such as

- immigration and reception of newcomers;
- socioeconomic issues, (un)employment;
- cultural differences;
- crime, violence, drugs, and deviance;
- ethnic relations, discrimination.

In other words, of the many possible topics, we again find a short, stereotypical list in which the categories are usually defined in a negative way. Thus, immigration is always defined as a fundamental problem, and never as a challenge, let alone as a boon to the country, often associated with a financial burden. The same is true for the other main topics. Crime or crime-related topics such as drugs are virtually always among the top five of minority portrayals – even focusing on what is seen as 'typical' ethnic crime, such as drug trafficking and sales, but also what is defined as political 'terrorism' (for instance about Arabs). Cultural differences tend to be overemphasized and cultural similarities ignored. The coverage of elite racism – which may provide a more balanced view of the 'negative' aspects of society – is rare in the press. Instead we read about popular resentment against immigration, against individual cases of discrimination, or about extremist racist parties. In other words, discrimination and racism, when discussed at all in elite discourse, are always *elsewhere*.

Whereas topics are undoubtedly the most important, while also the most memorable, aspect of news, they merely tell us what the media report about ethnic issues, not how they do so. Although we have less detailed insight into the local aspects of meaning, style, and rhetoric of news reporting on 'race', there are a few findings that appear to be fairly reliable.

We already have observed for headlines that responsible agency may be enhanced or backgrounded by active or passive sentences. In the same way, backgrounding agency may occur in nominalizations, or word order of sentences. Again, the (largely unintentional) strategy that governs such local structures is the combined polarized tendency of positive self-presentation and negative other-presentation. Thus, we may find references to 'resentment' or 'discrimination' in the country, but it is not always spelled out who resents or discriminates against *whom*, as if discrimination or racism were phenomena of nature instead of practices of dominant group members.

Besides such aspects of discursive surface forms (syntax), it is especially the rich system of *meaning* that incorporates the many underlying beliefs that represent mental models of ethnic events, or more general, shared social representations of ethnic groups or ethnic relations. Following the now familiar ideological square, we thus may expect, and indeed do find, that in general information that is positive about Us or negative about Them will get highlighted, and vice versa. Semantically this means that such information will tend to be explicit rather than implicit, precise rather than vague, specific rather than general, asserted rather than presupposed, detailed instead of dealt with in abstractions. Thus, our intolerance, everyday racism, or discrimination will seldom be reported in much concrete detail, but their crimes, violence and deviance will.

Taking into account the cognitive interface discussed above, we suppose that such meaning structures are a function of underlying mental representations which simply portray ethnic events and ethnic groups in that way. These may be ad hoc, personal mental models with personal opinions, but also widely shared stereotypes, prejudices and ideologies. And the less these are conscious (as is often the case for more subtle forms of racism), the more the consensus is intertwined with dominant ethnic ideologies. Indeed, detailed news analysis about ethnic events provides a rich source for a study of contemporary social cognition.

Note though that what people say and mean in discourse is not only a direct function of their ethnic beliefs, but also a function of *context*, such as the setting, genre, speakers/writers, the audience, and so on. Thus news on ethnic affairs in serious broadsheets and in tabloids is very different for those contextual reasons, even if the journalists' underlying mental models about the ethnic events would be roughly the same. These contextual differences especially manifest themselves in the variable surface structures of style (layout, syntax, lexicalization, rhetorical devices).

News reports also have an important intertextual dimension. Newsmaking is largely based on the processing of a large number of source texts, such as other news reports, press conferences, interviews, scholarly studies, and so on. Such intertextuality in news reports shows in various forms of citation and other references to other discourses. Thus, it comes as no surprise that newspapers will generally take (white) elite source texts (e.g., of government, scholars, or the police) as being more credible and newsworthy than source texts of minority group members. Indeed, minority groups have little direct access to the media. If they are cited, they are always accompanied by declarations of credible majority group members. Statements about discrimination and racism will often be downgraded to the dubious status of allegations.

Whereas these and many other aspects of news reporting about race clearly express and reproduce dominant ethnic attitudes and ideologies, and hence crucially influence racism, it should finally be emphasized that problematization and marginalization do not only apply to minorities in the news, but also in the newsroom. Especially in Western Europe, leading reporters are virtually always white Europeans. No wonder that these will follow a beat, search for sources and believe opinions that are consistent with their own and other members of their group, and much less those of minority groups. So far, thus, minority journalists have had less access to the media, especially in leading positions. As we have seen, the elites, especially in Europe, are virtually always white, and they also control the contents, forms, style and goals of news and newsmaking. And it comes as no surprise therefore that the mass media, and especially the right-wing tabloid press, is rather part of the problem of racism than part of its solution.

Textbooks

Arguably, after the mass media, educational discourse is most influential in society, especially when it comes to the communication of beliefs that are not usually conveyed in everyday conversation or the media. All children, adolescents and young adults are daily confronted for many hours with lessons and textbooks – the only books that are obligatory reading in our culture. That is, there is no comparable institution and discourse that is as massively inculcated as that of school.

The bad news is that this is also true for lessons about Them – immigrants, refugees, minorities and peoples in the Third World – and that such discourses are often very stereotypical and sometimes plainly prejudiced. The good news is that there is no domain or institution in society where alternative discourses have more possibilities to develop than in education.

Many studies have been carried out on the portrayal of minorities and Third World people in textbooks. Even simple content analyses have repeatedly shown that such portrayal, at least until recently, tends to be biased, stereotypical, and Eurocentric, and in early textbooks even explicitly racist (Blondin, 1990; Klein, 1985; Preiswerk, 1980; van Dijk, 1993a).

As suggested, much has changed in contemporary textbooks. Whereas minorities were earlier virtually ignored or marginalized in textbooks, at least until the late 1980s, and despite their prominent presence in the country and even in the classroom, current textbooks in the social sciences as well as other fields seem finally to have discovered that there are also minorities to write about. And whereas information about Us that could be negative (such as colonialism) used to be ignored or mitigated, there is now a tendency to want to teach children also about the less glorious aspects of 'our' history or society.

And yet, this is a tendency but still far from the rule. Many contemporary textbooks in many western countries remain basically Eurocentric: not only our economy or technology but also our views, values, societies, and politics are invariably superior. They keep repeating stereotypes about minorities and other non-European people. Third World countries tend to be treated in a homogeneous way, despite the huge differences. As is the case in the press, the Others are invariably associated with Problems, for which however We tend to offer a solution. All this is equally true for minorities in the country, which largely are dealt with in terms of cultural differences and deviance, and seldom in terms of their everyday life, work and contributions to both culture and the economy. Finally, textbook assignments too often ignore the presence of minority children in the classroom, and if not, these may be spoken about as Them, and not always addressed as part of Us.

These and many other properties of textbooks obviously are hardly an ideal preparation for the acquisition of ethnic beliefs that prepare children adequately for contemporary, increasingly multicultural and diverse societies in Western Europe, North America, and elsewhere where Europeans are dominant over non-Europeans. As is the case for the media and the adult population, textbooks and lessons based on them form the discursive crucible for the everyday reproduction of biased ethnic beliefs and the often discriminatory practices based on them. We have argued that racism is learned and not natural or innate. This learning process already begins at school.

Political Discourse: Parliamentary Debates

Finally, among the influential symbolic elites of society, that is, those who have special access to and control over public discourse, we should mention the politicians. Indeed, sometimes even before the mass media, leading politicians have already preformulated a definition of the ethnic situation. State institutions such as the immigration service and the police, as well as their sustaining bureaucracies, are often the first to actually 'talk to' new immigrants, as well as talk about them. Such discourse will rapidly become official, both as to meaning/content and style, and routinely adopted by the media which cover these agencies and institutions, thus spreading dominant definitions of the ethnic situation among the population at large. Also depending on political parties and contexts, such discourses may again be stereotypical, biased, or even racist, or indeed take a dissident, anti-racist position based on human rights, multiculturalism and diversity (see, e.g., Hargreaves and Leaman, 1995; Hurwitz and Peffley, 1998; Solomos, 1993).

Historically, political discourse on the Others, whether minorities within the country or non-Europeans in Third World countries or colonies, has been among the most blatantly racist forms of elite discourse (Lauren, 1988). Until at least World War II, leading politicians would openly derogate people of Asian or African origin, and claim their white, western superiority. But due to the Holocaust and World War II, and as a result of the discrediting of racist beliefs because of their use by the Nazis, post-war political discourse has become increasingly less blatant on the Right, and more anti-racist on the Left. This development, however, should not be seen as a steady form of progress because in the 1990s problematizing and stigmatizing discourse on refugees and immigrants has reappeared more openly, even in mainstream parties.

Analysis of parliamentary debates on minorities, immigration, refugees and ethnic issues more generally shows many features that are consistent with those of other elite discourses we have examined above (van Dijk, 1993a). Specific for this discourse genre are of course especially its contextual characteristics: the political domain, the institution of parliament, the overall sociopolitical act of legislation, the participants in many different roles (politicians, party members, MPs, representatives, opposition members, etc.) and the local acts involved, such as defending or opposing a bill, giving a speech, criticizing the government, attacking opponents, and so on.

Large parts of parliamentary debates on immigration and ethnic issues are organized as a function of these context dimensions. Thus, populist strategies of talk, in which the will of the people is invoked, for instance, to restrict immigration, is of course a function of the position of MPs needing votes to stay in office or to toe the party line. Positions on ethnic policies taken and defended in parliament, thus, are not primarily personal opinions, but expressions of shared political party attitudes. And topics selected are those that are a function of the actual business of legislation at hand, such as dealing with an immigration bill or the arrival of refugees from Bosnia or Kosovo.

Political context similarly defines the nationalism that transpires in debates on immigration and minorities. In the same way as we find disclaimers in everyday talk, parliamentary speeches may begin with long sections of positive self-presentation in the form of nationalist glorification of 'long traditions of tolerance' or 'hospitality for the oppressed'. But of course, 'we cannot let them all in', 'we have no money', and so forth. That is, the rest of such debates will often be quite negative when it comes to the characterization of the others or the legitimation of further restrictions on immigration. That at least is the dominant voice – because occasionally we also find more tolerant, anti-racist, dissident voices which make appeal to human rights and universal principles.

Structurally speaking, parliamentary debates are organized sequences of speeches, by government and opposition speakers respectively. Given the respective political positions and roles, thus, each speaker will speak 'to' a specific issue, such as a recent ethnic event or a bill, and argue for or against a number of standpoints, for instance, aspects of ethnic or immigration policy. This means that such debates and their speeches will be largely argumentative and rhetorical.

Apart from the well-known rhetoric of nationalism, populism, or human rights mentioned above, what is perhaps most fascinating in parliamentary debates on immigration are the *argumentative moves*, for instance, those that are used to legitimate immigration restrictions. Many of these moves have become standard arguments or *topoi*, such as the reference to our ('white man's') financial burden, the regrettable reference to 'resentment' in the country, the suggestion of receiving refugees in their own country, the need to listen to the will of the people, and so on. Similarly, such argumentations are replete with *fallacies* of various kinds. Credibility rather than truth is managed by referring to authoritative sources or opinion makers, such as scholars or the Church. Selected but emotionally effective examples are used either of immigration fraud or of torture by foreign regimes in order to argue against or for liberal immigration laws for refugees, in both cases giving in to the fallacy of generalization from single cases. Again, the overall strategy in the selection of argumentative moves is positive self-presentation and negative other-presentation. The Others in such a case may be not only the immigrants, but also those members of (opposed) political parties who defend their rights or, vice versa, those who are seen to infringe upon such rights.

Parliamentary debates are public, for the record and official. This means that both content and style are strictly controlled, especially in written speeches. There is less formality in spontaneous debate, with large variation according to countries: in France such debates may be heated, with many interruptions, heckling and many rhetorical styles, unlike the Netherlands and Spain, where parliamentary debates are formal and polite. This also applies to meanings and style of debates on minorities and immigration.

Self-control and public exposure prohibits, for instance, explicit forms of derogation or lexical selection that is obviously biased. This means that such official discourse will seldom appear very racist. On the contrary, tolerance and understanding may be extensively topicalized. But we have seen that this may also be a move, a disclaimer that introduces more negative topics. And in order to legitimate immigration restrictions, thus, speakers need to spell out why immigrants or immigration are bad for Us, and such an overall statement can only be conveyed by the general strategy, implemented at all levels of discourse, of negative other-presentation. Thus, in parliament, there will be references to fraud, drugs, or crime of immigrants, as well as to cultural differences and conflicts, and to the disastrous impact on the job market.

Concluding Remark

In sum, we see that influential public discourses, namely, that of the elites and elite institutions, show a large number of related characteristics. These not only reflect similar underlying mental models and social representations shared by the elites, but also similar ways of social interaction, communication, persuasion and public opinion formation. Differences are mostly contextual, that is, depend on the aims, functions, or participants involved in them. But given similar aims, namely, the management of public opinion, legitimation and decision-making, we may assume that very similar structures and strategies will be at work in such discourse types. We will encounter stereotypical topics, conventional topoi, disclaimers that save face and hence manage impression formation; they engage in similar argumentative fallacies, make similar lexical selections when talking about Them, or use the same metaphors to emphasize some of their (bad) characteristics. All these different structures at different levels, and of different elite genres, contribute to the overall strategy of positive self-presentation and negative other-presentation. We have seen that precisely such structures may derive from and be geared towards the construction of similar mental structures, that is, negative attitudes and ideologies on minorities and immigration. And since among the elites as well as among the population at large such dominant group cognitions will again inspire similarly negative discourses and social practices, we may begin to understand how discourse, and especially public elite discourse, is crucially involved in the reproduction of racism.

6

Discourse and the Denial of Racism

Discourse and Racism

One of the crucial properties of contemporary racism is its denial, typically illustrated in such well-known disclaimers as 'I have nothing against blacks, but . . .'. This chapter examines the discursive strategies, as well as the cognitive and social functions, of such and other forms of denial in different genres of text and talk about ethnic or racial affairs.

The framework of this study is an interdisciplinary research programme at the University of Amsterdam that deals with the reproduction of racism through discourse and communication. In this research programme several projects have been carried out that analysed everyday conversations, textbooks, news in the press, parliamentary discourse and other forms of public and organizational communication (van Dijk, 1984a, 1987a, 1987b, 1991).

The guiding idea behind this research is that ethnic and racial prejudices are prominently acquired and shared within the white dominant group through everyday conversation and institutional text and talk. Such discourse serves to express, convey, legitimate or indeed to conceal or deny such negative ethnic attitudes. Therefore, a systematic and subtle discourse analytical approach should be able to reconstruct such social cognitions about other groups.

It is further assumed in this research programme that talk and text about minorities, immigrants, refugees or, more generally, about people of colour or Third World peoples and nations, also have broader societal, political and cultural functions. Besides positive self-presentation and negative other-presentation, such discourse signals group membership, white ingroup allegiances and, more generally, the various conditions for the reproduction of the white group and their dominance in virtually all social, political and cultural domains.

The theoretical framework that organizes this research programme is complex and multidisciplinary. Systematic descriptions of text and talk require an explicit theory of discourse. Relating such discourse structures to mental representations such as models, attitudes and ideologies about ethnic events, groups and the ethnic organization of society and culture, presupposes a sophisticated psychology of social cognitions. And a study of the functions of discourse in the reproduction of white group dominance should take place within the broader perspective of a social and cultural theory of racism and ethnicism.

Such a multidisciplinary approach to the role of discourse and communication in the reproduction of racism first operates at the societal micro level of everyday situated interactions, discourse and social cognitions of individual group members. Secondly, this micro level 'reality' of racism 'implements' the overall structures and processes of dominance and inequality at the meso and macro levels of groups, social formations, neighbourhoods, institutions, organizations and even nations and whole world regions. At the same time, the study of the interdependency of the micro and macro structures of racism, also requires an analysis of the relations between cognition and action, that is, at the micro level, between mental models of group members and their practices, and at the macro level, between social group attitudes and ideologies, on the one hand, and societal structures, on the other hand.

Another important hypothesis that emerges from this earlier work is that political, media, academic, corporate and other elites play an important role in the reproduction of racism. They are the ones who control or have access to many types of public discourse, have the largest stake in maintaining white group dominance and are usually also most proficient in persuasively formulating their ethnic opinions. Although there is of course a continuous interplay between elite and popular forms of racism, analysis of many forms of discourse suggests that the elites in many respects 'preformulate' the kind of ethnic beliefs of which, sometimes more blatant, versions may then get popular currency. Indeed, many of the more 'subtle', 'modern', 'everyday' or 'new' forms of cultural racism, or ethnicism, studied below, are taken from elite discourse (see van Dijk, 1987b, 1993a, for detail). This hypothesis is not inconsistent with the possibility that (smaller, oppositional) elite groups also play a prominent role in the preformulation of anti-racist ideologies.

Within this complex theoretical framework, our earlier studies of text and talk examined, among other structures, dominant topics of discourse, text schemata, for instance those of story-telling and argumentation, as well as local semantic moves (such as the disclaimer mentioned above), style, rhetoric and specific properties of conversational interaction.

We suggested above that one of the results of this earlier work was that in text and talk about ethnic or racial minorities, many white people follow a double strategy of positive self-presentation, on the one hand, and a strategy of expressing subtle, indirect or sometimes more blatant forms of negative other-presentation, on the other hand. Indeed, especially in public discourse, outgroup derogation seldom takes place without expressions of ingroup favouritism or social face-keeping.

The Denial of Racism

The denial of racism is one of the moves that is part of the latter strategy of positive ingroup presentation. General norms and values, if not the law, prohibit (blatant) forms of ethnic prejudice and discrimination, and many if not most white group members are both aware of such social constraints and, up to a point, even share and acknowledge them (Billig, 1988). Therefore, even the most blatantly racist discourse in our data routinely features denials or at least mitigations of racism. Interestingly, we have found that precisely the more racist discourse tends to have disclaimers and other denials. This suggests that language users who say negative things about minorities are well aware of the fact that they may be understood as breaking the social norm of tolerance or acceptance.

Denials of racism, and similar forms of positive self-presentation, have both an *individual* and a *social* dimension. Not only do most white speakers individually resent being perceived as racists, also, and even more importantly, such strategies may at the same time aim at defending the ingroup as a whole: 'We are not racists', 'We are not a racist society'.

Whereas the first, individual, form of denial is characteristic of informal everyday conversations, the second is typical for public discourse, for instance in politics, the media, education, corporations and other organizations. Since public discourse potentially reaches a large audience, it is this latter, social form of denial that is most influential and, therefore, also most damaging: it is the social discourse of denial that persuasively helps construct the dominant white consensus. Few white group members would have reason or interest to doubt, let alone to oppose, such a claim.

Face-keeping or positive self-presentation are well-known phenomena in social psychology, sociology and communication research, and are part of the overall strategy of impression management (Brewer, 1988; Brown and Levinson, 1987; Goffman, 1959; Schlenker, 1980; Tedeschi,

1981). In interaction, people try to act, and hence to speak, in such a way that their interlocutors construct an 'impression' of them that is as positive as possible, or at least speakers try to avoid a negative impression (Arkin, 1981).

Theoretically, impressions are person representations, that is, mental schemata that feature an organized set of categories by which people are judged, usually along several dimensions and with respect to several social norms, interests or criteria. Such judgements may be local or situational, and pertain to current actions or cognitions, but they may also be about more permanent, context independent, 'personality' characteristics of an individual.

It may be assumed that, whereas people may want to avoid a negative impression in any situation, they are probably more anxious to avoid a general negative evaluation about their personality than to avoid a negative judgement about one particular action in one specific situation. To be categorized as 'a racist' or even as being 'intolerant' presupposes a more enduring characteristic of people, and is therefore a judgement that is particularly face-threatening. Hence, when speakers emphasize that 'they have nothing against blacks' (or other minority groups), such disclaimers focus on a more permanent attitude, rather than on the specific (negative) opinion now being expressed about some specific outgroup member or some specific ethnic or racial action or event.

What such disclaimers try to do, thus, is to block inferences from this particular instance to a more general impression. After all, a specific negative opinion about a particular ethnic group member or a particular act, may well be found to be justified, whereas a more general negative opinion about ethnic minorities might be seen as constitutive of a racist attitude.

In the latter case, a negative attitude may be found acceptable only when pertaining to a specific characteristic of a group, for instance when someone assumes that refugees often enter the country illegally, or when blacks are seen as insufficiently 'motivated' to get a good education or to get a job. In that case, the judgement may be warranted with references to (alleged) negative actions or attitudes of the outgroup. It is not surprising, therefore, that when such negative judgements are qualified as 'racist', racism is emphatically denied.

We see below that in such cases the charge is often reversed: the person who accuses the other as racist is in turn accused of inverted racism against whites, as oversensitive and exaggerating, as intolerant and generally as 'seeing racism where there is none', as right-wing British newspapers like to put it (van Dijk, 1991). Accusations of racism, then,

soon tend to be seen as more serious social infractions than racist attitudes or actions themselves, e.g., because they disrupt ingroup solidarity
and smooth ingroup encounters: they are felt to ruin the 'good atmos-
phere' of interactions and situations. Moreover, such accusations are seen
to impose taboos, prevent free speech and a 'true' or 'honest' assessment
of the ethnic situation. In other words, denials of racism often turn into
counter-accusations of intolerant and intolerable anti-racism.

Types of Denial

We see that denials come in many forms, each with its own cognitive,
emotional, social, political and cultural functions. We have situational and
general denials, personal ones and group-based ones. Although people
who speak about other groups usually talk as ingroup members, there
may well be a tension between individual opinions and those shared by
the ingroup. Those who deny that they are racists usually imply that they
comply with the general, official group norm that prohibits racism, and
that, therefore, they are decent citizens. Such individual disclaimers often
presuppose that the whole group is not racist.

On the other hand, there may be situations where individuals deny
racist opinions or practices while acknowledging that the group as a
whole, or at least some or many other group members, may not share
such tolerance. Such combined denials/admissions are rare, however,
since criticizing the ingroup may be a characteristic strategy of anti-
racists (Taguieff, 1988), whereas denials of individual racism are often
typical of racist opinions. On the other hand, individual denials of racism
may strategically be made by comparison to 'others', e.g., one's neighbours or customers, and then takes the form of a *transfer* move: 'I have
nothing against them, but you know my customers don't like to deal
with black personnel.'

The act of denial itself, thus, also comes in different guises. Generally,
denials are part of a strategy of *defence*, presupposing explicit or implicit
accusations. In that case, people may deny to have engaged in negative
acts, to have broken the law or some social norm, or to have some negative, overall personality characteristic of which they are *actually* accused
by an interlocutor. On the other hand, denials may also be preemptive, as
is the case in positive self-presentation or face-keeping, that is, they may
focus on *possible* inferences of the interlocutor.

Action is theoretically analysed as a combination of cognition (intention) and activity. One may admit having engaged in an action that may
have been interpreted as negative, but at the same time deny the nega-

tive cognitive counterpart: 'I did not intend it that way.' That is, in strategies of defence, the crucial condition of responsibility for negative action lies in intentions: good intentions are seen as implementations of good attitudes, and hence as characteristic of good social membership or good citizenship.

This distinction between intention and activity also permeates many aspects of criminal law, and for instance distinguishes between murder and manslaughter. Intention, especially long-term planning and willingly engaging in criminal offences, is at least an aggravating condition of crime. On the other hand, accidents, incidents, 'on the spur of the moment', or emotionally defined acts, and similarly non-planned actions are partly excusable and hence less serious. This is, by definition, especially the case in spontaneous everyday interaction.

Note that intention denials, as we may call them, are strategically very effective, since the accuser has few ways to actually prove negative intentions. This is particularly also the case in discrimination trials, where it is often hard to prove that the negative action was not committed because of other, acceptable reasons. For instance, a newspaper may repeatedly and prominently publish reports about minority crime, but may at the same time defend such practices by claiming to publish 'the truth', and thus deny prejudiced opinions about minority crime and hence deny spreading such prejudices with the intention of discrediting minorities or inciting racial hatred. This is among the most classical cases of media racism (van Dijk, 1991).

On the other hand, although intentionally committed crimes are usually evaluated as more serious, people are assumed to have control over their activities, and hence also over their intentions. This may mean, for instance, that people are responsible for the *possible* consequences of their actions, even when such consequences may not have been the actual purpose of such actions. That is, if it can be shown that people could have known that their acts have negative consequences, then they are at least partially responsible for such consequences, especially if these would not have occurred without their actions. For instance, a politician who gives an interview that criticizes welfare cheating by minorities knows that such allegations will be published, and that such a publication may further confirm negative prejudices among the media audience. Such a politician may deny discriminatory intent or purpose, and claim that he or she only wanted to 'tell the truth'.

In other words, we now have the following types of denials:

1   act-denial ('I did not do/say that at all');

2   control-denial ('I did not do/say that on purpose', 'It was an acci-
     dent');
3   intention-denial ('I did not mean that', 'You got me wrong');
4   goal-denial ('I did not do/say that, in order to . . .').

In the last case, there is also a denial of responsibility: if there were
negative consequences, I did not have control over them. We have already
suggested that especially the media routinely deny responsibility for what
the audience may do with media contents. Theoretically, legally and
morally, these are the more difficult dimensions of the denial of racism.
In most cases, one would need repeated acts/texts of the same kind, in
different situations, and occasional expressions of plans, intentions or
goals in order to 'prove' negative intentions or goals. It is not surprising,
therefore, that also in discrimination lawsuits, intentions may sometimes
be declared irrelevant, and that people are judged only by the direct or
even indirect (statistical) consequences of their actions.

Another form of denial is the class of acts that may be categorized as
mitigations, such as downtoning, minimizing or using euphemisms when
describing one's negative actions: 'I did not threaten him, but gave him
friendly advice,' 'I did not insult her, but told her my honest opinion,' etc.
Mitigation strategies are particularly important in social situations where
the relevant norms are rather strong. Thus, we may assume that the more
stringent the norm against discrimination and racism, the more people
will tend to have recourse to denials and hence also to mitigations.

Indeed, the very notion of 'racism' may become virtually taboo in
accusatory contexts because of its strong negative connotations. If used at
all in public discourse, for instance in the media, it will typically be
enclosed by quotes or accompanied by doubt or distance markers such
as 'alleged', signalling that this is a possibly unwarranted if not preposterous accusation, e.g., by minorities themselves or by (other) anti-racists.
Acts in which racism is undeniable tend to be described in terms of
'discrimination', 'prejudice', 'stereotypes', 'bias', 'racial motivation', but
not as 'racist'. Generally, the notions of 'racism' and 'racist' in European
and US public discourse are reserved for *others*, for instance, extremist,
right-wing, fringe groups and parties outside of the consensus. Also, the
notion of 'racism' may be used to describe racism abroad or in the past,
as is the case for apartheid in South Africa or the period of slavery, reconstruction and segregation in the USA. As a general term denoting a
whole system of racial or ethnic inequality, exclusion or oppression in
western societies, racism is used primarily by minority groups or other
anti-racists. In other words, the use of euphemisms presupposes the denial

of systemic racism of the ingroup or dominant society. This is also the case in much scholarly discourse about ethnic relations (Essed, 1987).

Note that this denial of racism should partly be attributed to the fact that the concept of racism is (still) largely understood in the classical, ideological sense, of seeing other ethnic or racial groups as being inferior, or as overt, official, institutional practices, as is the case for apartheid (Miles, 1989). The more 'modern', subtle and indirect forms of ethnic or racial inequality, and especially the 'racism', or rather 'ethnicism' based on constructions of cultural difference and incompatibility, is seldom characterized as 'racism', but at most as xenophobia and, more often than not, as legitimate cultural self-defence (Barker, 1981; Dovidio and Gaertner, 1986).

Besides denial proper, there are also a number of cognitive and social strategies that are more or less closely related to denials. The first is *justification*, as we already saw in the case of the newspaper justifying special attention for minority crime by referring to the 'truth' or the 'right to know' of its readers. Similarly, in everyday conversations, people may justify a negative act or discourse relative to a minority group member by justifying it as an act of legitimate defence, or by detailing that the other person was indeed guilty and, therefore, deserved a negative reaction. In other words, in this case, the act is not denied, but it is denied that it was negative, and explicitly asserted that it was justified (for details, see Antaki, 1988; Scott and Lyman, 1968; Tedeschi and Reiss, 1981).

Similarly, negative acts may be acknowledged as such, but at the same time *excused* (Cody and McLaughlin, 1988). In this case, at least part of the blame may be put on special circumstances, or rather on others. Owners of clubs may admit to having discriminated against blacks by not letting them in, but may make an appeal to the circumstance that already so many other blacks were in the club. The same is routinely the case in immigration debates at a higher political level: we do not let in more immigrants or refugees in order to avoid aggravating the ethnic tensions in the inner cities. The latter case may in fact be presented as a justification and not as an excuse, because the act of refusing entry is not admitted to be a negative act, but a constitutional privilege of states.

Stronger excuse strategies are alleging *provocation* and *blaming the victim*. Thus, the police may feel justified to act harshly against young black males, as is the case in many European and US cities, because of alleged provocations, drug offences, or other stereotypically assigned negative actions of young blacks. Government policies, again both in Europe and the US, routinely justify or excuse 'tough' measures against minorities by claiming that they are themselves to blame: lack of integration, failing to learn the language, lacking motivation to find a job and cultural deviance are among the grounds for such blaming. Unemployment, lacking success in education, miserable housing and welfare dependence, among other things, are thus routinely attributed to negative characteristics of the 'victims' themselves. Note that such stronger strategies usually imply a denial of own failing policies.

Finally, the strongest form of denial is *reversal*: 'We are not guilty of negative action, *they* are' and '*We* are not the racists, *they* are the *real* racists.' This kind of reversal is the stock-in-trade of the radical Right, although less extreme versions also occur in more moderate anti-anti-racism (Murray, 1986). The British tabloids, as we see later, thus tend to accuse the anti-racists of being intolerant busybodies and the real racists. Similarly, the French Front National typically accuses those who are not against immigration of non-Europeans as engaging in 'anti-French racism'. More generally, anti-racists tend to be represented as the ones who are intolerant, while lightly accusing innocent and well-meaning citizens (i.e., us) of racism. We see that reversals are no longer forms of social defence, but part of a strategy of (counter-)attack.

Sociocultural and Political Functions

Although usually manifesting itself, at the micro-level of social organization, in everyday conversation and interpersonal communication, the denial of racism not only has individual functions. We have seen that people deny, mitigate, justify or excuse negative acts towards minorities in order to emphasize their compliance with the law or with norms and to stress their role as competent, decent citizens. That is, even in interpersonal situations, the moral dimension of denial has social presuppositions. It does not make sense to deny racist acts as a moral or legal transgression if the group or society as a whole agrees with you, as is/was the case during official apartheid policies in South Africa, or during the reconstruction and segregation period in US history. Indeed, more generally, it may be said that when racism, ethnicism or ethnocentrism are openly advocated or legitimated by the elites and the leading institutions of society, the less we should find denials, let alone excuses, of racist acts and discourse.

However, in present-day European and US societies, where discrimination and racism are officially banned, and norms have developed that do not tolerate blatant expressions of outgroup hate, denial takes a much more prominent role in discourse on ethnic affairs. We suggested that this is not only true at the personal level. Also groups, institutions or organizations as a whole, at a meso or macro level of social organization, may engage in such strategies of denial. In that case, denials may take the form of a shared opinion, as a consensus about the ethnic situation. For instance, since discrimination and racism are legally and morally prohibited, most western countries share the official belief that therefore discrimination and racism no longer exist as a structural characteristic of society or the state. If discrimination or prejudice still exist, it is treated as an incident, as a deviation, as something that should be attributed to, and punished at, the individual level. In other words, institutional or systemic racism is denied.

Hence, positive self-presentation and face-keeping are not limited to individuals but also, if not more strongly, characterizes the more public discourse of institutions and organizations. Universities in the USA routinely print on their letterhead that they are 'Equal Opportunity Employers', not only because such employment practices are the law, but also because this is good PR. Organizations, no more than individuals, do not want to be known as racist among their personnel, among their customers or among the public at large. Moreover, ethnic and racial tolerance, and even affirmative action, are symbols of social progress and modernity which by association may be related to the quality of the products or services of an organization. This is of course most literally true when organizations employ highly talented members from minority groups who may enhance quality of products and especially services for a growing clientele of minorities. Self-interest in this case may well be consistent with ideologies of social policy.

However, social policies may conflict with organizational or business interests and ideologies, for instance in more consequential forms of affirmative action such as quota. In this case, other values, such as the freedom of enterprise, and especially economic competitiveness, are posed against the values that underlie social policy. Refusing quotas, therefore, is most emphatically denied to be an expression of discrimination or racism, for instance, because it is seen as quality-degrading instead of equality-enhancing and to be an unacceptable form of group-favouring. Thus, ultimately, also in state or business organizations, the acceptance of affirmative action will move within strict boundaries defined by the interests and the power of the (white) elites that control them.

The social functions of the institutional denial of racism are obvious. If liberal democracies in Europe and the US have increasingly adopted laws and norms that presuppose or guarantee equality, freedom, if not brother- or sisterhood for all the ethnic or racial inequalities implied by discrimination or racism, would be inconsistent with official ideologies.

Instead of recognizing such 'imperfection', it is more expedient to deny such fundamental inconsistency, or at least to explain it away as incidental and individual, to blame it on the victims, or to characterize it as a temporary phenomenon of transition, for instance for new immigrants.

If racism is defined as a system of racial or ethnic dominance, it is likely that the denial of racism also has a prominent role in the very reproduction of racism. This is indeed the case. Dominance and inequality provoke resistance. However, when the dominant consensus is that there is no racism, minority groups and their protests or other forms of resistance have a very hard time to be taken seriously (Essed, 1991). In systems of apartheid and officially sanctioned segregation, things are clear-cut, and the power difference so blatant that the enemy is well defined, and resistance well focused.

However, in modern, increasingly pluralist societies that have laws and even prevalent norms against (blatant) prejudice, discrimination and racism, this is much less the case. If tolerance is promoted as a national myth, as is the case for the Netherlands, it is much more difficult for minority groups to challenge remaining inequalities, to take unified action and to gain credibility and support among the (white) dominant group. Indeed, they may be seen as oversensitive, exaggerating or overdemanding. The more flexible the system of inequality, the more difficult it is to fight it.

The white consensus that denies the prevalence of racism thus is a very powerful element in its reproduction, especially since successful resistance requires public attention, media coverage and at least partial recognition of grievances. If leading politicians and the media refuse to acknowledge that there is a serious problem, there will be no public debate, no change of public opinion and hence no change in the system of power relations. Change in that case can only be put on the agenda by actively creating the kind of public 'problems' that can no longer be overlooked, such as demonstrations or even 'riots'. Other serious problems, such as high minority unemployment or educational 'underachievement', may well be recognized by the elites, but it is routine to deny that they have anything to do with racism. 'Occasional, unintentional discrimination' is merely taken as one marginal element in such social problems.

We see that the social functions of the denial of racism are closely associated with the political ones. Decision-making, agenda-setting and public opinion management, both nationally and locally, favour a definition of the ethnic or racial situation in which the element of 'racism' is carefully eliminated, simply because it implies that we are the real problem, and not they. Immigration, employment, education or social policies, thus, need to be founded on an ideology that skilfully combines humanitarian values and self-interest.

By selectively attributing racism to the extreme Right, it is both denied as being a characteristic of the own ingroup of moderate white citizens, and at the same time is better manageable, for instance by occasionally prosecuting the more overt right-wing racists. Recognizing that many subtle forms of everyday racism are rife throughout society would be lending support to a form of sociopolitical analysis that is no longer manageable: if it is true, how can it be changed? After all, we already have laws against discrimination, and if these do not work properly, what else can we do to change the 'mentality' of the people? The result of such complex underlying structures of political decision-making is that overall denial is flexibly coupled with incidental admissions of the more blatant 'exceptions' to the rule.

We see that the denial of racism is not only part of a strategy of personal, institutional or social impression management and ideological self-defence, it also is a form of sociopolitical management. It helps control resistance, and at the same time makes political problems of an ethnically or racially pluralist society more manageable. In sum, denial is a major management strategy.

Finally, we may ask whether the denial of racism also has more specific cultural functions. Obviously, since different groups and their respective cultures are involved, and racism also requires definition in terms of cultural hegemony, its denial should also have cultural dimensions. One such dimension is the combination of denying racism or ethnocentrism with the self-affirmation of tolerance as a feature of contemporary 'western' culture. In the same way that democracy, technology, Christianity and western values are thus, at least implicitly, presented in textbooks, political discourse and the media as superior to other cultures, western 'tolerance' is contrasted with, for example, intolerant cultures, at present especially with Muslim fundamentalism (Said, 1981).

Western discourse during the Rushdie affair is a clear case in point. Public debate during this affair focused not only on freedom of speech and the arts, but at the same time on stereotypes about the fundamentalist if not 'fanatical' elements of Muslim culture. That anti-Arab racism played a prominent role in this debate was emphatically denied, e.g., by claiming universality of western values. In other words, in the same way as white people may deny racism and at the same time present themselves as tolerant citizens, western culture as a whole may deny racism or ethnocentrism, and emphasize tolerance.

That such cultural claims are closely linked with the management of world politics, as was also shown during the Gulf War, hardly needs to be spelled out. The same is true, more generally, in the management of the relations between the North and the South, e.g., through strategies of denying neo-colonialism or imperialism, self-interest in international aid and by affirming the 'leading' role of the western world. In sum, the western denial of racism and ethnocentrism, and its social, political and cultural implications, plays a role from the level of interpersonal relations, to the global level of intercultural and international relations. At all levels, such denial functions essentially to manage resistance, dissent and opposition and hence as a strategy in the reproduction of hegemony (Lauren, 1988).

Conversation

Everyday conversation is at the heart of social life. Whether in informal situations, with family members or friends, or on the job with colleagues or clients or within a multitude of institutions, informal talk constitutes a crucial mode of social interaction. At the same time, conversations are a major conduit of social 'information-processing', and provide the context for the expression and persuasive conveyance of shared knowledge and beliefs.

In ethnically mixed societies, minority groups and ethnic relations are a major topic of everyday conversation. Whether through direct personal experience, or indirectly through the mass media, white people in Europe and North America learn about minorities or immigrants, formulate their own opinions and thus informally reproduce – and occasionally challenge – the dominant consensus on ethnic affairs through informal everyday talk.

Our extensive discourse analytical research into the nature of such everyday talk about ethnic affairs, based on some 170 interviews conducted in the Netherlands and California, shows that such informal talk has a number of rather consistent properties (van Dijk, 1984a, 1987a):

1   Topics are selected from a rather small range of subjects, and focus on sociocultural differences, deviance and competition. Most topics explicitly or implicitly deal with interpersonal, social, cultural or economic 'threats' to the dominant white group, society or culture.
2   Story-telling is not, as would be usual, focused on entertaining, but

takes place within an argumentative framework. Stories serve as the strong, while personally experienced, premises of a generally negative conclusion, such as 'We are not used to that here,' 'They should learn the language' or 'The government should do something about that.'

3   Style, rhetoric and conversational interaction generally denote critical distance, if not negative attitudes towards minorities or immigration. However, current norms of tolerance control expressions of evaluations in such a way that discourse with strangers (such as interviewers) is generally rather mitigated. Strong verbal aggression tends to be avoided.

4   Overall, speakers follow a double strategy of positive self-presentation and negative other-presentation.

It is within this latter strategy also that disclaimers, such as 'I have nothing against Arabs, *but* . . .' have their specific functions (Scott and Lyman, 1968). Such a denial may be called 'apparent', because the denial is not supported by evidence that the speaker does not have anything against 'them'. On the contrary, the denial often serves as the face-keeping move introducing a generally negative assertion, following the invariable, sometimes stressed, as in the following example from a Dutch woman:

(1) uhh . . . how they are and that is mostly just fine, people have their own religion have their own way of life, and I have *absolutely* nothing against that, *but*, it is a fact that if their way of life begins to differ from mine to an *extent* that . . .

Talking about the main topic of cultural difference, the denial here focuses on relative tolerance for such cultural differences which, however, is clearly constrained. The differences should not be too great. So, on the one hand, the woman follows the norm of tolerance, but on the other hand, she feels justified to reject others when they 'go too far'. In other words, the denial here presupposes a form of limited social acceptance.

Speakers who are more aware of discrimination and racism, as is the case in California, are even more explicit about the possible inferences of their talk:

(2) It sounds prejudiced, but I think if students only use English . . .

The use of English, a prominent topic for 'ethnic' conversations in the

USA, may be required for many practical reasons, but the speaker realizes that, whatever the good arguments he or she may have, it may be heard as a form of prejudice against immigrants. Of course the use of 'It sounds' implies that the speaker does not think he is really prejudiced.

One major form of denial in everyday conversation is the denial of discrimination. Indeed, as also happens in the right-wing media (see below), we also find reversal in this case: we are the real victims of immigration and minorities. Here are some of the ways people in Amsterdam formulate their denials:

(3) Yes, they have exploited them, that's what they say at least, you know, but well, I don't believe that either. . . .

(4) Big cars, they are better off than we are. If anybody is being discriminated against, our children are. That's what I make of it.

(5) And the only thing that came from her mouth was I am being discriminated against and the Dutch all have good housing, well it is a big lie, it is not true.

(6) And they say that they are being dis . . . discrim . . . [*sic*] discriminated against. That is not true.

(7) Listen, they always say that foreigners are being discriminated against here. No, *we* are being discriminated against. It is exactly the reverse.

In all these situations, the speakers talk about what they see as threats or lies by immigrants: a murder in (3), cheating on welfare in (4), a radio programme where a black woman says she is discriminated against in (5) and neighbourhood services in (6) and (7). In conversations such reversals may typically be heard in working-class neighbourhoods where crime is attributed to minorities, or where alleged favouritism (e.g., in housing) is resented. Poor whites thus feel that they are victims of inadequate social and urban policies but, instead of blaming the authorities or the politicians, they tend to blame the newcomers who, in their eyes, are so closely related to the changing, i.e., deteriorating, life in the inner city. And if they are defined as those who are responsible, such a role is inconsistent with the claim that they are discriminated against (Phizacklea and Miles, 1979).

Note that this consensus is not universal. Negative behaviour may be observed, but without generalization and with relevant comparisons to Dutch youths:

(8) And that was also, well I am sorry, but they were foreigners, they were apparently Moroccans who did that. But God, all young people are aggressive, whether it is Turkish youth, or Dutch youth, or Surinamese youth, is aggressive. Particularly because of discrimination uhh that we have here . . .

Here discrimination is not reversed, and the young immigrants are represented as victims of discrimination, which is used to explain and hence to excuse some of their 'aggressiveness'. Such talk, however, is rather exceptional.

The Press

Many of the 'ethnic events' people talk about in everyday life are not known from personal experiences, but from the media. At least until recently, in many parts of Western Europe and even in some regions of North America, most white people had few face-to-face dealings with members of minority groups. Arguments in everyday talk, thus, may be about crime or cultural differences they read about in the press, and such reports are taken as 'proof' of the negative attitudes the speakers have about minorities.

Our analyses of thousands of reports in the press in Britain and the Netherlands (van Dijk, 1991) largely confirm the common-sense interpretations of the readers: a topical analysis shows that crime, cultural differences, violence ('riots'), social welfare and problematic immigration are among the major recurrent topics of ethnic affairs reporting. In other words, there are marked parallels between topics of talk and media topics.

Overall, with some changes over the last decade, the dominant picture of minorities and immigrants is that of *problems* (Hartmann and Husband, 1974). Thus the conservative and right-wing press tends to focus on the problems minorities and immigrants are seen to create (in housing, schooling, unemployment, crime, etc.), whereas the more liberal press (also) focuses on the problems minorities have (poverty, discrimination), but which we (white liberals) do something about. On the other hand, many topics that are routine in the coverage of white people, groups or institutions tend to be ignored, such as their contribution to the economy, political organization, culture and in general all topics that characterize the everyday lives of minorities and their own, active contributions to the society as a whole. Thus, in many respects, except when involved in conflicts or problems, minorities tend to be 'denied' by the press (Boskin, 1980).

Practices of newsgathering as well as patterns of quotation also show that minorities and their institutions have literally little to say in the press. First of all, especially in Europe, there are virtually no minority journalists, so that the perspective, inside knowledge and experience, prevailing attitudes and necessary sources of journalists tend to be all-white, as are also the government agencies, police and other institutions that are the main sources of news in the press (van Dijk, 1988a, 1988b). Even on ethnic events, minority spokespersons are less quoted, less credibly quoted and, if they are quoted, their opinions are often 'balanced' by the more 'neutral' comments of white spokespersons. Especially on delicate topics, such as discrimination, prejudice and racism, minority representatives or experts are very seldom heard in a credible, authoritative way. If at all, such quotes are often presented as unwarranted or even ridiculous accusations.

It is at this point where the overall strategy of denial has one of its discursive manifestations in press reports. Of course, as may be expected, there is a difference between liberal, conservative and right-wing newspapers in this respect. Note, however, that there are virtually no explicitly anti-racist newspapers in Europe and North America. The official norm, even on the Right, is that 'we are all against racism', and the overall message is, therefore, that serious accusations of racism are a figment of the imagination.

Liberal newspapers, however, do pay attention to stories of explicit discrimination, e.g., in employment (though *rarely* in their own newsrooms or news reports), whereas right-wing extremism is usually dealt with in critical terms, although such coverage may focus on violent or otherwise newsworthy incidents rather than on racist attitudes per se. By such means ethnic or racial inequality is redefined as marginal, that is, as individualized or outside the consensus. Thus, the Dutch liberal press extensively reports cases (accusations) of discrimination and the same is true in the USA. In the right-wing press, discrimination is also covered, but from a different perspective. Here, it is usually covered as a preposterous accusation, preferably against 'ordinary' people, or embedded in explanations or excuses (the act was provoked).

Whereas discrimination gets rather wide attention in the press, racism does not. Indeed, discrimination is seldom qualified as a manifestation of racism. One of the reasons for this is that racism is still often understood as an ideology of white supremacy, or as the kind of practices of the extreme Right. Since the large majority of the press does not identify with the extreme Right, any qualification of everyday discriminatory practices as 'racism' is resolutely rejected.

For large sections of the press, only anti-racists see such everyday racism as racism which results in the marginalization of anti-racists as a radical, 'loony' group. For much of the press, at least in Britain, the real enemies, therefore, are the anti-racists: they are intolerant, anti-British, busybodies, who see racism everywhere, even in 'innocent' children's books, and even in the press.

It is not surprising, therefore, that reports on general aspects of racism in one's own society or group tend to be rare, even in the liberal press. Anti-racist writers, researchers or action groups have less access to the media, and their activities or opinions tend to be more or less harshly scorned, if not ridiculed. For the right-wing press, moreover, they are the real source of the 'problems' attributed to a multicultural society, because they not only attack venerable institutions (such as the police, government or business), but also provide a competing but fully incompatible definition of the ethnic situation. It is this symbolic competition for the definition of the situation and the intellectual struggle over the definition of society's morals that pitches the right-wing press against left-wing, anti-racist intellectuals, teachers, writers and action groups.

Let us examine in more detail how exactly the press engages in this denial of racism. Most of our examples are taken from the British press, but it would not be difficult to find similar examples in the Dutch, German and French press. Because of its long history of slavery and segregation, the notion of white racism is more broadly accepted in the USA, even when today's prevailing ideology is that, now minorities have equal rights, racism is largely a thing of the past.

Racism and the press

The denial of racism in and by the press is of course most vehement when the press itself is the target of accusations. Reflecting similar reactions by other editors of Dutch newspapers to our own research on racism in the press, the Editor-in-Chief of a major elite weekly, *Intermediair*, catering especially for social scientists and the business community, writes the following in a letter:

> (9) In particular, what you state about the coverage of minorities remains unproven and an unacceptable caricature of reality. Your thesis 'that the tendency of most reports is that ethnic minorities cause problems for us' is in my opinion not only not proven, but simply incorrect. (*Translated from the Dutch*)

This reaction was inspired by a brief summary of mostly international research on the representation of minorities in the press. The editor's denial is not based on (other) research, but simply stated as a 'fact'. It is not surprising that the article, on recent news research, was not published despite my having been initially invited to write such a piece.

Other editors take an even more furious stand and challenge the very academic credentials of the researcher and the university, as is the case for the editor of the major conservative popular daily in the Netherlands, *De Telegraaf*, well-known for its biased reporting on minorities, immigrants and refugees:

> (10) Your so-called scientific research does not in any sense prove your slanderous insinuations regarding the contents of our newspaper, is completely irrelevant and raises doubt about the prevailing norms of scientific research and social prudence at the University of Amsterdam. (*Translated from the Dutch*)

We see that whatever 'proof' may be brought in one's painstaking analyses of news reports, the reaction is one of flat denial and counter-attack by discrediting the researcher. Examples like these may be multiplied at random. No newspaper, including (or especially) the more liberal ones, will accept even a moderate charge of being biased, while allegations of racism are rejected violently. Recall that these newspapers, especially in Europe, generally employ no, or only one or two token, minority journalists.

With such an editorial attitude towards racism, there is a general reluctance to identify racist events as such in society at large. Let us examine the principal modes of such denials in the press. Examples are taken from the British press coverage of ethnic affairs in 1985 (for analysis of other properties of these examples, see van Dijk, 1991). Brief summaries of the context of each fragment of news discourse are given in parentheses.

Positive self-presentation

The semantic basis of denial is 'truth' as the writer sees it. The denial of racism in the press, therefore, presupposes that the journalist or columnist believes that his or her own group or country is essentially 'tolerant' towards minorities or immigrants. Positive self-presentation, thus, is an important move in journalistic discourse and should be seen as the argumentative denial of the accusations of anti-racists:

> (11) [Handsworth] Contrary to much doctrine, and acknowledging a small malevolent fascist fringe, this is a remarkably tolerant society. But tolerance would be stretched were it to be seen that enforcement of law adopted the principle of reverse discrimination. (*Daily Telegraph*, Editorial, 11 September 1985)
> (12) [Racial attacks and policing] If the ordinary British taste for decency and tolerance is to come through, it will need positive and unmistakable action. (*Daily Telegraph*, Editorial, 13 August 1985)

(13) [Racial attacks against Asians] . . . Britain's record for absorbing people from different backgrounds, peacefully and with tolerance, is second to none. The descendants of Irish and Jewish immigrants will testify to that. It would be tragic to see that splendid reputation tarnished now. (*Sun*, Editorial, 14 August 1985)

(14) [Immigration] Our traditions of fairness and tolerance are being exploited by every terrorist, crook, screwball and scrounger who wants a free ride at our expense. . . . Then there are the criminals who sneak in as political refugees or as family members visiting a distant relative. (*Mail*, 28 November 1985)

(15) We have racism too – and that is what is behind the plot. It is not white racism. It is black racism. . . . But who is there to protect the white majority? . . . Our tolerance is our strength, but we will not allow anyone to turn it into our weakness. (*Sun*, 24 October 1985)

These examples not only assert or presuppose white British 'tolerance', but at the same time define its boundaries. Tolerance might be interpreted as a position of weakness and, therefore, it should not be 'stretched' too far, lest 'every terrorist', 'criminal' or other immigrant, takes advantage of it. Affirmative action or liberal immigration laws, thus, can only be seen as a form of reverse discrimination, and hence as a form of self-destruction of white Britain. Ironically, therefore, these examples are self-defeating because of their internal contradictions. It is not tolerance per se that is aimed at, but rather the limitations preventing its 'excesses'. Note that in example (15) positive self-presentation is at the same time combined with the well-known move of reversal. 'They are the real racists', 'We are the real victims.' We shall come back to such reversal moves below.

Denial and counter-attack

Having constructed a positive self-image of white Britain, the conservative and tabloid press especially engages in attacks against those who hold a different view, at the same time defending those who agree with its position, as was the case during the notorious Honeyford affair (Honeyford was headmaster of a Bradford school who was suspended, then reinstated and finally let go with a golden handshake, after having written articles on multicultural education which most of the parents of his mostly Asian students found racist). The attacks on the anti-racists often embody denials of racism:

(16) [Reaction of 'race lobby' against Honeyford] Why is it that this lobby have chosen to persecute this man. . . . It is not because he is a racist; it is precisely

because he is not a racist, yet has dared to challenge the attitudes, behaviour and approach of the ethnic minority professionals. (*Daily Telegraph*, 6 September 1985)

(17) [Honeyford and other cases] Nobody is less able to face the truth than the hysterical 'anti-racist' brigade. Their intolerance is such that they try to silence or sack anyone who doesn't toe their party-line. (*Sun*, 23 October 1985, column by John Vincent)

(18) [Honeyford] For speaking commonsense he's been vilified; for being courageous he's been damned, for refusing to concede defeat his enemies can't forgive him. . . . I have interviewed him and I am utterly convinced that he hasn't an ounce of racism in his entire being. (*Mail*, 18 September 1985, column by Lynda Lee-Potter)

(19) [Honeyford quits] Now we know who the true racists are. (*Sun,* Editorial, 30 November 1985)

These examples illustrate several strategic moves in the press campaign against anti-racists. First, as we have seen above, denial is closely linked to the presupposition of 'truth': Honeyford is presented as defending the 'truth', namely the failure and anti-British nature of multiculturalism. Secondly, consequent denials often lead to the strategic move of reversal: *we* are not the racists, *they* are the 'true racists'. This reversal also implies, thirdly, a reversal of the charges: Honeyford, and those who sympathize with him, are the victims, not his Asian students and their parents. Consequently, the anti-racists are the enemy: *they* are the ones who persecute innocent, ordinary British citizens, *they* are the ones who are intolerant. Therefore, victims who resist their attackers may be defined as folk heroes, who 'dare' the 'anti-racist brigade'.

Note also, in example (17), that the 'truth', as the supporters of Honeyford see it, is self-evident, and based on common sense. Truth and common sense are closely related notions in such counter-attacks, and reflect the power of the consensus, as well as the mobilization of popular support by 'ordinary' (white) British people. Apart from marginalizing Asian parents and other anti-racists by locating them outside the consensus, and beyond the community of ordinary people like 'us', such appeals to common sense also have powerful ideological implications: self-evident truth is seen as 'natural', and hence the position of the others as 'unnatural' or even as 'crazy'. The anti-racist Left, therefore, is often called 'crazy' or 'loony' in the right-wing British press.

Moral blackmail

One element that was very prominent in the Honeyford affair, as well as in similar cases, was the pretence of censorship: the anti-racists not only ignore the 'truth' about multicultural society, they also prevent others (us) from telling the truth. Repeatedly, thus, journalists and columnists argue that this 'taboo' and this 'censorship' must be broken in order to be able to tell the 'truth', as was the case after the disturbances in Tottenham:

(20) [Tottenham] The time has come to state the truth without cant and without hypocrisy . . . the strength to face the facts without being silenced by the fear of being called racist. (*Mail*, 9 October 1985, column by Lynda Lee-Potter)

Such examples also show that the authors feel morally blackmailed, while at the same time realizing that to 'state the truth', meaning 'to say negative things about minorities', may well be against the prevalent norms of tolerance and understanding. Clamouring for the 'truth', thus, expresses a dilemma, even if the dilemma is only apparent: the apparent dilemma is a rhetorical strategy to accuse the opponent of censorship or blackmail, not the result of moral soul-searching and a difficult decision. After all, the same newspapers extensively *do* write negative things about young blacks, and never hesitate to write what they see as the 'truth'. Nobody 'silences' them, and the taboo is only imaginary. On the contrary, the right-wing press in Britain reaches many millions of readers.

Thus, this strategic play of denial and reversal at the same time involves the construction of social roles in the world of ethnic strife, such as allies and enemies, victims, heroes and oppressors. In many respects, such discourse mimics the discourse of anti-racists by simply reversing the major roles: victims become oppressors, those who are in power become victims.

Subtle denials

Denials are not always explicit. There are many ways to express doubt, distance or non-acceptance of statements or accusations by others. When the official Commission for Racial Equality (CRE) in 1985 published a report on discrimination in the UK, outright denial of the facts would hardly be credible. Other discursive means, such as quotation marks, and the use of words like 'claim' or 'allege', presupposing doubt on the part of the writer, may be employed in accounting for the facts, as is the case in the following editorial from the *Daily Telegraph*:

(21) In its report which follows a detailed review of the operation of the 1976 Race Relations Act, the Commission claims that ethnic minorities continue

to suffer high levels of discrimination and disadvantage. (*Daily Telegraph*, 1 August 1985)

Such linguistic tricks do not go unnoticed, as we may see in the following reaction to this passage in a letter from Peter Newsam, then director of the CRE.

(22) Of the Commission you say 'it claims that ethnic minorities continue to suffer high levels of discrimination and disadvantage'. This is like saying that someone 'claims' that July was wet. It was. And it is also a fact supported by the weight of independent research evidence that discrimination on racial grounds, in employment, housing and services, remains at a disconcertingly high level. (*Daily Telegraph*, 7 August 1985)

Denials, thus, may be subtly conveyed by expressing doubt or distance. Therefore, the very notion of 'racism' usually appears between quotation marks, especially also in the headlines. Such scare quotes are not merely a journalistic device for reporting opinions or controversial points of view. If that were the case, the opinions with which the newspaper happens to agree would also have to be put between quotes, which is not always the case. Rather, apart from signalling journalistic doubt and distance, the quotes also connote 'unfounded accusation'. The use of quotes around the notion of 'racism' has become so much routine, that even in cases where the police or the courts themselves established that racism was involved in a particular case, the conservative press may maintain the quotes out of sheer habit.

Mitigation

Our conceptual analysis of denial already showed that denial may also be implied by various forms of mitigation, such as downtoning, using euphemisms or other circumlocutions that minimize the act itself or the responsibility of the accused. In the same Editorial of the *Daily Telegraph* quoted above, we find the following statement:

(23) [CRE report] No one would deny the fragile nature of race relations in Britain today or that there is misunderstanding and distrust between parts of the community. (*Daily Telegraph*, Editorial, 1 August 1985)

Thus, instead of inequality or racism, race relations are assumed to be 'fragile', whereas 'misunderstanding and distrust' is also characteristic of these relations. Interestingly, this passage also explicitly denies the prevalence of denials and, therefore, might be read as a concession: there *are* problems. However, the way this concession is rhetorically presented by way of various forms of mitigation suggests, in the context of the rest of the same Editorial, that the concession is apparent. Such apparent concessions are another major form of disclaimer in discourse about ethnic relations, as we also have them in statements like: 'There are also intelligent blacks, but . . .', or 'I know that minorities sometimes have problems, but . . .'. Note also that in the example from the *Daily Telegraph* the mitigation not only appears in the use of euphemisms, but also in the *redistribution of responsibility*, and hence in the denial of blame. It is not we (whites) who are mainly responsible for the tensions between the communities, but everybody is, as is suggested by the use of the impersonal existential phrase: 'There is misunderstanding . . .' Apparently, one effective move of denial is to either dispute responsible agency or to conceal agency.

Defence and offence

On the other hand, in its attacks against the anti-racists, the right-wing press is not always that subtle. On the contrary, they may engage precisely in the 'diatribes' they direct at their opponents:

(24) [Anti-fascist rally] The evening combined emotive reminders of the rise of Nazism with diatribes against racial discrimination and prejudice today. (*Daily Telegraph*, 1 October 1985)

(25) [Black sections] In the more ideologically-blinkered sections of his [Kinnock's] party . . . they seem to gain pleasure from identifying all difficulties experienced by immigrant groups, particularly Afro-Caribbeans, as the result of racism . . . (*Daily Telegraph*, Editorial, 14 September 1985).

(26) [Worker accused of racism] . . . The really alarming thing is that some of these pocket Hitlers of local government are moving into national politics. It's time we set about exposing their antics while we can. Forewarned is forearmed. (*Mail*, Editorial, 26 October 1985).

These examples further illustrate that denial of discrimination, prejudice and racism is not merely a form of self-defence or positive self-presentation. Rather, it is at the same time an element of attack against what they define as 'ideologically blinkered' opponents, as we have also seen in the reversal move in other examples. Anti-racism is associated with the 'loony left', and attacking it therefore also has important ideological and political implications, and not just moral ones.

'Difficulties' of the Afro-Caribbean community may be presupposed, though not spelled out forcefully and in detail, but such presuppositions rather take the form of an apparent concession. That is, whatever the causes of these 'difficulties', as they are euphemistically called, they cannot be the result of racism. Implicitly, by attributing 'pleasure' to those who explain the situation of the blacks, the newspaper also suggests that the Left has an interest in such explanations and, therefore, even welcomes racism. This strategy is familiar in many other attacks against anti-racists: 'If there were no racism, they would invent it.' It hardly needs to be spelled out that such a claim again implies a denial of racism.

The amalgamation of comparisons and metaphors used in these attacks is quite interesting. That is, in one example an ironic reference is made to the 'emotive reminders' of Nazism, and in another these same opponents of Nazism are qualified as 'pocket Hitlers'. Yet, this apparent inconsistency in sociopolitical labelling has a very precise function. By referring to their opponents in terms of 'pocket Hitlers' the newspapers obviously distance themselves from the fascist opinions and practices that are often part of the more radical accusations against the Right. At the same time, by way of the usual reversal, they categorize their opponents precisely in terms of their own accusations, and thus put them in a role these opponents most clearly would abhor.

Thus, the anti-racist Left is associated with fascist practices, ideological blinkers and antics. Apart from their anti-racist stance, it is, however, their (modest) political influence which particularly enrages the right-wing press – although virtually powerless at the national level, and even within their own (Labour) party, some of the anti-racists have made it into local councils, and therefore control (some) money, funding and other forms of political influence. That is, they have at least some counter-power, and it is this power and its underlying ideology that is challenged by a press which itself controls the news supply to millions of readers. What the denial of racism and the concomitant attacks against the anti-racists in education or politics is all about, therefore, is a struggle over the definition of the ethnic situation. Thus, their ideological and political opponents are seen as symbolic competitors in the realm of moral influence. Whether directed at a headmaster or against other ordinary white British or not, what the right-wing press is particularly concerned about is its own image: by attacking the anti-racists, it is in fact defending itself.

Parliamentary Discourse

In close symbiosis with the mass media, politics plays a prominent role in the definition of the ethnic situation. In Western Europe, decision-making by the administration and the bureaucracy and parliamentary debates in the 1980s and 1990s increasingly deal with ethnic affairs, immigration and refugees. Persistent social inequalities, unemployment, affirmative action, educational 'disadvantage', popular resentment against immigration and the arrival of 'waves' of new refugees from the South are among the major topics on the political agenda.

Our analysis of elite discourse, therefore, also needs to pay attention to parliamentary discourse, because different ideologies, opinions and interests may openly clash there, especially over 'delicate' issues such as minorities and immigration. Therefore, we examined some major debates on these topics in the parliaments of the UK, the Netherlands, France and Germany, as well as in the US Congress.

Note that such discourse, perhaps more than any other discourse, is 'for the record'. All speeches and even spontaneous interruptions are recorded and published, even if some countries allow later 'editing'. Speeches, therefore, are seldom spontaneous, and usually carefully prepared, written statements read out loud. For delicate topics such as ethnic affairs, we may expect that such discourse is heavily monitored, politically as well as morally. With the exception of some extremist right-wing parties, e.g., the Front National in France, blatantly racist talk is very rare in present day western parliaments.

However, as we have seen above, there are more indirect and subtle ways to express underlying opinions and attitudes, whether more liberal or more conservative ones. Despite the difference in style and function, we found that parliamentary discourse has some striking resemblances to other forms of talk about ethnic minorities, such as positive self-presentation, denial of racism and negative other-presentation. Therefore, let us examine, finally, what specific patterns the denial of racism takes in western parliaments.

Nationalist self-glorification

Parliament is the prime forum for nationalistic rhetoric. This is particularly true when international norms and values, such as democracy, equal rights and tolerance are involved. Accusations of racism in such a context may easily be heard as a moral indictment of the nation as a whole, and are therefore permitted, though resented, only in partisan debates, in which one party accuses the other of racism. After all, racism is always *elsewhere*, and always a property of the *others*.

Against this background, it may be expected that any debate on ethnic affairs, and particularly those in which the rights of minorities or immigrants are at stake, nationalist positive self-presentation is an important strategic prelude to statements that precisely intend to limit such rights. Let us give some examples from each of these parliaments. All examples are taken from the parliamentary records of the respective countries and from debates held between 1985 and 1990. The detailed context of the discussion is not given here, nor are the speakers or parties identified. For the purpose of this chapter we merely identify the countries involved, e.g., in order to show the similarity of such talk across national boundaries.

(27) Our debate today not only regards the refugees, but our whole society, and the responsibility of Europe and the Netherlands to maintain fundamental human rights in the world. The right of asylum is the national component of a consistent human rights policy. (*The Netherlands*)

(28) I believe that we are a wonderfully fair country. We stick to the rules unlike some foreign governments. (*UK*)

(29) Our country has long been open to foreigners, a tradition of hospitality going back, beyond the Revolution, to the *Ancien Régime*. (*France*)

(30) France, which has shown the world the road to democracy and to human rights, France land of welcome and asylum, France present on five continents, could not yield to racial hate. (*France*)

(31) I know of no other country on this earth that gives more prominence to the rights of resident foreigners than does this bill in our country. (*Germany*)

(32) This is a nation whose values and traditions now excite the world, as we all know. I think we all have a deep pride in American views, American ideals, American government, American principles, which excite hundreds of millions of people around the world who struggle for freedom. (*USA*)

(33) There are so many great things about our country, all the freedoms that we have, speech, religion, the right to vote and choose our leaders and of course our greatness lies in our mobility, the ability to each and every one of us, regardless of the circumstances of our birth, to rise in American society, to pursue our individual dreams. (*USA*)

Although nationalist rhetoric may differ in different countries (it is usually more exuberant in France and in the USA, for instance), the basic strategy of positive self-presentation appears in all Houses: we are fair, respect human rights, have a long tradition of tolerance, etc. It is not uncommon to hear in each parliament that at least some representatives think of their own country as the most liberal, freedom-loving, democratic, etc. in the world.

Fair, but . . .

Such self-glorification, especially when introducing a debate on minorities or immigration, has various functions in parliamentary discourse. For those groups or parties that oppose legislation in favour of minorities or immigrants, positive self-presentation often functions as a disclaimer, that is, as an introduction for a '*but*', followed by arguments in favour of special restrictions, as is also the case in the following fragments from a radio interview with Dutch Prime Minister Ruud Lubbers:

(34) In practice, we should come to opportunities and possibilities for them, but in practice we should also come to a less soft approach. There should be a line like: we also hold them responsible [literally: 'we address them'].

Elsewhere we find a nearly routine combination of fairness on the one hand, and firmness, realism, pragmatism, etc., on the other hand.

(35) National and international responsibility for people in emergency situations, combined with obligations that follow from agreements, are our policy principles. This should remain as it is. But of course we need to take measures, especially when it is clear that many improper, not bona fide, apparently unfounded applications for asylum are being made, and that in some cases also the problems people experience are being exploited for commercial ends. (*The Netherlands*)

(36) It is fair to establish visa controls as long as there is mutual agreement about them between the countries involved. They are the best way to control immigration fairly, so that those who properly qualify to come here or to leave this country to visit other countries can do so. Such controls make sure that people have the right qualifications for travel. (*UK*)

(37) If we are to work seriously for harmony, non-discrimination and equality of opportunity in our cities, that has to be accompanied by firm and fair immigration control. (*UK*)

(38) The period of expansion of our country has been at an end for more than 15 years, and this population of foreigners lives in the midst of a French population that is deeply touched by recession and unemployment, a question we must deal with humanely but also reasonably, because I do not hesitate to say that after the time of illusions comes necessarily that of realism. (*France*).

(39) It belongs to this fair balance of interests that the further immigration of foreigners must be limited, because for each society there are limits to the ability and the readiness to integrate. (*Germany*).

(40) This substitute offers the House of Representatives an opportunity to enact a landmark civil rights bill that is both fair and pragmatic. (*USA*)

This remarkably similar rhetoric of fairness ('fair, but strict', etc.) in the different countries also seeks to combine two opposed ideological or political aims, namely the humanitarian values of tolerance or hospitality on the one hand, and the common-sense values of 'realism' on the other. In other words, the humanitarian aims are recognized, but at the same time they are rejected as being too idealistic and, therefore, impractical in the business of everyday political management and decision-making. The reference to fairness also serves as an element in a 'balance', namely in order to mitigate the negative implications of proposed legislation, such as limitations on further immigration in the European debates, and limitations on the 1990 Civil Rights Bill (eventually vetoed by President Bush) in the USA.

Positive presentation of such legislation, and of the parties or groups who support it, also involves strategic argumentative moves such as apparent altruism ('It is in their own best interests'), choice of the lesser evil ('Restriction of immigration prevents conflicts in the inner cities') and other moves that emphasize that the speaker or party has the national interest, the interests of their own (white) population, as well the interests of the minorities and the immigrants or refugees in mind. Such a 'predicament' is sketched by the Dutch Secretary of Foreign Affairs, Mr van den Broek:

(41) The government is confronted with a Dutch society which reacts dividedly to the increasing number of asylum applications. [Some people want a liberal admission policy.] On the other hand, there are more or less latent movements who consider the influx of aliens as a threat to Dutch society.

Interestingly, governments tend to listen especially to those citizens who agree with the attitudes such governments have helped to create in the first place, as was the case with the refugee scare in the Netherlands during the last few years. That is, there is no real predicament, only a semblance of balancing popular feelings and interests. By using the populist argument for immigration control, thus, the government is able to legitimate its own policies by claiming support it has manufactured itself. This is done by creating a panic about 'waves' of refugees entering the country, a definition of the situation that is largely adopted also by the press, so that it also reaches the public at large (van Dijk, 1988c).

Denial of racism

In such a political context of public impression management, the denial of racism plays a prominent role. Whatever the political orientation or party involved, including the extremist Right, all parliamentarians emphatically reject any accusation or suggestion of prejudice, discrimination or racism. Indeed, the more racist the opinions professed, the more insistent are the denials of racism, as may be apparent in the following quotes from representatives of the Front National in the French Assemblée Nationale:

(42) We are neither racist nor xenophobic. Our aim is only that, quite naturally, there be a hierarchy, because we are dealing with France, and France is the country of the French.

(43) No, the French are neither racist, nor antisemitic, nor xenophobic nor revisionist. They may be worried in the face of an immigration which is out of control, in the face of an Islam pure and hard that might cross the Mediterranean. But the French stay tolerant.

Note that in both cases, an explicit or implicit *but* follows the denial. In the first case, the speaker (the leader of the Front National, Le Pen) even claims that it is 'natural' to have a hierarchy between the own group, the French, and the immigrants. This assignment of a 'natural' right to a superior position is at the heart of racist ideologies. The second example is more indirect, and focuses on the 'worries' of ordinary French people, faced with a different culture and a different religion. Besides the discursive and political strategy of populism, which is very prominent in such debates ('The people would resent it', 'You should listen to what ordinary French, English . . . people say'), we also find the element of euphemism: we are not racist, only worried. Here is a more sophisticated example of such a strategy:

(44) The French are not racist. But, facing this continuous increase of the foreign population in France, one has witnessed the development, in certain cities and neighbourhoods, of reactions that come close to xenophobia. In the eyes of the French unemployed man, for instance, the foreigner may easily become a rival, towards whom a sentiment of animosity may threaten to appear.

Following the usual *but*, we do not find, as in other disclaimers, a negative statement about immigrants, but rather an explanation of the reaction of the 'common man' (women are apparently not involved). Note that the way this explanation is formulated ('continuous increase', 'rival') suggests understanding, if not an excuse, as in the usual accounts of racism in terms of economic competition. The denial of racism itself is rather complex, however. It is a denial that holds for the French in general. It is followed by a partial concession, duly limited by heavy mitigation and hedging ('coming close to xenophobia', 'a sentiment of animosity may threaten to appear'), as well as limited in place ('In certain cities'). In other words, prejudice, discrimination and racism are local incidents, and should also be seen as being provoked by continuous immigration, arguments we also found in the right-wing British press.

When restrictive measures are being debated, those who support them feel impelled to remind their audience, and the public at large, that such political decisions have nothing to do with prejudice or racism:

(45) I hope that people outside, whether they are black or white and wherever they come from, will recognize that these are not major changes resulting from prejudice. (*UK*)

(46) My Hon. Friend and I will continue to apply a strict but fair system of control, not because we are prejudiced or inhumane, but because we believe that control is needed if all the people who live in our cities are to live together in tolerance and decent harmony. (*UK*)

Such denials need argumentative support. Saying only that the measures are 'fair' may be seen as too flimsy. Therefore, we find the moves we have found earlier, such as concern for the inner cities. Note that such arguments also imply a move of transfer: we are not racist, but the poor people in the inner cities are, and we should avoid exacerbating the mood of resentment among the population at large. This argument is rather typical of what we have called 'elite racism', which consistently denies racism among the own elite group but recognizes that others, especially poor, white people, may fail to be as tolerant.

Denial and reproach

In the analysis of the British press, we have found that denials of racism easily transform into attacks against anti-racists. Such a strategy may also be found in parliamentary discourse. Thus, conservative representatives will not accept accusations or even implicit suggestions that their stricter immigration or ethnic minority policies are categorized as racist by other politicians. Since the official norm is 'that we are all tolerant citizens', such allegations are declared unacceptable:

(47) Addressing myself to the people of the left, I repeat again that we are. I have noted in your words, my God, terms such as racism and xenophobia, that those who do not support your proposals would be judged with the same

terms. It should be understood once and for all: we are not racists because we combat your text.   (*France*)

(48)   You will allow me to tell you that in no circumstance this debate should be prejudged by insinuating that, on these benches, the only anti-racists are over there, whereas we, by opposition, would be racists.   (*France*)

(49)   Well, now can we also agree this afternoon that you can have different philosophies about how to achieve through law civil rights and equal opportunities for everybody without somehow being anti-civil rights or being a racist or something like that.   (*USA*)

One interesting case may be found in a German debate on the new Aliens Bill. When one of the Green Party representatives qualifies the provisions of the Bill as 'racist', a term that is as unusual in official German discourse as it is in the Netherlands, conservative representatives are furious. Even the Speaker of the Bundestag intervenes:

(50)   A chill ran down my back when our colleague . . . said that this bill was a form of institutionalized racism. Whereas the older ones among us had to live twelve years under institutionalized racism, Ladies and Gentlemen, I beg you, and in particular our younger colleagues, to show respect for these terrible experiences, and not to introduce such concepts to our everyday political business.

In other words, evaluations in terms of racism are limited only to the Nazi past, and are banned from official political discourse. At most, the term *Ausländerfeindlichkeit* (literally: animosity against foreigners) may be used. 'Racism' thus is by definition too strong, if only because the present situation cannot be compared to the monstrosities of the Nazis. A similar attitude exists in the Netherlands, where racism is also avoided as a term in public (political, media) discourse because it is understood only in terms of extremist, right-wing ideologies of racial superiority.

Reversal

Although moderate reproaches directed against anti-racist delegates are not uncommon in parliament, reversal is rather exceptional. However, it is quite typical for right-wing party representatives, such as those of the Front National in France. Being routinely accused, also explicitly, of racism, they go beyond mere denial, and reverse the charges. For them, this means that the others, and especially the socialists, allegedly letting in so many immigrants and granting them equal rights, are guilty of what they call 'anti-French racism':

(51) There exists a form of racism, my dear colleagues [interruptions] that is passed over silently, but of which the manifestations nowadays reach an insupportable level and a scope that should concern us: that is anti-French racism. Another way of reversing the charges is to accuse the anti-racists of being themselves responsible for creating racism, if only by not listening to the people and by letting so many non-European immigrants enter the country.

(52) Well, France today, according to what those creatures of the world tell us who often have come to take refuge in our country . . . France is the least racist country that exists in the world. We can't tolerate hearing it said that France is a racist country. . . . In this respect, this law proposal, because of the debate that is taking place at this moment, secretes and fabricates racism!

These examples taken from several western parliaments show that although the debate may be couched in less extremist terms than in much of the right-wing or tabloid press, or in everyday conversations, rather similar strategies and moves are used to talk about ethnic affairs. Most characteristic of this kind of political discourse is not merely the nationalist self-praise, but also the strategic management of impression: whatever we decide, we are fair. Since, especially in Europe, ethnic minorities, let alone new immigrants and refugees, have virtually no political power, this 'balancing act' of presenting policies as 'firm but fair' is obviously addressed primarily to the dominant white public at large. When defined as humane without being too soft, thus, the government and its supporting parties may be acceptable as essentially reasonable: we take energetic measures, but we are not racist.

In other words, besides managing impressions, such political discourse also manages its own legitimation by manufacturing consent on ethnic policies, and at the same time manages the politics of ethnic affairs, immigration and international relations.

Conclusions

Whether in the streets of the inner city, in the press or in parliament, dominant group members are often engaged in discourse about 'them': ethnic minority groups, immigrants or refugees, who have come to live in the country. Such discourses, as well as the social cognitions underlying them, are complex and full of contradictions. They may be inspired by general norms of tolerance and acceptance but also, and sometimes at the same time, by feelings of distrust, resentment or frustration about those 'others'.

Topics, stories and argumentation may thus construct a largely negative picture of minorities or immigrants, e.g., in terms of cultural differences, deviance or competition, as a problem or as a threat to 'our' country, territory, space, housing, employment, education, norms, values, habits or language. Such talk and text, therefore, is not a form of individual discourse, but social, group discourse, and expresses not only individual opinions, but rather socially shared representations.

However, negative talk about minority groups or immigrants may be heard as biased, prejudiced or racist, and as inconsistent with general values of tolerance. This means that such discourse needs to be hedged, mitigated, excused, explained or otherwise managed in such a way that it will not 'count' against the speaker or writer. Face-keeping, positive self-presentation and impression management are the usual strategies that language users have recourse to in such a situation of possible 'loss of face': they have to make sure that they are not misunderstood and that no unwanted inferences are made from what they say.

One of the major strategic ways white speakers and writers engage in such a form of impression management is the denial of racism. They may simply claim they did not say anything negative, or focus on their intentions: it may have sounded negative, but was not intended that way. Similarly, they may mitigate their negative characterization of the others by using euphemisms, implications or vague allusions. They may make apparent concessions, on the one hand, and on the other hand support their negative discourse by arguments, stories or other supporting 'facts'.

Also, speakers and writers may abandon their position of positive self-presentation and self-defence and take a more active, aggressive counter-attack: the ones who levelled the accusations of racism are the real problem, if not the real racists. They are the ones who are intolerant, and they are against 'our' own people. We are the victims of immigration, and we are discriminated against.

It is interesting to note that despite the differences in style for different social groups, such discourse may be found at any social level, and in any social context. That is, both the 'ordinary' white citizens as well as the white elites need to protect their social self-image, and at the same time they have to manage the interpretation and the practices in an increasingly variegated social and cultural world. For the dominant group, this means that dominance relations must be reproduced, at the macro as well as at the micro level, both in action as well as in mind.

Negative representations of the dominated group are essential in such a reproduction process. However, such attitudes and ideologies are inconsistent with dominant democratic and humanitarian norms and ideals. This means that the dominant group must protect itself, cognitively and discursively, against the damaging charge of intolerance and racism. Cognitive balance may be restored only by actually being or becoming anti-racist, by accepting minorities and immigrants as equals, or else by denying racism. It is this choice white groups in Europe and North America are facing. So far they have largely chosen the latter option.

7

Political Discourse and
Political Cognition

Relating Politics, Cognition and Discourse

The aim of this chapter is to explore some of the relations between political discourse and political cognition. Separately, both interdisciplinary fields have recently received increasing attention, but unfortunately the connection between the two has largely been ignored: political psychology has not shown much interest in discourse, and vice versa, most scholars interested in political discourse disregard the cognitive foundations of such discourse.

And yet, the relationships involved are as obvious as they are interesting. The study of political cognition largely deals with the mental representations people share as political actors. Our knowledge and opinions about politicians, parties or presidents are largely acquired, changed or confirmed by various forms of text and talk during our socialization (Merelman, 1986), formal education, media usage and conversation. Thus, political information processing often is a form of discourse processing, also because much political action and participation is accomplished by discourse and communication.

On the other hand, a study of political discourse is theoretically and empirically relevant only when discourse structures can be related to properties of political structures and processes. The latter however usually require an account at the macro level of political analysis, whereas the former rather belong to a micro-level approach. This well-known gap can only be adequately bridged with a sophisticated theory of political cognition. Such a theory needs to explicitly connect the individual uniqueness and variation of political discourse and interaction with the socially shared political representations of political groups and institutions. Thus, a biased text about immigrants may derive from personal beliefs about immigrants, and these beliefs in turn may be related to the shared racist attitudes or ideologies of a larger group.

The theoretical framework of this chapter is complex and multidisciplinary. It relates various levels and dimensions of the political domain. The base level consists of individual political actors, as well as their beliefs, discourses and (other) interactions in political situations. The intermediate level, constituted by the base level, consists of political groups and institutions, as well as their shared representations, collective discourse, relations and interactions. The top level, which in turn is based on the intermediate level, is constituted by political systems, and their abstract representations, orders of discourse, and sociopolitical, cultural and historical processes.

Of course these levels are related in many ways, so that the micro and the macro levels seem to manifest themselves at the same time. Thus, a representative giving a speech in parliament speaks as an individual and thus expresses his or her personal political beliefs in a unique way and in a unique context. At the same time, that person speaks as a member of parliament or Congress, as a member of a party and as a representative of a constituency, thus possibly 'doing' opposition against another party or against the government, and expressing the attitudes or ideologies of the own group. And finally, by doing so he or she is enacting a system of parliamentary democracy, reproducing the discourse order of democracy and democratic ideologies, and presupposing a historically variable Common Ground of cultural knowledge, norms and values, shared by all other groups of the same culture.

This chapter will focus on some of the relationships between the first two, lower, levels of political analysis, that is, on how political text and talk of individuals are related to socially shared political representations and collective interactions of groups and institutions.

Given the complexity of these relations between the individual and collective levels of analysis, this chapter must be limited to a few main topics. The first topic that needs to be examined in somewhat more detail is the role of the political context of discourse and how this context is cognitively defined and managed by political actors in the production and comprehension of political text and talk. Secondly, I shall show that political discourse structures (such as political topics, pronouns and metaphors) also require description and explanation in terms of 'underlying' mental representations, which in turn may be related to political structures and processes.

In terms of the three levels distinguished above, this means that discourse and politics can be related in essentially two ways: (a) at a socio-political level of description, political processes and structures are constituted by situated events, interactions and discourses of political actors in political contexts; and (b) at a sociocognitive level of description, shared political representations are related to individual representations of these discourses, interactions and contexts. In other words, political cognition serves as the indispensable theoretical interface between the personal and the collective dimensions of politics and political discourse.

An example

In order to illustrate the theoretical argument of this chapter, let us take a concrete example of political discourse, viz., a fragment of a speech given in the British House of Commons on 5 July 1989, by Sir John Stokes, a (very) conservative MP representing Halesowen and Stourbridge. His speech is a contribution to a debate on immigration and DNA testing, and supports further immigration restrictions of the Thatcher government, which the Labour opposition (by mouth of Roy Hattersley) at the start of the same debate called 'racially discriminatory'. This is what Sir John Stokes has to say:

In the past 25 years, we have allowed hundreds of thousands of immigrants	1
into this small island so that we now have ethnic minorities of several million	2
people and in some cases, as we all know, their birth rate far exceeds that of	3
the indigenous population. This is primarily a problem for England, as the	4
other countries in the United Kingdom have much smaller immigrant	5
populations. Why are we English Members of Parliament here today? I ask	6
that question of the Opposition, too. Are we not the trustees of this beloved	7
England for posterity? What is the future of our country to be in another 25	8
years, even if all immigration is stopped tomorrow? What will be the effect	9
on our religion, morals, customs, habits and so on? Already there have been	10
some dangerous eruptions from parts of the Muslim community. Having	11
served with the Muslims during the war, may I say that I greatly admire	12
many of them and their religion. I also very much like the letter which my	13
Hon. Friend the Minister of State, Home Office, wrote to Muslim leaders	14
and which was published in the newspapers today. It is foolish to ignore the	15
problems and the fears that those dangerous eruptions engender among the	16
ordinary people whom we are supposed to represent. We must not allow our	17
feelings of guilt over our treatment of immigrants to cloud our judgement.	18
We in England are a gentle, kind, tolerant and peace-loving people. We have	19
already absorbed large numbers of newcomers. Except occasionally, there	20
have not been the riots and bloodshed that some people prophesied. The	21
burden of receiving and coping with these newcomers in our midst has fallen	22

not on the intellectuals, Labour Members of Parliament and others of that ilk   23
but on ordinary English working-class people. Surely they are entitled to a   24
voice here. Vast changes have been made in the cities because of the large   25
numbers of immigrants living there. The local English people were never   26
asked about this. They never had to vote on it. They must have views about   27
the future of this influx. They look to us to safeguard their position. Everyone 28
here – immigrant or non-immigrant – wants to safeguard our position. As I   29
said, fortunately we have not had much bloodshed or rioting, and relations   30
generally are good, but as the figures on those who are still coming in are   31
published, more and more people are starting to say, 'Will this go on, or can   32
we say enough is enough?' This is a small attempt to have a little more   33
control, and very wise it is. It should be welcomed by everyone in the House   34
and outside.   (*Hansard*, 5 July, 1989, columns 390–1).   35

In order to fully understand this fragment, a few remarks are in order
about its political context. The speech was given in the summer of the
year the *fatwah* against Salman Rushdie was issued by the Ayatollah
Khomeiny, because of his book *The Satanic Verses*. This religious death
sentence also raised tensions in the British Muslim community, some of
whose members supported the *fatwah*. This even led to demonstrations
and public burning of Rushdie's book. These are the 'dangerous eruptions' Sir John Stokes refers to (line 11). He also refers to a letter written
by his conservative colleague, Secretary of the Home Office, Douglas
Hurd, to the Muslim community, warning them that undemocratic
behaviour would not be tolerated in Great Britain.

Let us now return to the theoretical argument, and use examples from
this speech by way of illustration.

The study of political cognition

The study of political cognition focuses on various aspects of 'political
information processing'. It essentially deals with the acquisition, uses and
structures of mental representations about political situations, events,
actors and groups. Typical topics of political cognition research are: the
organization of political beliefs; the perception of political candidates;
political judgement and decision-making; stereotypes, prejudices and
other sociopolitical attitudes; political group identity; public opinion;
impression formation; and many other topics that deal with memory
representations and the mental processes involved in political understanding and interaction (for details, see, e.g., Hermann, 1986; Iyengar
and McGuire, 1993; Lau and Sears, 1986; Lodge and McGraw, 1995).

A review of this research is beyond the scope of this chapter. My aim is rather to construct a new framework that focuses on the relations between political discourse and political cognition. Of course, many of the dimensions of such a framework will also be relevant for a theory of the relations between political cognition and various other components of political structures and processes, as mentioned above. (Although there is virtually no specific work that combines systematic political discourse analysis with political cognition research, there is work that relates political psychology with the analysis of communication; see e.g., Crigler, 1996; Kraus, 1990; Kraus and Perloff, 1985. One of the few scholars in political cognition who studies various discourse types, though with content analytical methods, is Tetlock, 1981, 1983, 1984, 1985a, 1985b; for a survey of this research, see Tetlock, 1993).

One crucial element of my framework that is lacking in other research on political cognition is that of mental models which serve as the necessary interface between socially shared political cognitions, on the one hand, and personal beliefs, on the other. These models also serve as the cognitive basis of political discourse and political action, and thus also relate the political macro structures of shared representations of groups and institutions with the political micro structures of the activities of political actors.

A Conceptual Framework

In order to be able to reconstruct the systematic relations between political cognition and political discourse, I shall briefly summarize some elementary psychological notions of the theoretical framework in which these relations will be analysed (for discussion of the relevance of such a framework for political information processing, see Wyer and Ottati, 1993).

1 Cognitive processes and representations are defined relative to an abstract mental structure called 'memor'.

2 A distinction is traditionally made between Short-Term Memory, STM (also called Working Memory) and Long-Term Memory (LTM). Actual processing of information (e.g., perception, discourse understanding and production, the monitoring of interaction, etc.) takes place in STM, and makes use of information (e.g., knowledge) stored in LTM.

3 A further distinction is made in LTM between Episodic Memory and Semantic Memory. Episodic memory stores personal experiences that result from processing (understanding) in STM, and

Semantic Memory stores more general, abstract and socially shared information, such as our knowledge of the language or knowledge of the world. Given the socially shared nature of the information in Semantic Memory, I shall call this 'Social Memory', in contrast to the more personal information stored in Episodic Memory.

4   Information in LTM is organized in various types of mental representations, each with their own schematic structure. For instance, general social knowledge about conventional episodes (such as shopping in a supermarket or participating in a scholarly conference) may be organized by 'scripts' consisting of a number of fixed categories, for instance categories for the typical setting, events, actions and participants of such episodes. Part of this social knowledge is also the general political knowledge people have, e.g., about politicians, parliamentary debates, elections, political propaganda or political demonstrations.

5   Knowledge is here defined as the organized mental structure consisting of shared factual beliefs of a group or culture which are or may be 'verified' by the (historically variable) truth criteria of that group or culture. Note that what may be 'knowledge' for one group (period or culture) may be deemed mere 'beliefs' or 'opinions' by other groups.

6   Besides knowledge, people also have other socially shared information, viz., group attitudes (including prejudices), ideologies, norms and values. Whereas knowledge is culturally defined as 'factual' or 'objective', that is as 'true beliefs' (of a group) attitudes are often defined as evaluative and (inter)subjective, because they essentially vary between different groups in society (see below, for details).

7   Although little is known about the organization of evaluative beliefs, it is likely that also attitudes and ideologies are organized by characteristic schemas, for instance about the own and other groups and their relationships. Thus, male chauvinist opinions about women and gender relations are probably stored in inter-related group schemata about men and about women as groups.

8   The overall 'architecture' of Social Memory is still unknown. Yet, I shall assume that its basis is constituted by a Common Ground of sociocultural beliefs, featuring generally shared (undisputed) cultural knowledge and opinions (for a related but different – more local and interactional – definition of 'common ground', see Clark, 1996). It is this cultural Common Ground that defines

such notions as 'common sense' and 'taken-for-grantedness'. Although fundamental for a given period or culture, even Common Ground beliefs may change historically. On the basis of this cultural Common Ground (which enables mutual understanding and communication) each social group may however develop its own group knowledge and opinions which in turn are organized by underlying ideologies. Sometimes (fragments of) specialized group beliefs will enter the Common Ground (e.g., our elementary knowledge about the earth as a planet). And vice versa, Common Ground beliefs of one period may become special group or sectarian beliefs in a later period (as is the case for Christianity).

9 Besides socially shared beliefs of the groups they are members of, people also may have personal experience and knowledge, as represented in their Episodic Memory. These personal experiences are represented in mental models which also have a schematic structure consisting of a number of fixed categories, e.g., for setting, actions and participants and their various roles.

10 Contrary to socially shared beliefs, models represent specific events such as the events debated in the parliamentary debate which we used as an example. Models are the personal interpretation (knowledge and opinion) of such an event. That is, models are subjective.

11 Models form the cognitive basis of all individual discourse and interaction. That is, both in production and understanding, people construct a model of an event or action, e.g., the event a text is about, or the action which people perceive or participate in. Models also serve as the referential basis of discourse and thus help define local and global coherence.

12 Models integrate new information (e.g., from text understanding or event observation), fragments of earlier experiences (old models), instantiations of more general personal information (personal knowledge, personality, Self), as well as instantiations of socially shared information (e.g., group beliefs or cultural knowledge scripts). In other words, models embody both personal and social information, and hence serve as the core of the interface between the social and the individual.

13 For the same reason, when shared, generalized, abstracted from and socially normalized, models may constitute the basis of experiential social and political learning. That is the general and abstract social representations of social memory are first of all

derived from our personal experiences as represented in our episodic models. Social and political knowledge may however also be acquired more directly, e.g., from general, abstract discourse, such as political treatises or propaganda.

This brief summary of some main features of the theoretical framework used to study the relations between political discourse and political cognition leaves out a host of details, only some of which will be spelled out below. Also, whereas some of these features are fairly generally accepted in psychology, others are less generally accepted or known, or even idiosyncratic to my approach. For instance, whereas the literature on political cognition does deal with knowledge, attitudes and ideologies, as well as their schematic organization and processing, it virtually ignores the theory of mental models, which however is quite generally accepted in the psychology of text processing (see, e.g., Garnham, 1987; Johnson-Laird, 1983; Morrow, 1994; Oakhill and Garnham, 1996; van Dijk and Kintsch, 1983; van Dijk, 1985a, 1987b; van Oostendorp and Zwaan, 1994).

Conversely, the psychology of text processing does integrate script theory and theories of knowledge, but virtually ignores evaluative beliefs (opinions) and socially shared attitudes and ideologies. We here find one of the consequences of the rather arbitrary division of labour between cognitive and social psychology. It is within this general framework that we shall now discuss a number of issues that define the relations between political discourse and political cognition.

Discourse processing

Language use in general, and the production and understanding of political text and talk in particular, may cognitively be analysed in terms of the theoretical framework summarized above (among many studies, see, e.g., Britton and Graesser, 1996; van Dijk and Kintsch, 1983; van Oostendorp and Zwaan, 1994; Weaver, Mannes and Fletcher, 1995).

Relevant for our discussion are (a) the relations between shared beliefs (political representations) on the one hand and personal beliefs (models) on the other hand; and (b) the relations of these social and personal representations with discourse structures.

In discourse production, we assume that speakers (or writers) will generally start from their personal mental model of an event or situation. This model organizes the subjective beliefs of the speaker about such a situation. Thus, in our example, the speech of Sir John is produced on the basis of his model of the current ethnic and immigration situation in England, a model that is evaluatively defined in terms of a macro proposition that he also expresses: 'a problem for England' (line 4). Part of his broader model about the current ethnic situation in the UK, there are more specific models of particular events, such as about the 'dangerous eruptions from parts of the Muslim community' and about the letter sent by Secretary Hurd to that community, both of which not only feature Sir John's interpretation of these actions, but also his opinions.

Sir John's models instantiate shared social and political beliefs, viz., those of all English people, in general, and those of the conservatives in particular. For instance, it is common knowledge that several hundreds of thousands of immigrants have come to England, and this general knowledge is here integrated into the model of the current situation. Similarly, as he claims himself, not only he but many others define such immigration as a 'problem'. And like others he specifically instantiates the racist attitude that (many) Muslims are 'dangerous'. Conversely, he represents 'us in England' as gentle, kind, tolerant, peace-loving people. This contrast between Us and Them thus not only characterizes the attitudes and ideologies he shares with other (mostly conservative, white) British people, but also polarizes the current personal model he has about the present situation in Britain. These examples show some of the relationships between personal knowledge and opinions, and socially shared ones, that is, between representations in Social Memory and personal models in Episodic Memory.

Once such a personal model of an event or situation is constituted, speakers may express fragments of such models in discourse, using a number of detailed linguistic and discursive strategies that will not be analysed here. It is however important to note that speakers usually only express a small part of their models, viz., only the information that is relevant in the current context. I shall come back to this contextual constraint below. In other words, a text is usually only the tip of the iceberg of all information speakers have about an event or situation they are talking about. Thus, Sir John undoubtedly knows more about the 'dangerous eruptions' of the Muslim community, but only summarizes the model he has of this event, viz., by expressing the evaluative macroproposition defining his model. The same is true for the expression of his model of Mr Hurd's letter to the Muslim community.

What has here been summarized for the process of discourse production also applies to discourse understanding. Thus, Sir John's audience, as well as we as readers of the *Hansard* text of his speech, understand what he says first through a complex process of decoding and understanding words and sentences, and ultimately by constructing our own models of what he is talking about. Of course, if we agree with him, we would accept his models as essentially true or 'correct'. If not, we may construct alternative models of the situation, depending again on our own personal knowledge of the current situation as well as on socially shared, group knowledge and evaluations. If recipients read or listen to many similar discourses of politicians or the mass media, and have no competing, alternative information, such models may in turn be generalized to socially shared abstract representations about Muslims, minorities, English people and immigration, for instance in ethnic prejudices and nationalist or racist ideologies.

This brief characterization of discourse processing shows several relations between political discourse and cognition. Thus, our example shows how conservative political attitudes and ideologies are used in the construction of an individual model of the current situation, and how some of this model information is selectively expressed in a parliamentary speech. Important for our argument is that this theoretical framework indeed offers the first elements of the necessary interface between the social and the individual, between group action and individual action and discourse.

That is, at the sociopolitical level of analysis, we witness how the Tories enact or defend a restrictive immigration bill and how such a political act of a group is actually 'realized' locally and contextually by a member (of parliament, of the Conservative Party) through a specific form of interaction, viz., a parliamentary speech. Similarly, and in parallel with the social–political connection between the social and the personal, at the cognitive level we find socially shared attitudes and ideologies and how these are related to specific opinions of a social actor in his models of the current situation and events.

This framework, however, is still very sketchy. It as yet says very little about the structures of shared political representations and of personal models, nor does it explain many of the properties of a parliamentary speech such as the one by Sir John. So, we need to introduce further theoretical instruments to provide more detailed insights into the relations between political discourse and political cognition.

Context models

It was found above that language users only express part of the models they have about specific situations and events, models we shall henceforth simply call 'event models' (but which were earlier called 'situation models', see van Dijk and Kintsch, 1983). Indeed, in most communicative situations it would be irrelevant to express all we know about an event, or inappropriate to express (all) our opinions. Moreover, much knowledge we have is already known to our interlocutors, and in some cases these even share our opinions.

In other words, in order for speakers to know what information from their models or social representations to actually include in their discourses, they need to know something about the current communicative situation of their text or talk – including the assumed beliefs of their recipients. Also, they must know on what occasion they are speaking, so that they may evaluate whether the expression of their beliefs is appropriate in the current social situation (cf. Fussell and Krauss, 1992). Certain kinds of things can, but others cannot be said in parliament. Similarly, members of a Government party will do so in a different way to members of the Opposition. Indeed, whereas Roy Hattersley speaks about 'racially discriminatory' regulations as proposed by the Thatcher government, Sir John speaks positively about them and explicitly 'welcomed' them (line 34).

These examples show something we all know about discourse, viz., that what we say (or understand) depends on structural constraints of the current context, including e.g., the setting, type of event, genre, aims, current actions, as well as on the participants, their roles and their knowledge (Duranti and Goodwin, 1992). And conversely, by speaking the way we do, we at the same time constitute or define such a context, and affect the ways participants in turn understand and evaluate us as a participant, and so on. For these and other reasons, language users multiply signal or 'index' their text and talk with elements of the context, as Sir John does with his question: 'Why are we English Members of Parliament here today?'. This question alone indexes the aim of the current session of parliament, the participants and their roles (MPs), as well as the setting (location and time).

This way of formulating the relations between text and context is the standard one. It does however have a serious theoretical shortcoming because it relates two types of entities that cannot simply be related in a direct way, viz., structures of a social situation (participants, settings, actions) and structures of discourse. Moreover, if such would be the case, all people in such a social situation would speak in the same way. That is, we again need a (cognitive) interface.

Indeed, it is not so much the social situation that makes Sir John speak as he does but rather his personal interpretation or model of that situation. What discourses signal or index, thus, is not the social context itself but the subjective mental models of the context as constructed by speech participants (for details, see van Dijk, 1997a, 1999). This allows personal differences between context models of different participants, and (different) personal opinions about the current communicative situation (including about ourselves and others in it). Context models also explain conflicts between speech participants because they have (and use) incompatible models of the current communicative situation. And perhaps most importantly, such personal models of the situation explain why all individual text and talk, even about the same topics, is always unique and different while based on unique personal models of both the event and context.

It follows that in the overall framework presented above, a crucial component was still missing between event models and discourse, viz., the context models of the participants in a communicative event. It is the (subjective) information stored in these models that ultimately controls how speakers and writers adapt their text and talk to the current situation, and how speech acts and conversational acts may be (more or less) appropriate in such a situation. Finally, context models also define the very notion of (pragmatic) relevance (Sperber and Wilson, 1986), namely in terms of those structures of the communicative situation that are constructed as context by the participants in their context models.

Context models are structured like any other model represented in episodic memory. More specifically, contexts feature such categories as a Setting (Time, Location, Circumstances, Props), Events, Participants and their various types of social, professional, communicative roles, the Actions they currently engage in, as well as current Cognition (aims, knowledge, opinions, emotions, etc.). At a fairly high level, they may feature an overall definition of the whole situation, which ultimately may be represented as constitutive of a specific social domain. (For earlier work on the structure of social situations and episodes see, e.g., Argyle, Furnham and Graham, 1981).

Thus, for our example we may assume that the MPs present in the parliamentary debate about immigration share information about the current domain (Politics rather than, say, Education), the current definition of the situation (Session of Parliament), the Setting (House of Commons, 5 July 1989), the Circumstances (a Bill presented by the cabinet), the various participants and their roles as MPs, representatives of their constituencies, the ongoing overall interaction or genre (a parliamentary debate), and a vast set of shared knowledge about the current issue (immigration, minorities, Muslims, England, etc.).

There are also elements where the models of the participants differ, more generally, and at any respective moment of the ongoing debate, in particular. Thus, obviously, there are differences of opinion, e.g., between the Tories and Labour, and possibly among Tory MPs as well (Sir John is notably more reactionary in his views than many other conservatives). Similarly, when speaking, Sir John has a different role and aim than the other participants, who have the role of listeners. These will in turn gradually confirm or change their opinion about what is being said, as well as about Sir John. Most crucially different and possibly changing during a discourse are the mutual perceptions of participants, that is the mental models they construct about each other (for perceptions and representations of politicians, see Granberg, 1993; Lodge and McGraw, 1995).

Similarly, the participants in this situation may have different emotions. Sir John may express fears of threatening overpopulation or Muslim violence, while at least some people in his audience may be angry about his racist remarks. More generally, emotion is an important factor in political context models (Roseman, Abelson and Ewing, 1986). Such a property of the context model will control specific properties (e.g., intonation, stress or lexicalization) of political discourse (Just, Crigler and Neuman, 1996).

Changing for all, dynamically, is also what has already been said at each moment, that is, the preceding discourse. This confirms the intuitive idea of reflexivity, viz., that the discourse is of course part of its own context. In other words, some elements of a context model are shared by all participants, and some are different; some are stable throughout the whole communicative event, whereas others dynamically change as a function of the ongoing interaction and discourse. In other words, context models, especially in verbal interaction, are dynamic, and gradually change.

Whereas mental models of events may be seen as the basis of the 'content' or meaning of discourse, context models typically control not only what is being said but especially how it is said. That is, they may be seen as the basis of the pragmatic and stylistic properties of discourse. The structures of context models define the appropriateness conditions of speech acts and interaction sequences more generally. They serve as the referential basis of deictic expressions. They control what 'relevant' information of event models is included in the semantic representation of a text. And they regulate how such meanings are variably formulated in syntactic structures, lexical items and phonological or graphical expressions. In sum, context models are vital for the production and comprehension of a large number of discourse structures, and prove how important the social situation and its interpretation are for discourse and communication.

Context models are particularly relevant for an explicit analysis of political discourse genres. Indeed, few structural properties of political discourse genres (as we shall see in more detail below) are exclusive but may be shared with other types of discourse. However, what is specific are the elements of the context of political text and talk, viz., the overall domain and definition of the situation, the setting, circumstances, participant roles, aims, opinions and emotions. In other words, the genre definition of political discourse may well be contextual rather than textual. Except from a few expressions explicitly denoting elements of the current situation, much of what Sir John says about immigration and minorities could be said in other social situations. Conversely, other genres, such as conversations, stories, poems, news reports, advertisements and scholarly articles are much more defined in terms of their specific structures, and not largely by their context.

Thus, we may provisionally conclude that political discourse genres are essentially defined by their functions in the political process, as represented by the categories of the political context model. Trivially: whatever a politician says is thus by definition a form of political discourse; and whatever anybody says with a political aim (viz., to influence the political process, e.g., decision-making, policies) is also a form of political discourse.

The cognitive processes involved in the construction, activation, uses or changes of both event models and context models are strategic (van Dijk and Kintsch, 1983). That is, they are on-line, goal-oriented, hypothetical operations that process information at various levels at the same time. These strategies are fast and efficient, but fallible, and may need correction on later occasions: Language users may be wrong about the interpretation of a social situation – and such errors may lead to typical communicative conflicts, for instance when a recipient interprets a promise as a threat, tells many things a recipient already knows, uses an inappropriate style, or the wrong politeness markers. There are various types of 'pragmatic' repairs that may correct such misunderstandings of context information.

The efficiency of strategic processing may require that often only part of the relevant situational information needs to be processed. Depending on aims, tasks or special requirements, thus, language users may interpret a communicative situation more or less superficially, resulting in more or less detailed context models. In some situations, only the most important top levels of context models need to be constructed, such as the overall definition of the situation, the overall ongoing actions, only a few participants and their most relevant role, and an approximate sub-model of the knowledge and opinions of the recipient(s). In our example, for instance, more casual or distracted recipients of Sir John's speech may only have to know that this is a speech within a parliamentary debate and that the speaker is a conservative MP. Detailed beliefs about the various roles of Sir John (for instance the district he represents) or his knowledge may not be necessary to arrive at a contextually more or less appropriate understanding of his discourse. Indeed, some may only represent Sir John in terms of his age or appearance, or his 'image', instead of his political opinions (see Wyer et al., 1991). Obviously, those appointed to criticize or comment upon his speech may need a much more detailed mental model of this situation, including of Sir John himself.

Political Cognition

After this discussion of the personal side of political cognition, that is, the models political actors construct in their episodic memory in order to produce or understand political discourse and action, we finally need to say some more about the socially shared dimension of political cognition. We have assumed that social memory is constituted by knowledge, attitudes, ideologies, values and norms. We have further assumed that at least some of these representations may be schematically organized, and how they are organized in the overall architecture of the social mind (Kuklinski, Luskin and Bolland, 1991; see the various contributions in Lau and Sears, 1986).

However, in order to understand the structures of political discourse, we also need to say more about the structures of general political representations. How, indeed, are political attitudes and ideologies represented, and what is the role of political values and norms in such representations? Also, we may want to know how such structures affect the content and structures of both event models and context models, and how finally they may appear in political discourse. Thus, Sir John claims that the birthrate of immigrants far exceeds that of the indigenous population, a general statement that might be a direct expression of his conservative ethnic attitudes about groups and their reproduction, although he claims ('as we all know') that this proposition is part of the general Common Ground. At the same time, he explicitly claims that he has a great admiration for many Muslims but, since little admiration for Muslims transpires in his speech, we may wonder whether his underlying attitudes about Muslims really are suffused by admiration, or whether this claim is essentially a strategic form of impression management and positive self-presentation, engaged in to disclaim possible prejudice or racism his audience might

attribute to him. In other words, the relations between political representations and discourse are not that straightforward. So let us briefly examine some of the components of social–political memory.

Knowledge

Unlike most philosophical and psychological approaches to knowledge,
I proposed above to distinguish between two types of knowledge, namely
the knowledge shared by a specific group, on the one hand, and the
general cultural knowledge shared across different groups throughout
society, on the other.

The latter, Common Ground knowledge is the basis of all interaction
and communication in society and is generally presupposed in discourse.
This kind of knowledge is generally undisputed, uncontroversial and
taken for granted, and taught in socialization and at school in a given
society. These generally shared 'factual' beliefs are accepted as (and called)
'knowledge' in society. In Sir John's speech, most of his words are based
on such shared knowledge: thus, we all know what 'parliament',
'Muslims' or 'immigration' are.

Secondly, there are factual beliefs that are only accepted as 'true' by
specific social groups, such as scientists, experts, professionals, members of
specific religions, members of a party, or any other kind of group. The
criteria applying for knowledge mentioned above also apply here (this
knowledge is also routinely undisputed, taken for granted, seen as
common sense, generally presupposed, etc.), but only at the group level.
This group knowledge is called 'knowledge' within the group itself.
Outside the group, however, such knowledge may well not be called
'knowledge' at all, but 'belief or 'opinion', that is, beliefs that are not
found to be true according to the truth criteria of the general culture, or
those of other groups (which does not mean that from an abstract
'universal' point of view such beliefs are false).

Much political knowledge is group knowledge and will often be seen
as 'mere political opinion' by opposing groups. Typically, knowledge of
feminists about male dominance in society may be rejected by many
men, and the same is true for the knowledge of environmental groups
about pollution which may be challenged by polluters. The converse is
equally true: racist groups have their group knowledge, even if many
other people in society may dispute such knowledge and treat it as
prejudiced beliefs.

In Sir John's speech, there is a typical example when he states that 'we
all know' that the birthrate (of Muslims) far exceeds that of the indige-

nous population. We may assume that this is a 'fact' for Sir John, whereas members of other (e.g., anti-racist) groups may qualify this as a prejudiced opinion, or at least as an exaggeration, or as a biased statement because it is incomplete, in the sense that the birthrate of immigrants, even when higher than that of the native population, usually quickly adapts to that of the majority. The fact that Sir John makes the statement about what 'we all know' suggests that this is precisely not general knowledge, otherwise he would have presupposed and not asserted it. He makes the statement because he knows that others in parliament would see it as an opinion or a biased belief, and his presentation of this knowledge as generally shared is thus a well-known rhetorical move to persuade the audience of the general validity of his group 'knowledge'. The same is true for his 'knowledge' about the 'large numbers' of immigrants Great Britain has absorbed and that ordinary English people were never asked their opinion about immigration.

Socially shared knowledge of specific groups or whole cultures needs to be applicable in many situations and therefore needs to be general and abstract. It may be about immigrants in general but is not about a specific immigrant or a specific event. We have argued that such specific knowledge is typically stored in mental (event) models in episodic memory. Hence, it makes sense to distinguish not only between cultural and group knowledge but also between social and personal knowledge.

Finally, there is a type of knowledge that embodies characteristics of both specific (model-based) knowledge, on the one hand, and socially shared knowledge on the other hand, namely historical knowledge. Such knowledge may be about specific events, e.g., the Holocaust or the Civil War in Bosnia, but at the same time it may be more or less generally known, and therefore even presupposed (to be true) in discourse and interaction. Much political knowledge is of that kind, and also Sir John's speech presupposes such historical-political knowledge.

Opinions and attitudes

The beliefs described above as various kinds of knowledge may be called 'factual' because persons, groups or whole cultures hold them to be true according to their respective truth criteria. There are, however, also sets of belief in social memory that are not dealt with in terms of truth criteria but shared on the basis of evaluative criteria (good vs. bad, etc.), namely opinions. As we have seen, however, what may be a factual belief for one group may be an evaluative belief or opinion for another.

Just as knowledge, such shared social opinions may be organized in larger structures for which we reserve the traditional term 'attitude' (for other conceptions of attitudes, see Eagly and Chaiken, 1993). Thus, shared group attitudes about abortion or immigration usually consist of more than one opinion. Note that in my framework attitudes are essentially social and associated with groups. Individuals may have personal opinions, but only share (in) attitudes as members of such groups.

Because of their evaluative nature, opinions and attitudes are typically not taken for granted, uncontroversial or undisputed and are therefore seldom part of the cultural Common Ground. Yet each culture may well have a number of opinions that are not disputed and hence have all the properties of other Common Ground beliefs.

In a speech about a controversial topic such as immigration given by a (very) conservative parliamentarian, we may expect many group opinions. These may either be expressed directly, in their general and abstract form, e.g., as premises in arguments, or through their instantiations in specific models, that is, applied to a special case by an individual speaker.

Thus, Sir John expresses the following general group opinions, among others,

(1)   This (large-scale immigration) is a problem for England.   (line 4)

(2)   We in England are a gentle, kind, tolerant and peace-loving people.   (line 19)

Most other opinions, however, are specified for the 'here' and 'now' of the present situation, and hence included in models for current events:

(3)   There have been some dangerous eruptions from parts of the Muslim community.   (lines 10–11)

(4)   It is foolish to ignore the problems and the fears that those dangerous eruptions engender among the ordinary people whom we are supposed to represent.   (lines 15–16)

(5)   We must not allow our feelings of guilt over our treatment of immigrants to cloud our judgement.   (lines 17–18)

(6)   This is a small attempt to have a little more control, and very wise it is. It should be welcomed by everyone in the House and outside.   (lines 34–35)

Evaluative beliefs are based on norms and values. Thus (3) is an opinion, given the use of 'dangerous' as an evaluative description of the 'eruptions' of the Muslims, an evaluation that presupposes the violation of the positive value of safety. Opinion (4) is an evaluative description of a mental act (ignore fears . . .) that violates the values of democracy. Similarly (5) is a normative statement based on the value of rationality. And finally in (6) the use of 'wise' is based on the value of wisdom, and it is predicated on the notion of 'control', which is also evaluative if 'being in control' is a positive value in British culture. All these opinions derive of course from socially shared political attitudes about the threat of foreigners in general, and of Muslims in particular, attitudes about what 'ordinary people' think, and more generally about immigration.

Finally, note that the text also features a number of opinions that are personal, such as his admiration of Muslims and their religion, and his liking for Douglas Hurd's letter to the Muslim community. However, even such personal opinions, when no further argued for, must be based on presupposed general opinions. Thus his positive remark about Muslims is based on the general opinion and value that other cultures are equal to ours, and his liking of the letter-writing an opinion derived from the conservative group attitude about law and order and the actions responsible politicians should take in order to keep the peace. In other words, opinions in personal mental models may be formed on the basis of shared social attitudes of groups.

Personal opinions, and the discourse expressing them, may thus be more or less in accordance with group attitudes, and more or less coherent. Empirical research suggests that such attitudinal coherence is more pronounced for those who have political expertise in a specific area than for novices (Judd and Downing, 1990). For the discussion of this chapter, this also means that extensive and well-structured political representations facilitate comprehension of political affairs (politicians, political issues, political stories in the media, etc.) (Fiske, Lau and Smith, 1990).

Ideologies

Finally, it will be assumed that the social representations (knowledge, attitudes) shared by a group may be organized by underlying ideologies. Ideologies are by definition general and abstract because they must apply to many different attitudes in different social domains. Thus, a racist ideology may control attitudes to immigration but also to housing, work, education or the culture of immigrants or minorities (for details, see van Dijk, 1991, 1998a).

The level of abstraction and complex control of social cognition requires extensive social learning from experience (models) or direct indoctrination. Therefore ideologies are acquired relatively late in development and not in the same detailed way by all group members. Some group experts (ideologues) will have more extensive ideologies than 'ordinary' group members (see Judd and Downing, 1990; Powell, 1989; Zaller, 1990).

However, to be a member of an ideological group (and to identify with such a group) will probably require that one accepts a few core ideological beliefs. Although classical work on political ideologies (Converse, 1964) as well as some directions in contemporary social psychology (Billig, 1991a, 1991b) deny that people have (stable) ideologies, it seems plausible that for those domains where people have social attitudes, such as those that organize their everyday lives, people do have ideologies that organize these attitudes (Milburn, 1987). Personal ideological variations expressed in surveys and (other) discourse can simply be explained in terms of personal opinions as embodied by models of events (personal experiences) and context, and because individuals are members of different social groups, each with their own attitudes and ideologies (Krosnick and Milburn, 1990).

It is assumed that ideologies are organized first of all by group self-schemata, with such categories as Membership Criteria, Activities, Goals, Values/Norms, Social Position and Resources. These are the categories in which the crucial information is represented that self-defines the own group, as well as its relation to other groups: who are we, what do we do, with what aims, etc. Within the Social Position category the – possibly – conflictual relationships with other groups may be represented.

In our example, the group knowledge and opinions expressed by Sir John may be organized by various ideologies, viz., those of nationalism, ethnocentrism, racism and democracy. Thus, a racist ideology will emphasize (group) knowledge about the vast number of immigrants, about birthrate and about the opposition of ordinary people against further immigration ('enough is enough'). It also controls the attitude about the criminality or aggressiveness of minorities in general, and the representation of Muslims in particular. Nationalist ideology controls shared social opinions about the positive qualities of Us, English (gentle, kind, tolerant, peace-loving), and about the homeland (beloved). Democratic ideology organizes the general attitudes about the need for ordinary people to have a voice, to be able to vote and to be able to express their views about their everyday lives and experiences, including immigration. More specifically, Sir John defends a populist version of democracy which claims to listen to the opinion of ordinary (working-class) people, while ignoring those of the elites (intellectuals, etc.). Obviously, Sir John's democratic credentials are strategically displayed as a form of positive self-presentation both of himself and of his party. Thus, rather typically, he ignores the democratic rights of immigrants.

Political cognition: concluding remarks

The theoretical analysis and descriptions of the specific example given above have shown that, in order to understand and explain political discourse, we also need to examine the underlying political cognition of participants in political communication. Instead of simply dealing with such cognition in terms of beliefs and belief systems, a complex framework needs to be elaborated that distinguishes between very different kinds of both personal and socially shared beliefs (see also Seliktar, 1986). Such beliefs may be organized in various schematic formats, clustered and assigned a theoretical place in the overall architecture of the social mind. Thus, it was assumed that for all members of a culture we should assume a general Common Ground, largely consisting of undisputed, common-sense knowledge. Similarly, for each group we may distinguish between group knowledge and group attitudes organized by fundamental group ideologies. These cultural and group cognitions serve as the basis of personal knowledge and opinions as stored in mental models. These models form the mental basis of all social practices, including discourse production and comprehension. It was finally argued that in order to describe and understand political discourse genres, the context especially, or rather a mental representation of the context (a context model), needs to be taken into account.

Political Discourse

After having examined various aspects of political cognition and the way they control the structures of political discourse, let us now reverse the direction of the analysis of the relation between discourse and cognition. That is, we shall focus on some prototypical properties of many political discourse genres, and then try to account for them in terms of underlying political cognition, and indirectly in terms of their functions in the political context and in politics more generally.

A review of even a fraction of earlier discourse analytical studies on political text and talk is beyond the scope of this chapter (see the many references to studies of political discourse in Chilton and Schäffner

(2002), and the introductions by Chilton and Schäffner, 1997 and van Dijk, 1997b). The same is true for the more specific analysis of parliamentary debates (for parliamentary debates on minorities and immigration see Carbó, 1992, 1995; Martin Rojo and van Dijk, 1997).

Instead, I shall proceed more theoretically, and merely discuss some structures of political discourse and their relations to political cognition and their functions in the political process. Given the importance of contextualization for the definition of political discourse, I shall pay special attention to the (cognitive) analysis of context.

Context

Before we deal with political discourse structures per se, let us briefly deal with their context. As suggested above, contexts should be defined in terms of participants' mental models of communicative events. That is, they are subjective and evaluative representations of self and other participants, and of the other discourse-relevant categories of communicative situations, such as, for example (van Dijk, 1997a, 1999):

- overall domain (e.g., politics);
- overall societal action (legislation);
- current setting (time, location);
- current circumstances (bill to be discussed);
- current interaction (political debate);
- current discourse genre (speech);
- the various types of role of participants (speaker, MP, member of the Conservative Party, white, male, elderly, etc.);
- the cognitions of the participants (goals, knowledge, beliefs, etc.).

It has also been suggested that the many genres of political discourse (parliamentary debates, laws, propaganda, slogans, international treaties, peace negotiations, etc.) are largely defined in contextual, rather than in textual, terms. Political discourse is not primarily defined by topic or style, but rather by who speaks to whom, as what, on what occasion and with what goals. In other words, political discourse is especially 'political' because of its functions in the political process (van Dijk, 1997b).

Thus, what Sir John has to say is an appropriate 'speech' in parliament only when a number of these specific contextual conditions are satisfied. The Speaker of the House of Commons is partly in control of such situational criteria. For instance, Sir John is only allowed to speak in parliament, for a specific amount of time, and during a specific parliamentary session or debate, because he is an MP, because he represents his party and because he has obtained the floor from the Speaker. And his speech is politically functional for the political process because he aims to defend a (Tory) Bill presented in parliament against criticism of the (Labour) Opposition.

That speakers are aware of such contextual categories is shown by their sometimes explicit indexical descriptions of them. Thus, Sir John explicitly refers to Setting, participant roles and aims, when he asks (rhetorically): 'Why are we English members of Parliament here today?' (line 6). And when in the next sentence he explicitly addresses the Opposition, he thus shows that the social–political role of Opponents or Opposition may be a relevant category in a political situation (for details, see e.g., Wilson, 1990). Many of the deictic expressions of Sir John's speech presuppose knowledge of other relevant contextual categories such as location ('this small Island') and time ('we now have ethnic minorities') and especially participants in various roles ('as we all know', 'our country', 'we are supposed to represent', 'we in England').

In particular, the use of the most typical political pronoun ('our') shows with which groups the speaker identifies himself. Note though that such group membership is not 'objective' but both part of the models and social representations of speakers as group members and in a particular speech also socially constructed for strategic purposes ('we democrats') and excluding others ('we in England', referring to white rather than black people). The discursive polarization of Us and Them, typical for political discourse, not only reflects mental representations of people talked about (English vs. Muslims), but also the categories of participants (represented in context models) talked to in a communicative situation (We Conservatives vs. Them of the Labour Opposition).

Context models also regulate style, such as the formality of designating expressions ('indigenous population', 'influx', etc.) as a function of formal, institutional interaction in parliament, or the use of popular expressions ('enough is enough') as a function of the persuasive strategy of positive self-presentation of a populist MP who claims to take the perspective of 'ordinary people'. Note that only some of these expressions (such as the use of 'honourable' – abbreviated as 'Hon' in the *Hansard* transcript – or 'friend' as used to address an MP of the same party) are typical for parliamentary debates.

As we have seen, context models also regulate semantic representations by controlling the selection of relevant information from event models. Sir John knows much more and has many more opinions about immigration and Muslims, but both time constraints, beliefs about the beliefs of the recipients and strategies of positive self-presentation will determine that some model information is selected for expression and other information remains implicit, presupposed or merely hinted at. And the conservative ideology of his party will be instantiated in a context model that favours the selection of beliefs about Our good characteristics and Their bad ones.

Context models regulate the pragmatic dimension of political discourse, e.g., the use of speech acts such as the 'rhetorical' questions being expressed in Sir John's speech. He knows that others know, or do not want to know, his opinion and hence he and his recipients know that his questions do not require answers. And indirectly, the use of derogatory terms like 'ilk' about the Labour Opposition, implies the accomplishment of an accusation (that Labour is soft on immigration) if we spell out all the relevant context categories of the current situation.

Note finally, that the relations between context, context models, discourse and cognition have several directions. Thus, context models constrain text production, resulting in context-bound discourse structures. These again will be interpreted by recipients as properties of the context model of the speaker (his or her interpretation of the Setting, the Current Interaction as well as his/her Goals, Knowledge and Opinions). That is, discourse structures may in turn influence recipient models of the context. They may accept these interpretations of the context and construe them, as suggested, in their own context models. On the other hand, they may represent and evaluate the current interaction and especially the speaker in a different way. Thus, whereas Sir John for instance represents white British, including himself, as tolerant, they may reject that opinion. Similarly, they may disagree with the rhetorically suggested problem of immigration, conveyed by him.

Political discourse structures

We have seen that many discourse structures are a function of context models. However, discourse is not only constrained by context models, but also by event models, that is, by the way the speaker interprets the events talked about, as well as by more general social representations shared by group members, as shown above. As suggested, important for the definition of political discourse is that such structures are relevant for political structures and processes. Thus, contextually, Sir John's speech functions as a contribution to parliamentary decision-making and legislation about immigration, which in turn plays a role in the reproduction of ethnic relations and racism in the UK (Solomos and Back, 1995;

Reeves, 1983; van Dijk, 1991, 1993a). More locally, in parliament, his speech functions as a defence of a Bill and as an attack on the Labour opposition.

Let us now briefly consider some discourse structures, and show how they are relevant for the political process, as well as for political cognition. We shall assume these structures as such to be known and in no need of theoretical analysis, and especially focus on their political functions. Overall, as we shall see, such structures will follow the global ideological or political strategy of positive self-presentation and negative other-presentation (for theoretical analysis and further examples, see van Dijk, 1987a, 1993a).

Topics: What information is defined and emphasized to be important or topical in (political and other) discourse, is a function of the event and context models of speakers. Thus, typically, negative information about Us, our own group (e.g., racism in Britain), will not be topicalized in Sir John's speech, whereas negative information about Them, the Others (e.g., their alleged aggression) tends to be topicalized. And vice versa: our positive characteristics (tolerance, hospitality) will be topical whereas Their positive characteristics will be ignored, downplayed or mentioned only in passing. Thus the main topics of Sir John's speech are an expression of his mental model of current immigration in the UK:

(T1) Massive immigration is a problem for England.
(T2) Immigrants are a threat to our country and culture.
(T3) Ordinary English people don't want more immigration.
(T4) We can exercise more control over immigration with this Bill.

The implied consequence of these topics is that the House should vote for this Bill. Apart from reproducing ethnic stereotypes, and from trying to persuade the House to adopt this Bill, this speech at the same time has a more direct political function, viz., to warn the Labour opposition not to ignore the 'voice of the people'. Sir John clearly implies with this warning that if we (or Labour) do not listen to ordinary white people, we won't have their support. Empirical research shows that overall topics, issue definitions or 'frames', as provided by the elites, may have a significant effect on interpretation and public opinion (Gamson, 1992; Kinder and Sanders, 1990).

Schemata: The global schematic organization of discourse is conventional and hence not directly variable because of context constraints: thus, a parliamentary speech has the same constituent categories whether engaged in by a Conservative or Labour MP. It is especially the order, prominence, kind and extent of the information included in these categories that may vary, and hence be highlighted or mitigated as a function of positive self-presentation and negative other-presentation. Thus, if such a speech would have a global Problem–Solution structure, Sir John might dwell more on the Problem category (the problems allegedly caused by immigrants) than on the Solution category.

Parliamentary debates are typically persuasive discourses, in which MPs take political positions, express their opinions and attack those of others within the framework of argumentative structures – one of the most characteristic schematic structures of discourse. Thus, Sir John intends to support a Bill that limits immigration. His arguments that lead to the Conclusion that such a limitation is good for Britain are therefore selected in both his mental models and his conservative attitudes in such a way that they optimally support that conclusion:

(a)   there are millions of immigrants;
(b)   they have a higher birthrate;
(c)   England is small and already has too many immigrants;
(d)   our culture is being threatened;
(e)   especially Muslims are dangerous;
(f)   ordinary English people will suffer;
(g)   ordinary people say it's been enough;
       etc.

Typical also is the rejection of possible counter-arguments which happens when he rejects emotional arguments: feelings of guilt should not cloud our judgement; and this restriction is not racist (as some may think) because the English are tolerant; and I am not a racist or anti-Muslim, because I admire Muslims.

In other words, the selection of negative propositions about immigrants from specific events models (e.g., recent 'eruptions' of Muslims) and general prejudices ('birthrates', etc.) obeys the overall constraint of negative other-representation, which in turn organizes all premises that need to lead to the negative conclusion, viz., that immigration must be curbed. This conclusion, which applies to the current context model, is thus at the same time a model of future action in the political context: immigrants are no longer let in. In sum, also, an analysis of political argumentation presupposes various strategic uses of various types of mental representations.

Local semantics: We have seen that political context models define what information of models of current events will be relevantly included in discourse or not. This is true both for global (topical) meanings, as well as for local meanings expressed in the actual sentences of text or talk. An important context category controlling this selection is the political ideology of the speaker and the recipients which may also influence the complexity of local meanings. Thus, the simplicity of Sir John's argument seems to confirm the often observed lack of conceptual complexity of (especially conservative) radical politicians (Tetlock, 1983, 1984, 1993). And conversely, specific semantic structures thus construed may influence the 'preferred' models of recipients who have no alternative knowledge sources (Lau, Smith and Fiske, 1991).

Thus, many propositions of Sir John's speech are persuasively selected as a function of his mental model of the situation in the UK which in turn is controlled by his conservative, nationalist and racist ideologies, and typically focus on details of Their negative characteristics:

(S1) we have allowed hundreds of thousands of immigrants;
(S2) we now have ethnic minorities of several million people;
(S3) their birthrate far exceeds that of the indigenous population;
(S4) what will be the effect on our religion, morals, customs habits and so on?
(S5) already there have been some dangerous eruptions from parts of the Muslim community;
(S6) the fears that those dangerous eruptions engender;
(S7) large numbers of immigrants are living there.

Exaggeration, numbers, contrast and metaphor ('eruption') and other rhetorical moves further enhance this ideologically biased selection of negative propositions from Sir John's event model. The overall implication of such propositions is that They (Muslims) are a threat to Us. The only positive proposition about Muslims (lines 12/13), might in such a dominant topology of negative meanings be read as a disclaimer that has the strategic function of positive self-presentation (van Dijk, 1987a, 1993a). Indeed, it is also the only part of the speech where Sir John speaks about himself.

On the other hand, the short speech does emphasize the positive qualities of (white) British people, as we have seen above, thus contrasting Us and Them, as usual, and as analysed before. Note though that his positive reference to ordinary English people need not be an expression of his social representations of ordinary people. As an arch-conservative, it is unlikely that Sir John is really fond of 'the people' and their will. Rather, then, his positive description is a 'populist' strategy of positive self-presentation (we are democratic; we listen to the people), and an implied critique of Labour (who does not listen to the people). That is, we see that not all meanings derive from ideologically based models of events but may also be inspired by context models featuring images of Us (Conservatives) and Them (Labour) and the goals of political action (to defend a Bill). For the same reason, critical recipients will probably hear such positive references to ordinary people not as genuine opinions but merely as moves of strategic political interaction.

More generally, then, a cognitively based political analysis of local meanings will try to relate the selection of propositions expressed in text and talk to underlying event and context models as well as socially shared (group) representations such as knowledge, attitudes and ideologies. Thus, whether or not local meaning is explicit or implicit, asserted or presupposed, detailed or global, general or specific, direct or indirect, or blatant or subdued, will typically be a function of the ideologically based event models. As is the case in our example, this will generally mean that negative meanings about the Others will tend to be selected, emphasized, explicit, detailed, specific, direct or blatant, whereas mitigations, disclaimers or denials are rather a function of positive self-presentation (or avoiding a bad impression) as regulated by context models.

Style and rhetoric: Finally, semantic representations are expressed in variable surface structures, that is, through specific lexicalization, syntactic structures and specific features of sound, printing or images, as well as by rhetorical devices that are geared towards the emphasis or de-emphasis of underlying meanings.

We have already suggested that cognitively such variation is partly a function of structures and opinions in event models. Thus, negative opinions about outgroups, as stored in event models and political attitudes, typically will be lexicalized by negative words, as we saw in the expression 'dangerous eruptions' for the description of demonstrations by Muslims, or 'ilk' when describing the Labour opposition. Such lexicalizations may not just be negative but also have a rhetorical function as hyperboles, for instance when Sir John refers to the birthrate of immigrants as 'far exceeding' that of the indigenous population. Conversely, positive lexicalizations ('gentle', 'tolerant', 'peace-loving') may be chosen to express positive self-images of the ingroup. The use of specific lexical variants may also have very different 'framing' effects on the activation of political attitudes and ideologies, and hence on the construction of event models. Elites may thus use specific terms in policy or media discourse in order to influence public opinion. For instance, defining affirmative action as 'unfair advantage' or as 'reverse discrimination' triggers a host of cognitive representations and strategies, and especially racist attitudes and ideologies, that result in a more negative opinion about affirmative action (Kinder and Sanders, 1990).

Many properties of style and rhetoric, however, are not expressions of underlying opinions or structures of models or political representations, but monitored by the various categories of context models. Certain terms are prototypical for the domain of politics, and the choice of formal words, such as 'indigenous' and 'influx' in Sir John's speech indexes the formality of the parliamentary speech and the session of this House of Commons. Participant roles and identities, for instance in parliamentary debates, are multiply indexed by pronouns ('we'; 'Us vs. Them'), forms of address ('honourable', 'friend') and politeness strategies, while at the same time expressing forms of political or social inclusion or exclusion.

Similarly, speech acts and rhetorical questions may be employed in order to express or confirm political identity and relationships. For instance, Sir John's direct address of the Labour Party in lines 6–10 is monitored by the underlying political roles of the participants, viz., as government and opposition parties, and as a means to accuse the opposition of not caring about the future of the country. All this is part of Sir John's definition of the current political context of his speech and hence appears in his context model and also surfaces in his speech, strategically, by self-representing Tories as being concerned, and the opposition as callous, if not as undemocratic (not listening to ordinary people, who should be their main constituents).

Conclusion

In this brief account of the structures of political discourse, we have found that virtually all of them can be accounted for in terms of a more sophisticated cognitive theory that links different types of mental representations to text and talk. Generally, then, both meanings and forms of political discourse variously derive from event models, or from general political representations, such as knowledge, attitudes and ideologies, in both cases as a function of context models. Of course, this insight is hardly new when we realize that these mental structures represent how participants understand specific political events, the political world, as well as the situation of political communication, respectively.

For our theoretical argument, this cognitive analysis of political discourse structures is not an exercise in applying cognitive psychology to political discourse studies. Rather, the cognitive analysis is essential to truly describe and explain in detail how political discourse expresses and plays its role in the political process. That is, political text and talk is related to the immediate political context and occasioning, as was Sir John's speech in a parliamentary debate about immigration. However, it appears that it is not the context itself that thus relates to discourse, but the models the participants construct of the interactional or communicative context. It is through a sociocognitively defined notion of relevance that we are able to demonstrate how exactly, and why, political situations constrain text and talk, and conversely.

Similarly, political discourse is seldom just personal, although it should not be forgotten that the converse is also true: it is not only social or political, but as individual text and talk also embodies individual characteristics. Only a cognitive theory is able to spell out this interface between the social and the personal, namely through the relations between episodic mental models and other personal representations, on the one hand, and the socially shared political representations of groups, on the other hand. Political groups or institutions are thus defined not only sociopolitically in terms of sets of interacting actors or collectivities and their interactions, but also sociocognitively in terms of their shared knowledge, attitudes, ideologies, norms and values. In other words, political discourse can only be adequately described and explained when we spell out the sociocognitive interface that relates it to the socially shared political representations that control political actions, processes and systems.

8

War Rhetoric of a Little Ally: Political Implicatures and Aznar's Legitimization of the War in Iraq

Introduction

In this chapter, we examine some properties of the belligerent parliamentary rhetoric of Spanish Prime Minister José Maria Aznar in support of military action of the USA and its allies against Saddam Hussein in 2003. One of the interesting contextual features of Aznar's speeches in the Cortes was that they defied a vast popular majority, of more than 90 per cent, against a war in Iraq without UN-backing, even among his own party, the Partido Popular. Aznar totally ignored both the biggest demonstrations ever held in Spain (more than a million people in Barcelona alone), as well as the opposition of all other parties, including his own coalition partners, and thus risked losing many votes in the approaching municipal elections of May 2003. Although he was not personally up for re-election at the next general elections in 2004, why would a prime minister thus commit political suicide by slavishly following President George W. Bush as a small-time ally-at-war who is barely taken seriously internationally? Because of the conservative ideology shared with the current US administration? Because of genuine worries about the weapons of mass destruction Saddam Hussein allegedly had? Or perhaps in order to enlist Bush's support for the local fight against the terrorist organization ETA? This chapter will not engage in these or other political speculations about Aznar's decisions to support the war against Iraq, but more concretely examine some of the properties of the speeches that are the discursive expressions of Aznar's public reasons. I

185

shall do so against the background of broader questions about the legitimization of state violence and war, especially after the attack against the
World Trade Center and the Pentagon, on 11 September 2001, and the
international anti-terrorist hysteria that followed it.

More specifically, I shall focus on what I shall call the political implicatures of Aznar's speech, that is, the specific political inferences that
participants in the communicative situation, for instance MPs in a parliamentary debate, may make on the basis of (their understanding of) this
speech and its context.

My general framework is a multidisciplinary brand of Critical
Discourse Analysis (CDA) that tries to 'triangulate' social issues in terms
of a combined study of discursive, cognitive and social dimensions of a
problem (van Dijk, 1993c, 2003a). Thus, in our case, we are interested not
just in describing some interesting properties of political rhetoric but, in
order to explain them, we need to relate them to such sociocognitive
representations as attitudes, norms, values and ideologies, e.g., those that
Aznar shares with his party, as well as to the sociopolitical context of his
speeches in contemporary Spain. That is, Aznar's political discourses and
their properties are ultimately to be treated not only as texts but also as
expressions of political cognition and political actions in political
processes, such as party propaganda and parliamentary decision-making
at the national level, as well as diplomacy, coalition building and power
politics at the international level. This is especially true for political
discourse whose analysis should not be limited to structural features of
text and talk, but also account for their conditions and functions in the
political process.

Our corpus consists of four interventions by Aznar held during parliamentary sessions on 5 and 19 February and 5 and 29 March 2003.
However, I shall cite examples only from his first speech of 5 February and
focus only on his own contributions, and ignore, in this chapter, the contributions of other politicians and the discursive interactions of the debate.

Theoretical Framework

Parliamentary debates

Against the background of earlier work in CDA in general, and on political discourse in particular, the theoretical framework of this study first of
all focuses on the structures and functions of parliamentary debates. Such
debates are forms of institutional verbal interaction as well as a specific
genre of political discourse, and their general properties may thus be

analysed in the broader frameworks of these discourse categories. As a genre of political discourse, parliamentary debates are local manifestations of the global political acts of legislation, governing and control of government. More specifically, such debates feature speeches of MPs and members of government that pragmatically function as presenting and legitimating government decisions and policies, supporting the government and engaging in opposition. Relevant analyses of parliamentary debates should therefore focus on these global functions, and it will thus be assumed that also the structures of the speeches in these debates may be described as implementing local moves in the overall realization of these global political functions. It is within this framework that I shall define and use the notion of 'political implicature' below.

Parliamentary debates have a number of formal properties that shall largely be ignored in my analysis, such as speaker and turn-taking control by the Speaker or President, order and change of speakers according to membership of government or opposition parties, ritualized form of address (e.g., 'Su Señoría' in Spanish), and the formal lexical and syntactic style of prepared addresses and official reactions to previous speeches. Also because our data are taken from the official record, there are hardly any spontaneous forms of speech and interactions, such as overlaps, repairs, false starts and incomplete sentences.

Politically more interesting in this case, and hence more relevant in a CDA framework, are the semantic and rhetorical properties of Aznar's speech. Thus, in a speech legitimating Spain's participation in the war in Iraq, we may not only expect the usual global strategies of legitimation, such as the legal, moral or political justification of such participation, but also the well-known global semantic strategies of positive self-presentation of *Us* and negative other-presentation of *Them*. As is the case for many other political discourses after September 11, *We* represent the western democracies that fight against terrorism or 'rogue states', and *They* are the terrorists or states that threaten us, in our case specifically Saddam Hussein. Such semantic polarization may be rhetorically emphasized in the usual way, e.g., by hyperboles and metaphors about *our* good things and *their* bad things.

Although there are few general semantic constraints on parliamentary debates, which after all may be about many different topics, these overall semantic and rhetorical strategies of ingroup and outgroup polarization are quite general and also dependent on the political functions of such debates. That is, governments and the MPs that back them will typically present their own policies and actions in a positive light, and opposition MPs will, by definition, do the 'opposite': negatively describe, condemn or attack such actions and policies. In my analysis I shall merely summarize some of the specific forms these semantics and rhetoric take in the speech of Aznar.

Context models

There is another fundamental aspect of parliamentary debates: context. That is, many of the formal, semantic and rhetorical aspects of parliamentary debates are hardly specific, and may be found also in other formal encounters or in other political discourse. This means that most of the unique properties of this genre of political discourse are contextual: who is speaking and listening, what are their roles, what kind of actions they do engage in, with what intentions, and so on. As suggested above, it is here that we must observe the *political* functions of the debates, as interactions between MPs, as engaging in specific political actions, and with specific political goals.

This formulation of the contextual dimension of parliamentary debates is however rather informal. Theoretically, it should be emphasized that there is no direct relationship between text and context when context is defined in terms of these aspects of the political *situation*: MPs and their roles, actions and goals. Rather, contexts can only influence what people say or understand when defined in terms of subjective, participant constructs. *It is not the social or political situation itself that influences text or talk, but rather the way individual participants represent, understand or otherwise construct the now-for them-relevant properties of such a situation.* Thus, contexts are not objective, or 'out there', but subjective constructs of participants. In terms of contemporary cognitive psychology, this means that contexts are mental models represented in episodic memory: context models. These context models control many of the properties of the production and comprehension of discourse: speech acts, style, lexical selection, formats, rhetoric, semantic strategies and so on.

Although unique in each communicative situation, while representing each participant's ad hoc construction of the communicative situation, the general format of context models is necessarily more general, though culturally variable. MPs need not invent each time the standard categories of the structure that organizes their context models of the debates they participate in.

Political implicatures

The feature of Aznar's speech I would like to focus on is the *political impli-*

catures of his speech. These implicatures must be defined within the framework of the theory of context briefly summarized above, that is, in terms of the participants' context models of their own political identities, roles, goals, actions and beliefs. I have chosen the term 'implicature' rather than 'implication' because the inferences involved are not semantic, but pragmatic or contextual. Aznar's speech of course also has many semantic implications, for instance when he describes the 'bad' behaviour of Saddam Hussein. Most of these semantic implications are, in our case, about Iraq and Spain's policy. That is, they are inferred from the topics talked about as well as from the general knowledge we have about Spain, terrorism, international policy, Iraq and so on. Much of the understanding of the speeches in this debate involves the production of these semantic inferences, some of which are quite general, others more personal and variable. Thus, when Aznar in the beginning of his speech defines the situation in Iraq as a 'crisis that confronts' the international community, then the (political) implication is that Iraq is a threat to 'us'.

Implicatures on the other hand are usually defined as weak semantic implications or pragmatically in terms of contexts (Atlas, 2000; Gazdar, 1979; Grice, 1989; Levinson, 2000). My use of the term will here be limited to the pragmatics of context, and I shall thus define *political implicatures* as implicatures that are specifically based on the political context. For example, if Aznar emphasizes that, despite his support for the war in Iraq, his policy is a peaceful one, he not only makes an assertion about the war in Iraq and his policies – to be analysed in semantic terms – but this assertion should also be understood as the defence of government policy of the Prime Minister, of the leader of the government party Partido Popular (PP), and as reacting to critique from citizens and the opposition parties, and with the political aim to legitimate highly controversial decisions.

Thus, each fragment of his speech may also be analysed in terms of its functions in the current political interaction, locally within parliament in the current debate and more globally in the current political situation, such as legitimating his own policies and delegitimating the opposition, among other strategies.

Political implicatures are assigned by the participants as inferences from three sources:

1 participants' representations of the structures of the discourse and its meanings (such as their mental model of the situation in Iraq);
2 participants' context model of the current communicative situation;

3   participants' more general knowledge about the political situation
      in the world and in the country. In the examples below, I shall
      show in more detail how such implicatures may be derived. This
      will be done more or less informally, but it should be stressed that
      in a theoretically more explicit account we would need to spell
      out in detail the contents of the context models, as well as the
      strategies of inference that allow participants – in this case MPs –
      to make such inferences. Approaches in CDA, conversation analy-
      sis and political discourse analysis that ignore a cognitive compo-
      nent either need to disregard such 'unobservable' implicatures or
      reduce them to properties of discourse or undefined contexts.
      Also, a satisfactory account of (pragmatic) political implicatures
      presupposes an explicit theory of context, as briefly summarized
      here.

   That such implicatures are actually *relevant* for political discourse
analysis is not only obvious for participants and analysts alike if they share
the relevant political knowledge of the current political situation, but
more specifically may also be explicitly *signalled* by the participants in
their reactions to previous speeches. This is, however, not a necessary
condition of our analysis – political implicatures may also be assessed
indirectly by later interviews of participants, or by other methods – and
need not be signalled explicitly in a speech by participants. Indeed, they
are routinely understood and only presupposed in later talk and text.
Later commentary in the media on parliamentary debates often precisely
focuses on these tacit political implicatures of such debates. Political
implicatures *explain* that and why political participants say the things they
do. They define the fundamental political *point* of parliamentary debates
in the first place, such as 'doing' government and 'doing' opposition, and
more generally the institutional and political power play enacted in
parliaments. Through an analysis of political implicatures, thus, we show
why ongoing political discourse is relevant for the political process.

Method

In my analyses below, I shall select a number of characteristic fragments
of Aznar's speech as they implement the usual properties of political
discourse as we know them from the literature, such as positive ingroup
and negative outgroup descriptions as well as other strategies of parliamentary debates. This selection and brief characterizations show how
Aznar is engaging in political discourse and its well-known structures

and strategies, and more specifically in the case of the debate about the war in Iraq. At the same time, these examples and their (largely semantic) analysis should provide insight into a political issue, namely how political leaders manage the legitimation of controversial policies. There is no explicit discovery procedure for these political discourse structures, and hence for the selection of the fragments analysed, other than those predicted by theories of political discourse in general, and theories of parliamentary debates in particular.

Besides these brief standard analyses, the analysis will focus in more detail on the political implicatures of each fragment, thus accounting for the political functions and rationale of this debate in the Spanish Cortes. I suggest that this is probably the way MPs and other observers, as well as the knowledgeable public at large, understand the debate. Obviously, a complete analysis of all political implicatures of this speech would require hundreds of pages of detailed description, so we shall limit ourselves to a limited number of characteristic examples.

Defining the Situation

Many types of discourse, such as editorials and also speeches in parliament, feature an initial schematic category that might be called *Defining the Situation*. Such a category is sequentially relevant in discourses whose main aim is to make comments on a social or political situation, to recommend specific actions, or to justify or legitimate actions. Thus, if one wants to explain or justify why one acted in a specific (usually criticized) way, it makes sense to describe a situation in which such acts appear necessary, logical, comprehensible, unavoidable or otherwise acceptable. Typically, there are normative rules (and international law) that in specific cases allow people or states to defend themselves when they are attacked – and US politicians, scholars and military have justified the Iraq war on such grounds (for analysis of such forms of legitimation, see, e.g., Borch and Wilson 2003; see also Nye, 2000; Dinstein, 2001; Rodin, 2002; Chomsky, 2003; Christopher, 2003; Daalder and Lindsay, 2003; Falk, 2003; Newhouse, 2003; Gareau, 2004; Waltzer, 2004).

Thus, if Aznar is required to defend his very unpopular Iraq policy, he first needs to lay out a political situation that makes such policy understandable, reasonable, and legitimate. This is indeed what he does, as from the first words of his intervention, in which he defines the situation as a crisis:

(1) El señor PRESIDENTE DEL GOBIERNO (Aznar López): Señora presi-

denta, señorías, al comenzar el periodo de sesiones, comparezco esta tarde ante
la Cámara para informar a SS.SS. de la posición del Gobierno ante la crisis
que enfrenta a la comunidad internacional con Irak.

*Mr President of the Government (Aznar López): Mrs Speaker, Honourable Members,
at the beginning of this session period, I this afternoon am   appearing before this
House in order to inform your Honourable Members about the position of the government facing the crisis with Iraq confronting the international community.*

Since politicians, parliaments and especially governments need to take
action when there is a 'crisis', this is a persuasive way to define the initial
situation. Indeed, also the opposition no doubt describes the current situation as a crisis, if only because of the looming war threatened by the
USA and the UK. Note though that even in this very first sentence,
Aznar does not blame the crisis on those who started it with their war
plans, such as the USA and the UK, but on Iraq. The obvious political
implication of his first definition of the situation, thus, is that it is Iraq
that is responsible for the crisis, and the choice of the word *'enfrenta'*
(confront) further confirms that 'we' are the victims of this confrontation.
Secondly, the crisis is not defined as facing Aznar's government alone, but
as a crisis that affects the whole international community. Such a formulation, and its (weak) implications, is one of the ways in which arguments
can be opposed that claim that this is a conflict only as defined by the
USA and its allies, and not by the international community.

Besides these (semantic) implications, there are however also a number
of political implicatures of this speech. From the start and throughout,
Aznar shows that he is acutely aware of his own position, that of his party,
as well as of the opposition and the population at large, in the question
of Iraq. In the current situation in parliament, thus, it is crucial that not
only the 'content' of his speech be an efficient contribution to the
general strategy of legitimation of his policies, but that he be seen and
accepted as a good, responsible party leader and prime minister and that,
hence, the opposition have no 'point'. Thus, instead of directly starting
with his report of the government's policy in Iraq, Aznar prefaces his
statement with an explicit deictic formula describing his own 'appearance' in parliament.

Such performatives may just be a more or less formal way of speaking, but in this case they also have specific political implicatures: Aznar
had been accused by the opposition as well as by the media and other
elites of ignoring parliament and public opinion by not informing them
about government policy on Iraq. Thus, by making his own 'appearance'

and 'report' for the MPs explicit in the very first sentence of his speech, he politically implicates that (i) he is doing his job as PM, (ii) he listens to the opposition and the country and hence is a good democrat, (iii) the earlier critique against him is not or no longer relevant, and (iv) those who formulated the critique – such as the oppositional PSOE – have no point. These and possibly other political implicatures may be seen as part of one of the forms of contextual polarization and face management, that is, of positive self-presentation and negative other-presentation, and of course of political counter-attack.

At the same time, Aznar politically implicates that his government is part of *us*, that is, the ingroup of the 'international community', an implicature that has a whole series of other political implicatures, namely that his policies are in line with the international community, and therefore legitimate, and that the opposition, which does not want to join the war (and which when they came to power in March 2004 immediately decided to withdraw Spanish troops from Iraq), is not part of the international community and hence less legitimate in its claims. Indeed, following the political logic of President George W. Bush, one might further infer that if the opposition is not *with* the 'international community' (that is, the USA, the UK and some other countries), then it is against them, and possibly even playing into the hands of the enemy, Saddam Hussein.

As suggested before, the formulation of these implicatures is informal, but will have to do for the purposes of this chapter. A more formal account would have to make explicit the precise context models of Aznar and the MPs, so that it can be shown how previous political knowledge, the representation of the situation and the mental model representing the semantic interpretation of this fragment all provide the information necessary to derive these plausible political inferences.

After this initial, and hence thematic or global, definition of the situation (as headlines at the beginning of a news article) and its overall contextual implicatures, Aznar needs to provide specifics of the situation of crisis and further arguments that allow him to define the situation as a crisis in the first place and that also explain the position of his government in this crisis. This is indeed what he does, by now explicitly attributing the crisis to Iraq:

(2) La crisis es consecuencia del reiterado incumplimiento por parte de Irak de sus obligaciones internacionales y de las resoluciones del Consejo de Seguridad de las Naciones Unidas. A poco que hagamos memoria, vemos que no es más que un nuevo episodio del problema surgido en 1990, cuando el régimen iraquí invadió Kuwait. (Rumores)

> *This crisis is the consequence of the repeated non-compliance on the part of Iraq with its international obligations and the resolutions of the Security Council of the United Nations. We hardly have to think to see that this is a new episode of the problem that emerged in 1990 when the Iraqi regime invaded Kuwait. (Noise)*

Note that Aznar here does much more than merely accuse Iraq as the cause of the crisis. Among other things, he says, does and implies the following:

(a) By modifying non-compliance of Iraq with the word 'repeated', he semantically emphasizes the seriousness of non-compliance, and hence the seriousness of the crisis, thereby adducing further grounds to accuse Iraq and to legitimize the war. Such a rhetorical emphasis presupposes the normative or legal inference that if a negative act (such as non-compliance) is not unintentional or exceptional, and does not occur for the first time, its repeated nature makes it intentional and the perpetrator more guilty.

(b) By referring to international obligations and the Security Council of the United Nations, he emphasizes that Iraq is defying the world's highest authority and official earlier resolutions. Again, this emphasizes the 'official' guilt of Iraq, as well as the legitimacy, if not the obligation, to condemn Iraq and take action against it.

(c) In the second sentence, Aznar refers to the (first) Gulf War, in which Iraq's (Saddam Hussein's) aggression was obvious because of its invasion of Kuwait. By calling the current situation a continuation of that invasion, Aznar politically implies at least two other things: that Iraq, despite the fact that it has not invaded another country now, is still guilty of provoking an international crisis, and secondly that, in the same way as in 1990, international (armed) action against Iraq is legitimate. That this implication is understood, but rejected as a legitimatization of war now, is obvious from the protests of other MPs (described here as 'rumores' – noise – in the transcript of the *Diario de las Sesiones*).

This further definition of the situation as a crisis provoked by Iraq at the same time emphasizes the seriousness of the crisis as well as the guilt of Iraq as a challenge to the highest authority in the world, as a form of politically aligning himself with such authority (the Security Council and the United Nations), and finally to legitimate international action because of the repeated and continuous challenges to the UN, already begun with the Iraqi invasion of Kuwait.

In other words, the initial definition of the situation is one that Aznar carefully articulates in a way that is consistent with his own policy. That is, his speech not only provides a description of an international crisis but also formulates it in such a way that the mental model of the event it expresses and conveys is the one preferred in this process of persuasion. At the same time, the implications of this definition provide as many arguments for the political legitimatization of his own policies: to define the current situation as a crisis, to accuse Iraq as being non-compliant and hence as in breach of international resolutions, to define this challenge as a continuation of the aggression against Iraq, and hence the legitimacy to confront Iraq with armed intervention as was the case in the Gulf War. Indeed, since there are many other dictatorships in the world, the fact that Saddam Hussein oppresses the people of Iraq is as such no international legitimization for war against him, so that it is imperative to marshal any evidence or argument that finds him guilty of current breaches of international law, or that defines his current position as the same as the one that provoked the earlier (legitimate) war. We see that Aznar carefully follows this legitimatization strategy in his speech. Although these implications are local legitimatizations of his own policy, they are at the same time international in scope, and overlapping with those of US and UK foreign policy.

But Aznar is not only aligning himself internationally with Bush and Blair, but in parliament he needs to defend such policy against fierce opposition and in Spain against a nearly unanimous popular condemnation. This means that we should also draw the political inferences of his speech in terms of the relation with the stance of the parliamentary opposition and public opinion, that is in terms of contextual implicatures. In other words, Aznar does not only speak about Iraq or about his government policy but also needs to manage his power in parliament and the country. He does so, implicitly, through a polarization according to which he associates himself with the Good Guys, and those who oppose the war as supporting Saddam Hussein, the enemy. Again, this move is part of the ideological strategy of positive self-presentation and negative other-presentation. By doing so, he not only legitimizes his own policy but also delegitimizes those who oppose the war, and especially also the political opposition parties, such as the PSOE, the Socialist Party of Spain. As suggested above, such political implicatures are inferred from a combined general knowledge of politics and a more contextual understanding of the current political situation, for instance in Spain. The sequence of political inferences might in that case be something like this:

- I am doing what I am supposed to do according to the rules.
- (Therefore) I am doing my job as prime minister.
- (Therefore) I follow the rules of our democracy.
- (Therefore) I am a democrat.
- (Therefore) I am a good politician.
- (Therefore) There is (now) no reason to criticize me or my government.
- (Therefore) The criticism of the opposition (or others) is unfounded.
- Therefore) The opposition is not doing its job well.
- (Therefore) The opposition is no good.

Empirically such inferences are warranted when consistent with the way competent political participants actually do understand Aznar's statements in this way, an understanding that may become manifest in the way they react to his speech.

Positive Self-presentation

As we have seen also for Aznar, speakers prefer to describe themselves in positive terms. This tendency is part of well-known interactional and sociocognitive strategy to present oneself in a positive light, or at least to avoid a negative impression and in general to manage the impression on our interlocutors. The same is of course true in most forms of public discourse, where making a good impression may even be more important than in informal everyday life conversations, for instance because of the more serious impact on a larger audience, as well as the possibility of professional or political damage that may be the result of a 'wrong' presentation of Self. This is particularly important in politics, where opposition politicians especially, as well as the media and indirectly the public at large, are listening critically, and where a faux pas may cost votes at the next elections. We may therefore expect that Aznar will also engage in extensive and varied forms of positive self-presentation, especially given the devastating critique his position on Iraq received in the media and from most other political parties, as well as from the vast majority of the population at large. Probably on few topics in recent Spanish history had opposition against government policy been so pervasive. In other words, Aznar has some serious image repair to do. Let us examine some of these moves. Here is a first example, right at the beginning of his speech:

Esta comparecencia continúa la información proporcionada a SS.SS. por el gobierno anteriormente. En concreto, el Gobierno ha informado sobre la situación de Irak por medio de la comparecencia de la ministra de Asuntos Exteriores en un total de cinco ocasiones, la última el viernes pasado ante la Comisión correspondiente. Yo mismo he comparecido para dar cuenta de la posición del Gobierno en otras dos ocasiones. El Gobierno también ha contestado por escrito a diversas preguntas que se le han formulado sobre la cuestión. A la comparecencia de hoy seguirán otras mías o de los ministros de Asuntos Exteriores y de Defensa, en función de los acontecimientos y según la forma que requiera la evolución de esta crisis, conforme al Reglamento de la Cámara.

My presentation continues the information previously made available by the Government to the Honourable Members. More specifically, the Government provided information on five occasions about the situation in Iraq by means of the presentation of the Minister of Foreign Affairs, on five occasions, the last time being last Friday for the corresponding committee. I myself have appeared here twice to account for the position of the Government. The Government has also responded in writing to various questions that had been formulated about this affair. After today's presentation, there will be others by me and the ministers of Foreign Affairs or of Defence, depending on the events and corresponding to what the development of this crisis requires, in accordance with the regulations of this House.

Why would Aznar enter so much detail about his repeated 'appearances' in parliament? The rather obvious answer is in terms of its relevance in relation to the (presupposed) critique of the opposition, the media and others, namely that Aznar, unlike Tony Blair, hardly tried to explain or justify his policies about Iraq, and thus had shown his arrogance in the face of massive public opposition to the war. That is, in order to show that he is *not* arrogant, but democratic, listens to the people and follows (as he says explicitly) the rules of parliament, he emphasizes his repeated compliance with the democratic rules. He need not explicitly say that he is democratic and otherwise respecting of the wishes of parliament, but this passage politically implicates such meanings for a politically knowledgeable audience. At each point of his speech, Aznar carefully measures the possible political implications of what he is saying, emphasizing the points that show that he (or his party) is complying with basic political rules of democracy, as well as with more general social norms and values – and conversely, justifying or de-emphasizing in many ways those elements of his words and his policies that might be interpreted negatively, thereby aiming to avoid or to challenge a bad impression.

Throughout his speeches, Aznar engages in many other forms of positive self-presentation. Let us examine some other examples:

(4) El Gobierno, señorías, desea la paz y está trabajando activamente para asegu-
     rarla.   (p. 11250)

     *The government, Honourable Members, wishes peace and is actively working to real-
     ize it.*

(5) España ha mantenido siempre una actitud constructiva en el conflicto de
     Oriente Medio.   (p. 11253)

     Spain has always maintained an constructive attitude in the Middle East conflict.

(6) Señora presidenta, señorías, soy bien consciente de que lo que esta tarde trata-
     mos en la Cámara es algo que afecta de manera profunda a los sentimientos,
     también a las convicciones y también, por supuesto, además, a la razón. Siento
     el mayor respeto por todas las posiciones que se puedan manifestar en esta
     sesión . . . (Rumores). (. . .) Nadie tiene el monopolio de la razón, como
     nadie tiene el monopolio de los buenos sentimientos. Comprendo que lo que
     tratamos son decisiones difíciles y que ninguno querríamos estar en la
     situación que estamos.

     *Mrs Speaker, Honourable Members, I am well aware of the fact that what we are deal-
     ing with this afternoon in this House profoundly affects our feelings, convictions and of
     course our intelligence. I have the greatest respect for all the positions that might be
     expressed in this session . . . (Noise) (. . .) No one has a monopoly on intelligence, as
     no one also has a monopoly on emotions. I understand that what we are dealing with
     are difficult decisions and that no one would like to be in the situation in which we
     find ourselves.*

These are three different types of self-presentation, namely when the
speaker speaks for his group or organization (here, the government), as in
example 4, when the speaker speaks for his country (example 5), and
when the speaker speaks for himself, as in the last and most significant
example. Whereas the first two kinds of self-praise are typically political,
the last one is personal, and intended to emphasize the good character of
the speaker. In all cases, these forms of self-congratulation are interactionally occasioned, and respond to real or possible criticisms of his
opponents – as they define the political context of Aznar's speech.
Example (5) is the most obvious case, since Aznar and his government
have been widely accused of warmongering, so he needs to emphasize
that he and his government are (of course) in favour of peace – a self-
evident and well-known topos, widely used even to legitimize war and
aggression, and part of the overall strategy of positive self-presentation
and negative other-presentation: *We* are peaceful and merely defending
ourselves, whereas *They* are aggressive and warmongering.

We shall see later that in this and many other passages, however, Aznar always adds that this peace should be peace 'with security'. The second case is more general and responds to the real or possible critique that, by joining the USA in a war against Iraq, Spain may lose its credit with the Arab states. The third form of self-presentation, which may also be described as the first part of a (complex) disclaimer, namely as a form of apparent empathy, is intended to show that he is not the ruthless statesman who disregards the feelings, opinions and reasons of all those who are against the war – namely the vast majority of the Spanish population and all political parties in parliament except his own. Disregarding these feelings and beliefs would not only allow the conclusion that he personally lacks feelings and consideration, but perhaps even more crucially that he is not democratic in not considering the opinions of all those who oppose the war. Indeed, respect is one of the major values both in everyday interaction as well as in politics. It is important that he emphasizes these characteristics, especially in the face of multiple critiques among other politicians, the media and the population at large that his pro-war policy ignores the opinion of the vast majority of the people in Spain. In the last part of example (6), he continues this important section of his speech with a topos of equality, formulated in the form of a repeated negation and parallelism to emphasize its effect. This fragment may also be interpreted as (part of) a standard disclaimer, namely as an apparent concession ('I may be wrong, but . . .'), but given the political context, the interpretation should rather be that Aznar does not accept that the 'good feelings' are only on the side of the opposition. However, in the rest of the sequence, as well as in the speech as a whole, Aznar nevertheless disregards these feelings of 'comprehension' and ask for a 'responsible' (and hence not emotional) support of his policies, so that his positive moves may be interpreted as the first part of a long disclaimer. Indeed, as suggested, in another move of positive self-presentation that also has a function as a legitimization of his policies, Aznar then adds that a 'firm and resolute' response to Saddam Hussein is a 'responsible' policy, because only in this way are the best interests of Spain served:

(7) [La posición] . . . que le corresponde tomar a un gobierno español que atienda a los intereses permanentes de nuestro país. (p. 11254)

[The position] . . . that ought to be taken by a Spanish Government that is concerned about the permanent interests of our country.

(8) Creo sinceramente que hoy estoy cumpliendo lo que reclamé cuando encabezaba la oposición, lo que me comprometí al ser elegido presidente del

Gobierno, lo que creo más razonable y lo que creo que conviene mejor a España y a los españoles.

I sincerely believe that what I am doing what I demanded when I was head of the opposition, and to what I committed myself when I was elected president of the Government, what I think is most reasonable and what I think is best for Spain and the Spaniards.

Note that in these examples, which are the final words of this speech before thanking the president of the Cortes, he interestingly combines various forms of positive self-presentation, such as a eulogy of his government, with an emphasis on personal commitment, reasonableness and sincerity. Politically most relevant, of course, is his claim that the policy of his government is good for the country. Personally and interactionally, however, it is more important that he comes across as credible and honest.

The analysis of these few examples is not merely another illustration of the well-known strategy of positive self-presentation and its functions in political speeches. My point, and the rationale for this chapter, is that the informal analysis of various types of positive self-presentation and facework provided above highlights a series of political implicatures that cannot simply be described in a semantic analysis, but presuppose detailed *contextual* knowledge of the current political situation in Spain and the world (the Iraq crisis) at a more global level, and the communicative and political situation in the Cortes during the speech at the local level. There are many ways and levels to 'understand' this speech, and a politically relevant one is what Aznar's political concerns are, and why each move in his speech also has a very specific function in the political process. These functions, although they are relevant and understood by all knowledgeable participants, are seldom made explicit and are embodied in the political implicatures that participants derive at each point of a political speech.

Negative Other-presentation

In political and other ideologically-based discourse, positive self-presentation is usually combined with *negative other-presentation*, or derogation, following the well-known social psycho-logic of ingroup–outgroup polarization. Thus, in speeches that are intended to justify or legitimize war, derogation of the 'enemy' is of course crucial, as we also have seen in the speeches of Bush, Blair and those who support them. Although first considered and supported as an ally (e.g., against Iran), especially since the occupation of Kuwait, Saddam Hussein was generally portrayed as the West's preferred villain, both in politics and the media (Martín Rojo, 1995). So it is not surprising that in the wake of the sudden interest of Bush and Co in 'rogue states' and 'global terrorism' after the September 11 attacks, Saddam Hussein soon become the Number One rogue, when Osama Bin Laden could not be captured after the attacks. This and related backgrounds and legitimatizations of the war against Iraq of course also play in the discourses of the allies of the USA, namely the UK and Spain, and we may therefore expect extensive derogation of Saddam Hussein also in Aznar's speeches. Moreover, these arguments are strong not only because Hussein was undoubtedly a dictator who had savagely oppressed the people of Iraq but also because these arguments could, as such, hardly be challenged by a leftist opposition that could not agree more. Thus, bashing Saddam is perfectly consistent with a humanitarian, leftist perspective, and therefore strategically an excellent ploy. If the war against Saddam Hussein was not strictly legal, there was at least a good argument for its legitimacy if the argument were purely humanitarian. However, as we know, in order not to break international legal conventions, the threat of weapons of mass destruction had to be alleged as the official motive for the war, and not because Saddam Hussein was a dictator or violating human rights – since that argument would apply to many other countries and dictators.

It is not surprising therefore that Aznar emphasizes the negative characteristics of the enemy, Saddam Hussein, such as in the following passage

(9) El de Sadam es un régimen de terror que no ha dudado en emplear armas de destrucción masiva en las guerras que ha promovido contra sus países vecinos y contra su propio pueblo.

Saddam's is a regime of terror, which has not hesitated to use weapons of mass destruction in the wars that it waged against its neighbours and against his own people.

An analysis of this and other passages is consistent with earlier work on political rhetoric in general and on Saddam Hussein in particular, and will not further detain us. Thus, we find the usual forms of hyperbole, extreme case formulations, and a specific set of lexical items (such as 'terror', 'armas de destrucción masiva') among many other forms of negative person and group characterization. My main point in this chapter is not merely the usual description of political rhetoric and legitimation but a study of some of the *contextual functions* of such strategies in the current political situation and the political process. Why is it *politically* relevant and important *now* to repeat and emphasize that Saddam Hussein is a very bad guy? After all, there is no disagreement about this at all with the opposition or public opinion at large, so there is no particular point for an argument or a form of persuasion here. So, what are the political implicatures of Aznar's current derogation of Saddam Hussein? Let us spell out a few of them:

- If the socialist opposition (mostly the PSOE) does not want to go to war against Saddam Hussein, then they are in fact playing into the hands of Saddam Hussein. Since we all know that he is an appalling dictator, the opposition are nevertheless supporting him, even against the interests of the Iraqi population. This is obviously inconsistent with the humanitarian and social values of the (social-ist) opposition. So, by not supporting the war against Saddam Hussein, and hence our policies, the socialist opposition is betray-ing its own principles, and hence cannot be trusted.
- On the other hand, since Aznar does want to support a coalition that wants to fight such a terrible dictator as Saddam Hussein (because he is a danger for the world and his own people), then Aznar is doing his duty as a responsible prime minister.
- By describing and emphasizing those characteristics of Saddam Hussein as they were highlighted also by the USA, such as the invasion of Kuwait, his earlier breaches of UN resolutions, the alleged weapons of mass destruction and the links with terrorist organizations, Aznar shows the alignment of his government and party with those of a powerful ally. That by itself may be seen as a legitimate policy, but also shows the political 'family resemblance' between Aznar and Bush, as fellow conservative politicians. For the same reason there is much less emphasis on the serious violations of human rights by Saddam Hussein – which would be much more typical for the opposition.
- By emphasizing the danger 'for all of us' of the possibility that the weapons of mass destruction may be used by terrorists, through their alleged links with Saddam Hussein, Aznar shows his legiti-mate concern as responsible leader, and at the same time politically implies that the opposition obviously does not have that concern and hence disregards its social responsibilities.

Of course, several other implicatures may be formulated, but the point is clear that what Aznar says about Saddam Hussein has little to do with his personal or 'real' opinions about the dictator but rather with the overall strategy of legitimating a war against such a tyrant. The political implicatures of such a negative other-presentation of the dictator is thus again a way of positively presenting his own position and policies, and hence those of his party and government, while at the same time disparaging those of the opposition. A detailed, negative description of the horrible violations of human rights by Saddam Hussein would not have satisfied these political functions: they would be inconsistent with the main arguments of the USA, against international rules (that do not allow removal of terrible dictators) and too consistent with the attitudes of the opposition. Indeed, awkward questions may then be asked about the earlier support of Saddam Hussein by the USA, e.g., through the supply of toxic gas and other weapons, when the dictator was their ally against Iran. In other words, negative other-presentations in political discourse are not just a description of a bad guy, but rather a politically relevant selection of, and emphasis on, what are the currently politically relevant 'bad' things that need to be highlighted in discourse. The analysis of political implicatures makes such tacit 'tactical' reasons explicit.

Peace, Security and Terrorism

Aznar's slogan in this debate, as is the case more generally, is *paz y seguridad*, peace and security, a slogan that is repeated in many forms in his speech, as in the following examples.

(10) Primero, el Gobierno está trabajando por restablecer la paz y la seguridad. El interés del Gobierno es obtener una situación de paz con seguridad.

First, the government is working to restore peace and to guarantee security. It is in the interest of the Government to arrive at peace with security.

(11) Desearía que convinieran conmigo en que una postura firme y resolutiva para desarmar a Irak en un plazo inmediato es lo responsable, lo lógico e inteligente para las aspiraciones de paz y seguridad de la comunidad internacional, que también son las de nuestro país.

I wish you could agree with me that a firm and reolute attitude to disarm Iraq in the short term is the most responsible thing to do, the most logical and intelligent and wise for the peace and security aspirations of the international community, which are also those of our country.

The first part of the binomial expression is in line with a major value, and shared by the majority of his opponents, even when these are not exactly pacifists but only oppose *this* war. It is the kind of value, aim and principle that is unassailable. However, it is the combination with the second concept that makes the slogan interesting, and characteristic of his conservative government, also in questions of immigration, and in line with similar slogans in the USA and Europe: security has become the keyword of post-September 11 politics, even in domains that have little to do with terrorism. In many countries, citizens are manipulated into believing that society has become increasingly insecure and are mobilized to support a sometimes draconian curtailment of their civil rights. Terrorist attacks are selectively (and gratefully) focused upon, both in politics and the media, to sustain that continuous fear. That many more citizens die of other avoidable causes that could be combated with much less money and less limitations of freedom is of course not an issue in such belligerent ideologies and policies. Thus, if we read the slogan as it is really intended, *Peace*, **but** *security*, it takes the more transparent form of a well-known disclaimer, that of the Apparent Concession, in which the first part is the part that satisfies the strategy of positive self-presentation ('we want peace', 'we are peaceful'), comparable to the well-known counterpart in racist disclaimers ('we are not racists'). The crucial, second part then becomes the essential condition and the principal aim of the discourse, consistent with the overall strategy of well-known security text and talk of the national security state. No further analysis is needed here on why terrorism serves Bush, his party, the Pentagon budget, the curtailment of civil liberties and especially the businesses involved in war and security. Such analyses have been provided repeatedly by other authors.

Besides the general semantic and political analysis of the disclaimer, relevant for us are the political implicatures of such a slogan: why does it serve Aznar here and how? Again, we witness that the fundamental contextual strategy is one of positive political self-presentation for the public or the voters at large, on the one hand, and the derogation of the opposition, on the other hand. In the same way as Law and Order is the slogan to combat crime and emphasize and implement conservative values, Peace and Security serves to appeal to the fears of people who feel insecure and need a strong government that will primarily satisfy the fundamental needs of security. Aznar, Bush and Blair know that most citizens – no more than they themselves – are not really worried in their daily life about what happens in Iraq or the Middle East, or about weapons of mass destruction, and maybe not even about lack of peace somewhere else in the world. Hence, to legitimate power policies and wars, it is essential to use the vague general concept that does matter for many people: feelings of (in)security. In (10), therefore, the slogan is not just that Aznar and his government want Peace and Security, but are actively engaged in trying to establish it ('*trabajando*'). At the same time, the corollary is the political implicature that if the opposition only wants peace, they are not offering what people want most: security. Thus Aznar is implicitly able to disqualify the leftist opposition as mere pacifists.

These implicatures also function locally – that is, they are relevant in the local political context in Spain – when Aznar indirectly and some-times directly links Iraq and Saddam Hussein with international terror-ism, and international terrorism with local terrorism of ETA. Peace in such a context may be a less appropriate term, but security of course is. In other words, the slogan at the same time functions politically as a way to emphasize the positive role of the conservative government in the fight against ETA, as also several other passages in his speech show:

(12) ... este Gobierno ha querido desempeñar un papel activo en esta crisis internacional pensando en la nueva amenaza que hoy supone el terrorismo, especialmente si tiene a su alcance medios de destrucción masiva.

this government has been willing to fulfil an active role in this international crisis, thinking of the new menace that terrorism constitutes today, especially when it has access to means of mass destruction.

(13) ... el Gobierno entiende que hay un riesgo gravísimo y un vínculo amenazador entre la proliferación de armas de destrucción masiva y el terrorismo. Sé bien que no es agradable precisar estos riesgos, pero sé muy bien que no estamos hablando, señorías, de ninguna fantasía. No son hipóte-sis de ciencia ficción. Hemos visto hace pocos días en Londres y también, por desgracia, en Barcelona que hay grupos terroristas dispuestos a atacar causando el mayor daño y destrucción posibles y que cuentan con sustan-cias que podrían causar centenares, si no miles, de muertos. Después del 11 de septiembre ningún gobernante responsable, ante su conciencia y ante su país, puede ignorar esta realidad.

... the government understands that there is a very grave risk and a menacing link between the proliferation of weapons of mass destruction and terrorism. I know well that it is not pleasant to specify such risks, but I also know that we are not speaking of some fantasy. We have seen, some days ago in London, and unfortunately in Barcelona, that there are terrorist groups that are prepared to attack, causing the most damage and destruction possible, and that share substances that are able to kill hundreds if not thousands of people. After the 11th of September, no responsible leader is able to ignore this reality when facing his own conscience and the country.

(14)   La lucha contra el terrorismo es el principal objetivo, apoyado por las fuerzas
       parlamentarias, de la política exterior española. Hemos impulsado la lucha
       contra el terrorismo y contra la proliferación de armas de destrucción
       masiva en nuestras relaciones bilaterales y en todos los foros internacionales.

       *The struggle against terrorism, supported by the parliamentary forces, is the main
       objective of Spanish international policy. In our bilerateral relations and in all inter-
       national forums, we have insisted on the struggle against terrorism and against the
       proliferation of the weapons of mass destruction.*

(15)   España ha impulsado con toda sus fuerzas estas políticas y vemos con satis-
       facción cómo la lucha contra estas lacras ha escalado posiciones en la agenda
       de la comunidad internacional hasta convertirse en objetivo básico de ésta.
       Sabemos que ello nos ayudará – ya lo está haciendo – en nuestra lucha
       contra el terrorismo de ETA y creemos que es un deber específico de
       España ofrecer su cooperación a otros países señalados por el terrorismo.
       Creo que la pasividad ante estas nuevas amenazas es nuestro mayor peligro.

       *Spain has energetically pushed for these policies and it is with satisfaction that we see
       how the struggle against this blight has risen in the priority of the agenda of the inter-
       national community, until becoming its basic objective. We know that this will help
       us – it already does – in our fight against ETA terrorism and we believe that it is
       Spain's special duty to offer its cooperation to other countries afflicted by terrorism. I
       believe that passivity before these new threats is our biggest danger.*

These examples barely need further contextual and political analysis.
International terrorism has become the main argument for the security
policies of Bush, Aznar and other leaders, especially when associated with
weapons of mass destruction. But although that alone is a sufficient legitimation for them to go to war, Aznar locally needs to do more than that.
So he repeatedly emphasizes the local relevance of this struggle by
constructing a link with local ETA terrorism. Since the public at large as
well as the socialist opposition share the main aims of the struggle against
ETA assassinations, Aznar strategically uses this argument to argue for a
broader, international struggle against terrorism by asserting that this will
also be relevant locally. That international terrorism, and of course Iraq,
has nothing to do with the actions of ETA is of course irrelevant for such
an argument – they simply have the concept of 'terrorism' in common –
a well-known move of amalgamation. Another political implicature is to
accuse the opposition of inconsistency: if you are against ETA terrorism,
you should also actively fight international terrorism. In the last sentence
of (15), he actually makes this implicature somewhat more explicit: the
danger consists in *not* taking action. Interestingly but typically, by the

well-known move of conversion, it is pacifism and not terrorism that is the main problem for Aznar. Note finally, that the topic of terrorism threat is thus becoming a standard argument that needs no further proof, that is a topos, that can be used in any argument, for instance to increase defence spending, engaging in war and to curtail human rights – all in order to enhance security.

When international terrorism finally also hit home, as it did one year later, on 11 March 2004 with the train massacre in Madrid, causing 190 deaths, Aznar seems to get the 'proof' he wants – namely that international terrorism is also locally relevant. Ironically, however, again for the same local reasons mentioned above – the alleged amalgam of international ('Islamist') terrorism and ETA terrorism – Aznar at first wanted to make the media and the public believe that the attacks were perpetrated by ETA, for the obvious reason that this would even more vindicate his aggressive anti-ETA policy and get him votes. However, the public and the media resented such obvious manipulation just two days before the national elections and voted him out of office. Independently of the public response, however, what we can learn about the political implicatures of Aznar's speech of 5 February 2003 is important. Namely, we learn that it is always crucial to sustain international policies with local policies and strategies to get votes and to delegitimate one's political opponents. Hence the link established with ETA and the focus on *national* security, and the feelings of safety of the citizens. Indeed, this is basically the same strategy Bush followed in the USA to legitimate the war against Iraq.

Other Strategies

With these examples of Aznar's political rhetoric we not only have witnessed some of the common properties of political discourse and legitimation, such as the strategy of positive self-presentation and negative other-presentation, but also some principles underlying the contextual interpretation of such discourse in terms of political implicatures. The other global and local strategies of Aznar's speech function in a similar way and may thus be summarized more briefly.

Internationalism

Aznar repeatedly refers to the UN and the international community, first of all in order to legitimate the war and his support for it as beneficial for the whole world – which, in the words of Bush, Blair and Co, will be 'safer without Saddam Hussein' – and secondly to hide that the war in Iraq was precisely not supported by the UN or the Security Council:

(16) El Gobierno ha mantenido desde el comienzo de esta última crisis una postura coherente con la legalidad internacional, la defensa de los intereses de la nación y sus obligaciones internacionales, por este orden.

Since the beginning of this last crisis, the Government has always maintained a coherent position with respect to international legality, the defence of the interests of the nation, and its international duties, in this order,

The political implicatures of this example are quite explicit by Aznar's emphasis that not only his policy is legitimate – and hence the aims of the opposition inconsistent with international 'legality' – but also that the government is *primarily* thinking of the national interest, and hence that international action is actually in the interests of Spanish citizens. This again politically implies that those who oppose that policy are not working in the best interests of Spanish citizens. Indeed, here and elsewhere Aznar actually emphasizes that the opposition is placing itself outside the international consensus – a well-known move of *conversion* when he knows that it is the war policy of Bush and himself that is nearly universally condemned. Hence his support for UN resolutions is mere political lip service. At the same time, emphasizing the interests of the nation is also a counterweight against possible critique, even in his own party, that 'internationalism' may be inconsistent with 'nationalism', on the Right, and the interests of the people, on the Left.

The number game

A well-known ploy of argumentation is the number game which we also know from the rhetoric against immigration. In Aznar's speech, the number game has several functions, such as to convey objectivity and precision, and hence credibility, and specifically to emphasize the truth about Saddam Hussein's non-compliance with international resolutions. The number game is also a rhetorical move of emphasis and hyperbole:

(17) No ha dado cuenta del agente nervioso VX producido y no declarado (Rumores.); no ha explicado el destino de 1.000 toneladas de agentes químicos que conservó tras la guerra con Irán; no ha dado cuenta de 6.500 proyectiles para carga química; no ha demostrado la destrucción de 8.500 litros de ántrax; no ha detenido la producción de misiles con un radio de más de 150 kilómetros: no ha revelado el destino de 380 propulsores de

misiles con agentes químicos que fueron introducidos de contrabando en el país el mes anterior.

> *It [Iraq] has not accounted for the nerve gas VX, produced but not declared (Noise); it has not explained the destination of 1,000 tons of chemical agents that were kept after the war with Iran; it has not accounted for 6,500 chemically loaded projectiles; it has not demonstrated the destruction of 8,500 litres of anthrax: it has not stopped the production of missiles with a range of more than 150 kilometres; it has not revealed the destination of 380 engines for missiles with chemical agents that a month ago were smuggled into the country.*

Obviously, the precise numbers do not matter here – the fact that even weeks after the occupation of Iraq none of this has been found shows that these numbers were largely speculative or relative to innocent chemicals. The political point and implicature of the number game however is its rhetoric of objectivity and credibility – Aznar shows that he is well-informed, that he has done his homework. The opposition in this case has less of a case against him, and cannot use numbers to support its pacifist policy. At the same time, Aznar of course uses these 'facts' as proof about the bad character of Saddam Hussein, which is again one argument in the legitimation of the support of the war. Hence, the number game is an example of a more general type of strategy that may be called 'facticity'. This strategy not only plays a role in argumentation and legitimation, but also in the context of political interaction, namely to signal truth and precision and hence competence and credibility. The facts as such matter little: the political point is to appear credible. The same is true for much media discourse.

Consensus

A well-known political move is that of Consensus, that is asking for or affirming that policies are not partisan but in the national interest, and hence should be supported by the opposition. Thus, Aznar uses this ploy to emphasize the relevance of the unanimity of Resolution 1441 of the UN which is now brought to bear in a request for support for action against Iraq. But as is also the case for immigration policies both in Spain and elsewhere, 'threats' from outside are typically met with a call for national consensus. This also happens here, when Aznar requires national unity in the fight against terrorism. The political implicature of this move is that opposition, and lacking support for government policies, in fact means acting against national interests and against political common sense – thereby discrediting the opposition. A somewhat stronger version of this move is that of Necessity: we have no other way than to honour our international obligations. This is not only a well-known and effective semantic strategy of argumentation and hence a valid form of legitimation, but again also has the political implicature that Aznar is taking his international 'obligations' seriously, and hence is an honourable statesman – whereas the 'pacifist' opposition on the other hand does not do so. There are many other moves in his speech that have similar functions, but the examples given above should suffice as illustrations of the nature of the war rhetoric and legitimation by Aznar in the Iraq crisis, as well as the relevance of the notion of political implicature.

Concluding Remark

Although this chapter cannot possibly do justice to all the structures, moves and strategies of Aznar's speeches in parliament about Iraq, we now have a first glimpse of some of the main characteristics of these speeches. There are few surprises, in the sense that the large majority of the moves and strategies are quite classical in political and ideological text and talk, such as positive self-presentation and negative other-presentation, as well as a number of familiar rhetorical and argumentative ploys, such as the use of statistics/numbers, consensus, internationalism, authorities, comparisons and examples to justify current policy and action.

Theoretically more interesting, however, is the notion of 'political implicature', based on inferences from combined general political knowledge and models of the current political situation. For Spain, this means not only that participants need to share knowledge about the current political situation in Spain as represented in their episodic mental models, but also of the context models that control the very speech of Aznar, including setting, participants, aims and so on. These implicatures are the political 'subtext' of the speeches, and the way he wants his audience to understand him. These political implicatures are also what define the political *functions* of the speech in the political process, and focus especially on Aznar's role as prime minister and party leader, as well as the legitimacy of his government and its international policies. At the same time, the implicatures have the function of derogating and attacking the opposition in the public sphere. It is this *political* analysis of the speech that may be a contribution to the study of the political function of the speech in the political process.

9

Discourse and Manipulation

Introduction

There are a number of crucial notions in Critical Discourse Analysis (CDA) that require special attention because they imply discursive power abuse. Manipulation is one of these notions. Yet, although this notion is often used in a more impressionistic way, there is no systematic theory of the structures and processes involved in manipulation. In this chapter, I examine some of these properties of manipulation, and do so within the 'triangulation' framework that explicitly links discourse, cognition and society (van Dijk, 2001). A discourse analytical approach is warranted because most manipulation, as we understand this notion, takes place through text and talk. Secondly, those being manipulated are human beings, and this typically occurs through the manipulation of their 'minds', so that a cognitive account is also able to shed light on the processes of manipulation. Thirdly, manipulation is a form of talk-in-interaction and, since it implies power and power abuse, a social approach is also important.

I have advocated many times that these approaches cannot be reduced to one or two of them (see, e.g., van Dijk, 1998, 2001). Although social, interactional and discursive approaches are crucial, I aim to show that a cognitive dimension is important as well because manipulation always involves a form of mental manipulation.

In this chapter, I do not deal with the form of 'manipulation' used in physics, computer science, medicine or therapy, among other uses more or less directly derived from the etymological meaning of 'manipulation' as moving things by one's hands. Rather, I deal with 'communicative' or 'symbolic' forms of manipulation as a form of interaction, such as politicians or the media manipulating voters or readers, that is, through some kind of discursive influence.

Conceptual Analysis

Before we embark on a more theoretical account and the analysis of some data, we need to be more explicit about the kind of manipulation we want to study. As suggested, manipulation as intended here is a communicative and interactional practice, in which a manipulator exercises control over other people, usually against their will or against their best interests. In everyday usage, the concept of manipulation has negative associations – manipulation is *bad* – because such a practice violates social norms.

It should therefore be borne in mind in the rest of this chapter that 'manipulation' is a typical observer's category, e.g., of critical analysts, and not necessarily a participant category; few language users would call their own discourse 'manipulative'. As is also the case for racist discourse, this shows that the well-known principle of some forms of ethnomethodology and Conversation Analysis (CA), namely to make explicit members' categories, is not always a useful method in more critical approaches. Indeed, this would make the (critical) study of sexist or racist discursive practices impossible.

Manipulation not only involves power but specifically *abuse* of power, that is, *domination*. More specifically, manipulation implies the exercise of a form of *illegitimate* influence by means of discourse: manipulators make others believe or do things that are in the interests of the manipulator and against the best interests of the manipulated (of the many studies on discourse and legitimation, see, e.g., Chouliaraki, 2005; Martín Rojo and van Dijk, 1997).

In a broader, semiotic sense of manipulation, such illegitimate influence may also be exercised with pictures, photos, movies or other media (van Leeuwen, 2005). Indeed, many forms of contemporary communicative manipulation, e.g., by the mass media, are multimodal, as is typically the case in advertising (Day, 1999; Messaris, 1997).

Without the negative associations, manipulation could be a form of (legitimate) persuasion (see, e.g., Dillard and Pfau, 2002; O'Keefe, 2002). The crucial difference in this case is that in persuasion the interlocutors are free to believe or act as they please, depending on whether or not they accept the arguments of the persuader, whereas in manipulation recipients are typically assigned a more passive role: they are *victims* of manipulation. This negative consequence of manipulative discourse typically occurs when the recipients are unable to understand the real intentions or to see the full consequences of the beliefs or actions advocated by the manipulator. This may be the case especially when the recipients lack the specific knowledge that might be used to resist manipulation (Wodak, 1987). A well-known example is governmental and/or media discourse about immigration and immigrants, so that ordinary citizens blame the bad state of the economy, such as unemployment, on immigrants and not on government policies (van Dijk, 1993a).

Obviously, the boundary between (illegitimate) manipulation and (legitimate) persuasion is fuzzy and context-dependent: some recipients may be manipulated by a message that is unable to manipulate others. Also the same recipients may be more or less manipulable in different circumstances, states of mind, and so on. Many forms of commercial, political or religious persuasion may formally be ethically legitimate but people may still feel manipulated by it, or critical analysts may judge such communication to be manipulating people. Provisionally, then, I shall assume that the crucial criteria are that people are being acted upon against their fully conscious will and interests, and that manipulation is in the best interests of the manipulator.

In the following theoretical account of discursive manipulation, I follow the overall multidisciplinary framework I have advocated in the last decade, triangulating a social, cognitive and discursive approach (see, e.g., van Dijk, 1998, 2001). That is, manipulation is a social phenomenon – especially because it involves interaction and power abuse between groups and social actors – a cognitive phenomenon because manipulation always implies the manipulation of the minds of participants, and a discursive–semiotic phenomenon because manipulation is being exercised through text, talk and visual messages. As claimed earlier, none of these approaches can be reduced to the other and all three of them are needed in an integrated theory that also establishes explicit links between the different dimensions of manipulation.

Manipulation and Society

To understand and analyse manipulative discourse, it is crucial to first examine its social environment. We have already assumed that one of the characteristics of manipulation, for instance as distinct from persuasion, is that it involves power and domination. An analysis of this power dimension involves an account of the kind of control that some social actors or groups exercise over others (Clegg, 1975; Luke, 1989; Wartenberg, 1990; see also Chapter 2). We also have assumed that such control is first of all a control of the mind, that is, of the beliefs of recipients, and indirectly a control of the actions of recipients based on such manipulated beliefs.

In order to be able to exercise such social control of others, however, social actors need to satisfy personal and social criteria that enable them to influence others in the first place. In this chapter, I limit my analysis to social criteria and ignore the influence of psychological factors, such as character traits, intelligence, learning, etc. In other words, I am not interested here in what might be a 'manipulating personality', or in the specific personal way by which people manipulate others.

Social conditions of manipulative control hence need to be formulated — at least at the macro level of analysis — in terms of group membership, institutional position, profession, material or symbolic resources and other factors that define the power of groups and their members. Thus, parents can manipulate their children because of their position of power and authority in the family, professors can manipulate their students because of their institutional position or profession and because of their knowledge, and the same is true for politicians manipulating voters, journalists manipulating the recipients of media discourse or religious leaders manipulating their followers. This does not mean that children cannot manipulate their parents, or students their teachers, but this is not because of their position of power, but as a form of opposition or dissent, or ad hoc, on the basis of personal characteristics.

Thus, the kind of social manipulation we are studying here is defined in terms of social domination and its reproduction in everyday practices, including discourse. In this sense, we are more interested in manipulation between groups and their members than in the personal manipulation of individual social actors.

A further analysis of domination, defined as power abuse, requires special access to, or control over, scarce social resources. One of these resources is preferential access to the mass media and public discourse, a resource shared by members of 'symbolic' elites, such as politicians, journalists, scholars, writers, teachers, and so on (see Chapter 3). Obviously, in order to be able to manipulate many others through text and talk, one needs to have access to some form of public discourse, such as parliamentary debates, news, opinion articles, textbooks, scientific articles, novels, TV shows, advertising, the internet, and so on. And since such access and control in turn depend on, as well as constitute, the power of a group (institution, profession, etc.), public discourse is at the same time a means of the social reproduction of such power. For instance, politicians can also exercise their political power through public discourse, and through such public discourse they at the same time confirm and reproduce their political power. The same is true for journalists and professors and their respective institutions — the media, the universities, etc.

We see that manipulation is one of the discursive social practices of dominant groups geared towards the reproduction of their power. Such dominant groups may do so in many (other) ways as well, e.g., through persuasion, providing information, education, instruction and other social practices that are aimed at influencing the knowledge, beliefs and (indirectly) the actions of the recipients.

We have seen that some of these social practices may of course be quite legitimate, e.g., when journalists or teachers provide information for their audiences. This means that manipulation, also in accordance with what has been said before about its negative characteristics, is characterized as an illegitimate social practice because it violates general social rules or norms. We define as illegitimate all forms of interaction, communication or other social practices that are only in the interests of one party, and against the best interests of the recipients.

We here touch upon the very social, legal and philosophical foundations of a just or democratic society, and of the ethical principles of discourse, interaction and communication (see, e.g., Habermas, 1984). A further discussion of these principles, and hence an explanation of why manipulation is illegitimate, is outside the scope of this article. We assume that manipulation is illegitimate because it violates the human or social rights of those who are manipulated but it is not easy to formulate the exact norms or values that are violated here.

One might venture as a norm that recipients are always duly informed about the goals or intentions of the speaker. However, this would be much too strict a criterion because in many forms of communication and interaction such intentions and goals are not made explicit but contextually attributed to speakers by recipients (or analysts) on the basis of general rules of discourse and interaction. Indeed, one might even postulate a social egoism principle, saying that (nearly) all forms of interaction or discourse tend to be in the best interests of the speakers. This means that the criteria of legitimacy must be formulated in other terms, as suggested, namely that manipulation is illegitimate because it violates the rights of recipients. This need not imply the norm that all forms of communication should be in the best interests of the recipients. Many types of communication or speech act are not, as is the case for accusations, requests, commands, and so on.

A more pragmatic approach to such norms and principles are the conversational maxims formulated by Grice (1975) which require contributions to conversations to be truthful, relevant, relatively complete, and so on. In actual forms of talk and text, however, such maxims are often hard to apply: People lie, which may not always be the wrong thing to do; people tell only half of a story for all kinds of, sometimes legitimate, reasons and irrelevant talk is one of the most common forms of every-day interaction.

In other words, manipulation is not (only) 'wrong' because it violates conversational maxims or other norms and rules of conversation, although this may be one dimension of manipulative talk and text. We therefore will accept without further analysis that *manipulation is illegitimate in a democratic society, because it reproduces, or may reproduce, inequality*: it is in the best interests of powerful groups and speakers, and hurts the interests of less powerful groups and speakers. This means that the definition is not based on the intentions of the manipulators, nor on the more or less conscious awareness of manipulation by the recipients, but in terms of its societal consequences (see also Etzioni-Halevy, 1989).

For each communicative event, it then needs to be spelled out how such respective interests are managed by manipulative discourse. For instance, if the mass media provide incomplete or otherwise biased information about a specific politician during an election campaign so as to influence the votes of the readers, we would have a case of manipulation if we further assume that the readers have a right to be 'duly' informed about the candidates in an election. 'Due' information in this case may then further be specified as balanced, relatively complete, unbiased, relevant, and so on. This does not mean that a newspaper may not support or favour its own candidate, but it should do so with arguments, facts, etc., that is through adequate information and persuasion, and not through manipulation, for instance by omitting very important information, by lying or distorting the facts, and so on. All these normative principles, as they are also laid down in the professional codes of ethics of journalism, are part of the specific implementation of what counts as 'legitimate' forms of interaction and communication. Each of them, however, is quite vague, and in need of detailed further analysis. Again, as suggested earlier, the issues involved here belong to the *ethics of discourse*, and hence are part of the *foundations* of CDA.

This informal analysis of the social properties of manipulation also shows that if manipulation is a form of domination or power abuse, it needs to be defined in terms of *social groups, institutions* or *organizations*, and not at the individual level of personal interaction. This means that it only makes sense to speak of manipulation, as defined, when speakers or writers are manipulating others in their role as a member of a dominant collectivity. In contemporary information societies, this is especially the case for the symbolic elites in politics, the media, education, scholarship, the bureaucracy, as well as in business enterprises, on the one hand, and their various kinds of 'clients' (voters, readers, students, customers, the general public, etc.) on the other. Thus, manipulation, socially speaking, is a discursive form of elite power reproduction that is against the best interests of dominated groups and (re)produces social inequality.

Obviously, this formulation is in terms of traditional macro-level categories, such as the power of groups, organizations and institutions. Especially relevant for discourse analysis is of course also the more local-situated micro-level of social structure, that of *interaction*. Manipulation is also very fundamentally a form of social practice and interaction, and we shall therefore pay more attention to those local forms of manipulation when we discuss discursive manipulation later in this chapter.

Manipulation and Cognition

Manipulating people involves manipulating their minds, that is, people's beliefs, such as the knowledge, opinions and ideologies which in turn control their actions. We have seen, however, that there are many forms of discourse-based mental influence, such as informing, teaching and persuasion, that also shape or change people's knowledge and opinions. This means that manipulation needs to be distinguished from these other forms of mind management, as we have done earlier in social terms, that is, in terms of the context of discourse. In order to be able to distinguish between legitimate and illegitimate mind control, we first need to be more explicit about how discourse can 'affect' the mind in the first place.

Since the mind is extraordinarily complex, the way discourse may influence it inevitably involves intricate processes that can only be managed in real time by applying efficient strategies. For our purposes in this chapter, such an account will be simplified to a few basic principles and categories of cognitive analysis. There are a vast number of cognitive (laboratory) studies that show how understanding can be influenced by various contextual or textual 'manipulations', but it is beyond the scope of this chapter to review these (for general accounts of discourse processing, see Britton and Graesser, 1996; Kintsch, 1998; van Dijk and Kintsch, 1983; Van Oostendorp and Goldman, 1999).

Manipulating short-term memory (STM)-based discourse understanding

First of all, discourse in general, and manipulative discourse in particular, involves processing information in short-term memory (STM), basically resulting in 'understanding' (of words, clauses, sentences, utterances and non-verbal signals), for instance in terms of propositional 'meanings' or 'actions'. Such processing is strategic in the sense of being on-line, goal-directed, operating at various levels of discourse structure and hypothetical: fast and efficient guesses and shortcuts are made instead of complete analyses.

One form of manipulation consists of controlling some of this, partly automatized, strategy of discourse understanding. For instance, by printing part of the text in a salient position (e.g., on top), and in larger or bold fonts; these devices will attract more attention, and hence will be processed with extra time or memory resources, as is the case for headlines, titles or publicity slogans – thus contributing to more detailed processing and to better representation and recall. Headlines and titles also function as the conventional text category for the expression of semantic macro structures, or topics, which organize local semantic structures; for this reason, such topics are better represented and recalled. Our point here is that specific features of text and talk – such as its visual representation – may specifically affect the management of strategic understanding in STM, so that readers pay more attention to some pieces of information than others.

Of course, this occurs not only in manipulation but also in legitimate forms of communication, such as news reports, textbooks and a host of other genres. *This suggests that, cognitively speaking, manipulation is nothing special: it makes use of very general properties of discourse processing.* So, as was the case for the social analysis of manipulation, we need further criteria that distinguish between legitimate and illegitimate influence on the processing of discourse. Manipulation in such a case may reside in the fact that by drawing attention to information A rather than B, the resulting understanding may be partial or biased, for instance when headlines emphasize irrelevant details rather than expressing the most important topics of a discourse – thus impairing understanding of details through top-down influence of topics. The further social condition that should be added in this case, as we have done earlier, is that such partial or incomplete understanding is in the best interests of a powerful group or institution, and against the best interests of a dominated group. Obviously, this is not a cognitive or textual condition but a normative social and contextual one: the rights of recipients to be adequately informed. Our cognitive analysis merely spells out how people are manipulated by controlling their minds, but cannot formulate why this is *wrong*. Similar processes are at play with many forms of non-verbal expressions, such as general layout, use of colour, photos, or drawings in written conversation, or gestures, facework and other non-verbal activity in oral discourse.

Since discourse processing in STM involves such different forms of analysis as phonetic, phonological, morphological, syntactic and lexical operations, all geared towards efficient understanding, each and any of these processes of STM may be influenced by various means. For instance, more distinct, slower pronunciation, less complex syntax and the use of basic lexical items, a clear topic on a subject the recipients know well, among many other conditions, will generally tend to favour understanding.

This also means that if speakers wish to hamper understanding, they will tend to do the opposite, that is, speak faster, less distinctly, with more complex sentences, with more abstruse words, a confused topic on a subject less familiar to the recipients – as may be the case, for instance, in legal or medical discourse that is not primarily geared towards better understanding by clients, and hence may assume manipulative forms when understanding is intentionally impaired.

In other words, if dominant groups or institutions want to facilitate the understanding of the information that is consistent with their interests, and hinder the comprehension of the information that is not in their best interests (and vice versa for their recipients), then they may typically engage in these forms of STM-based manipulation of discourse understanding. We see that cognitive, social, discursive and ethical dimensions are involved in this case of illegitimate hindering or biasing of the process of discourse comprehension. The ethical dimension also may involve the further (cognitive) criterion whether such control of comprehension is *intentional* or not – as is the case for the distinction between murder and manslaughter. This means that in the context models of the speakers or writers there is an explicit plan to impair or bias understanding.

Episodic manipulation

STM-based manipulation takes place on-line and affects strategic processes of the understanding of specific discourses. However, most manipulation is geared to more stable results, and hence focuses on long-term memory (LTM), that is, knowledge, attitudes and ideologies, as we shall see in a moment. Also forming part of LTM, however, are the personal memories that define our life history and experiences (Neisser and Fivush, 1994), representations that are traditionally associated with 'episodic' memory (Tulving, 1983). That is, our memory of communicative events – which are among our everyday experiences – is stored in episodic memory, namely as specific mental models with their own schematic structures. Telling a story means formulating the personal, subjective mental model we have of some experience. And understanding a news report or a story involves the construction of such a (subjective) mental model by the recipients.

In episodic memory, the understanding of situated text and talk is thus related to more complete models of experiences. Understanding is not merely associating meanings with words, sentences or discourses but constructing mental models in episodic memory, including our own personal opinions and emotions associated with an event we hear or read about. It is this mental model that is the basis of our future memories, as well as the basis of further learning, such as the acquisition of experience-based knowledge, attitudes and ideologies.

Note that mental models are unique, ad hoc and personal: it is *my* individual interpretation of this particular discourse in this specific situation. Of course, such personal models also involve the 'instantiation' of general, socially shared knowledge or beliefs − so that we can actually understand other people and communication and interaction are possible in the first place − but the mental model as a whole is unique and personal. There are other notions of (mental, cognitive) models that are used to represent socially shared, cultural knowledge (see, e.g., Shore 1996), but that is not the kind of model I am referring to here.

Mental models not only define our understanding of talk and text itself (by representing what a discourse is about) but also the understanding of the whole communicative event. Such understandings are represented in 'context models' which at the same time, for the speakers, operate as their − dynamically changing − plans for speaking (van Dijk, 1999).

Given the fundamental role of mental models in speaking and understanding, manipulation may be expected to especially target the formation, activation and uses of mental models in episodic memory. If manipulators are aiming for recipients to understand a discourse as *they* see it, it is crucial that the recipients form the mental models the manipulators want them to form, thus restricting their freedom of interpretation or at least the probability that they will understand the discourse against the best interests of the manipulators.

We shall later examine some of the discourse strategies that are geared in this way towards the formation or activation of 'preferred' models. More generally, the strategy is to discursively emphasize those properties of models that are consistent with our interests (e.g., details of our good deeds), and discursively de-emphasize those properties that are inconsistent with our interests (e.g., details of our bad deeds). Blaming the victim is one of the forms of manipulation in which dominant groups or institutions discursively influence the mental models of recipients, for instance by the re-attribution of responsibility of actions in their own interests. Any discursive strategy that may contribute to the formation or reactivation of preferred models may thus be used in manipulative discourse use. As is the case for STM processing, much model formation and activation tends to be automatized, and subtle control of mental models is often not even noticed by language users, thus contributing to manipulation.

Manipulating social cognition

Discursively manipulating how recipients understand one event, action or discourse is at times quite important, especially for such monumental events as the attack on the World Trade Center in New York on 11 September 2001, or the bomb attack on Spanish commuter trains on 11 March 2004. Indeed, in the latter case, the conservative Spanish government led by José María Aznar tried to manipulate the press and citizens into believing that the attack was committed by ETA instead of by Islamist terrorists. In other words, through his declarations as well as those of his Minister of the Interior, Acebes, Aznar wanted to influence the structure of the mental model of the event by emphasizing the preferred agent of the attack – a model that would be consistent with the government's own anti-ETA policies. Since it soon became clear that this time it was not ETA but Al-Qaida that was responsible for the attack, the voters in the upcoming elections felt manipulated and voted Aznar and the government of the Partido Popular out of office.

Although these and similar events, as well as the many discourses accompanying, describing and explaining them, give rise to mental models that may have a special place in episodic memory so that they are well recalled even much later, the most influential form of manipulation does not focus on the creation of specific preferred mental models but on more general and abstract beliefs such as knowledge, attitudes and ideologies. Thus, if a political party wants to increase its popularity with the voters, it will typically try to positively change voters' attitudes towards such a party, because a general, socially shared attitude is far more stable than the specific mental models (and opinions) of individual language users. Influencing attitudes implies influencing whole groups, and on many occasions. Thus, if governments want to restrict immigration, they will try to form or modify the attitudes of citizens (including other elites) about immigration (van Dijk, 1993a; Wodak and Van Dijk, 2000). In this case, they need not engage in multiple persuasion attempts every time immigrants want to enter the country. Manipulation thus focuses on the formation or modification of more general, socially shared representations – such as attitudes or ideologies – about important social issues. For instance, governments may do so for the issue of immigration by associating increased immigration with (fears of) increasing delinquency, as former Prime Minister Aznar – as well as other European leaders – did in the past decade.

We see that the cognitive processes of manipulation assume that LTM not only stores subjectively interpreted personal experiences as mental models, but also more stable, more permanent, general and socially shared beliefs, sometimes called 'social representations' (Augoustinos and Walker, 1995; Moscovici, 2001). Our sociocultural knowledge forms the core of these beliefs and allows us to meaningfully act, interact and communicate with other members of the same culture. The same is true for the many social attitudes and ideologies shared with other members of the same social group, e.g., pacifists, socialists, feminists, on the one hand, or racists and male chauvinists, on the other (van Dijk, 1999). These social representations are gradually acquired throughout our lifetime and, although they can be changed, they do not typically change overnight. They also influence the formation and activation of the personal mental models of group members. For instance, a pacifist will interpret events such as the US-led attack on Iraq, or news reports about them, in a different way from a militarist, and hence form a different mental model of such an event or sequence of events.

We have assumed that mental models on the one hand embody the personal history, experiences and opinions of individual persons, but on the other hand also feature a specific instantiation of socially shared beliefs. Most interaction and discourse is thus produced and understood in terms of mental models that combine personal and social beliefs – in a way that *both* explains the uniqueness of all discourse production and understanding, *and* the similarity of our understanding of the same text. Despite the general constraints of social representations on the formation of mental models and hence on discourse production and understanding, no two members of the same social group, class or institution, not even in the same communicative situation, will produce the same discourse or interpret a given discourse in the same way. In other words, mental models of events or communicative situations (context models) are the necessary interface between the social, the shared and the general, as well as the personal, the unique and the specific in discourse and communication.

Whereas manipulation may concretely affect the formation or change of unique personal mental models, the general goals of manipulative discourse are the control of the shared social representations of groups of people because these social beliefs in turn control what people do and say in many situations and over a relatively long period. Once people's attitudes are influenced, for instance on terrorism, little or no further manipulation attempts may be necessary in order for people to act according to these attitudes, for instance to vote in favour of anti-terrorism policies (Chomsky, 2003; Sidel, 2004).

It comes as no surprise that, given the vital importance of social representations for interaction and discourse, manipulation will generally focus on social cognition, and hence on groups of people rather than on individuals and their unique personal models. It is also in this sense that manipulation is a discursive practice that involves both cognitive and social dimensions. We should therefore pay special attention to those discourse strategies that typically influence socially shared beliefs.

One of these strategies is generalization, in which case a concrete specific example that has made an impact on people's mental models is generalized to more general knowledge or attitudes, or even fundamental ideologies. The most striking recent example is the manipulation of US and world opinion about terrorism after 9/11, in which very emotional and strongly opinionated mental models held by citizens about this event were generalized to more general, shared fears, attitudes and ideologies about terrorism and related issues. This is also a genuine example of massive manipulation because the resulting social representations are not in the best interests of the citizens when such attitudes are being manipulated in order to dramatically raise military spending, legitimate military intervention and pass legislation that imposes severe restrictions on civil rights and freedoms (such as the Patriot Act). Manipulation in this case is an abuse of power because citizens are manipulated into believing that such measures are taken in order to protect them (of the many books on manipulating public opinion after the September 11 attacks in the USA, see, e.g., Ahmed, 2005; Chomsky, 2003; Greenberg, 2002; Halliday, 2002; Palmer, 2003; Sidel, 2004; Žižek, 2002).

This notorious example of national and international manipulation by the US government, partly supported and carried out by the mass media, also shows some of the cognitive mechanisms of manipulation. Thus, first of all a very emotional event with a strong impact on people's mental models is being used in order to influence these mental models as desired – for instance in terms of a strong polarization between Us (good, innocent) and Them (evil, guilty). Secondly, through repeated messages and the exploitation of related events (e.g., other terrorist attacks), such a preferred model may be generalized to a more complex and stable social representation about terrorist attacks, or even an anti-terrorist ideology.

Of importance in such a case is that the (real) interests and benefits of those in control of the manipulation process are hidden, obscured or denied, whereas the alleged benefits for 'all of us', for the 'nation', etc. are emphasized, for instance in terms of increased feelings of safety and security. That through anti-terrorist actions and military intervention not only the military and business corporations who produce arms and security outfits may profit, but more terrorism may actually be promoted, and hence security of the citizens further endangered, is obviously not part of the preferred attitudes that are the goals of such manipulation. Thus, one crucial cognitive condition of manipulation is that the targets (persons, groups, etc.) of manipulation are made to believe that some actions or policies are in their own interests, whereas in fact they are in the interests of the manipulators and their associates.

The examples of immigration, political violence and anti-terrorist ideologies involve strong opinions, attitudes and ideologies, and are textbook examples of governments and media manipulating the population at large, as they also were manipulated, for instance, during the 'Red scare' of anti-communist ideologies and manipulation in the Cold War and McCarthyism in the USA (Caute, 1978).

However, manipulation of social cognition may also involve the very basis of all social cognition: general, socioculturally shared *knowledge*. Indeed, one of the best ways to detect and resist manipulation attempts is specific knowledge (e.g., about the current interests of the manipulators) as well as general knowledge (e.g., about the strategies of maintaining the military budget at a high level). It will thus be in the best interests of dominant groups to make sure that relevant and potentially critical general knowledge is *not* acquired, or that only partial, misguided or biased knowledge is allowed distribution.

A well-known example of the latter strategy was the claim with which the US and its allies legitimated the attack on Iraq in 2003: 'knowledge' about weapons of mass destruction, knowledge that later turned out to be false. Information that may lead to knowledge that may be used critically to resist manipulation, for instance about the real costs of the war, the number of deaths, the nature of the 'collateral damage' (e.g., civilians killed in massive bombing and other military action), and so on, will typically be hidden, limited or otherwise made less risky, and hence discursively de-emphasized, for instance by euphemisms, vague expressions, implicitness, and so on.

Manipulation may affect social representations in many ways, both as to their contents as well as to their structures. Although as yet we know little about the internal organization of social representations, they are likely to feature schematic categories for participants and their properties as well as the typical (inter)actions they (are thought to) perform, how, when and where. Thus, attitudes about terrorist attacks may feature a script-like structure, with terrorists as main actors, associated with a number of prototypical attributes (cruel, radical, fundamentalist, etc.), using violent means (e.g., bombs) to kill innocent civilians, and so on.

Such attitudes are gradually acquired by generalization and abstraction from mental models formed by specific news stories, government declarations as well as films, among other discourses. It is important in this case that 'our' forms of political violence, such as military intervention or the actions of the police, are spoken and written about in such a way that they do not give rise to mental models that can be generalized as terrorist attacks, but as a legitimate form of (armed) resistance or punishment. And, vice versa, terrorist attacks need to be represented in such a way that no legitimation of such political violence may be construed in mental models and attitudes. The very notion of 'state terrorism' for this reason is controversial and used largely by dissidents, while blurring the distinction between illegitimate terrorist action and legitimate government and military action (Gareau, 2004). Mainstream media therefore consequently avoid describing state violence in terms of 'terrorism', not even when they are critical of the foreign policy of a country, as was the case for many European media in regard to the US attack against Iraq in 2003.

Finally, the manipulation of social cognition may affect the very norms and values used to evaluate events and people and to condemn or legitimate actions. For instance, in the manipulation of globalized world opinion, those who advocate neoliberal market ideologies will typically emphasize and try to get adopted the primary value of 'freedom', a very positive value, but in such a case specifically interpreted as the freedom of enterprise, the freedom of the market, or the freedom from government interference with the market. In the case of terrorist threats and actions, anti-terrorist discourse celebrates the value of security, assigning it a higher priority than, for instance, the value of civil rights, or the value of equality (Doherty and McClintock, 2002).

We see how the cognitive dimension of manipulation involves strategic understanding processes that affect processing in STM, the formation of preferred mental models in episodic memory, and finally and most fundamentally the formation or change of social representations, such as knowledge, attitudes, ideologies, norms and values. Groups of people who thus adopt the social representations preferred by dominant groups or institutions henceforth barely need further manipulation: they will tend to believe and act in accordance with these – manipulated – social cognitions anyway, because they have accepted them as their own. Thus, as we have seen, racist or xenophobic ideologies, manipulated in this way by the elites, will serve as a permanent basis for the discrimination (such as blaming the victim) of immigrants: a very effective strategy for steering critical attention away from the policies of the government or other elites (van Dijk, 1993a).

Discourse

Manipulation as defined here takes place through discourse in a broad sense, that is, including non-verbal characteristics, such as gestures, face-work, text layout, pictures, sounds, music, and so on. Note though that, as such, discourse structures are not manipulative; they only have such functions or effects in specific communicative situations and the way in which these are interpreted by participants in their context models. For instance, as stipulated, manipulation is a social practice of power abuse, involving dominant and dominated groups, or institutions and their clients. This means that in principle the 'same' discourse (or discourse fragment) may be manipulative in one situation, but not in another situation. That is, the manipulative meaning (or critical evaluation) of text and talk depends on the context models of the recipients – including their models of the speakers or writers and their attributed goals and intentions. Manipulative discourse typically occurs in public communication controlled by dominant political, bureaucratic, media, academic or corporate elites. This means that further contextual constraints prevail, namely on participants, their roles, their relations and their typical actions and cognitions (knowledge, goals). In other words, *discourse is defined to be manipulative first of all in terms of the context models of the participants.* That is, as critical analysts, we evaluate discourse as manipulative first of all in terms of their context categories, rather than in terms of their textual structures.

And yet, although discourse structures per se need not be manipulative, some of these structures may be more efficient than others in the process of influencing the minds of recipients in the speaker's or writer's own interests. For instance, as suggested earlier, headlines are typically used to express topics and to signal the most important information of a text, and may thus be used to assign (extra) weight to events that in themselves would not be so important. And, vice versa, discourse about events or states of affairs that are very relevant for citizens or clients may eschew headlines that emphasize the negative characteristics of dominant groups and institutions. To wit, the press never publish stories about racism, let alone emphasize such information by prominent headlines on the front page (van Dijk, 1991).

The overall strategy of positive self-presentation and negative other-presentation is very typical in this biased account of the facts in favour of the speaker's or writer's own interests, while blaming negative situations and events on opponents or on the Others (immigrants, terrorists, youths, etc.). This strategy can be applied to the structures of many discourse levels in the usual way (for examples and detail, see, e.g., van Dijk, 2003a):

- *Overall interaction strategies*
  - Positive self-presentation
  - Negative other-presentation
- *Macro speech act implying Our 'good' acts and Their 'bad' acts, e.g., accusation, defence*
- *Semantic macrostructures: topic selection*
  - (De-)emphasize negative/positive topics about Us/Them.
- *Local speech acts implementing and sustaining the global ones, e.g., statements that prove accusations*
- *Local meanings Our/Their positive/negative actions*
  - Give many/few details
  - Be general/specific
  - Be vague/precise
  - Be explicit/implicit
  etc.
- *Lexicon: Select positive words for Us, negative words for Them*
- *Local syntax*
  - Active vs. passive sentences, nominalizations: (de)emphasize Our/Their positive/negative agency, responsibility
- *Rhetorical figures*
  - Hyperboles vs. euphemisms for positive/negative meanings
  - Metonymies and metaphors emphasizing Our/Their positive/negative properties
- *Expressions: sounds and visuals*
  - Emphasize (loud, etc.; large, bold, etc.) positive/negative meanings
  - Order (first, last: top, bottom, etc.) positive/negative meanings

These strategies and moves at various levels of discourse are hardly surprising because they implement the usual ideological square of discursive group polarization (de-emphasize good/bad things of Us/Them) one finds in all ideological discourse (van Dijk, 1998a, 2003a). Since sociopolitical manipulation as discussed here also involves domination (power abuse), it is likely that such manipulation is also ideological. Thus, in the manipulative discourses that followed the September 11 and March 11 terrorist attacks in New York and Madrid, nationalist, anti-terrorist, anti-Islam, anti-Arab and racist ideologies were rife, emphasizing the evil nature of terrorists and the freedom and democratic principles of the 'civilized' nations. Thus, if Bush and Co. want to manipulate the politicians and/or the citizens in the USA into accepting going to war in Iraq, engaging in worldwide actions against terrorists and their protectors (beginning with Afghanistan) and adopting a bill that severely limits the civil rights of the citizens, such discourse would be massively ideological. That is, they do this by emphasizing 'Our' fundamental values (freedom, democracy, etc.) and contrasting these with the 'evil' ones attributed to Others. They thus make the citizens, traumatized by the attack on the Twin Towers, believe that the country is under attack, and that only a 'war on terrorism' can avert a catastrophe. And those who do not accept such an argument may thus be accused of being unpatriotic.

Much more detailed analyses of these discourses have shown that they are fundamentally ideological in this way, and it is likely that socio-political manipulation always involves ideologies, ideological attitudes and ideological discourse structures (see the special double issue of *Discourse & Society* 15 (3–4), 2004, on the discourses of September 11, edited by Jim Martin and John Edwards). If many Western European leaders, including former Prime Minister Aznar, and more recently also Tony Blair, want to limit immigration so as to increase support from the voters, then such manipulative policies and discourses are also very ideological, involving nationalist feelings, Us/Them polarization and a systematic negative representation of the Others in terms of negative values, characteristics and actions (delinquency, illegal entry, violence, etc.).

Although sociopolitical manipulation is usually ideological, and manipulative discourses often feature the usual ideological polarization patterns at all levels of analysis, the discursive structures and strategies of manipulation cannot simply be reduced to those of any other ideological discourse. Indeed, we may have sociopolitical discourses that are persuasive but not manipulative, such as persuasive parliamentary debates or a discussion in a newspaper or on television. That is, given our analysis of the social and cognitive contexts of manipulative discourse, we need to examine the specific constraints formulated earlier, such as the dominant position of the manipulator (for instance), the lack of relevant knowledge of the recipients and the condition that the likely consequences of the acts of manipulation are in the interest of the dominant group and against the best interests of the dominated group, thus contributing to (illegitimate) social inequality.

As suggested earlier, it is not likely that there are discursive strategies that are only used in manipulation. Language is seldom that specific – it is used in many different situations and by many different people, also by people of different ideological persuasions. That is, the same discourse structures are used in persuasion, information, education and other legitimate forms of communication, as well as in various forms of dissent.

However, given the specific social situation, there may be distinctive strategies preferred in manipulation, that is, 'manipulative prototypes'. Specific kinds of fallacies might be used to persuade people to believe or do something, for instance those that are hard to resist, such as the Authority fallacy consisting of presenting devote Catholics with the argument that the Pope believes or recommends a certain action, or addressing Muslims and pointing out that a certain action is recommended by the Koran.

We thus introduce a contextual criterion that recipients of manipulation – as a form of power abuse – may be defined as victims, and this means that somehow they need to be defined as lacking crucial resources to resist, detect or avoid manipulation. Crucially, this may involve:

(a) incomplete or lack of relevant knowledge – so that no counterarguments can be formulated against false, incomplete or biased assertions;
(b) fundamental norms, values and ideologies that cannot be denied or ignored;
(c) strong emotions, traumas, etc. that make people vulnerable;
(d) social positions, professions, status, etc. that induce people into tending to accept the discourses, arguments, etc. of elite persons, groups or organizations.

These are typical conditions of the cognitive, emotional or social situation of the communicative event, and also part of the context models of the participants, i.e., controlling their interactions and discourses. For instance, if recipients of manipulative discourse feel afraid of a speaker, then this will be represented in their context models, and the same is true for their relative position and the power relation between them and the speaker. Conversely, in order for manipulation to be successful, speakers need to have a mental model of the recipients and their (lack of) knowledge, their ideologies, emotions, earlier experiences, and so on.

Obviously, it is not necessary for all recipients to have the ideal properties of the target of manipulation. It may be sufficient that a large group
or a majority has such properties. Thus, in most real-life situations there
will be critical, sceptical, cynical, incredulous or dissident people who are
impervious to manipulation. But as long as these people do not dominate the mainstream means of communication, or the elite institutions
and organizations, the problem of counter-discourses is less serious for
the manipulators.

Again, the most typical recent example has been the US-led war
against Iraq, in which the majority of the mainstream media supported
the government and congress, and critical voices were effectively marginalized, especially in the USA.

As soon as such dissident voices become more powerful (for instance,
when part of the mainstream media supports them) and more widespread, as was the case during the war against Vietnam, manipulation
functions less efficiently and finally may become useless because citizens
have enough counter-information and arguments to resist manipulative
discourse. Indeed, as was the case after the terrorist bomb attack in
Madrid, citizens may resent manipulation so much that they will turn
against the manipulators – and vote them out of office.

Given these contextual constraints, we may focus on those discourse
structures that specifically presuppose such constraints:

(a) emphasize the position, power, authority or moral superiority of
     the speaker(s) or their sources – and, where relevant, the inferior
     position, lack of knowledge, etc. of the recipients;
(b) focus on the (new) beliefs that the manipulator wants the recipi-
     ents to accept as knowledge, as well as on the arguments, proofs,
     etc. that make such beliefs more acceptable;
(c) discredit alternative (dissident, etc.) sources and beliefs;
(d) appeal to the relevant ideologies, attitudes and emotions of the
     recipients.

In sum, and in quite informal terms, the overall strategy of manipulative discourse is to discursively focus on those cognitive and social characteristics of the recipients that make them more vulnerable and less
resistant to manipulation, that make them credulous or willing victims
who accept beliefs and do things they otherwise would not do. It is here
that the essential conditions of domination and inequality play a role.

As formulated earlier, these general strategies of manipulative
discourse appear to be largely semantic, i.e., focused on manipulating the

'content' of text and talk. However, as is the case for the implementation of ideologies, these preferred meanings may also be emphasized and de-emphasized in the usual ways, as explained: by (de-)topicalization of meanings, by specific speech acts, more or less precise or specific local meanings, manipulating explicit vs. implicit information, lexicalization, metaphors and other rhetorical figures as well as specific expression and realization (intonation, volume, speed; text layout, letter type, photos, etc.). Thus, the powerful position of the speaker may be emphasized by a very formal setting, attire, tone of voice, lexical choice, and so on, such as an official discourse of the president addressing the nation or Congress. The reliability of sources may be further enhanced by mentioning authoritative sources, using photographs, and so on – for example, the demonstration of the presence of weapons of mass destruction in Iraq. People's emotions may be roused and appealed to by specially selected words, dramatic rhetoric (hyperboles, etc.), photographs, and so on. Opponents and dissidents may be discredited by the usual display of Us/Them polarization mentioned earlier. All these discourse features of manipulation need to be examined in closer detail to see how they are formulated, how they function in text and talk and how they achieve their contextual functions and effects.

An Example: Tony Blair Legitimating the War against Iraq

Instead of continuing to theorize about these properties, however, let us examine an example of well-known manipulative discourse, e.g., when the UK Prime Minister (PM) Tony Blair in March 2003 legitimated his government's decision, in line with that of US President George W. Bush, to go to war and invade Iraq. This is a classic example that has attracted much attention in the press as well as from academic analysts from different disciplines. The case is important because, until the following general elections in May 2005, Tony Blair was permanently accused of having misled UK citizens about this decision.

Examine the following initial fragment of this debate:

Extract 1

At the outset, I say that it is right that the House debate this issue and pass   1
judgement. That is the democracy that is our right, but that others struggle for   2
in vain. Again, I say that I do not disrespect the views in opposition to mine.   3
This is a tough choice indeed, but it is also a stark one: to stand British troops   4

down now and turn back, or to hold firm to the course that we have set. I   5
believe passionately that we must hold firm to that course. The question most   6
often posed is not 'Why does it matter?' but 'Why does it matter so much?' Here   7
we are, the Government, with their most serious test, their majority at risk, the   8
first Cabinet resignation over an issue of policy, the main parties internally   9
divided, people who agree on everything else: 10
                                                                            11
[Hon. Members: 'The main parties?']   12
                                                                            13
Ah, yes, of course. The Liberal Democrats – unified, as ever, in opportunism and   14
error.   15
                                                                            16
[Interruption]   17

Tony Blair begins his speech with a well-known *captatio benevolentiae*, which at the same time is a specific move in the overall strategy of positive self-presentation, by emphasizing his democratic credentials: respect for the House and other opinions, as well as recognizing the difficulty of the choice about whether or not to go to war. The manipulative effect here consists of suggesting that the UK Parliament (still) had the right to decide about going to war, although it later became clear that this decision had already been made the previous year. In the following sentences, Blair also insists that he/we/they must 'hold firm', which is also a strategic move of positive self-presentation. And when he finally refers to his 'passionate beliefs', we see that, in addition to the rational arguments, Blair is also presenting his emotional (and hence vulnerable) side, thus emphasizing the strength of his beliefs.

He even concedes that the matter is so serious that for the first time – due to the opinions and votes, even in his own party, against the war in Iraq – his government majority is at risk. Secondly, he construes the well-known polarized opposition between Us (democracies) and Them (dictatorship), thereby politically implying that those who are opposed to the war might be accused of supporting Saddam Hussein – trying, in this way, to silence opposition. Going to war, thus, is a way of defending democracy, an implicit – fallacious – argument that is quite common in manipulation, namely by associating recipients with the enemy and hence possibly as traitors. This move is further sustained by another – ideological – move, namely that of nationalism when he refers to 'British troops' that cannot be stood down, which also politically implicates that not supporting British troops is disloyal and also a threat to the UK, democracy, and so on. Finally, after protests from the House about mentioning only the major parties (Labour and Conservatives), he discredits the opposition of the Liberal Democrats by ridiculing them and calling them opportunistic.

We see that even in these few lines all aspects of manipulation are evident:

(a) ideological polarization (Us/Democracies vs. Them/ Dictatorships; nationalism: supporting the troops);

(b) positive self-presentation by moral superiority (allowing debate, respect for other opinions, struggling for democracy, holding firm, etc.);

(c) emphasizing his power, despite the opposition;

(d) discrediting the opponents, the Liberal Democrats, as being opportunistic;

(e) emotionalizing the argument (passionate beliefs). In sum, those who oppose the decision to go to war are implicitly being accused (and once explicitly, such as the Liberal Democrats) as being less patriotic, as being unwilling to resist dictatorship, etc.

Consider the next paragraph of Blair's speech

Extract 2

The country and the Parliament reflect each other. This is a debate that, as time 1
has gone on, has become less bitter but no less grave. So why does it matter so 2
much? Because the outcome of this issue will now determine more than the 3
fate of the Iraqi regime and more than the future of the Iraqi people who have 4
been brutalized by Saddam for so long, important though those issues are. It 5
will determine the way in which Britain and the world confront the central 6
security threat of the 21st century, the development of the United Nations, the 7
relationship between Europe and the United States, the relations within the 8
European Union and the way in which the United States engages with the rest 9
of the world. So it could hardly be more important. It will determine the 10
pattern of international politics for the next generation. 11

Manipulation in this fragment becomes even more explicit. First, Blair continues his positive self-presentation by emphasizing his generosity and democratic credentials (recognizing opposition in parliament and the country). Secondly, he rhetorically enhances the seriousness of the matter (with the litotes 'no less grave'). Thirdly, he continues the ideological polarization strategy (We/Democracy vs. Them/Dictatorship). Fourthly, he uses hyperboles ('brutalized') to enhance that the Other is evil. And finally and crucially, he extends the ideological opposition between Us and Them, to an ingroup of Us, Europe, the United States and the rest of the world, facing its major security threat. To summarize, what in reality is (among many other things) getting control with the USA of a key (oil) country in the Middle East, using as an excuse weapons of mass destruction and the support of terrorism, is now presented as defending the whole 'free' world against its major threat. Besides the extension of the ingroup from 'Us' in the UK to the rest of the 'free' world (a move one might call 'ideological globalization'), we also witness several other hyperbolic moves to emphasize the seriousness of the situation, e.g., the extension of time: 'for the next generation'.

Thus we see that manipulative discourse focuses on several crucial and fundamental issues: the international struggle between Good and Evil, national and international solidarity, the seriousness of the situation as an international conflict, positive self-presentation as a strong ('firm') and morally superior leader, and negative other-presentation (e.g., of the opposition) as opportunistic.

In the rest of his speech, not analysed here, Blair engages in the following manipulative moves:

(a) history of the aftermath of the previous war with Iraq, the importance of the issue of the WMD, Saddam Hussein's bad intentions and misleading UN weapons inspections, etc.;
(b) description of the WMD: anthrax, etc.;
(c) repeated expressions of doubts about Saddam Hussein's credibility;
(d) repeated positive self-presentation: details of willingness to compromise, as being reasonable ('Again, I defy anyone to describe that as an unreasonable proposition').

In other words, this part is essentially what was missing in the earlier part: a detailed account of the 'historical facts', up to Resolution 1441 of the Security Council, as a legitimation to go to war.

Although this single example obviously does not present all the relevant strategies of manipulative discourse, we have found some classic examples of manipulative strategies, such as emphasizing one's own power and moral superiority, discrediting one's opponents, providing details of the 'facts', polarization between Us and Them, negative other-presentation, ideological alignment (democracy, nationalism), emotional appeals, and so on.

Members of parliament are not exactly stupid people and there is little doubt that they would perfectly understand many of Blair's moves of legitimation and manipulation. This means that if they are not powerless victims, and there is no consequential political inequality, we may have a form of political persuasion but not of manipulation, as stipulated earlier.

Yet there is a crucial point where parliament and the opposition are less powerful than the government: they lack the crucial information, e.g. from the secret services, about the WMD, in order to be able to accept the legitimacy of the invasion of Iraq. Secondly, the Labour majority in the House, even when many of them opposed the invasion of Iraq – as did the majority of the British people – can hardly reject Blair's motion without putting the Labour government at risk. We know that only a few Labour politicians openly defied the party leadership and thus were willing to risk losing their jobs. Thirdly, such a rejection would also mean defying the USA and damaging the friendship between the UK and the USA. Fourthly, no one in the House can morally defend showing any lack of solidarity with British troops abroad – and hope to get re-elected. Finally, withholding support for this motion could indeed be (and has been) explained as defending Saddam Hussein: a double bind or Catch 22 situation in which those on the left wing in particular, who are most explicitly engaged in the struggle against dictatorships, can hardly disagree with the manipulative argument.

In this specific case, we see that some relevant context properties of this speech help us to distinguish between manipulation and legitimate persuasion, although in real life the two kinds of mind control overlap. That is, many of the strategies used may also be applied in perfectly legitimate political rhetoric in parliament. However, in this case of what is defined as a national and international emergency, even a powerful parliament like that of the UK may be manipulated into accepting the Prime Minister's policy of joining the USA in what is presented as a war against tyranny and terrorism. Both contextually (the speaker as leader of the Labour party and PM, the recipients as MPs and British, etc.) as well as textually, Blair defines the situation in such a way that few MPs can refuse, even when they know they are being manipulated and probably lied to.

In sum, the MPs are 'victims' of the political situation in several ways, and can thus be manipulated, as happened in the USA and Spain, by those in power. By accepting the reasons provided by Blair in his speech legitimating the war, they are manipulated not only into accepting specific beliefs, e.g., on international security, but also into the concrete act of accepting the motion and thereby sending troops to Iraq.

Final Remark

In this chapter, we have taken a multidisciplinary approach to an account of discursive manipulation. In order to distinguish such discourse from other forms of influence, we first *socially* defined it as a form of power abuse or domination. Secondly, we focused on the *cognitive* dimensions of manipulation by identifying what exactly the 'mind control' dimension of manipulation means. And finally, we analysed the various *discursive* dimensions of manipulation by focusing on the usual polarized structures of positive self-presentation and negative other presentation expressing ideological conflict. In addition, we found that manipulation involves: enhancing the power, moral superiority and credibility of the speaker(s), and discrediting dissidents, while vilifying the Others, the enemy; the use of emotional appeals; and adducing seemingly irrefutable proofs of one's beliefs and reasons. Future work will need to provide much more detail about the discursive, cognitive and social aspects of manipulation.

10

Contextualization in Parliamentary Discourse: Aznar, Iraq and the Pragmatics of Lying

The Relevance of 'Context'

One of the new developments in discourse studies is the growing interest in the analysis of context. This development should be seen against the background of the increasingly multidisciplinary approach to the analysis of text and talk in most of the humanities and social sciences. It is no longer adequate to just examine the 'linguistic' structures of discourse 'itself', and not even to limit oneself to the autonomous interaction structures of conversation but to look beyond discourse and examine its cognitive, social, political, cultural and historical *environments*:

- in linguistics, and especially in Systemic Linguistics, several proposals have been made to analyse context (Ghadessy, 1999; Leckie-Tarry, 1995; see also Fetzer, 2004; see also the critical analysis of this approach in van Dijk, 2008a);
- conversation analysis (CA) itself has extended its scope since the early 1990s to the study of the institutional and organizational context of talk in interaction (Boden and Zimmerman, 1991; Drew and Heritage, 1992; Sarangi and Roberts, 1999);
- anthropological linguistics obviously has a disciplinary interest in the study of the cultural aspects of talk, and hence in the situated aspects of face-to-face interaction (Duranti, 1997, 2001; see also Duranti and Goodwin, 1992);

- interactional sociolinguistics, especially with the seminal work of John Gumperz (see, e.g., Gumperz, 1982a, 1982b, 1992), has paid special attention to the subtle 'contextualization cues' of discourse (see also Auer and Di Luzio, 1992);
- Critical Discourse Studies (CDS) by definition studies talk and text within their societal contexts, with specific attention to relationships of power, domination, and social inequality (Fairclough, 1995a; Wodak and Meyer, 2001; Wodak and Chilton, 2005);
- the same is true, more specifically, for feminist discourse studies, interested in the critical study of gender domination and its reproduction in discourse (Lazar, 2005);
- even in more formal approaches in discourse studies, for instance in Artificial Intelligence and related fields, it is being recognized that automatic language production and comprehension is impossible without modelling the context of communication (see, e.g., Akman et al., 2001).
- Earlier work on situations and episodes in social psychology might be taken as an example for more detailed studies of context (Argyle, Furnham and Graham, 1981; Forgas, 1979; 1985; Scherer and Giles, 1979).

In sum, at least since the 1990s, we witness diverse but steady attention being paid to the relevance of context analysis in various areas of discourse studies and the humanities and social sciences in general. However, although there seems to be a widespread consensus about the relevance of such an extension of discourse studies, there is hardly any agreement about what the notion of context actually means, or should mean. Generally speaking, and quite vaguely, context is seen as the explanatory 'environment' of discourse, but the problem is how to define, that is to de-limit, such an environment without running the risk of engaging in a theory-of-everything. Thus, in a parliamentary debate, the context may be limited to the setting of the Spanish Cortes, the *diputados* present and some other obvious candidates for contextual categories, but what about such 'contexts' as the current situation in the country, or the current international situation, or Spanish foreign policy, etc.? Most such environments may well be relevant to the study of such discourse but the question is also whether they were actually *relevant* for the speakers in parliament themselves. Hence, usually contexts are limited to the *relevant* aspects of the environment. This, however, begs the question because in that case we need to define what is relevant and what not, and we may end up with a circular definition.

More specifically, for instance in Conversation Analysis, has been the tendency to be very parsimonious in admitting (relevant) 'context' and only when somehow aspects of such context are 'procedurally consequential' for talk (Schegloff, 1987, 1991, 1992). This seems to restrict contextual influence on talk quite seriously, but even then we do not have a solution because the influence of the context may be on the assignment of meanings or functions in discourse that are obvious to the participants, but not explicitly expressed. That is, such a definition is empiricist and even behaviourist because it only admits 'observable' evidence, and not other evidence or methods of inquiry (experiments, post hoc explanations, introspection, participant protocols, etc.). Still, it provides at least one (superficial) criterion for the elusive notion of 'relevance'.

In Critical Discourse Studies (CDS), the admission of 'contextual' evidence is obviously more liberal, and any property of discourse, at any level, that seems to require a contextual description or explanation may thus be accounted for, for instance in terms of dominance relations between speakers and recipients, or in terms of organizational roles or positions of speakers or authors. But such an account is wide open to the critique that there is no limit to the analysis of possibly relevant context in terms of social structures (e.g., of domination) that impinge on discourse.

Towards a New Theory of Context

It is against this general background in discourse studies in various disciplines, and in view of developing a general, multidisciplinary theory of context that integrates these various directions of research, that I have been proposing, also since the 1990s, a new theory of context in terms of a specific kind of mental model of experience: *context models* (van Dijk, 1999, 2001, 2004, 2005; 2008a, 2008b). This new theory was also premised on the obvious limitations of a more formal approach to context in my earlier book on text and context (van Dijk, 1977).

The fundamental idea behind this proposal is that contexts are not some kind of objective 'social situation' – which is the dominant, informal view of context in linguistics, discourse studies and other disciplines. Rather, for contexts to be relevant for text and talk, as required, they should be characterized as being *subjective*, namely as *definitions of the relevant aspects of the communicative situation by the participants themselves.*

This idea, as such, is not new and has been formulated, without much detail, especially in various studies in social psychology and the social sciences (Brown and Fraser, 1979; Duranti and Goodwin, 1992). The notion of 'the definition of the situation' is famous in the history of sociology (Thomas, 1966). However, the more subjectivist definitions have hardly been taken seriously because they seem to be inconsistent with the social perspective of these various approaches to language use, discourse and communication. Indeed, a subjectivist approach is typically rejected as individualist, and hence incompatible both with microsociological ('interactional') approaches, as well as with macrosociological ('system') approaches.

Moreover, the fact that the very concept of 'defining the situation' by participants also has obvious *cognitive* aspects makes such a subjectivist approach even more suspicious in most of the socially oriented approaches to discourse (see van Dijk, 2006; special issue of *Discourse Studies*). And yet, it is precisely this cognitive aspect that provides the necessary theoretical and empirical bridge or interface between social situation and social structure, on the one hand, and the necessarily personal nature of each individual discourse, on the other hand. That is, contexts can only be shown to be relevant if they are *relevant-for-the-participant*. This can only be shown when it is being shown for individual participants, without abstractions and generalizations towards higher level interactions or groups or social structures.

Such context definitions are relevant for participants in interaction and hence they are construed under the influence of other participants and the interaction itself, but they still remain definitions of individual participants. Indeed, the participants of an interaction, as well as writers and readers in written communication, may not have the same definition of the communicative situation in the first place, as is typically the case, and actually shown in communicative conflicts.

In sum, although some of the ideas behind my concept of context as a subjective definition of the communicative situation can be found in the literature, no systematic theory has been formulated about the precise nature and influence of such definitions.

Contexts as mental models

In the broader perspective of contemporary cognitive science, and more specifically within the framework of cognitive model theory (Johnson-Laird, 1983; van Dijk and Kintsch, 1983), I thus have proposed to formulate the notion of context in terms of a specific kind of memory representation of participants, namely as mental models (van Dijk, 1999, 2008a, 2008b). Like all our personal experiences, these mental models are stored in the personal (autobiographical) memory, episodic memory, of language users (Neisser and Fivush, 1994; Tulving, 1983). Thus, 'experiencing', 'being aware of' a communicative event in which one participates, is what we call a context model, or simply a context. This notion of mental model includes exactly the kind of properties we usually ascribe to contexts: they are subjective, they are definitions of the situation and they may be incomplete, biased, prejudiced, etc. and hence nothing like an 'objective situation'. That is, they are participant *constructs*. In this sense, my proposal is consistent with a constructionist approach to discourse in social psychology (Edwards and Potter, 1992), but, unlike such an approach, the only explicit way such constructs can be formulated is in terms of cognitive representations of some kind, and *without reduction to other kinds of objects, such as discourse or interaction.*

Thus, *contexts are subjective episodic models (experiences) of participants dynamically construed (and updated) during interaction.* As we know from more informal context studies and experiences, such context models have a profound influence on discourse, and vice versa; discourse has a profound influence on the definitions of the situation by the participants. That is, there is ongoing, dynamic mutual influence between talk or text and its production or comprehension on the one hand, and the way the participants see, interpret and construe the other, 'environmental' aspects of such discourse, such as the setting, the participants, the ongoing action, as well as the goals and knowledge of the participants.

In terms of the psychology of discourse production, this means that context models control this production process, and thus guarantee that what is said, and especially also how it is said, is *adequate* or *appropriate* in the current situation. This would mean control over much of the (variable) sound structure, the syntax, lexical choice and any other discourse structures that may vary in the situation.

The precise cognitive process model of this kind of control is beyond the scope of this chapter (see van Dijk, 2008a). Suffice it to say that this kind of theoretical approach is perfectly compatible with contemporary studies of discourse processing (van Dijk and Kintsch, 1983; van Oostendorp and Goldman, 1999) and in fact supplies an important missing link in this approach, namely the fundamental context dependency of discourse processing. Such context dependency was usually ignored or dealt with in an ad hoc way in cognitive psychology, for instance in terms of independent variable control in laboratory experiments (age, gender, etc. of subjects) which obviously are only a very imperfect simulation of 'real' communicative contexts.

One of the many attractive aspects of the theory is that the 'pragmatic' kind of context model here proposed combines very well with the kind of 'semantic' (situation) models previously proposed as the basis for the meaning and reference production and comprehension of discourse (Johnson-Laird, 1983; van Dijk and Kintsch, 1983; van Oostendorp and Goldman, 1999). That is, both pragmatic and semantic 'understanding' of discourse are based on mental models in episodic memory, that is, on the ways participants subjectively understand the situation they talk or read about, on the one hand, and the situation *in which* they are now communicating, on the other – two kinds of representation that are obviously related, and that also define the boundaries between semantic and pragmatics.

By definition, context models have the same structure as other kinds of models, such as the (semantic) models participants construct of the events they write/speak or read/hear *about*, or *refer* to.

Also, in order to be able to function adequately in fractions of seconds, that is, realistically and online, context models obviously cannot have dozens, let alone hundreds, of possible categories representing communicative situations. Rather, the number of fundamental categories, as is usual in such cases, is probably around seven (Miller, 1956), although this might be multiplied by seven if each main category has seven subcategories. For instance, if we have a main category 'Participants', subcategories may be: communicative roles (Speaker, Recipient, Overhearer, etc.); social identities (gender, ethnicity, class, etc.); social roles (father, friend, etc.), relations between participants (competitors, etc.), etc.

Of course, empirical research needs to establish which are the categories that are relevant in each culture, assuming that such cultural variation is to be expected – even when some categories may be universal (there is always a Speaker role, and always speakers assume that Recipients share knowledge with them, etc.). In this way, the same general frame-of-context models may be strategically – and hence very rapidly – construed and dynamically adapted during the understanding of the social situation of a discourse.

Micro and macro contexts

Most studies of context focus on the immediate, face-to-face situation of interaction, that is, on the micro context. Yet, there are reasons to assume that language users also construe some kind of 'macro' context (van Dijk, 2006). Thus, when teaching a class, I am not only aware of the students present, of myself as a teacher, and some other typical context characteristics of teaching, but in line with the usual (but problematical) distinction in sociology between micro and macro accounts of society (Knorr-Cetina and Cicourel, 1981), I may also represent myself as a member of a profession and as a member of an institution, the University, and hence as performing locally something that also can be represented globally: the university educating students, that is, teaching as a macro notion.

Such macro contexts need not be a permanent awareness during my actual (micro) teaching at the level of interaction, but the overall functionality or 'sense' of what I am now doing sometimes need to be construed or activated, and sometimes also will be made explicit. *Indeed, we thus also have an elegant way to link micro and macro levels of society, not as levels or categories of the analyst, but as participant categories.*

As is the case for semantic and pragmatic micro and macro structures (van Dijk, 1980), also macro contexts have the same structure as micro contexts: Settings, Participants, Actions, Aims, etc., but only at another level, e.g., that of cities or countries, groups or organizations, collective and repetitive actions, overall goals, and so on, as when it is represented that the university in Spain teaches the students such and such, or when the Spanish Cortes voted for military action in Iraq.

Note though that, because of the usual processing constraints also, macro contexts cannot consist of a vast amount of categories and presupposed knowledge: it will only be a partial construction of *now* relevant aspects of social structure, and much of the time such knowledge will remain backgrounded in some kind of long term 'working' memory.

Knowledge

The usual properties of social situations construed to be relevant in both traditional concepts of contexts, as well as in the sociocognitive approach to context defined as context models, are especially Setting (Time, Place), Participants and their various Identities, Roles or Relations, the ongoing Action and the Goals of the participants.

Usually forgotten as a crucial category of contexts, however, is the *knowledge* of the participants, and especially the mutual knowledge about each other's knowledge (van Dijk, 2005). Yet, obviously such an epistemic component is necessary in order to describe and explain how speakers or writers are able to manage the very complex task of adapting their talk and text to the (assumed) knowledge of the recipients. In each sentence, and for each word, they need to know not only that the recipients know the words used by them, but also what the recipients already know about the events spoken or written about. Thus, if it is assumed that the recipients already know some 'fact' (proposition, etc.), then such a fact must be *presupposed* if it is assumed that it is readily accessible in memory (inferrable), or it must be *recalled* if such a fact, usually a concrete event, might have been forgotten even when it was probably known earlier.

Language users can only do this in the few (fractions of) seconds they have in the production of each word or sentence, when their context models keep track of the kind of knowledge which kind of recipients have. This does not mean that speakers need to have hypotheses about the hundreds of thousands of facts recipients know – something which would be totally impossible within the very limited size of context models.

Rather, speakers use handy strategies (van Dijk and Kintsch, 1983) to calculate what knowledge recipients have. For instance, for communication among members of the same social group or community, the easiest strategy is simply to assume that other members have the same general sociocultural knowledge as I have. For personal communication among friends, family members or acquaintances, such shared knowledge is not the sociocultural shared knowledge of groups or communities, but the kind of knowledge that has been shared in previous interactions, and that hence is stored in 'old' context models. In this case, speakers only need to activate old context models and check whether some proposition has been communicated before. If in doubt, they will make sure to repeat or remind the recipients of the 'old' information. More difficulties exist for the management of knowledge among people from different cultures, that is, from different epistemic communities, although here too much 'universal human' knowledge may be presupposed.

The K-device of the context models consists of these kinds of strategy for the activation, expression, presupposition, reminding or repeating of shared or new knowledge. At each moment in the context model, it strategically 'calculates' what information of the speaker, as stored in mental models about public or private events or in sociocultural knowledge, is probably shared by the recipient or not, and hence what may or must be presupposed, recalled, repeated or newly asserted.

My approach to knowledge is rather pragmatic and discursive than semantic and logical. That is, unlike in epistemology, I do not define knowledge as 'justified true beliefs', which is an abstract, semantic definition in terms of the relations between beliefs and the 'world' (see, among a vast number of books, e.g., the reader by Bernecker and Dretske, 2000). *Truth* in my view is not a property of beliefs but a property of discourse about the world. The crucial condition of human knowledge is not whether or not beliefs abstractly correspond with (refer to, etc.) some state of affairs in some world or situation, but *whether such a belief is shared by other members of a community, the knowledge-community.* That is, we only say that someone knows something when we as observers or speakers know the same thing, that is, share a belief with that person. In other words, saying that X knows *p* presupposes that the speaker also knows *p*. This is true both for (inter)personal knowledge as well as for socioculturally shared knowledge. In the latter case, it is presupposed that each and any member of a community shares some belief.

Moreover, and contrary to the shared beliefs we call opinions, or indeed (mere) 'beliefs', knowledge is shared belief that has been or can be certified by the knowledge criteria of some community. These may be the common-sense criteria of everyday life (observation, inference or reliable sources) but also those of specialized communities, such as those of the mass media, science or social movements. Obviously, since these criteria may change historically, and vary culturally, knowledge is by definition relative, as it should be. But note that also this relativity is relative – as it should be – because *within* an epistemic community beliefs that have been accepted or certified according to the criteria of that community are considered to be knowledge, even when from outside the community (or in a later stage of the community) we may deem such beliefs to be mere beliefs, opinions or superstitions. Thus, we may say that in the Middle Ages people from their own perspective *knew* that the earth was flat, and hence presupposed it in public discourse. It also follows that all that we claim to know today is *our knowledge*, and may well be defined differently elsewhere or in the future. Such relativism is nothing to worry about because for all practical purposes we act and speak in terms of, or on the basis of, this (relative) knowledge, and it is this knowledge that is socioculturally shared with others.

Lying

Lying is a verbal act that involves the illegitimate manipulation of knowledge in interaction and communication. It is not a speech act in the classical sense because it does not satisfy the usual appropriateness conditions: there are no systematic conditions that must be fulfilled in order to lie 'appropriately'.

Rather, lying should be defined as a violation of the specific pragmatic conditions of appropriate affirmation and at the same time, more generally, as a violation of the general ethical norms of truthfulness that are at the basis of all human interaction. Note though that if in some situation speaking the truth violates other norms or values (e.g., those of politeness, discretion, face-keeping, legitimate secrecy, and so on), lying may

well be ethically permitted. For instance, lying to the enemy in an inter-
rogation may be considered ethically correct. Obviously, each of these
situations needs its own definition and hence its own context model.

In this sense, lying is generally illegitimate if it hurts the interests of
the recipient or others. In a broader sense of social and political legitimacy, this is especially the case if the liar (as a person or institution) is
thus able to establish or confirm its domination, and thus abuses of its
power, for instance through its control over the means of communication
and public discourse, and hence over the public access to knowledge (see,
e.g., Barnes, 1994; Lewis and Saarni, 1993; Wortham and Locher, 1999).

We see that lying is a complex phenomenon that may be dealt with
in philosophical (ethical), semantic, pragmatic, psychological, social, political and cultural terms. In the limited framework of this paper, however,
we shall merely deal with it in terms of context-based pragmatics,
although I shall later also include more fundamental criteria of legitimacy. In those terms, lying is a communicative act controlled by a
context model in which the speaker knows that p is not the case, but has
the purpose to make the recipient believe that p is the case. In other
words, if a lie is successful, speaker and hearer have a different mental
model of the events referred to.

If appropriate assertions presuppose that the speakers know what they
assert, then lies are not appropriate assertions. However, recipients may
not know that this condition is not satisfied and interpret a lie as an
appropriate assertion, and change their knowledge accordingly. We see
that in order to describe what lies are we need context models that are
able to represent speakers and recipients and their knowledge and goals.

Lies are members of a larger family of communicative acts that violate
the conditions of previous knowledge, such as deception, self-deception,
misleading someone, errors, mistakes, confabulations, fiction, and so on,
that shall not further be analysed here.

Thus, the crucial (ethical) difference is that when lying speakers know
that what they assert is false, whereas in other communicative acts (errors,
self-deception) they may not know so, or not be aware of it.

There are various intermediate cases, for instance when the speaker
believes what is asserted but is not sure, which also suggest that the
knowledge component of the context model should be scalar, making
lies more or less 'blatant'. Similarly, what may be a genuine assertion from
the point of view of the speaker may be a lie for the recipient when the
recipient believes that the speaker knowingly asserts a falsehood.

Note that all these conditions can easily be formulated in terms of
context models, which for each participant spell out not only her or his

knowledge but also the beliefs about the knowledge, intentions and goals of the other participants.

Parliamentary Discourse

As is the case for all discourse genres, parliamentary discourse (and its lies) is also largely defined by its context properties (van Dijk, 2000, 2004; see also the other studies in Bayley, 2004; Steiner, 2004).

Although there are several kinds of linguistic or discursive structures that characterize parliamentary discourse, such as speeches delivered in a parliamentary debate, these are seldom unique. Rather, parliamentary debates share with other formal genres a number of characteristics of style and interaction, such as speaker and turn control by a Chair, time allocation for turns, a formal lexicon, elaborate syntax and the usual structures of argumentation and persuasion characteristic of debates. Only some of these, such as forms of address ('my honourable friend'), may be quite typical and unique, for instance in the UK House of Commons, or 'Sus señorías' in the Spanish Cortes. Similarly, contents may be constrained in terms of topics that have to do with public affairs, the country, and so on – but also these, for instance 'immigration', may also be topics in news reports, editorials or everyday conversation. And formal grammatical style will be similar to the grammatical style of any formal meeting, e.g., the board meeting of a company. Note though that in isolation, none of these categories are *exclusive* for parliamentary discourse, their combination may well be quite *(proto)typical* of parliamentary discourse.

What *is* exclusive to parliamentary debates as a genre, however, are such obvious context categories as the Setting (House of Parliament), the Participants (MPs, opposition, etc.), the Aims (policies, etc.) and the political knowledge and ideologies of the participants. In other words, although content and even style of what is said in parliament may be shared by other types of communicative events, the *function* of such structures should be established in relation to the specific political situation: the speakers/MPs 'do' politics, legislate, represent the voters, govern the country, and so on. In the rest of this chapter I shall examine such categories in more detail and apply the results in a study of a specific parliamentary debate.

Thus, the question is what speakers in parliamentary debates need to know about the specific communicative situation in order to be able to speak appropriately. And secondly, how does such (presupposed) knowledge influence their talk? The latter question is important not only as an empirical check on what otherwise might be pure theoretical speculation, but also as part of a discovery procedure because we have few other methods to access the knowledge of participants. Note though that the general criterion of relevance or of procedural consequentiality for the recognition of context elements should not be limited to directly 'observable' features of talk, lest we adhere to a behaviourist conception of talk and text. Knowledge is generally defined as shared factual belief of a community and, by definition, presupposed. This means that also in interaction, such knowledge is seldom formulated, expressed or manifest. Thus, in a parliamentary debate, all participants know they are MPs, and hence seldom actually need to say so, unless in very specific situations, in which such identity needs to be affirmed, displayed and made explicit. Similarly, the aim of parliamentary debates may be to persuade the recipients but, again, such aims will seldom be made explicit. Thus, the participants presuppose many if not all of the properties of the communicative situation, as subjectively represented in their context models, but the analyst can only infer these from indirect expressions or manifestations, for instance in order to explain properties of talk.

Contextual Analysis of a Fragment of a Parliamentary Debate

In the rest of this chapter, I shall examine some context categories through a partial analysis of a fragment of a debate in the Spanish Cortes on 12 Marc 2003, on the war in Iraq. In this debate, Prime Minister José María Aznar defends his decision to support US intervention in Iraq, against the opposition led by PSOE leader José Luís Rodríguez Zapatero, currently Prime Minister. From this debate I have selected a fragment in which Aznar and Zapatero directly confront each other (see the full text of this fragment in the Appendix).

Note that this analysis is not like any other analysis of discourse or talk in interaction which would require a vast account of all the properties of this fragment of parliamentary interaction. Rather, we focus on those elements of this talk that are understandable only in light of the putative context models of the two participants. We may call this a *contextual analysis*. But since context models are also complex, these can only be analysed partially. I shall therefore focus on the point highlighted above: the management of knowledge in such debate, and especially what some participants, outside observers or analysts call lying (see also van Dijk, 2003b).

It should also be stressed that we only have the written transcript as made available in the official *Diario* of the Spanish Cortes, and not the usual, much more detailed, transcript of spoken interaction.

Forms of address and presentation

Before we deal with the crucial aspect of knowledge, we should briefly deal with other aspects of context models and their control of discourse. Thus the forms of address used in this debate and in this fragment presuppose that the participants know whom they are talking to. Thus, when the President of the Cortes gives the floor to Zapatero, she addresses him by his full first and last name, as well as by his current function of *diputado* (MP) and honorary title *(don)*. Note that the address is not direct, in the form of a second person pronoun, but indirect, in a third person pronoun, which makes the invitation or permission to speak rather a form of presentation of the next speaker. But since she has the official right to distribute turns, this presentation of the next speaker is at the same time directed at Zapatero, namely as an invitation to take the floor. The *Diario* itself describes the position of the President of the Cortes as such *(Presidenta)*, but such is not part of the debate itself, but rather a property of its transcript, as is the case for the identification-descriptions of all speakers.

Finally, as part of her presentation of the next speaker, the President also mentions the type of institutional speech act (a question), as well as its number. In many other forms of interaction, this would be anomalous, because speakers can hardly know what the next speaker is going to say or do. So, this presupposes an institutional condition, in which the action of the next speaker has already been announced earlier, and that interventions, or at least the beginning of interventions, by rule need to be in the form of questions, for instance, as in this case after the intervention of the Prime Minister, Aznar. All this, obviously, already presupposes quite some contextual knowledge, namely about the sequence of speakers, their functions (MP, President), the nature of their speech acts, the conditions of such speech acts, the formal relations between the speakers, as well as the formality of the event, requiring honorary titles such as *don*. Since the function of the President is only described by the *Diario*, but not expressed or otherwise signalled in the debate until the next move by Zapatero, this function is implicit by the very action of presenting and inviting the next speaker. The consequentiality of this context feature (Function of Participant) in this case is thus not formulated but only enacted. That Zapatero may speak next similarly presupposes that he is an MP, but in this case such a function is explicitly described by the President.

Similar forms of interaction may be found in the next turn, when Aznar is not named but only described as *Señor presidente del Gobierno*. On later presentations in this fragment, Zapatero is just presented by his name and without the description of his function (*diputado*) or his honorary title (*don*).

When Zapatero takes the floor, he not only addresses the President of the Cortes in polite terms, that is, in terms of her function and acknowledges being invited to speak next with a routine speech act of thanking (*Muchas gracias*) but in the same turn addresses his 'real' addressee in this debate, namely Aznar, but only with his last name, and the minimally polite form of address *señor*, without any further honorifics, or even his function.

Political roles and relations

We see that the simple interaction in the first few turns in this debate is premised on shared general knowledge about parliamentary interaction rules, on the one hand, and on the specific context models of the three participants. That is, each is able to play its specific role in this exchange, the President of the Cortes presenting next speakers, allocating turns, and Aznar and Zapatero appropriately addressing her and each other.

In addition to this rather general routine, which is very similar in other formal encounters, the context models need to specify the specific political *roles* and *relations* of the participants, so that Aznar can speak first, and that Zapatero, as leader of the opposition speaks first after him. This is crucial to interpret Zapatero's question in line 5–7, *because this is not merely a question, but also intended and interpreted as a form of political opposition*. This may also be seen by the reaction of Aznar, who not merely replies with 'Yes', but reformulates and hence implicitly disagrees with the proposition presupposed by the question: instead of defining it as a 'military intervention', he defines it 'as disarming the regime of Saddam Hussein', that is, in more positive terms. Politically speaking, this implies that he rejects the implicit critique of the opposition by defending government policy as a positive action. That is, in order to be able to engage in *political* interaction, the participants need to represent themselves and each other in terms of their institutional roles and relationships, and each contribution to the debate needs to be interpreted in this framework. A question that literally (in another context) may be interpreted as a request for information or an expression of an opinion is thus intended, heard and reacted to as a form of political opposition in parliament. In the same framework it is then expected that the leader of the opposition won't be satisfied by that simple reply of the Prime Minister, and in the next turn will challenge that reply, as indeed happens as from line 20. Such political inferences are only possible when the participants have context models in which such political inferences can be made (van Dijk, 2005).

Knowing and lying

In Zapatero's next turn (line 20–39), in which he details his question and opposition directed at Aznar, he accuses Aznar of hiding his real position and decision regarding the intervention in Iraq and of being less credible each time. Again, in general interactional terms an affirmation directed at a recipient implying that the recipient, does not respond (to questions) and does not say what he really wants, may be heard as an accusation, especially if general norms or rules require people to be honest and tell the truth.

This would be the analysis of a similar exchange in a mundane conversation (but formulated in less formal style, of course). However, in this specific political situation, such an indirect accusation, formulated by the head of the Opposition and directed against the head of the government, is a fundamental form of opposition. If the Prime Minister is accused of lying, this implies he has lied to the nation and, especially in case of military intervention, this may be a breach of crucial norms of a democratic state. In other words, by indirectly accusing Aznar of lying, Zapatero at the same time accuses him of political misconduct, of misleading the nation and the people, and as a Prime Minister who cannot be trusted. These *political implicatures* are not derivable from the meaning of what Zapatero says, nor from the meaning of the interaction (an accusation) but from the contents of the context models of the participants who interpret this exchange as an interaction between Prime Minister and Head of the Opposition (van Dijk, 2005).

Note also that the style of this intervention indexes the *formality* of the encounter in general, and the formality of parliamentary interaction in particular. Apart from formal lexical items (*auténticas posiciones*, etc.), thus, Zapatero has recourse to a polite euphemism. Instead of telling Aznar in so many words that he is a liar, he says that Aznar is *cada día menos creíble*, a euphemism that has the usual combined function of saving face and expressing politeness and respect, as is due to the Prime Minister. Again, such a way of speaking presupposes that Zapatero's context model represents such conditions (the definition of the situation, the parliamentary session, his own role as leader of the Opposition, the recipient's role of Prime Minister, etc.).

In the rest of his intervention, Zapatero continues his accusation against Aznar and his government, as may be expected from the head of the Opposition. The overall strategy in this accusation is to show the inconsistency between the findings (or rather the *lack* of findings) of the experts (Blix, Baradei) of the United Nations and the decisions of Bush and Aznar not to allow more time for the inspections, and wanting to intervene militarily right away. At the same time Zapatero emphasizes that what is being given as reasons for the interaction (weapons of mass destruction, links with terrorism) are actually false. In lines 32–3 the accusation is formulated in terms of what Aznar's government (and specifically the Minister of Foreign Affairs) has done, namely sign a resolution that does not give more time to the inspectors. That is, the phrases *usted ha firmado . . . usted acaba a través de su gobierno* show that Zapatero defines and addresses Aznar not as any person or politician, but as head of the government. We see how the (semantic) model of the situation talked about (what happens at the UN and in Iraq) is combined with the context model representing the respective definitions of the participants of the current situation. Aznar and Zapatero share their definitions of the current (parliamentary) Setting, and the roles of the participants, but as soon as Zapatero accuses Aznar, the definition of the situation of course is no longer the same: Zapatero accuses Aznar of being a liar and of deceiving the nation, and obviously Aznar has another definition of himself.

Zapatero's rhetorical questions in lines 35ff imply that according to him Aznar cannot know more than the experts who have done local research in Iraq – an expertise that is rhetorically enhanced by emphasizing the time of their work (years of investigation). Since Aznar cannot possibly know more than the experts, the tacit conclusion is that either he must have secret information or that he, Bush and Blair are misleading the world about the intervention in Iraq by inventing a pretext. Opposition elsewhere, for instance in the USA and the UK, engaged in the same strategy, namely of focusing on what later turned out to be the lies of their leaders about the situation in Iraq (Allman, 2004; Boyle, 2004; Fossà and Barenghi, 2003; O'Shaughnessy, 2004; Stothard, 2003).

Contextually relevant here is not just the accusation (and its formulation) but also the management of knowledge. We here reach the heart of the matter and this debate, both in Spain as well as elsewhere, pitching one camp (Bush, Blair, Aznar and their advisors) against another doubting or challenging the official reasons for the war: the alleged weapons of mass destruction and the link between the Iraqi regime and the terrorists.

In this specific debate, this means that Zapatero voices the doubts of the opposition about the veracity of the official grounds for the intervention. He thus not only indirectly accuses Aznar of lying but also, politically, of misleading the nation, and hence of being a 'bad' leader of a 'bad' government, as is his task as the leader of the Opposition. That is, for all those participants in this session, this is a normal and legitimate act, according to their context models.

Note that as we have seen above much of the interaction in this debate is related to this issue of (mutual) knowledge and lying. Thus, the negation of the concepts expressed by the lexical items *auténticas* and *creibles* already provides an expression of the context model of Zapatero about Aznar. That is, he does not merely say what is false but that the speaker, Aznar, is becoming less credible – i.e., is probably lying, or at least mistaken. Secondly, this opinion is argumentatively supported by the next propositions in his intervention (lines 23 ff), which feature the usual authority move, citing the UN experts Blix and Baradei, rhetorically emphasizing their expertise (*'informe exhaustivo'*, *'maxima autoridad'*, *'afirmaciones muy claras'*, etc.).

Similarly, the rhetorical question (line 35ff) – *'Por qué sabe Usted más que el señor Blix'?* – also focuses on and challenges the knowledge of Aznar, presupposing that Aznar cannot know more than an expert who was in Iraq, and hence implying again that either Aznar is lying or has secret knowledge he does not want to divulge. In either case, Aznar is misleading the nation, and is hence a bad Prime Minister. Obviously, such arguments in a public debate in parliament at the same time presuppose that Zapatero knows that all or most MPs know that Aznar cannot know more than the experts, and hence must be lying or have been lied to himself. Thus, pragmatically, Zapatero accuses Aznar of lying (or of being manipulated), which is already serious, but much more important is the political implicature of the accusation, namely that Aznar is either incompetent, or being manipulated by Bush and Blair, or misleading the nation. Such inferences can be shared in parliament or in the public sphere only when the context models of the participants construe Aznar as PM, Zapatero as leader of the Opposition and Aznar as head of a conservative government colluding with (also conservative) President Bush, and so on. If we want to understand what goes on in this parliamentary debate, we at least need to simulate these context models of the participants: it is their definition of the communicative situation that controls what they say and how they say it.

We also see that with such definitions of the communicative event, Zapatero can legitimately accuse Aznar of lying, although he does so indirectly. Also, in the rest of his intervention he challenges the veracity of the claims of Aznar, Blair and Bush, for instance by referring in lines 47ff. to the lack of proof and the falsity of some claims. This means that Zapatero makes explicit some of the knowledge criteria of our culture, e.g., empirical proof, which again does double duty: delegitimizing Aznar as PM, but at the same time legitimizing his own opposition by requiring legitimate proof for a policy that affects the whole country.

In a next move (lines 54ff), Zapatero further emphasizes that his doubts are not merely his, but are general. That is, he moves from personal opinions and context models to generally shared beliefs, and hence to knowledge. Thus, he again both emphasizes that he is right and Aznar is wrong, a political polarization that is in line with the opinions and acts of the leader of the opposition. By referring to public opinion and the Spanish people, this move of evidentiality (Chafe and Nichols, 1986) not only supports his own judgement but also emphasizes his support by the people, thus politically legitimizing himself. On the basis of this accumulated evidence, and concluding that Aznar's position is untenable, Zapatero finally and rhetorically asks Aznar to vote against the war in Iraq.

Since Zapatero focused his opposition on Aznar's lack of the proven necessity to intervene in Iraq, it may be expected that Aznar in his reaction (lines 74ff) does so to. After trying to delegitimize Zapatero and his discourse by degrading it to that of demonstration slogans and banners, he immediately focuses on the question of 'proof' and asserts that none is needed – for which he claims the relevance of UN resolution 1441. In order to interactionally avoid the burden of proof, Aznar thus changes the topic by emphasizing that Saddam Hussein needs to provide proof. And once focusing on Saddam Hussein as the dictator and emphasizing that Zapatero does not require anything from *him*, Aznar associates his opponent with the one who is generally considered to be the bad guy, thereby delegitimizing Zapatero by the suggestion of collusion or association. When talking about Saddam Hussein, Aznar activates the usual, ideologically based mental models and general attitudes about the dictator, thus taking distance from the current, contextually defined, accusation of Zapatero. But by then counter-accusing Zapatero of not requiring proof from Saddam Hussein, he again brings the focus back to what is politically relevant in this debate, namely defending himself against the opposition (and public opinion) and accusing them of colluding with the enemy.

We see that in order to be able to draw such inferences from the debate we need to assume that the participants construct and continuously update context models. These context models need to feature general sociocultural and political knowledge as well as specific knowledge about specific events, on the one hand, and a representation of the political identities (PSOE, PP), the political roles (PM, leader of the opposition), the political relations (political antagonists) and political goals (delegitimize, etc.) of the participants. Only then are we able to understand what the participants are really doing (politically) and especially how they are able to do it. Without such an approach, that is, in pure interactional terms, we would be limited to a rather superficial account of questions and answers, accusations and defences, and so on. Even if we would acknowledge that the debate takes place in parliament, we would be able to account only for the formal style, and perhaps the specific turn allocation and distribution rules of the institution. But the *political point* of this debate would remain unanalysed or underanalysed if we did not also construe the political situation as being subjectively and personally, as well as collectively, located in the context models of the participants.

Conclusions

The study of discourse should not be limited to an 'autonomous' analysis of text and talk but also develop a theory of context. It has been assumed in this chapter that such a context should not be formulated in terms of objective social situations or even their relevant properties, but rather in terms of mental models: context models. Such models represent the subjective definitions of the communicative situation and control each participant's contribution to interaction.

Besides the usual categories of social situations, such as Setting and Participants (and their identities, roles, relations, etc.), context models also should feature the 'cognitive' aspects of the situation, such as the goals and the knowledge of the participants. The knowledge of the participants in particular is crucial in the management of what information remains implicit and what is being explicitly expressed, recalled or presupposed in discourse. The K-device of the context model does just that: strategically controlling knowledge in interaction.

Such strategies are also crucial for the management of lies. In order to be able to lie successfully, speakers must know what recipients know or do not know. And vice versa, when recipients know that what speakers assert is false, they can accuse them of lying. That is, lies not so much need a semantic account in terms of the truth of propositions but rather a pragmatic approach in terms of how knowledge is being managed by context models.

In political debates such management of lies is crucial for the legitimacy of the participants. I therefore analysed one of the debates in the Spanish Cortes on the occasion of the looming war in Iraq, pitching Prime Minister Aznar against Opposition leader Zapatero. As was the case in the USA, the UK and elsewhere, here also the crucial point was whether Aznar was lying about the real reasons for going to war, amidst serious doubts about Saddam Hussein's alleged possession of weapons of mass destruction and links with international terrorism. In this analysis it is shown that, in addition to the usual structures and strategies of discourse and interaction, a contextual approach accounts for the constraints of institutional interaction, such as forms of address and presentation, speaker order and turn allocation. More specifically it is shown that context models feature a knowledge component that controls the strategies of lying, accusations of lying and defending oneself against such accusations. Moreover, it is shown that in this way not only can the debate be analysed in general contextual terms but more specifically as a form of *political* interaction.

Appendix

Fragment of the debate in the Spanish Cortes on March 12, 2003, on the war in Iraq (English translation below).

La señora **PRESIDENTA:** Pregunta número 17 que formula el diputado	1
don José Luis Rodríguez Zapatero.	2
	3
El señor **RODRÍGUEZ ZAPATERO:** Muchas gracias, señora presidenta. Señor Aznar, ¿cree necesaria una intervención militar en Irak?	4
	5
	6
La señora **PRESIDENTA:** Muchas gracias, señor Rodríguez Zapatero. Señor presidente del Gobierno.	7
	8
	9
El señor **PRESIDENTE DEL GOBIERNO** (Aznar López): Creo que es necesario el desarme del régimen de Sadam Husein.	10
	11
	12
La señora **PRESIDENTA:** Muchas gracias, señor presidente. Señor Rodríguez Zapatero.	13
	14
	15
El señor **RODRÍGUEZ ZAPATERO:** Señor Aznar, a fuerza de no responder y no decir las auténticas posiciones y las auténticas decisiones que usted ha tomado, va a resultar cada día menos creíble. En la última reunión del Consejo de Seguridad de Naciones Unidas hemos visto un	16
	17
	18
	19

informe exhaustivo, supongo que respetable de los señores Blix y El 20
Baradei, los inspectores que tienen la máxima autoridad en todo este 21
debate y que hicieron afirmaciones muy claras. La frase, creo, más 22
importante es: ¿cuánto tiempo necesitamos para verificar el desarme 23
de Irak? Textualmente, dijeron: ni años ni semanas, meses. Y usted ha 24
firmado una resolución que da apenas unos días, y usted acaba, a través 25
de su Gobierno, de su ministra de Asuntos Exteriores, de decir que 45 26
días es inaceptable y está en contra. Pero, ¿por qué sabe usted más que 27
el señor Blix? ¿Por qué suplanta la autoridad del señor Blix, que lleva 28
años y meses trabajando, buscando lo que hace y lo que tiene que 29
cumplir, que es el mandato de Naciones Unidas? **(Rumores.)** 30
31
La señora **PRESIDENTA:** Señor Mancha. 32
33
El señor **RODRÍGUEZ ZAPATERO:** Mire, señor Aznar, hay 34
que defender la justicia y la legalidad internacionales, y en este juicio 35
que todos estamos viendo ustedes han perdido la razón; no han 36
presentado pruebas y algunas han sido falsas. Los peritos o los inspec- 37
tores han dicho lo que han dicho, que acabo de referirle, no han 38
demostrado ninguna vinculación con el terrorismo internacional, 39
ninguna, ni con Al Qaeda ni con el terrorismo mal llamado islámico 40
y, claro, cuando las razones no existen, la diplomacia hemos visto que 41
se ha convertido no en más pruebas sino en dólares, no en poner 42
razones y argumentos sino en hacer ofertas. Por eso, prácticamente ya 43
nadie defiende sus tesis, ni las de su Gobierno, ni en el Consejo de 44
Seguridad, ni en la opinión pública, ni en la ciudadanía española. Señor 45
Aznar, debe de tener un momento de reflexión y de no llevar a este 46
país a una posición indefendible, a la luz del derecho internacional, de 47
la razón y de autoridad de Naciones Unidas, que no respeta ni el 48
embajador que usted ha nombrado allí en la persona de su secretario 49
general. Abandone su posición, señor Aznar. Vote el próximo día, si es 50
que llega a haber votación en el Consejo, a favor de las tesis razonables 51
que ha presentado Blix y no de Bush, vote con la Europa cercana, vote 52
con la legalidad internacional, vote por el tiempo para la paz y no para 53
... **(Aplausos.)** 54
55
La señora **PRESIDENTA:** Muchas gracias, señor Rodríguez 56
Zapatero. Señor presidente del Gobierno. 57
58
El señor **PRESIDENTE DEL GOBIERNO** (Aznar López): Ya 59
sabíamos que S.S. saldría con pancarta otra vez, pero no hace falta que 60
nos adelante su discurso **(Rumores.),** ya comprendo que llevaba 15 61
días sin ir detrás de una pancarta y debe ser una cosa bastante inso- 62
portable de aguantar, señoría. Quiero decirle, para que S.S. comprenda, 63

que la Resolución 1441 no obliga a nadie a presentar pruebas nada   64
más que a Sadam Husein, que es al único al que usted no le exige que   65
cumpla nada, al único. Al único que las resoluciones de Naciones   66
Unidas obliga a presentar pruebas de desarme desde hace 12 años,   67
señor Rodríguez Zapatero, es a Sadam Husein, que es al único al que   68
usted, cuando habla de graves consecuencias no le advierte de ninguna   69
grave consecuencia. Usted admite graves consecuencias para el   70
Gobierno, para todo aquel que no está de acuerdo con usted, pues el   71
único que está advertido por la comunidad internacional de la cual   72
nosotros nos tenemos que alejar, de que si no le respeta y no prueba   73
su desarme está sometido a serias consecuencias, es exactamente aquel   74
que usted olvida en todos sus discursos, en todas sus actuaciones y en   75
todas sus pancartas sistemáticamente, señoría, el único que está oblig-   76
ado a hacerlo, el único. **(Aplausos.)** Desde hace 12 años, señoría, lo 77
lleva haciendo, y desde hace 12 años lo lleva incumpliendo, y las   78
resoluciones de Naciones Unidas dicen exactamente lo que yo le he   79
dicho, y los inspectores dicen que si hubiese cooperación podrían   80
terminar el trabajo rápidamente. ¿Cuál es el problema? ¿Por qué hay   81
armas de destrucción masiva? Porque no se quieren deshacer de las   82
armas de destrucción masiva. Usted lo que nos pide, señoría, es que no   83
hagamos nada o que aliviemos la presión, lo cual es el mejor mensaje   84
para todos los dictadores que quieren tener armas de destrucción   85
masiva, incluido también Sadam Husein, y eso, señoría, nosotros no lo   86
vamos a hacer. Y eso significa respetar la legalidad y eso significa   87
respetar el Consejo de Seguridad de Naciones Unidas. Sin duda que si   88
eso no ocurre así, habrá graves consecuencias, señoría, para el pueblo   89
iraquí, porque seguirá estando bajo una tiranía, y para el pueblo kurdo, 90
que seguirá siendo también atacado por ese dictador, y agrava las   91
consecuencias para la seguridad del mundo. No habrá un mundo más   92
inseguro que un mundo en el que no se respete la ley, pero vamos a   93
intentar que eso no sea así. Si lo conseguimos, señoría, no le debere-   94
mos nada a su actuación. Muchas gracias, señora presidenta.   95
(Prolongados aplausos).   96
                                                                           97
                                                                           98

Translation   99
                                                                          100

   Mrs. **PRESIDENT**: Question number 17 formulated by Member   101
of Parliament Don Jose Luis Rodriguez Zapatero.   102
                                                                          103

   Mr. **RODRÍGUEZ ZAPATERO**: Thank you very much Mrs.   104
President. Mr. Aznar, do you think that a military intervention in Iraq   105
is necessary?   106

Mrs. **PRESIDENT**: Thank you very much, Mr. Rodriguez   107
Zapatero. Mr. President of the Government.   108
     109

Mr. **PRESIDENT OF THE GOVERNMENT** (Aznar Lopez):   110
I believe that the disarmament of the regime of Saddam Hussein is   111
necessary.   112
     113

Mrs. **PRESIDENT**: Thank you very much, Mr. President.   114
     115

Mr. **RODRIGUEZ ZAPATERO**: Mr. Aznar, by virtue of not   116
responding and not telling us the real positions and the real decisions   117
that you have taken, you are less credible every day. In the last meet-   118
ing of the Security Council of the United Nations we have seen an   119
exhaustive and presumably respectable report of the gentlemen Blix   120
and Baradei, the inspectors who have the utmost authority in all this   121
debate and who made very clear statements. I believe that the more   122
important questions should be phrased as follows: how long do we   123
need to verify the disarmament of Iraq? They said literally: neither   124
years, nor weeks, months. And you have signed a resolution that hardly   125
gives days, and you have just said, through your Government, by your   126
minister of Foreign Affairs, that 45 days is unacceptable and that you   127
are against that. But, why do know you more than Mr. Blix? Why do   128
you claim to have the authority of Mr. Blix, who for years and months   129
has been working and looking for what he [Saddam Hussein] does and   130
what he must fulfil, by mandate of the United Nations. **(Noises)**   131
     132

Mrs. **PRESIDENT**: Mr. Mancha.   133
     134

Mr. **RODRIGUEZ ZAPATERO**: Look, Mr. Aznar, it is neces-   135
sary to defend international justice and legality, and in this trial we are   136
all witnessing at the moment, you really have no case: you have not   137
presented any proof and some have been false. The experts or the   138
inspectors have said what they said, and what I have just referred to,   139
namely that they have not demonstrated any link with international   140
terrorism, none, neither with Al Qaeda nor with ill-named Islamic   141
terrorism. So, of course, when there exist no reasons, the diplomacy we   142
have seen has changed from more proofs to more dollars, not by giving   143
more reasons and arguments but by making offers. That's why practi-   144
cally nobody still defends your theses, neither those of your   145
Government, nor in the Security Council, nor in public opinion, nor   146
among the Spanish citizens. Mr. Aznar, you must have a little while for   147
reflection and not take this country into a situation that is indefensi-   148
ble according to international law and according to the authority of   149
the United Nations, which not even the ambassador respect who you   150

have appointed there in the person of its Secretary General. Abandon   151
you position, Mr. Aznar. Vote the next day, if there will be any vote at   152
all in the Council, in favour of the reasonable theses presented by Blix   153
and not for those of Bush; vote with Europe, which is nearer, vote with   154
international legality, vote for the time for peace and not for ...   155
(Applause.)   156
                                                                               157
Mrs. **PRESIDENT**: Thank you very much, Mr. Rodriguez   158
Zapatero. Mr. President of the Government.   159
                                                                               160
Mr. **PRESIDENT OF THE GOVERNMENT** (Aznar Lopez):   161
We knew already that Your Honour would again come with your   162
placards, but you need not show these already here: I understand that   163
it has been 15 days without going behind a placard and that must be   164
quite unbearable, Sir. I want to tell you, so that the Honourable   165
Member understands, that Resolution 1441 does not force anyone to   166
present proof but Saddam Hussein, who is the only one whom you do   167
not demand to fulfil anything, the only one. The only one who the   168
resolutions of the United Nations oblige to present proof of disarma-   169
ment, for 12 years, Mr. Rodriguez Zapatero, is Saddam Hussein, who   170
is the only one whom you, when you speak of serious consequences,   171
do not warn of any serious consequences. You predict serious conse-   172
quences for the Government, for all those who are not in agreement   173
with you, although he is the only one who has been warned by the   174
international community, with respect to which we keep our distance,   175
and by whom he will be submitted to serious consequences if he does   176
not respect it and does not prove that he has disarmed, and he is the   177
only one you systematically forget in all your speeches, all your   178
performances and all your placards, Honourable Member, he is the   179
only one who is obliged to do it, the only one. **(Applause.)** He has   180
been asked to do so for 12 years, Honourable Member, and for 12   181
years he has been failing to comply, and the resolutions of the United   182
Nations say exactly what I am saying to you, and the inspectors say   183
that if there were cooperation they could finish the job quickly. So,   184
what is the problem? Why are there weapons of mass destruction?   185
Because they do not want to get rid of the weapons of mass destruc-   186
tion. What you ask from us, Honourable Member, is that we don't do   187
anything or that we alleviate the pressure, which is the best message   188
for all the dictators who want to have weapons of mass destruction,   189
including Saddam Hussein, and that, Honourable Member, is not what   190
we are going to do. And that means respecting legality and that means   191
respecting the Security Council of the United Nations. Undoubtedly,   192
if that does not happeny, there will be serious consequences,   193
Honourable Member, for the Iraqi people, because they will continue   194

living under a tyranny, and for the Kurdish people, who will also 195
continue being attacked by that dictator, thereby aggravating the 196
consequences for the security of the world. There will be no world 197
more uncertain than a world in which the law is not respected, but we 198
are going to try that that will not be the case. If we manage to do that, 199
Honourable Member, it will not be because of your performance. 200
Thank you very much, Mrs. President. 201
   (Prolonged applause.) 202

References

Abercrombie, N., Hill, S. and Turner, B. S. (1980) *The Dominant Ideology Thesis* (London: George Allen and Unwin).

Adelswärd, V., Aronsson, K., Jansson, L. and Linell, P. (1987) 'The unequal distribution of interactional space: Dominante and control in courtroom interaction'. *Text*, 7: 313–46.

Agger, B. (1992a) *Cultural Studies as Critical Theory* (London: Falmer Press).

Agger, B. (1992b) 'The discourse of domination', in *The Frankfurt School to Postmodernism* (Evanston, IL: Northwestern University Press).

Ahmed, N. M. (2005) *The War on Truth: 9/11: Disinformation and the Anatomy of Terrorism* (New York: Olive Branch Press).

Akman, V., Bouquet, P., Thomason, R. and Young, R. A. (eds.) (2001) *Modeling and Using Context: Proceedings of the Third International and Interdisciplinary Conference, CONTEXT 2001, Dundee, UK, 27–30 July 2001* (Berlin: Springer-Verlag).

Albert, E. M. (1972) 'Culture Patterning of Speech Behavior in Burundi', in J. J. Gumperz and D. Hymes (eds.), *Directions in Sociolinguistics: The Ethnography of Communication* (New York: Holt, Rhinehart & Winston), pp. 72–105.

Alexander, J. C., Giesen, B., Munch, R. and Smelser, N. J. (eds.) (1987) *The Micro–Macro Link* (Berkeley, CA: University of California Press).

Allman, T. D. (2004) *Rogue State: America and the World under George W. Bush* (New York: Thunder's Mouth Press).

Allport, G. W. (1954) *The Nature of Prejudice* (Garden City, NY: Doubleday, Anchor).

Altheide, D. (1985) *Media Power* (Beverly Hills, CA: Sage).

Anderson, D. A., Milner, J. W. and Galician, M. L. (1988) 'How Editors View Legal Issues and the Rehnquist Court'. *Journalism Quarterly*, 65: 294–8.

Antaki, C. (1988) 'Structures of Belief and Justification', in C. Antaki (ed.), *The Psychology of Ordinary Explanations of Social Behaviour* (London: Academic Press) pp. 60–73.

Apple, M. W. (1979) *Ideology and Curriculum* (London: Routledge & Kegan Paul).

Argyle, M., Furnham, A. and Graham, J. A. (1981) *Social Situations* (Cambridge, Cambridge University Press.

Arkin, R. M. (1981) 'Self-Presentation Styles', in J. T. Tedeschi (ed.), *Impression Management: Theory and Social Psychological Research* (New York: Academic Press), pp. 311–33.

Aronowitz, S. (1988) *Science as Power: Discourse and Ideology in Modern Society* (Minneapolis: University of Minnesota Press).

Atkinson, J. M. (1984) *Our Masters' Voices: The Language and Body Language of Politics* (London: Methuen).

Atkinson, J. M. and Drew, P. (1979) *Order in Court: The Organisation of Verbal Interaction in Judicial Settings* (London: Methuen).

Atkinson, J. M. and Heritage, J. (eds.) (1984) *Structures of Social Action: Studies in Conversational Analysis* (Cambridge: Cambridge University Press).

Atkinson, P., Davies, B. and Delamont, S. (eds.) (1995) *Discourse and Reproduction: Essays in Honor of Basil Bernstein* (Cresskill, NJ: Hampton Press).

Atlas, J. D. (2000) *Logic, Meaning and Conversation: Semantical Underdeterminacy, Implicature, and the Semantics/Pragmatics Interface* (New York: Oxford University Press).

Atwood, L. E., Bullion, S. J. and Murphy, S. M. (1982) *International Perspectives on News* (Carbondale: Southern Illinois University Press).

Auer, P. and di Luzio, A. (eds.) (1992) *The Contextualization of Language* (Amsterdam: John Benjamins).

Aufderheide, P. (1992) *Beyond PC: Toward a Politics of Understanding* (Saint Paul, MN: Graywolf Press).

Augoustinos, M. and Walker, I. (1995) *Social Cognition: An Integrated Introduction* (London: Sage).

Bachem, R. (1979) *Einführung in die Analyse politischer Texte. (Introduction to the Analysis of Political Discourse)* (Munich: Oldenbourg Verlag).

Bagdikian, B. H. (1983) *The Media Monopoly* (Boston: Beacon Press).

Barker, A. J. (1978) *The African Link: British Attitudes to the Negro in the Era of the Atlantic Slave Trade, 1550–1807* (London: Frank Cass).

Barker, M. (1981) *The New Racism* (London: Junction Books).

Barnes, J. A. (1994) *A Pack of Lies: Towards a Sociology of Lying* (New York: Cambridge University Press).

Barrett, M., Corrigan, P., Kuhn, A. and Wolff, J. (eds.) (1979) *Ideology and Cultural Production* (London: Croom Helm).

Bauman, R. and Scherzer, J. (eds.) (1974) *Explorations in the Ethnography of Speaking* (Cambridge: Cambridge University Press).

Bavelas, J. B., Rogers, L. E. and Millar, F. E. (1985) 'Interpersonal Conflict', in T. A. van Dijk (ed.), *Handbook of Discourse Analysis. Vol. 4: Discourse Analysis in Society* (pp. 9–26) (London: Academic Press).

Bayley, P. (ed.) (2004) *Cross-cultural Perspectives on Parliamentary Discourse* (Amsterdam Philadelphia: John Benjamins).

Becker, J., Hedebro, G. and Paldán (eds.) (1986) *Communication and Domination: Essays to Honor Herbert I. Schiller* (Norwood, NJ: Ablex).

Ben-Tovim, G., Gabriel, J., Law, I. and Stredder, K. (1986) *The Local Politics of Race* (London: Macmillan).

Berger, C. R. (1985) 'Social power and interpersonal communication', in M. L. Knapp and G. R. Miller (eds.), *Handbook of Interpersonal Communication* (Beverly Hills, CA: Sage), pp. 439–96.

Bergsdorf, W. (1983) *Herrschaft und Sprache: Studie zur politischen Termnologie der Bundesrepublik Deutschland* (Pfullingen: Neske Verlag).

264 References

Bergvall, V. L. and Remlinger, K. A. (1996) 'Reproduction, resistance and gender in educational discourse: the role of critical discourse analysis'. *Discourse and Society*, 7(4): 453–79.

Berman, P. (1992) *Debating PC: The Controversy over Political Correctness on College Campuses* (New York: Bantam-Dell).

Bernecker, S. and Dretske, F. I. (eds.) (2000) *Knowledge: Readings in Contemporary Epistemology* (Oxford: Oxford University Press).

Bernstein, B. (1971–1975) *Class, Codes, Control* (3 vols) (London: Routledge & Kegan Paul).

Bernstein, B. (1975) *Class, Codes and Control. Vol. 3: Towards a Theory of Educational Transmissions* (London: Routledge and Kegan Paul).

Bernstein, B. (1990) *The Structuring of Pedagogic Discourse* (London: Routledge & Kegan Paul).

Billig, M. (1988) 'The Notion of "Prejudice": Some Rhetorical and Ideological Aspects'. *Text*, 8: 91–110.

Billig, M. (1991a) 'Consistency and Group Ideology: towards a Rhetorical Approach to the Study of Justice', in R. Vermunt and H. Steensma (eds), *Social Justice in Human Relations* (Plenum Press: New York), pp. 169–94.

Billig, M. (1991b) *Ideology and Opinions: Studies in Rhetorical Psychology* (London, Sage).

Birnbaum, N. (1971) *Toward a Critical Sociology* (New York: Oxford University Press).

Blair, R., Roberts, K. H. and McKechnie, P. (1985) 'Vertical and network communication in organizations', in R. D. McPhee and P. K. Tompkins (eds.), *Organizational Communication: Traditional Themes and New Directions* (Beverly Hills, CA: Sage), pp. 55–77.

Blondin, D. (1990) *L'apprentissage du racisme dans les manuels scolaires* (Montreal, Quebec: Editions Agence d'Arc).

Boden, D. (1994) *The Business of Talk: Organizations in Action* (Cambridge: Polity).

Boden, D. and Zimmerman, D. H. (eds) (1991) *Talk and Social Strucutre: Studies in Ethnomethodolgy and Conversation Analysis* (Berkeley: University of California Press).

Borch, F. L. and Wilson, P. S. (2003) *International Law and the War on Terror* (Newport, R. I.: Naval War College).

Boskin, J. (1980) 'Denials: The Media View of Dark Skins and the City', in B. Rubin (ed.), *Small Voices and Great Trumpets: Minorities and the Media* (New York: Praeger), pp. 141–7.

Bourdieu, P. (1977) *Outline of a Theory of Practice* (Cambridge: Cambridge University Press).

Bourdieu, P. (1984) *Home Academicus* (Paris: Minuit).

Bourdieu, P. (1989) *La noblesse d'état. Grandes écoles et esprit de corps* (Paris: Minuit).

Bourdieu, P. and Passeron, J.-C. (1977) *Reproduction in Education, Society and Culture* (Beverly Hills, CA: Sage).

Bourdieu, P., Passeron, J. C. and Saint-Martin, M. (1994) *Academic Discourse: Linguistic Misunderstanding and Professorial Power* (Cambridge: Polity).

Boyd-Barrett, O. and Braham, P. (eds.) (1987) *Media, Knowledge and Power* (London: Croom Helm).

Boyle, F. A. (2004) *Destroying World Order: US Imperialism in the Middle East Before and After September 11* (Atlantic, GA: Clarity Press).

Bradac, J. J. and Mulac, A. (1984) 'A Molecular view of Powerful and Powerless Speech Styles'. *Communication Monographs*, 51: 307–19.

Bradac, J. J. and Street, R. (1986) 'Powerful and Powerless Styles Revisited: A Theoretical Analysis'. Paper presented at the annual meeting of the Speech Communication Association, Chicago.

Bradac, J. J., Hemphill, M. R. and Tardy, C. H. (1981) 'Language Style on Trial: Effects of 'Powerful' and 'Powerless' Speech upon Judgments of Victims and Villains'. *Western Journal of Speech Communication*, 45: 327–41.

Brewer, M. B. (1988) 'A Dual Process Model of Impression Formation', in T. K. Srull and R. S. Wyer (eds.) *Advances in Social Cognition*, Vol. 1 (Hillsdale, NJ: Lawrence Erlbaum).

Britton, B. K. and Graesser, A. C. (eds.) (1996) *Models of Understanding Text* (Mahwah, NJ: Erlbaum).

Brooke, M. E. and Ng, S. H. (1986) 'Language and Social Influence in Small Conversational Groups'. *Journal of Language and Social Psychology*, 5: 201–10.

Brown, J. D., Bybee, C. R., Wearden, S. T. and Murdock, D. (1982) 'Invisible Power: News Sources and the Limits of Diversity'. Paper presented at the annual meeting of the Association for Education in Journalism, Athens, OH.

Brown, L. B. (1973) *Ideology* (Harmondsworth: Penguin).

Brown, P. and Fraser, C. (1979) 'Speech as a Marker of Situation', in K. R. Scherer and H. Giles (eds.), *Social Markers in Speech* (Cambridge: Cambridge University Press), pp. 33–62.

Brown, P. and Levinson, S. C. (1978) 'Universals in Language Use: Politeness Phenomena', in E. N. Goody (ed.), *Questions and Politeness* (Cambridge: Cambridge University Press), pp. 56–289.

Brown, P. and Levinson, S. C. (1987) *Politeness: Some Universals in Language Use* (Cambridge: Cambridge University Press).

Brown, R. (1995) *Prejudice: Its Social Psychology*, Dates, J. L. and Barlow, W. (eds.) (1990) *Split Image: African Americans in the Mass Media* (Washington, DC: Howard University Press) (Oxford: Blackwell).

Brown, R. and Ford, M. (1972) 'Address in American English', in S. Moscovici (ed.), *The Psychosociology of Language* (Chicago: Markham), pp. 243–62.

Brown, R. and Gilman, A. (1960) 'The Pronouns of Power and Solidarity', in T. A. Sebeok (ed.), *Style in Language* (Cambridge: MIT Press), pp. 253–77.

Bruhn Jensen, K. (1986) *Making Sense of the News* (Aarhus, Denmark: Aarhus University Press).

Burton, F. and Carlen, P. (1979) *Official Discourse: On Discourse Analysis, Government Publications, Ideology and the State* (London: Routledge & Kegan Paul).

Caldas-Coulthard, C. R. and Coulthard, M. (eds.) (1996) *Texts and Practices: Readings in Critical Discourse Analysis* (London: Routledge & Kegan Paul).

Calhoun, C. (1995) *Critical Social Theory* (Oxford: Blackwell).

Cameron, D. (ed.) (1990) *The Feminist Critique of Language: A Reader* (London: Routledge and Kegan Paul).

Cameron, D. (1992) *Feminism and Linguistic Theory*. Second edn (London: Macmillan).

Candlin, C., Burton, J. and Coleman, H. (1980) Dentist–patient Communication: A Report to the General Dental Council (Lancaster, England: University of Lancaster, Department of Linguistics and Modem English Language).

Carbó, T. (1992) 'Towards an Interpretation of Interruptions in Mexican Parliamentary Discourse'. *Discourse and Society*, 3(1): 25–45.

Carbó, T. (1995) 'El discurso parlamentario mexicano entre 1920 y 1950: Un estudio de caso en metodologia de analisis de discurso'. (Mexican parliamentary discourse between 1920 and 1950: A Case Study in the Methodology of Discourse Analysis) (2 vols) (Mexico, CIESAS and Colegio de Mexico).

Caute, D. (1978) *The Great Fear: The Anti-Communist Purge under Truman and Eisenhower* (London: Secker and Warburg).

Centre for Contemporary Cultural Studies (1978) *On Ideology* (London: Hutchinson).

Chafe, W. and Nichols, J. (eds) (1986) *Evidentiality: The Linguistic Coding of Epistemology* (Norwood, NJ: Ablex).

Chaffee, S. H. (ed.) (1975) *Political Communication* (Beverly Hills, CA: Sage).

Charrow, V. R. (1982) Language in the Bureaucracy. In R. J. Di Pietro (ed.), *Linguistics and the Professions* (Norwood, NJ: Ablex), pp. 173–88.

Chibnall, S. (1977) *Law and Order News: An Analysis of Crime Reporting in the British Press* (London: Tavistock).

Chilton, P. A. (ed.) (1985) *Language and the Nuclear Arms Debate: Nukespeak Today* (London and Dover, NH: Frances Printer).

Chilton, P. A. (1988) *Orwellian Language and the Media* (London: Pluto Press).

Chilton, P. A. (1996) *Security Metaphors: Cold War Discourse from Containment to Common House* (Bern: Lang).

Chilton, P. A. (2004) *Political Discourse Analysis* (London: Routledge).

Chilton, P. and Lakoff, G. (1995) 'Foreign Policy by Metaphor', in C. Schäffner and A. L. Wenden (eds.), *Language and Peace* (Aldershot: Dartmouth), pp. 37–59.

Chilton, P. and Schäffner, C. (1997) 'Discourse and Politics', in T. A. van Dijk (ed.), *Discourse Studies: . A Multidisciplinary Introduction, vol. 2: Discourse as Social Interaction* (London, Sage), pp. 206–30.

Chilton, P. A. and Schäffner, C. (eds) (2002) *Politics as Text: Analytic Approaches to Political Discourse* (Amsterdam: John Benjamins).

Chomsky, N. (2003) *Hegemony or Survival: America's Quest for Global Dominance* (New York: Metropolitan Books).

Chouliaraki, L. (2005) 'The Soft Power of War: Legitimacy and Community in Iraq War Discourses', special issue of *Journal of Language and Politics*, 4(1).

Christopher, P. (2003) *The Ethics of War and Peace. An Introduction to Legal and Moral Issues* (Upper Saddle River, N J: Pearson/Prentice Hall).

Cicourel, Aaron V. (1973) *Cognitive Sociology* (Harmondsworth: Penguin).

Clark, H. H. (1996) *Using Language* (Cambridge, Cambridge University Press).

Clegg, S. (1975) *Power, Rule and Domination: A Critical and Empirical Understanding of Power in Sociological Theory and Organizational Life* (London: Routledge & Kegan Paul).

Clegg, S. R. (1989) *Frameworks of Power* (London: Sage).

Cody, M. J. and McLaughlin, M. L. (1988) 'Accounts on Trial: Oral Arguments in Traffic Court', in C. Antaki (ed.) *Analysing Everyday Explanation: A Casebook of Methods* (London: Sage), pp. 113–26.

Cohen, S. and Young, J. (eds.) (1981) *The Manufacture of News: Deviance, Social Problems and the Mass Media* (London: Constable).

Coleman, H. (ed.) (1984) 'Language and Work 1: Law, Industry, Education'. *International Journal of the Sociology of Language*, 49 (special issue).

Coleman, H. (1985a) 'Talking Shop: An Overview of Language and Work'. *International Journal of the Sociology of Language*, 51: 105–29.

Coleman, H. (ed.) (1985b) 'Language and Work 2: The Health Professions'. *International Journal of the Sociology of Language*, 51 (special issue).

Coleman, H. and Burton, J. (1985) 'Aspects of Control in the Dentist–Patient Relationship'. *International Journal of the Sociology of Language*, 51: 75–104.

Collins, R., Curran, J., Garnham, N., Scannell, P., Schlesinger, P. and Sparks, C. (eds.) (1986) *Media, Culture and Society* (London: Sage).

Converse, P. E. (1964) 'The Nature of Belief Systems in Mass Publics'. *International Yearbook of Political Behavior Research*, 5: 206–62.

Cook-Gumperz, J. (1973) *Social Control and Socialization* (London: Routledge & Kegan Paul).

Coulthard, R. M. (ed.) (1994) *Advances in Written Text Analysis* (London: Routledge & Kegan Paul).

Crigler, A. N. (ed.) (1996) *The Psychology of Political Communication* (Ann Arbor, MI: The University of Michigan Press).

Culley, J. D. and Bennett, R. (1976) 'Selling Women, Selling Blacks'. *Journal of Communication*, 26: 160–74.

Daalder, I. H. and Lindsay, J. M. (2003) *America Unbound: The Bush Revolution in Foreign Policy* (Washington, DC : Brookings Institution).

Dahl, R. A. (1957) 'The Concept of Power'. *Behavioural Science*, 2: 201–15.

Dahl, R. A. (1961) *Who Governs? Democracy and Power in an American City* (New Haven, CT: Yale University Press).

Danet, B. (1980) 'Language in the Legal Process'. *Law and Society Review*, 14: 445–65.

Danet, B. (ed.) (1984) 'Legal Discourse'. *Text*, 4(1/3) (special issue).

Dates, J. L. and Barlow, W. (eds) (1990) *Split Image: African Americans in the Mass Media* (Washington, DC: Howard University Press).

Davis, H. and Walton, P. (eds.) (1983) *Language, Image, Media* (Oxford: Blackwell).

Davis, K. (1988) *Power under the Microscope. Toward a Grounded Theory of Gender Relations in Medical Encounters* (Dordrecht: Foris).

Day, N. (1999) *Advertising: Information or Manipulation?* (Springfield, NJ: Enslow).

Debnam, G. (1984) *The Analysis of Power* (London: Macmillan).

Derian, J. D. and Shapiro, M. J. (1989) *International Intertextual Relations* (Lexington, MA: D. C. Heath).

Di Pietro, R. J. (1982) *Linguistics and the Professions* (Norwood, NJ: Ablex).

Diamond, J. (1996) *Status and Power in Verbal Interaction: A Study of Discourse in a Close-knit Social Network* (Amsterdam: Benjamin).

Dillard, J. P. and Pfau, M. (2002) *The Persuasion Handbook: Developments in Theory and Practice* (Thousand Oaks, CA: Sage).

Dines, G. and Humez, J. M. M. (eds.) (1995) *Gender, Race and Class in Media. A Text-Reader* (London, CA: Sage).

Dinstein, Y. (2001) *War, Aggression and Self-Defense* (Cambridge, UK and New York: Cambridge University Press).

Dittmar, N. and von Stutterheim, C. (1985) 'On the Discourse of Immigrant Workers', in T. A. van Dijk (ed.), *Handbook of Discourse Analysis: Vol. 4. Discourse Analysis in Society* (London: Academic Press), pp. 125–52.

Doherty, F. and McClintock, M. (2002) *A Year of Loss: Reexamining Civil Liberties since September 11* (New York: Lawyers Committee for Human Rights).

Domhoff, G. W. (1978) *The Powers that Be: Processes of Ruling Class Domination in America* (New York: Random House).

Domhoff, G. W. (1983) *Who Rules American Now? A View from the 1980s* (Englewood Cliffs, NJ: Prentice Hall).

Domhoff, G. W. and Ballard, H. B. (eds.) (1968) *C. Wright Mills and the Power Elite* (Boston: Beacon Press).

Donald, J. and Hall, S. (eds.) (1986) *Politics and Ideology* (Milton Keynes: Open University Press).

Dorfman, A. and Mattelart, A. (1972) *Para leer el Pato Donald. Comunicación de Masa y Colonialismo. (How to Read Donald Duck. Mass Communication and Colonialism)* (Mexico: Siglo XXI).

Dovidio, J. F. and Gaertner, S. L. (eds.) (1986) *Prejudice, Discrimination and Racism* (New York: Academic Press).

Downing, J. (1980) *The Media Machine* (London: Pluto).

Downing, J. (1984) *Radical Media: The Political Experience of Alternative Communication* (Boston: South End Press).

Drew, P. and Heritage, J. (eds.) (1992) *Talk at Work: Interaction in Institutional Settings* (Cambridge: Cambridge University Press).

D'Souza, D. (1995) *The End of Racism: Principles for Multiracial Society* (New York: Free Press).

Duin, A. H., Roen, D. H. and Graves, M. F. (1988) 'Excellence or Malpractice: The Effects of Headlines on Readers' Recall and Biases'. National Reading Conference (1987, St Petersburg, Florida). *National Reading Conference Yearbook*, 37: 245–50.

Duranti, A. (1997) *Linguistic Anthropology* (Cambridge, UK and New York, NY: USA: Cambridge University Press).

Duranti, A. (ed.) (2001) *Linguistic Anthropology: A Reader* (Malden, MA: Blackwell).

Duranti, A. and C. Goodwin (eds.) (1992) *Rethinking Context: Language as an Interactive Phenomenon* (Cambridge: Cambridge University Press).

Duszak, A. (ed.) (1997) *Culture and Styles of Academic Discourse* (Berlin: Mouton de Gruyter).

Dyer, G. (1982) *Advertising as Communication* (London: Methuen).

Eagly, A. H. and Chaiken, S. (1993) *The Psychology of Attitudes* (Orlando, Harcourt Brace Jovanovich).

Eakins, B. W. and Eakins, B. W. and Eakins, R. G. (1978) *Sex Differences in Human Communication* (Boston: Houghton Mifflin).

Ebel, M. and Fiala, P. (1983) *Sous le consensus, la xénophobie* (Lausanne: Institut de Science Politique).

Edelman, M. (1964) *The Symbolic Uses of Politics* (Urbana: University of Illinois Press).

Edelman, M. (1974) 'The Political Language of the Helping Professions'. *Politics and Society*, 4: 295–310.

Edwards, D. and Potter, J. (1992) *Discursive Psychology* (London: Sage Publications).

Ehlich, K. (ed.) (1989) *Sprache im Faschismus (Language under Fascism)* (Frankfurt: Suhrkamp).

Ehlich, K. (ed.) (1995) *The Discourse of Business Negotiation* (Berlin: Mouton de Gruyter).

Erickson, B., Lind, A. A., Johnson, B. C. and O'Barr, W. M. (1978) 'Speech Style and Impression Formation in a Court Setting: The Effects of "powerful" and "powerless" speech'. *Journal of Experimental Social Psychology*, 14: 266–79.

Erickson, F. and Shultz, J. (1982) *The Counselor as Gatekeeper: Social Interaction in Interviews* (New York: Academic Press).

Ervin-Tripp, S. and Strage, A. (1985) 'Parent–Child Discourse', in T. A. van Dijk (ed.), *Handbook of Discourse Analysis: Vol. 3. Discourse and Dialogue* (London: Academic Press), pp. 67–78.

Ervin-Tripp, S., O'Connor, M. C. and Rosenberg, J. (1984) Language and Power in the Family', in C. Kramarae, M. Schulz and W. M. D'Elan (eds.), *Language and Power* (Beverly Hills, CA: Sage), pp. 116–25.

Essed, P. J. M. (1984) *Alledaags Racisme [Everyday Racism]* (Amsterdam: Sara; English version published by Claremont, CA: Hunter House).

Essed, P. J. M. (1987) *Academic Racism: Common Sense in the Social Sciences* (University of Amsterdam: Centre for Race and Ethnic Studies, CRES Publications), no. 5.

Essed, P. J. M. (1991) *Understanding Everyday Racism: An Interdisciplinary Theory* (Newbury Park, CA: Sage).

Etzioni-Halevy, E. (1989) *Fragile Democracy: The Use and Abuse of Power in Western Societies* (New Brunswick, NJ: Transaction).

Fairclough, N. (1995) *Critical Discourse Analysis: The Critical Study of Language* (London: Longman).

Fairclough, N. L. (1992a) *Discourse and Social Change* (Cambridge: Polity Press).

Fairclough, N. L. (ed.) (1992b) *Critical Language Awareness* (London: Longman).

Fairclough, N. L. (1995a) *Critical Discourse Analysis: The Critical Study of Language* (Harlow, UK: Longman).

Fairclough, N. L. (1995b) *Media Discourse* (London: Edward Arnold).

Fairclough, N. L. and Wodak, R. (1997) 'Critical Discourse Analysis', in T. A. van Dijk (ed.), *Discourse Studies: A Multidisciplinary Introduction, Vol. 2. Discourse as Social Interaction* (London: Sage), pp. 258–84.

Falbo, T. and Peplau, L. A. (1980) 'Power strategies in intimate relationships'. *Journal of Personality and Social Psychology*, 38: 618–28.

Falk, R. A. (2003) *The Great Terror War* (New York: Olive Branch Press).

Fascell, D. B. (ed.) (1979) *International News: Freedom under Attack* (Beverly Hills, CA: Sage).

Fay, B. (1987) *Critical Social Science* (Cambridge: Polity).

Fedler, F. (1973) 'The Media and Minority Groups: A Study of Adequacy of Access'. *Journalism Quarterly*, 50(1): 109–17.

Fernandez, J. P. (1981) *Racism and Sexism in Corporate Life* (Lexington, MA: Lexington Books).

Ferree, M. M. and Hall, E. J. (1996) 'Rethinking Stratification from a Feminist Perspective: Gender, Race and Class in Mainstream Textbooks'. *American Sociological Review*, 61(6): 929–50.

Ferro, M. (1981) *Comment on raconte l'Histoire aux enfants à travers le monde entier* (Paris: Payot).

Fetzer, A. (2004) *Recontextualizing Context* (Amsterdam: Benjamins).

Fielding, G. and Evered, C. (1980) 'The Influence of Patients' Speech upon Doctors: The Diagnostic Interview', in R. N. St. Clair and H. Giles (eds.), *The Social and Psychological Contexts of Language* (Hillsdale, NJ: Lawrence Erlbaum), pp. 51–72.

Fisher, S. (1995) *Nursing Wounds. Nurse Practitioners, Doctors, Women Patients and the Negotiation of Meaning* (New Brunswick, NJ: Rutgers University Press).

Fisher, S. and Todd, A. D. (1983) *The Social Organization of Doctor–Patient Communication* (Washington, DC: Center for Applied Linguistics).

Fisher, S. and Todd, A. D. (eds.) (1986) *Discourse and Institutional Authority. Medicine, Education and Law* (Norwood, NJ: Ablex).

Fishman, M. (1980) *Manufacturing the News* (Austin: University of Texas Press).

Fishman, P. (1983) 'Interaction: The Work Women Do'', in B. Thorne, C. Kramarae and N. Henley (eds.), *Language, Gender, and Society* (New York: Pergamon Press), pp. 89–101.

Fiske, S. T. and Taylor, S. E. (1991) *Social Cognition*, 2nd edn (New York: Mcgraw-Hill)

Fiske, S. T., Lau, R. R. and Smith, R. A. (1990) 'On the Varieties and Utilities of Political Expertise'. *Social Cognition*, 8(1): 31–48.

Forgas, J. P. (1979) *Social Episodes: The Study of Interaction Routines* (London and New York: Published in cooperation with the European Association of Experimental Social Psychology by Academic Press).

Forgas, J. P. (ed.) 91985) *Language and Social Situations* (New York: Springer).

Fossà, G. and Barenghi, R. (2003) *The Bush Show: Verità e bugie della guerra infinita* (San Lazzaro di Savena (Bologna): Nuovi mondi media).

Fowler, R. (1985) 'Power', in T. A. van Dijk (ed.), *Handbook of Discourse Analysis: Vol. 4. Discourse Analysis in Society* (London: Academic Press), pp. 61–82.

Fowler, R. (1991) *Language in the News. Discourse and Ideology in the Press* (London: Routledge & Kegan Paul).

Fowler, R., Hodge, B., Kress, G. and Trew, T. (1979) *Language and Control* (London: Routledge and Kegan Paul).

Fox, C. J. and Miller, H. T. (1995) *Postmodern Public Administration. Toward Discourse* (London, CA: Sage).

Fox, D. R. and Prilleltensky, I. (1997) *Critical Psychology: An Introduction* (London: Sage).

Freeman, S. H. and Heller, M. S. (1987) 'Medical Discourse'. *Text*, 7 (special issue).

Fussell, S. R. and Krauss, R. M. (1992) 'Coordination of Knowledge in Communication: Effects of Speakers' Assumptions about What Others Know'. *Journal of Personality and Social Psychology*, 62(3): 378–91.

Galbraith, J. K. (1985) *The Anatomy of Power* (London: Corgi).

Galtung, J. and Ruge, M. H. (1965) 'The Structure of Foreign News'. *Journal of Peace Research*, 2: 64–91.

Gamble, A. (1986) ' The Political Economy of Freedom', in R. Levitas (ed.), *The Ideology of the New Right* (Cambridge, MA: Polity), pp. 25–54.

Gamson, W. A. (1992) *Talking Politics* (Cambridge: Cambridge University Press).

Gans, H. (1979) *Deciding What's News* (New York: Pantheon Books).

Giles, H. and Powesland, P. F. (1975) *Speech Style and Social Evaluation* (London: Academic Press).

Gareau, F. H. (2004) *State Terrorism and the United States: From Counterinsurgency to the War on Terrorism* (Atlanta, GA: Clarity Press).

Garnham, A. (1987) *Mental Models as Representations of Discourse and Text* (Chichester: Ellis Horwood).

Gazdar, G. (1979) *Pragmatics: Implicature, Presupposition and Logical Form* (New York: Academic Press).

Ghadessy, M. (ed.) (1999) *Text and Context in Functional Linguistics* (Amsterdam Philadelphia: John Benjamins).

Giles, H. and Powlesland, P. F. (1975) *Speech Style and Social Evaluation* (London: European Association of Experimental Social Psychology by Academic Press).

Giles, H. and Smith, P. M. (1979) 'Accommodation Theory: Optimal Levels of Convergence', in H. Giles and R. N. St Clair (eds.), Language and Social Psychology (Oxford: Basil Blackwell), pp. 45–65.

Giroux, H. (1981) *Ideology, Culture and the Process of Schooling* (London: Falmer Press).

Glasgow University Media Group (1976) *Bad News* (London: Routledge & Kegan Paul).

Glasgow University Media Group (1980) *More Bad News* (London: Routledge).

Glasgow University Media Group (1982) *Really Bad News* (London: Writers and Readers).

Glasgow University Media Group (1985) *War and Peace News* (Milton Keynes and Philadelphia: Open University Press).

Glasgow University Media Group (1993) Getting the Message', in J. Eldridge (ed.), *News, Truth and Power* (London: Routledge & Kegan Paul).

Glasser, T. L. and Salmon, C. T. (eds.) (1995) *Public Opinion and the Communication of Consent* (New York: Guilford Press).

Gleason, Y. B. and Geif, E. B. (1986) 'Men's Speech to Young Children', in B. Thome, C. Kramarae and N. Henley (eds.), *Language, Gender and Society* (Rowley, MA: Newbury House), pp. 140–50.

Goffman, E. (1959) *The Presentation of Self in Everyday Life* (Garden City, NY: Doubleday).

Goffman, E. (1967) *Interaction Ritual: Essays on Face-to-Face Behavior* (Garden City, NY: Doubleday).

Goffman, E. (1979) *Gender Advertisements* (New York: Harper & Row).

Golding, P. and Murdock, G. (1979) 'Ideology and the Mass Media: The Question of Determination', in M. Barrett, P. Corrigan, A. Kuhn and J. Wolff (eds.), *Ideology and Cultural Production* (London: Croom Helm), pp. 198–224.

Graber, D. A. (1980) *Crime News and the Public* (New York: Praeger).

Graber, Doris A. (1984) *Processing the News* (New York: Longman).

Graesser, A. C. and Bower, G. H. (eds.) (1990) *Inferences and Text Comprehension: The Psychology of Learning and Motivation*, Vol. 25 (New York: Academic Press).

Gramsci, A. (1971) *Prison Notebooks* (New York: International Publishers).

Granberg, D. (1993) 'Political Perception', in S. Iyengar and W. J. McGuire (eds.), *Explorations in Political Psychology: Duke Studies in Political Psychology* (Durham NC, Duke University Press), pp. 70–112.

Greenberg, B. S. (ed.) (2002) *Communication and Terrorism: Public and Media Responses to 9/11* (Cresskill, NJ: Hampton Press).

Greenberg, B. S. and Mazingo, S. L. (1976) 'Racial Issues in Mass Media Institutions', in P. A. Katz (ed.), *Towards the Elimination of Racism* (New York: Pergamon), pp. 309–40.

Greenberg, J., Kirkland, S. and Pyszczynski, T. (1987) 'Some Theoretical Notions and Preliminary Research Concerning Derogatory Labels', in G. Smitherman-Donaldson & T. A. van Dijk (eds.), *Discourse and Communication* (Detroit, MI: Wayne State University Press).

Grice, H. (1975) 'Logic and Conversation', in P. Cole and J. Morgan (eds.) *Syntax and Semantics, Vol. 3: Speech Acts* (New York: Academic Press), pp. 68–134.

Grice, H. P. (1989) *Studies in the Way of Words* (Cambridge, Mass: Harvard University Press).

Guespin, L. (ed.) (1976) Typologie du discours politique [Typology of political discourse], *Languages*, 41.

Gumperz, J. J. (1982a) *Discourse Strategies* (Cambridge: Cambridge University Press).

Gumperz, J. (ed.) (1982b) *Language and Social Identity* (Cambridge: Cambridge University Press).

Gumperz, J. J. (1992) 'Contextualization and Understanding', in A. Duranti and C. Goodwin (eds.), *Rethinking Context: Language as an Interactive Phenomenon* (Cambridge: Cambridge University Press), pp. 229–52.

Habermas, J. (1984) *The Theory of Communicative Action* (Boston, MA: Beacon Press).

Hall, S., Critcher, C., Jefferson, T., Clarke, J. and Roberts, B. (1978) *Policing the Crisis: Mugging, the State and Law and Order* (London: Methuen).

Hall, S., Hobson, D., Lowe, A. and Willis, P. (eds.) (1980) *Culture, Media, Language* (London: Hutchinson).

Halliday, F. (2002) *Two Hours that Shook the World: September 11, 2001: Causes and Consequences* (London: Saqi).

Halloran, J. D., Elliott, P. & Murdock, G. (1970) *Demonstrations and Communication: A Case Study* (Harmondsworth: Penguin).

Hamilton, D. (ed.) (1981) *Cognitive Processes in Stereotyping and Intergroup Behavior* (Hillsdale, NJ: Lawrence Erlbaum).

Hargreaves, A. G. and Leaman, J. (eds.) (1995) *Racism, Ethnicity and Politics in Contemporary Europe* (Aldershot, UK: Elgar).

Hariman, R. (ed.) (1990) *Popular Trials: Rhetoric, Mass Media and the Law* (Tuscaloosa, AL: University of Alabama Press).

Harris, S. (1984) 'Questions as a Mode of Control in Magistrates' Court'. *International Journal of the Sociology of Language*, 49: 5–27.

Hart, R. P. (1984) *Verbal Style and the Presidency* (Orlando, FL: Academic Press).

Hartmann, P. and Husband, C. (1974) *Racism and the Mass Media* (London: Davis-Poynter).

Helmreich, W. B. (1984) *The Things They Say Behind your Back. Stereotypes and the Myths Behind Them* (New Brunswick, NJ: Transaction Books).

Herman, E. S. and Chomsky, N. (1988) *Manufacturing Consent: The Political Economy of the Mass Media* (New York: Pantheon).

Hermann, M. G. (ed.) (1986) *Political Psychology* (San Francisco, Jossey-Bass).

Holly, W. (1990) *Politikersprache: Inszenierungen und Rollenkonflikte im informellen Sprachhandeln eines Bundestagsabgeordneten [Politician's Language: Dramatization and Role Conflicts in the Informal Speech Acts of a Bundestag Delegate]* (Berlin: Mouton de Gruyter).

Houston, M. and Kramarae, C. (eds.) (1991) *Women Speaking from Silence. Discourse and Society*, 2(4), special issue.

Hudson, K. (1978) *The Language of Modern Politics* (London: Methuen).

Hujanen, T. (ed.) (1984) 'The Role of Information in the Realization of the Human Rights of Migrant Workers', report of international conference, Tampere (Finland) (University of Tampere: Dept of Journalism and Mass Communication).

Hurwitz, J. and Peffley, M. (eds.) (1998) *Perception and Prejudice: Race and Politics in the United States* (New Haven, CT: Yale University Press).

Hymes, D. (ed.) (1972) *Reinventing Anthropology* (New York: Vintage Books).

Ibañez, T. and Íñiguez, L. (eds.) (1997) *Critical Social Psychology* (London: Sage).

Irvine, J. T. (1974) 'Strategies of Status Manipulation in the Wolof Greeting', in R. Bauman and J. Sherzer (eds.), *Explorations in the Ethnography of Speaking* (Cambridge: Cambridge University Press, pp. 167–91.

Iyengar, S. and McGuire, W. J. (1993) *Explorations in Political Psychology* (Durham: Duke University Press).

Jäger, S. (1992) *Brandsätze. Rassismus im Alltag [Inflammatory Sentences/Firebombs. Racism in Everyday Life]* (Duisburg, Germany: DISS).

Jäger, S. and Link, J. (1993) *Die vierte Gewalt: Rassismus and die Medien [The Fourth Power. Racism and the Media]* (Duisburg, Germany: DISS).

Jaworski, A. (1983) 'Sexism in Textbooks'. *British Journal of Language Teaching*, 21(2): 109–13.

Jaynes, G. D. and Williams, R. M. (eds.) (1989) *A Common Destiny: Blacks and American Society* (Washington, DC: National Academy Press).

Jenkins, R. (1986).*Racism and Recruitment: Managers, Organisations and Equal Opportunity in the Labour Market* (Cambridge: Cambridge University Press).

Johnson, K. A. (1987) *Media Images of Boston's Black Community*. William Monroe Trotter Institute, Research Report (Boston, MA: University of Massachusetts).

Johnson-Laird, P. N. (1983) *Mental Models* (Cambridge: Cambridge University Press).

Judd, C. M. and J. W. Downing. (1990) 'Political Expertise and the Development of Attitude Consistency'. *Social Cognition*, 8(1): 104–24.

Just, M. R., A. N. Crigler and W. R. Neuman. (1996) 'Cognitive and Affective Dimensions of Political Communication', in A. N. Crigler (ed.), *The Psychology of Political Communication* (Ann Arbor, MI: The University of Michigan Press), pp. 133–48.

Kalin, R. and Rayko, D. (1980) 'The Social Significance of Speech in the Job Interview', in R. N. St Clair and H. Giles (eds.), *The Social and Psychological Contexts of Language* (Hillsdale, NJ: Lawrence Erlbaum), pp. 39–50.

Katz, P. A. and Taylor, D. A. (eds.) (1988) *Eliminating Racism: Profiles in Controversy* (New York: Plenum Press).

Kelly, J. W. (1985) 'Storytelling in High Tech Organizations: A Medium for Sharing Culture'. Paper presented at the annual meeting of the Western Speech Communication Association, Fresno, CA.

Kennedy, S. (1959) *Jim Crow guide to the USA* (London: Lawrence and Wishart).

King, J. and Stott, M. (eds.) (1977) *Is this your life? Images of women in the media* (London: Virago).

Kinloch, G. C. (1981) *Ideology and Contemporary Sociological Theory* (Englewood Cliffs, NJ: Prentice-Hall).

Klein, G. (1986) *Reading into Racism* (London: Routledge & Kegan Paul).

Kinder, D. R. and L. M. Sanders. (1990) 'Mimicking Political Debate with Survey

Questions: The Case of White Opinion on Affirmative-Action for Blacks'. *Social Cognition*, 8(1): 73–103.

King, J. and Stott, M. (eds) (1977) *Is this Your life? Images of Women in the Media* (London: Virago).

Kintsch, W. (1998) *Comprehension: A Paradigm for Cognition* (Cambridge: Cambridge University Press).

Klapper, J. T. (1960) *The Effects of Mass Communication* (New York: Free Press).

Klaus, G. (1971) *Sprache der Politik [Language of Politics]* (Berlin: VEB Deutscher Verlag der Wissenschaften).

Klein, G. (1985) *Reading into Racism: Bias in Children's Literature and Learning Materials* (London: Routledge & Kegan Paul).

Klein, W. and Dittmar, N. (1979) *Developing Grammars: The Acquisition of German by Foreign Workers* (Heidelberg and New York: Springer-Verlag).

Knorr-Cetina, K. and Cicourel, A. V. (eds.) (1981) *Advances in Social Theory and Methodology: Towards an Integration of Micro- and Macrosociologies* (London: Routledge & Kegan Paul).

Kochman, T. (1981) *Black and White Styles in Conflict* (Chicago: University of Chicago Press).

Kotthoff, H. and Wodak, R. (eds.) (1997) *Communicating Gender in Context* (Amsterdam: John Benjamins).

Kramarae, C. (1980) *Voices and Words of Women and Men* (Oxford and New York: Pergamon).

Kramarae, C. (1983) *Women and Men Speaking* (Rowley, MA: Newbury House).

Kramarae, C., Schulz, M. and O'Barr, W. M. (1984) 'Towards an Understanding of Language and Power', in C. Kramarae, M. Schulz and W. M. O'Barr (eds.), *Language and Power* (Beverly Hills, CA: Sage).

Kramarae, C., Thorne, B. and Henley, N. (1983) 'Sex Similarities and Differences in Language, Speech and Nonverbal Communication: An Annotated Bibliography', in B. Thorne, C. Kramarae and N. Henley (eds.), *Language, Gender and Society* (Rowley, MA: Newbury House), pp. 151–331.

Kraus, S. (ed.) (1990) *Mass Communication and Political Information Processing* (Hillsdale NJ: Lawrence Erlbaum).

Kraus, S. and R. M. Perloff (eds.) (1985) *Mass Media and Political Thought* (Beverly Hills CA, Sage).

Kress, G. (1985) 'Ideological Structures in Discourse', in T. A. van Dijk (ed.), *Handbook of Discourse Analysis*, Vol. 4: *Discourse Analysis in Society* (London: Academie Press), pp. 27–42.

Kress, G. and Hodge, B. (1979) *Language and Ideology* (London: Routledge & Kegan Paul).

Krosnick, J. A. and M. A. Milburn. (1990) 'Psychological Determinants of Political Opinionation'. *Social Cognition* 8: 49–72.

Kuklinski, J. H., Luskin, R. C. and Bolland, J. (1991) 'Where is the Schema: Going Beyond the S-Word in Political Psychology?'. *American Political Science Review*, 85(4): 134–56.

Labov, W. (1972) 'Rules for Ritual Insults', in D. Sudnow (ed.), *Studies in Social Interaction* (New York: Free Press), pp. 120–69.

Lakoff, R. T. (1990) *Talking Power. The Politics of Language* (New York: Basic Books).

Lau, R. R. and Sears, D. O. (eds.) (1986) *Political Cognition* (Hillsdale, NJ: Erlbaum).

Lau, R. R., Smith, R. A. and Fiske, S. T. (1991) 'Political Beliefs, Policy Interpretations and Political Persuasion'. *Journal of Politics*, 53(3): 644–75.

Lauren, P. G. (1988) *Power and Prejudice. The Politics and Diplomacy of Racial Discrimination* (Boulder, CO: Westview Press).

Lavandera, B. R., Garcia Negroni, M. M., Lopez OcOn, M., Luis, C. R., Menendez, S. M., Pardo, M. L., Raiter, A. G. and Zoppi-Fontana, M. (1986) 'Analisis sociolingüístico del discurso politico'. *Cuadernos del Institute de Lingüística*, 1(1) (Buenos Aires: Instituto de Linguistica, Universidad de Buenos Aires).

Lavandera, B. R., Garcia Negroni, M. M., Lopez OcOn, M., Luis, C. R., Menendez, S. M., Pardo, M. L., Raiter, A. G. and Zoppi-Fontana, M. (1987) 'Analisis sociolingüístico del discurso politico (II)'. *Cuadernos del Institute de Lingüística* (Buenos Aires: Instituto de Linguistica, Universidad de Buenos Aires).

Lazar, M. (ed.) (2005) *Feminist Critical Discourse Analysis: Gender, Power and Ideology in Discourse* (Houndsmills, UK: Palgrave Macmillan).

Leckie-Tarry, H. (1995) *Language and Context. A Functional Linguistic Theory of Register*. Edited by David Birch (London: Pinter).

Leet-Pellegrini, H. (1980) 'Conversational Dominance as a Function of Gender and Expertise', in H. Giles, W. P. Robinson and P. Smith (eds.), *Language: Social Psychological Perspectives* (Oxford: Pergamon Press), pp. 97–104.

Leimdorfer, F. (1992) *Discours academique et colonisation. Themes de recherche sur l'Algerie pendant la periode coloniale [Academic Discourse and Colonization: Research on Algeria during the Colonial Period]* (Paris: Publisud).

Lein, L. and Brenneis, D. (1978) 'Children's Disputes in Three Speech Communities'. *Language in Society*, 7: 299–323.

Levinson, S. C. (2000) *Presumptive Meanings: The Theory of Generalized Conversational Implicature* (Cambridge, MA: MIT Press).

Lewis, M. and Saarni, C. (eds.) (1993) *Lying and Deception in Everyday Life* (New York, NY: Guilford Press).

Liebes, T. and Katz, E. (1990) *The Export of Meaning: Cross-cultural Readings of 'Dallas'* (New York: Oxford University Press).

Lind, E. A. and O'Barr, W. M. (1979) 'The Social Significance of Speech in the Courtroom', in H. Giles and R. N. St Clair (eds.), *Language and Social Psychology* (Oxford: Basil Blackwell), pp. 66–87.

Lindegren-Lerman, C. (1983) 'Dominant Discourse: The Institutional Voice and the Control of Topic', in H. Davis and P. Walton (eds.), *Language, Image, Media* (Oxford: Basil Blackwell), pp. 75–103.

Linell, P. and Jonsson, L. (1991) 'Suspect Stories: Perspective-setting in an Asymmetrical Situation', in I. Markova and K. Foppa (eds.), *Asymmetries in Dialogue: The Dynamics of Dialogue* (Savage, MD: Barnes and Noble Books/Bowman and Littlefield Publishers/ Harvester Wheatsheaf), pp. 75–100.

Lodge, M. and K. M. McGraw (eds.) (1995) *Political Judgement: Structure and Process* (Ann Arbor MI: University of Michigan Press).

Lorimer, R. (1984) 'Defining the Curriculum: The Role of the Publisher'. Paper presented at the annual meeting of the American Educational Research Association, New Orleans.

Luke, T. W. (1989) *Screens of Power: Ideology, Domination, and Resistance in Informational Society* (Urbana: University of Illinois Press).

Lukes, S. (1974) *Power: A Radical View* (London: Macmillan).

Lukes, S. (ed.) (1986) *Power* (Oxford: Blackwell).

Mankekar, D. R. (1978) *One-Way Flow: Neo-Colonialism via News Media* (New Delhi: Clarion).

Manning, D. J. (ed.) (1980) *The Form of Ideology* (London: George, Allen & Unwin).

Manstead, T. and McCullogh, C. (1981) 'Sex Role Stereotyping in British Television Ads'. *British Journal of Social Psychology*, 20: 171–80.

Marable, M. (1985) *Black American Politics* (London: Verso).

Martin Rojo, L. (1994) 'Jargon of Delinquents and the Study of Conversational Dynamics'. *Journal of Pragmatics*, 21(3): 243–89.

Martín Rojo, L. (1995) 'Division and Rejection: From the Personification of the Gulf Conflict to the Demonisation of Saddam Hussein'. *Discourse & Society* 6(1): 49–79.

Martin Rojo, L. and T. A. van Dijk. (1997) '"There was a problem and it was solved!" Legitimating the Expulsion of "Illegal" Immigrants in Spanish Parliamentary Discourse'. *Discourse and Society*, 8(4): 523–66.

Martindale, C. (1986) *The White Press and Black America* (New York: Greenwood Press).

Mattelart, A. (1979) *The Multinational Corporations and the Control of Culture: The Ideological Apparatus of Imperialism* (Atlantic Highlands, NJ: Harvester).

Maynard, D. W. (1985) 'The analysis of plea bargaining discourse', in T. A. van Dijk (ed.), *Handbook of Discourse Analysis: Vol. 4. Discourse Analysis in Society* (London: Academic Press), pp. 153–79.

Mazingo, S. (1988) 'Minorities and Social Control in the Newsroom: Thirty Years after Breed', in G. Smitherman-Donaldson and T. A. van Dijk (eds.), *Discourse and Discrimination* (Detroit, MI: Wayne State University Press), pp. 93–130.

McHoul, A. W. (1986) 'Writing, Sexism and Schooling: A Discourse-Analytic Investigation of Some Recent Documents on Sexism and Education in Queensland', in S. Fisher and A. D. Todd (eds.), *Discourse and Institutional Authority: Medicine, Education and Law* (Norwood, NJ: Ablex), pp. 187–202.

McLaughlin, M. L. (1984) *Conversation: How Talk is Organized* (Beverly Hills, CA: Sage).

McPhee, R. D. and Tompkins, P. K. (eds.) (1985) *Organizational Communication: Traditional Themes and New Directions* (Beverly Hills, CA: Sage).

Mead, R. (1985) 'Courtroom Discourse'. English Language Research, Discourse Analysis Monographs, 9 (University of Birmingham).

Mehan, H. (1979) *Learning Lessons* (Cambridge, MA: Harvard University Press).

Mehan, H. (1986) 'The Role of Language and the Language of Role in Institutional Decision Making', in S. Fisher and A. D. Todd (eds.), *Discourse and Institutional Authority: Medicine, Education and Law* (Norwood, NJ: Ablex), pp. 140–63.

Mercer, N. (1995) *The Guided Construction of Knowledge. Talk Amongst Teachers and Learners* (Clevedon: Multilingual Matters).

Merelman, R. M. (1986) 'Revitalizing Political Socialization', in M. G. Hermann (ed.), *Political Psychology* (San Francisco, Jossey-Bass), pp. 279–319.

Merten, K. (1986) *Das Bild der Ausländer in der deutschen Presse* (Frankfurt: Gagyeli Verlag).

Messaris, P. (1997) *Visual Persuasion: The Role of Images in Advertising* (Thousand Oaks, CA: Sage).

Mey, J. (1985) *Whose Language: A Study in Linguistic Pragmatics* (Amsterdam: Benjamins).

Milburn, M. A. (1987) 'Ideological Self-Schemata and Schematically Induced Attitude Consistency'. *Journal of Experimental Social Psychology*, 23(5): 383–98.

Miles, R. (1989) *Racism* (London: Routledge).

Milliband, R. (1983) *Class Power and State Power* (London: Verso).

Mills, C. W. (1956) *The Power Elite* (New York: Oxford University Press).

Miller, G. A. (1956) 'The Magical Number Seven, Plus or Minus Two: Some Limits on our Capacity for Processing Information'. *Psychological Review*, 63: 81–97.

Milner, D. (1983) *Children and Race: Ten Years On* (London: Ward Lock Educational).

Minority Participation in the Media (1983) Hearings before the Subcommittee on Telecommunications, Consumer Protection and Finance, of the Committee on Energy and Commerce, House of Representatives, 98th Congress, 19 and 23 September, 1983.

Mishler, E. G. (1984) *The Discourse of Medicine: Dialectics in Medical Interviews* (Norwood, NJ: Ablex).

Morrow, D. G. (1994) 'Spatial Models Created from Text', in H. van Oostendorp and R. A. Zwaan (eds.), *Naturalistic Text Comprehension* (Norwood, NJ: Ablex), pp. 57–78.

Moscovici, S. (2001) *Social Representations: Explorations in Social Psychology* (New York: New York University Press).

Mueller, C. ('1973) *The Politics of Communication: A Study of the Political Sociology of Language, Socialization and Legitimation* (New York: Oxford University Press).

Mumby, D. K. (1988) *Communication and Power in Organizations: Discourse, Ideology and Domination* (Norwood, NJ: Ablex).

Mumby, D. K. (ed.) (1993) *Narrative and Social Control: Critical Perspectives* (Newbury Park, CA: Sage).

Mumby, D. K. and Clair, R. P. (1997) 'Organizational Discourse', in T. A. van Dijk (ed.), *Discourse as Social Interaction: Discourse Studies. A Multidisciplinary Introduction*, vol. 1 (London: Sage), pp. 181–205.

Murray, N. (1986) 'Anti-Racists and Other Demons – The Press and Ideology in Thatcher's Britain'. *Race and Class*, 27: 1–19.

Natal, M., Entin, E. and Jaffe, J. (1979) 'Vocal Interruptions in Dyadic Communication as a Function of Speech and Social Anxiety'. *Journal of Personality and Social Psychology*, 37: 865–78.

Neisser, U. and Fivush, R. (eds.) (1994) *The Remembering Self: Construction and Accuracy in the Self-Narrative* (Cambridge: Cambridge University Press).

Nesler, M. S., Aguinis, H., Quigley, B. M. and Tedeschi, J. T. (1993) 'The Effect of Credibility on Perceived Power'. *Journal of Applied Social Psychology*, 23(17): 1407–25.

Newhouse, J. (2003) *Imperial America. The Bush Assault on the World Order* (New York: Knopf).

Ng, S. H. and Bradac, J. J. (1993) *Power in Language* (Newbury Park: Sage).

Nimmo, D. D. and Sanders, K. R. (eds.) (1981) *Handbook of Political Communication* (Beverly Hills, CA: Sage).

Nye, J. S. (2000) *Understanding International Conflicts. An Introduction to Theory and History* (New York: Longman).

O'Keefe, D. J. (2002) *Persuasion: Theory and Research* (Thousand Oaks, CA: Sage).

Oakhill, J. and A. Garnham, A. (eds.) (1996) *Mental Models in Cognitive Science. Essays in Honour of Phil Johnson-Laird* (Hove, UK: Psychology Press).

O'Barr, W. M. (1982) *Linguistic Evidence: Language, Power and Strategy in the Courtroom* (New York: Academic Press).

O'Barr, W. M., Conley, J. M. and Lind, A. (1978) 'The Power of Language: Presentational Style in the Courtroom'. *Duke Law Journal*, 14: 266–79.

Omi, M. and Winant, H. (1994) *Racial Formation in the United States. From the 1960s to the 1990s* (London: Routledge).

O'Shaughnessy, N. J. (2004) *Politics and Propaganda: Weapons of Mass Seduction* (Ann Arbor: University of Michigan Press).

Osler, A. (1994) 'Still Hidden from History: The Representation of Women in Recently Published History Textbooks'. *Oxford Review of Education*, 20(2): 219–35.

Owsley, H. H. and Scotton, C. M. (1984) The Conversational Expression of Power by Television Interviewers'. *Journal of Social Psychology*, 123: 696–735.

Packard, V. (1957) *The Hidden Persuaders* (New York: Pocket Books).

Palmer, M. T. (1989) 'Controlling conversations: turns, topics, & interpersonal control'. *Communication Monographs*, 56(1): 1–18.

Palmer, N. (ed.) (2003) *Terrorism, War and the Press* (Teddington, Middlesex: Hollis).

Pardo, M. L. (1996) 'Derecho y lingüística: Como se juzga con palabras' [Law and Linguistics: How to Judge with Words] (Buenos Aires: Nueva Visión).

Parkinson, M. G., Geisler, D. and Pelias, M. H. (1983) 'The Effects of Verbal Skills on Trial Success'. *Journal of the American Forensic Association*, 20: 16–22.

Pasierbsky, F. (1983) *Krieg und Frieden in der Sprache [War and Peace in Language]* (Frankfurt: Fischer).

Pêcheux, M. (1969) *Analyse automatique du discours* (Paris: Dunod).

Pêcheux, M. (1975) 'Analyse du discours. Langue et ideologies'. *Langages*, 37.

Pêcheux, M. (1982) *Language, Semantics and Ideology* (New York: St Martin's Press).

Percy, L. and Rossiter, J. R. (1980) *Advertising Strategy: A Communication Theory Approach* (New York: Praeger).

Pettigrew, A. M. (1972) 'Information Control as a Power Resource'. *Sociology*, 6: 187–204.

Pettigrew, A. M. (1973) *The Politics of Organizational Decision Making* (London: Tavistock).

Petty, R. E. and Cacioppo, J. T. (1981) *Attitudes and Persuasion: Classic and Contemporary Approaches* (Dubuque, IA: Wm. C. Brown).

Pfeffer, J. (1981) *Power in Organizations* (Marshfield, MA: Pitman).

Phizacklea, A. and Miles, R. (1979) 'Working Class Racist Beliefs in the Inner City', in R. Miles and A. Phizacklea (eds.), *Racism and Political Action in Britain* (London: Routledge & Kegan Paul), pp. 93–123.

Powell, L. W. (1989) 'Analyzing Misinformation: Perceptions of Congressional Candidates Ideologies'. *American Journal of Political Science*, 33: 272–93.

Preiswerk, R. (1980) *The Slant of the Pen: Racism in Children's Books* (Geneva: Programme to Combat Racism, World Council of Churches).

Radtke, I. (ed.) (1981) *Die Sprache des Rechts und der Verwaltung. Vol. 2. Deutsche Akademie für Sprache und Dichtung, Die öffentliche Sprachgebrauch* [The Language of the Law and the Administration. Vol. 2. German Academy of Language and Literature, Official Language Use]. (Stuttgart: Klett-Cotta).

Ragan, S. L. (1983) 'Alignment and Conversational Coherence', in R. T. Craig and K. Tracy (eds.), *Conversational Coherence* (Beverly Hills, CA: Sage), pp. 157–71.

Rasmussen, D. M. (ed.) (1996) *The Handbook of Critical Theory* (Oxford: Blackwell).

Reeves, F. (1983) *British Racial Discourse. A Study of British Political Discourse about Race and Race-Related Matters* (Cambridge: Cambridge University Press).

Richstad, J. and Anderson, M. H. (eds.) (1981) Crisis in international news. New York: Columbia University Press.

Riley, P. (1983) 'A Structurationist Account of Political Culture'. *Administrative Science Quarterly*, 28: 414–37.

Robinson, J. P. and Levy, M. R. (1986) *The Main Source. Learning from Television News* (Beverly Hills, CA: Sage).

Rodin, D. (2002) *War and Self-Defense* (Oxford: Clarendon Press and New York: Oxford University Press).

Roloff, M. E. and Berger, C. R. (eds.) (1982) *Social Cognition and Communication* (Beverly Hills, CA: Sage).

Roloff, M. E. and Miller, G. R. (eds.) (1980) *Persuasion: New Directions in Theory and Research* (Beverly Hills, CA: Sage).

Roseman, I., Abelson, R. P. and Ewing, M. F. (1986) 'Emotion and Political Cognition: Emotional Appeals in Political Communication', in R. R. Lau and D. O. Sears (eds.), *Political Cognition* (Hillsdale NJ, Lawrence Erlbaum), pp. 279–94.

Rosenblum, M. (1981) *Coups and Earthquakes: Reporting the World to America* (New York: Harper Row).

Sabsay, S. and Platt, M. (1985) *Social Setting, Stigma and Communicative Competence* (Amsterdam: John Benjamins).

Sacks, H., Schegloff, E. A. and Jefferson, G. A. (1974) 'A Simplest Systematics for the Organization of Turn Taking for Conversation'. *Language*, 50: 696–735.

Said, E. W. (1979) *Orientalism* (New York: Random House (Vintage)).

Said, E. W. (1981) *Covering Islam: How the Media and the Experts Determine How We See the Rest of the World* (New York: Pantheon).

Sarangi, S. and Roberts, C. (eds.) (1999) *Talk, Work and Institutional Order: Discourse in Medical, Mediation and Management Settings* (Berlin New York: Mouton de Gruyter).

Saville-Troike, M. (1982) *The Ethnography of Communication* (Oxford: Basil Blackwell).

Schatzman, L. and Strauss, A. (1972) 'Social Class and Modes of Communication', in S. Moscovici (ed.), *The Psychosociology of Language* (Chicago: Markham), pp. 206–21.

Schegloff, E. A. (1987) 'Between Macro and Micro: Contexts and Other Connections', in J. Alexander, R. M. B. Giesen and N. Smelser (eds.), *The Micro-Macro Link* (Berkeley: University of California Press), pp. 207–34.

Schegloff, E. A. (1991) Reflections on Talk and Social Structure', in: Boden, D., D. H. Zimmerman (eds.), *Talk and Social Structure: Studies in Ethnomethodology and Conversation Analysis* (Cambridge: Polity Press), pp 44–71.

Schegloff, E. A. (1992) 'In Another Context', in Alessandro, Duranti and Charles Goodwin (eds.), *Rethinking Context: Language as an Interactive Phenomenon* (Cambridge, UK: Cambridge University Press). pp. 191–227.

Scherer, K. R. and Giles, H. (1979) *Social Markers in Speech* (Cambridge: Cambridge University Press).

Schiller, H. L. (1973) *The Mind Managers* (Boston: Beacon Press).

Schlenker, B. R. (1980) *Impression Management: The Self-concept, Social Identity and Interpersonal Relations* (Monterey, CA: Brooks/Cole).

Schramm, W. and Atwood, E. (1981) *Circulation of News in the Third World: A Study of Asia* (Hong Kong: Chinese University Press).

Scott, M. and Lyman, S. (1968) 'Accounts'. *American Sociological Review*, 33: 46–62.

Seibold, D. R., Cantrill, J. G. and Meyers, R. A. (1985) Communication and Interpersonal Influence', in M. L. Knapp and G. R. Miller (eds.), *Handbook of Interpersonal Communication* (Beverly Hills, CA: Sage), pp. 551–611.

Seidel, G. (1985) Political discourse analysis', in T. A. van Dijk (ed.), *Handbook of*

Discourse Analysis:Vol. 4. Discourse Analysis in Society (London:Academic Press), pp. 43–60.

Seidel, G. (1987a) 'The White Discursive Order: The British New Rights's Discourse on Cultural Racism, with Particular Reference to the Salisbury Review', in I. Zavala, T. A. van Dijk and M. Diaz-Diocaretz (eds.), *Literature, Discourse, Psychiatry* (Amsterdam: John Benjamins), pp. 39–66.

Seidel, G. (1987b) 'The British New Right's "Enemy within":The Anti-Racists', in G. Smitherman-Donaldson and T. A. van Dijk (eds.), Discourse and Discrimination (Detroit:Wayne State University Press).

Seidel, G. (ed.) (1988) *The Nature of the Right. A Feminist Analysis of Order Patterns* (Amsterdam: John Benjamins), pp. 131–43.

Seliktar, O. (1986) 'Identifying a Society's Belief Systems', in M. G. Hermann (ed.), *Political Psychology* (San Francisco: Jossey-Bass), pp. 320–54.

Shapiro, M. (ed.) (1984) *Language and Politics* (Oxford: Basil Blackwell).

Shohat, E. and Stam, R. (1994) *Unthinking Eurocentrism. Multiculturalism and the Media* (London: Routledge & Kegan Paul).

Shore, B. (1996) *Culture in Mind: Cognition, Culture and the Problem of Meaning* (New York: Oxford University Press).

Shuy, R. W. (1986) 'Some Linguistic Contributions to a Criminal Court Case', in S. Fisher & A. D. Todd (eds.), *Discourse and Institutional Authority: Medicine, Education and Law* (Norwood, NJ: Ablex), pp. 234–49.

Shuy, R. W. (1992) *Language Crimes. The Use and Abuse of Language Evidence in the Court Room* (Oxford: Blackwell).

Sidel, M. (2004) *More Secure, Less Free? Antiterrorism Policy and Civil Liberties after September 11* (Ann Arbor: University of Michigan Press).

Sierra, M. T. (1992) Discurso, cultura y poder. El ejercio de la autoridad en los pueblos hfiethiifis del Valle del Mezquital. [Discourse, Culture and Power. The Exercise of Authority in the Hfialtfui (Otomli) Villages of the Mezquital Valley]. Gobierno del Estado de Hidalgo: Centro de Investigaciones y Estudios Superiores en Antropologia Social.

Sinclair, J. McH. and Brazil, D. (1982) *Teacher Talk* (Oxford: Oxford University Press).

Singh, R. (ed.) (1996) *Towards a Critical Sociolinguistics* (Amsterdam: John Benjamins).

Slobin, D. I., Miller, S. H. and Porter, L. W. (1972) 'Forms of Address and Social Relations in a Business Organization', in S. Moscovici (ed.), *The Psychosociology of Language* (Chicago: Markham), pp. 263–72.

Smith, D. E. (1991) 'Writing Women's Experience into Social Science'. *Feminism and Psychology*, 1(1): 155–69.

Smitherman-Donaldson, G. and van Dijk, T. A. (eds.) (1988) *Discourse and Discrimination* (Detroit:Wayne State University Press).

Sniderman, P. M.,Tetlock, P. E. and Carmines, E. G. (eds.) (1993) *Prejudice, Politics, and the American Dilemma* (Stanford, CA: Stanford University Press).

Snow, C. and Ferguson, C. (eds.) (1977) *Talking to Children* (New York: Cambridge University Press).

Solomos, J. (1989) *Race and Racism in Contemporary Britain* (London: Macmillan).

Solomos, J. (1993) *Race and Racism in Britain* (New York: St. Martin's Press).

Solomos, J. and Back, L. (1995) *Race, Politics and Social Change* (London: Routledge).

Spender, D. (1980) *Man-made Language* (London: Routledge & Kegan Paul).

Sperber, D. and D. Wilson (1986) *Relevance: Communication and Cognition* (Cambridge, MA: Harvard University Press).

Steiner, J. (2004) *Deliberative Politics in Action. Analysing Parliamentary Discourse* (New York: Cambridge University Press).

Stoll, E. A. (1983) A Naturalistic Study of Talk in the Classroom. Unpublished doctoral dissertation, University of Utah.

Stothard, P. (2003) *Thirty Days: Tony Blair and the Test of History* (New York: HarperCollins).

Strong, P. M. (1979) *The Ceremonial Order of Me Clinic: Parents, Doctors and Medical Bureaucracies* (London: Routledge & Kegan Paul).

Sykes, M. (1985) 'Discrimination in discourse', in T. A. van Dijk (ed.), *Handbook of Discourse Analysis: Vol. 4. Discourse Analysis in Society* (London: Academic Press), pp. 83–101

Sykes, M. (1987) 'From "rights" to "needs": Official Discourse and the "welfarisation" of race', in G. Smitherson-Donaldson and T. A. van Dijk (eds), *Discourse and Discrimination* (Detroit, MI: Wayne State University Press), pp. 176–205.

Taguieff, P.-A. (1988) *La force du préjugé. Essai sur le racisme et ses doubles* (Paris: Éditions de la Découverte).

Tajfel, H. (1981) *Human Groups and Social Categories* (Cambridge: Cambridge University Press).

Tannen, D. (1994a) *Gender and Discourse* (New York: Oxford University Press).

Tannen, D. (1994b) *Talking from 9 to 5: How Women's and Men's Conversational Styles Affect Who Gets Heard, Who Gets Credit, and What Gets Done at Work* (New York: Morrow).

Tedeschi, J. T. (ed.) (1981) *Impression Management: Theory and Social Psychological Research* (New York: Academic Press).

Tedeschi, J. T. and Reiss, M. (1981) 'Identities, the Phenomenal Self, and Laboratory Research', in J. T. Tedeschi (ed.), *Impression Management. Theory and Social Psychological Research* (New York: Academic Press), pp. 3–22.

Ter Wal, J. (1997) 'The Reproduction of Ethnic Prejudice and Racism through Policy and News Discourse: The Italian Case (1988–92)' (Florence: PhD, European Institute).

Tetlock, P. E. (1993) 'Cognitive Structural Analysis of Political Rhetoric: Methodological and Theoretical Issues', in S. Iyengar and W. J. McGuire (eds.), *Explorations in Political Psychology*. Duke Studies in Political Psychology (Durham NC, Duke University Press), pp. 380–405.

Tetlock, P. E. (1981) 'Personality and Isolationism: Content Analysis of Senatorial Speeches'. *Journal of Personality and Social Psychology*, 41: 737–43.

Tetlock, P. E. (1983) 'Cognitive Style and Political Ideology'. *Journal of Personality and Social Psychology*, 45(1): 118–26.

Tetlock, P. E. (1984) 'Cognitive Style and Political Belief Systems in the British House of Commons'. *Journal of Personality and Social Psychology*, 46: 365–75.

Tetlock, P. E. (1985a) 'Integrative Complexity of Policy Reasoning', in S. Kraus and R. Perloff (eds.), *Mass Media and Political Thought* (Beverly Hills CA, Sage).

Tetlock, P. E. (1985b) 'Toward an Intuitive Politician Model of Attribution Processes', in B. R. Schlenker (ed.), *The Self and Social Life* (New York, McGraw-Hill).

Therborn, G. (1980) *The Ideology of Power and the Power of Ideology* (London: Verso).

Thomas, J. (1993) *Doing Critical Ethnography* (Newbury Park: Sage).

Thomas, W. I. (1966 [1928]) 'Situational Analysis: The Behavior Pattern and the Situation', in M. Janovitz (ed.), *W. I. Thomas on Social Organization and Social Personality* (Chicago: Chicago University Press).

Thorne, B. and Henley, N. (eds.) (1975) *Language and Sex: Difference and Dominance* (Rowley, MA: Newbury House).

Thorne, B., Kramarae, C. and Henley, N. (eds.) (1983) *Language, Gender and Society* (Rowley, MA: Newbury House).

Tolmach Lakoff, R. (1981) 'Persuasive Discourse and Ordinary Conversation: With Examples from Sdvertising', in D. Tannen (ed.), *Analyzing Discourse: Text and Talk* (Washington, DC: Georgetown University Press), pp. 25–42.

Treichler, P., Frankel, R. M., Kramarae, C., Zoppi, C. and Beckman, H. B. (1984) 'Problems and Problems: Power Relationships in a Medical Interview', in C. Kramarae, M. Schultz and W. M. O'Barr (eds.), *Language and Power* (Beverly Hills, CA: Sage), pp. 43–61.

Troyna, B. (1981) *Public Awareness and the Media: A Study of Reporting on Race* (London: The Commission for Racial Equality).

Trömel-Plötz, S. (ed.) (1984) *Gewalt durch Sprache: Die Vergewaltigung von Frauen in Gesprächen* (Frankfurt: Fischer).

Tuchman, G. (1978) *Making News* (New York: Free Press).

Tuchman, G., Daniels, A. K. and Benet, J. (eds.) (1978) *Hearth and Home: Images of Women in the Mass Media* (New York: Oxford University Press).

Tulving, E. (1983) *Elements of Episodic Memory* (Oxford: Oxford University Press).

Turkel, G. (1996) *Law and Society. Critical Approaches* (Boston, MA: Allyn and Bacon).

Turow, J. (1983) 'Learning to Portray Institutional Power: The Socialization of Creators of Mass Media Organization', in R. D. McPhee and P. K. Tompkins (eds.), *Organizational Communication: Traditional Themes and New Directions* (Beverly Hills, CA: Sage), pp. 211–34.

UNESCO. (1977) *Ethnicity and the Media* (Paris: UNESCO).

UNESCO. (1980) *Many Voices, One World*. Report by the International Commission for the Study of Communication Problems (chaired by Sean MacBride) (Paris: UNESCO and London: Kogan Page).

van Dijk, T. A. (1977) *Text and Context* (London: Longman).

van Dijk, T. A. (1980) *Macrostructures: An Interdisciplinary Study of Global Structures in Discourse, Interaction and Cognition* (Hillsdale, NJ : Lawrence Erlbaum).

van Dijk, T. A. (1981) *Studies in the Pragmatics of Discourse* (The Hague and Berlin: Mouton/de Gruyter).

van Dijk, T. A. (1983) *Minderheden in de media* [*Minorities in the media*] (Amsterdam: Socialistische Uitgeverij Amsterdam).

van Dijk, T. A. (1984a) *Prejudice in Discourse. An Analysis of Ethnic Prejudice in Cognition and Conversation* (Amsterdam: Benjamins).

van Dijk, T. A. (1984b) 'Structures of International News. A Case Study of the World's Press'. Unpublished manuscript (University of Amsterdam, Department of General Literary Studies, Section of Discourse Studies).

van Dijk, T. A. (1985c) 'Cognitive Situation Models in Discourse Processing: The Expression of Ethnic Situation Models in Prejudiced Stories', in J. P. Forgas (ed.), *Language and Social Situations* (New York: Springer), pp. 61–79.

van Dijk, T. A. (1987a) *Communicating Racism: Ethnic Prejudice in Thought and Talk* (Beverly Hilas, CA: Sage).

van Dijk, T. A. (1987b) 'Elite Discourse and Racism', in I. Zavala, T. A. van Dijk and M. Diaz-Diocaretz (eds.), *Approaches to Discourse, Poetics and Psychiatry* (Amsterdam: John Benjamins), pp. 81–122.

van Dijk, T. A. (1987c) 'Episodic Models in Discourse Processing', in R. Horowitz and S. J. Samuels (eds.), *Comprehending Oral and Written Language* (San Diego CA, Academic Press), pp. 161–96.

van Dijk, T. A. (1987d) *Schoolvoorbeelden van racism* [*Textbook examples of racism*] (Amsterdam: Socialistische Uitgeverij Amsterdam).

van Dijk, T. A. (1987e) 'How "they" Hit the Headlines: Ethnic Minorities in the Press', in G. Smitherman-Donaldson and T. A. van Dijk (eds.), *Discourse and Discrimination* (Detroit: Wayne State University Press), pp. 221–62.

van Dijk, T. A. (1988a) *News Analysis. Case Studies of International and National News in the Press* (Hillsdale, NJ: Lawrence Erlbaum).

van Dijk, T. A. (1988b) *News as Discourse* (Hillsdale, NJ: Lawrence Erlbaum).

van Dijk, T. A. (1988c) 'The Tamil Panic in the Press', in T. A. van Dijk, *News Analysis* (Hillsdale, NJ: Lawrence Erlbaum, pp. 215–54.

van Dijk, T. A. (1989) 'Structures of Discourse and Structures of Power', in J. A. Anderson (ed.), *Communication Yearbook 12* (Newbury Park, CA: Sage), pp. 18–59.

van Dijk, T. A. (1990) 'Social Cognition and Discourse', in H. Giles and R. P. Robinson (eds.), *Handbook of Social Psychology and Language* (Chichester: Wiley), pp. 163–83.

van Dijk, T. A. (1991) *Racism and the Press* (London: Routledge).

van Dijk, T. A. (1993a) *Elite Discourse and Racism* (Newbury Park, CA: Sage).

van Dijk, T. A. (1993b) 'Discourse and Cognition in Society', in D. Crowley and D. Mitchell (eds.), *Communication Theory Today* (Oxford: Pergamon), pp. 104–26.

van Dijk, T. A. (1993c) 'Principles of Critical Discourse Analysis'. *Discourse and Society*, 4(2): 249–83.

van Dijk, T. A. (1996) 'Discourse, Power and Access', in C. R. Caldas-Coulthard and M. Coulthard (eds.), *Texts and Practices: Readings in Critical Discourse Analysis* (London: Routledge), pp. 84–104.

van Dijk, T. A. (1997a) 'Cognitive Context Models and Discourse', in M. Stamenow (ed.), *Language Structure, Discourse and the Access to Consciousness* (Amsterdam, John Benjamins), pp. 189–226.

van Dijk, T. A. (1997b) 'What is Political Discourse Analysis?', in J. Blommaert and C. Bulcaen (eds.), *Political Linguistics* (Amsterdam: John Benjamins), pp. 11–52.

van Dijk, T. A. (1998) *Ideology: A Multidisciplinary Approach* (London: Sage).

van Dijk, T. A. (1999) ' Towards a Theory of Context and Experience Models in Discourse Processing', in H. van Oostendorp and S. Goldman (eds.), *The Construction of Mental Models during Reading* (Hillsdale, NJ: Lawrence Erlbaum), pp. 123–48.

van Dijk, T. A. (2000) 'Parliamentary Debates', in: R. Wodak and T. A. van Dijk (eds.), *Racism at the Top. Parliamentary Discourses on Ethnic Issues in Six European States* (Klagenfurt, Austria: Drava Verlag), pp. 45–78.

van Dijk, T. A. (2001) 'Multidisciplinary CDA: A Plea for Diversity', in Ruth Wodak and Michael Meyer (eds.), *Methods of Critical Discourse Analysis* (London: Sage), pp. 95–120.

van Dijk, T. A. (2002) 'Political discourse and political cognition', in: Paul A. Chilton and Christina Schäffner (eds.), *Politics as Text and Talk: Analytical Approaches to Political Discourse* (Amsterdam: John Benjamins), pp. 204–36.

van Dijk, T. A. (2003a) *Ideología y discurso* (Barcelona: Ariel).

van Dijk, T. A. (2003b) 'Knowledge in Parliamentary Debates'. *Journal of Language and Politics*, 2(1): 93–129.

van Dijk, T. A. (2004) 'Text and Context of Parliamentary Debates', in Paul Bayley (ed.), *Cross-Cultural Perspectives on Parliamentary Discourse* (Amsterdam: John Benjamins), 339–72.

van Dijk, T. A. (2005) 'Contextual Knowledge Management in Discourse Production. A CDA Perspective', in Ruth Wodak and Paul Chilton (eds.), *A New Agenda in (Critical) Discourse Analysis* (Amsterdam: John Benjamins), pp. 71–100.

van Dijk, T. A. (2008a) *Discourse and Context: A Sociocognitive Approach* (Cambridge: Cambridge University Press).

van Dijk, T. A. (2008b) *Society and Discourse: How Contexts Influence Text and Talk* (Cambridge: Cambridge University Press).

van Dijk, T. A. (ed.) (1985a) *Handbook of Discourse Analysis* (4 vols.) (London: Academic Press).

van Dijk, T. A. (ed.) (1985b) *Discourse and Communication. New Approaches to the Analysis of Mass Media Discourse and Communication* (Berlin: de Gruyter).

van Dijk, T. A. (ed.) (1997) *Discourse Studies: A Multidisciplinary Introduction* (London: Sage).

van Dijk, T. A. (ed.) (2006) 'Discourse, Interaction and Cognition'. Special issue of *Discourse Studies*, 8(1).

van Dijk, T. A. and Kintsch, W. (1983) *Strategies of Discourse Comprehension* (New York: Academic Press).

van Leeuwen, T. (2005) *Introducing Social Semiotics* (London: Routledge).

van Oostendorp and Goldman, S. R. (eds.) (1999) *The Construction of Mental Representations during Reading* (Mahwah, NJ: Lawrence Erlbaum).

van Oostendorp, H. and Zwaan, R. A. (eds.) (1994) *Naturalistic Text Comprehension* (Norwood NJ, Ablex).

van Zoonen, L. (1994) *Feminist Media Studies* (London: Sage).

Walker, A. G. (1982) 'Patterns and Implications of Co-speech in a Legal Setting', in R. J. Di Pietro (ed.), *Linguistics and the Professions* (Norwood, NJ: Ablex), pp. 110–12.

Walker, A. G. (1986) 'The Verbatim Record: The Myth and the Reality', in S. Fisher and A. D. Todd (eds.), *Discourse and Institutional Authority: Medicine, Education and Law* (Norwood, NJ: Lawrence Erlbaum), pp. 205–22.

Waltzer, M. (2004) *Arguing about War* (New Haven, CT: Yale University Press).

Wartenberg, T. E. (1990) *The Forms of Power: From Domination to Transformation* (Philadelphia, PA: Temple University Press).

Weaver, C. A., Mannes, S. and Fletcher, C. R. (eds.) (1995) *Discourse Comprehension: Essays in Honor of Walter Kintsch* (Hillsdale, NJ: Lawrence Erlbaum).

Wellman, D. T. (1993) *Portraits of White Racism* (Cambridge, UK: Cambridge University Press).

Werner, F. (1983) *Gesprächsverhalten von Männern and Frauen* (Frankfurt: Lang).

West, C. (1984) *Routine Complications: Troubles with Talk between Doctors and Patients* (Bloomington: Indiana University Press).

West, C. and Zimmerman, D. H. (1983) 'Small Insults: A Study of Interruptions in Cross-Sex Conversations between Unacquainted Persons', in B. Thorne, C. Kramarae and N. Henley (eds.), *Language, Gender and Society* (Rowley, MA: Newbury House), pp. 102–17.

West, C. and Zimmerman, D. H. (1985) 'Gender, Language and Discourse', in T. A van Dijk (ed.), *Handbook of Discourse Analysis: Vol. 4. Discourse Analysis in Society* (London: Academic Press), pp. 103–14.

Wetherell, M. and Potter, J. (1992) *Mapping the Language of Racism: Discourse and the Legitimation of Exploitation* (New York: Columbia University Press).

White, D. M. (1976) *The Concept of Power* (Morristown, NJ: General Learning Press).

Wilkinson, L. C. (ed.) (1982) *Communicating in the Classroom* (New York: Academic Press).

Williams, J. (ed.) (1995) *PC Wars: Politics and Theory in the Academy* (New York: Routledge and Kegan Paul).

Willis, P. (1977) *Learning to Labour: How Working Class Kids Get Working Class Jobs* (London: Saxon House).

Wilson, C. C. and Gutiérrez, F. (1985) *Minorities and the Media* (Beverly Hills, CA, and London: Sage).

Wilson, J. . (1990) *Politically Speaking* (Oxford, Blackwell).

Wodak, R. (1984) 'Determination of Guilt: Discourses in the Courtroom', in C. Kramarae, M. Schulz and W. M. O'Barr (eds.), *Language and Power* (Beverly Hills, CA: Sage), pp. 89–100.

Wodak, R. (1985) 'The Interaction between Judge and Defendant', in T. A. van Dijk (ed.) *Handbook of Discourse Analysis, Vol. 4, Discourse Analysis in Society* (London: Academic Press), pp. 181–91.

Wodak, R. (1987) '"And Where Is the Lebanon?" A Socio-Psycholinguistic Investigation of Comprehension and Intelligibility of News', *Text* 7(4): 377–410.

Wodak, R. (1996) *Disorders of Discourse* (London: Longman. London: Sage).

Wodak, R. (1997) Gender and Discourse: Judge and Defendant', in T. A. van Dijk (ed.), *Handbook of Discourse Analysis. Vol. 4. Discourse Analysis in Society* (pp. (London: Academic Press), pp. 181–91.

Wodak, R. (ed.) (1989) *Language, Power and Ideology. Studies in Political Discourse* (Amsterdam: John Benjamins).

Wodak, R. and Chilton, P. (eds.) (2005) *A New Agenda in (Critical) Discourse Analysis* (Amsterdam: John Benjamins).

Wodak, R. and Meyer, M. (eds.) (2001) *Methods of Critical Discourse Analysis* (London: Sage).

Wodak, R., Nowak, P., Pelikan, J., Gruber, H., de Cillia, R. and Mitten, R. (1990) 'Wir sind alle unschuldige Täter', Diskurshistorische Studien zum Nachkriegsantisemitismus ['We are All Innocent Perpetrators'. Discourse Historic Studies in Postwar Antisemitism] (Frankfurt/Main: Suhrkamp).

Wodak, R. and Van Dijk, T. A. (eds.) (2000) *Racism at the Top: Parliamentary Discourses on Ethnic Issues in Six European States* (Klagenfurt, Austria: Drava Verlag).

Wortham, S. and Locher, M. (1999) 'Embedded Metapragmatics and Lying Politicians'. *Language and Communication*, 19(2): 109–25.

Wrong, D. H. (1979) *Power: Its Forms, Bases and Uses* (Oxford: Basil Blackwell).

Wyer, R. S. J. and V. C. Ottati (1993) 'Political Information Processing', in S. Iyengar and W. J. McGuire (eds.), *Explorations in Political Psychology. Duke Studies in Political Psychology* (Durham, NC: Duke University Press), pp. 264–95.

Wyer, R. S., Budesheim, T. L., Shavitt, S., Riggle, E. D., and Kuklinski, J. H. (1991) Image, Issues and Ideology: The Processing of Information about Political Candidates'. *Journal of Personality and Social Psychology*, 61(4): 533–45.

Young, M. (ed.) (1971) *Knowledge and Control: New Directions for the Sociology of Education* (London: Collier-Macmillan).

Zaller, J. R. (1990) 'Political Awareness, Elite Opinion Leadership and the Mass Survey Response'. *Social Cognition*, 8(1): 125–53.

Zanna, M. P. and Olson, J. M. (eds.) (1994) *The Psychology of Prejudice: The Ontario Symposium. Vol. 7* (Hillsdale, NJ: Lawrence Erlbaum).

Zimmerman, H. D. (1969) *Die politische Rede: Der Sprachgebrauch Bonner Politiker* [*Political Speech: Language Use of Bonn's Politicians*] (Stuttgart: Kohlhammer).

Žižek, S. (2002) *Welcome to the Desert of the Real! Five Essays on 11 September and Related Dates* (London: Verso).

Further Reading

The discussion in Chapter 1 has taken place against the background of a vast scholarly literature on power, domination, discourse, cognition and society. Much of this literature is cited in the following chapters. However, for those who would like to have a separate list of literature suggestions for the main fields and topics dealt with in this book, here are some general suggestions for further reading. To limit a potentially vast bibliography, we cite only books in English.

Discourse and conversation analysis

Blommaert, J. (2005) *Discourse: A Critical Introduction* (Cambridge: Cambridge University Press).

Brown, G. and Yule, G. (1983) *Discourse Analysis* (Cambridge: Cambridge University Press).

Georgakopoulou, A. and Goutsos, D. (1997) *Discourse Analysis: An Introduction* (Edinburgh: Edinburgh University Press).

Jaworski, A. and Coupland, N. (1999) *The Discourse Reader* (London: Routledge).

Johnstone, B. (2002) *Discourse Analysis* (Oxford: Blackwell).

Renkema, J. (2004) *Introduction to Discourse Studies* (Amsterdam Philadelphia: John Benjamins).

Schiffrin, D. (1993) *Approaches to Discourse* (Oxford: Blackwell).

Schiffrin, D., Tannen, D. and Hamilton, H. E. (eds.) (2001) *The Handbook of Discourse Analysis* (Malden, MA: Blackwell).

Stubbs, M. (1983) *Discourse Analysis: The Sociolinguistic Analysis of Natural Language* (Chicago: University of Chicago Press and Oxford: Blackwell).

Ten Have, P. (2007) *Doing Conversation Analysis: A Practical Guide*, 2nd edn (London: Sage).

van Dijk, T. A. (ed.) (1985) *Handbook of Discourse Analysis*, 4 vols (London: Academic Press).

van Dijk, T. A. (ed.) (1997a) *Discourse as Structure and Process: Discourse Studies: A Multidisciplinary Introduction, Vol. 1* (Thousand Oaks, CA: Sage Publications).

van Dijk, T. A. (ed.) (1997b) *Discourse as Social Interaction: Discourse Studies: A Multidisciplinary Introduction, Vol. 2* (Thousand Oaks, CA: Sage Publications)

van Dijk, T. A. (ed.) (2007) *Discourse Studies*, 5 vols. Sage Benchmark series (New Delhi: Sage).

Wooffitt, R. (2005) *Conversation Analysis and Discourse Analysis. A Comparative and Critical Introduction* (London: Sage).

Critical Discourse Studies

Bloor, M. and Bloor, T. (2007) *The Practice of Critical Discourse Analysis: An Introduction* (London: Hodder Arnold).

Caldas-Coulthard, C. R. and Coulthard, M. (eds.) (1995) *Texts and Practices: Readings in Critical Discourse Analysis* (London: Routledge).

Chilton, P. (2004) *Analysing Political Discourse* (London: Routledge).

de Beaugrande, R. (1997) *New Foundations for a Science of Text and Discourse: Cognition, Communication, and the Freedom of Access to Knowledge and Society* (Norwood, NJ: Ablex Publishing).

Fairclough, N. (1989) *Language and Power* (London: Longman).

Fairclough, N. (1995) *Critical Discourse Analysis: The Critical Study of Language* (London: Longman).

Fowler, R. (1991) *Language in the News: Discourse and Ideology in the British Press* (London: Routledge).

Fowler, R., Hodge, B., Kress, G. and Trew, T. (1979) *Language and Control* (London: Routledge & Kegan Paul).

Lazar, M. (ed.) (2005) *Feminist Critical Discourse Analysis: Gender, Power and Ideology in Discourse* (Basingstoke: Palgrave Macmillan).

Lemke, J. L. (1995) *Textual Politics: Discourse and Social Dynamics* (London: Taylor & Francis).

Toolan, M. J. (ed.) (2002) *Critical Discourse Analysis: Critical Concepts in Linguistics* (New York: Routledge).

van Dijk, T. A. (1993) *Elite Discourse and Racism* (Newbury Park, CA: Sage).

van Leeuwen, T. (2005) *Introduction to Social Semiotics* (London: Routledge).

Weiss, G. and Wodak, R. (eds.) (2003) *Critical Discourse Analysis: Theory and Interdisciplinarity* (Basingstoke: Palgrave Macmillan).

Wodak, R. (1989) *Language, Power and Ideology: Studies in Political Discourse* (Amsterdam: Benjamins).

Wodak, R. (ed.) (1997) *Gender and Discourse* (London: Sage).

Wodak, R. and Meyer, M. (eds.) (2001) *Methods of Critical Discourse Analysis* (London: Sage).

Young, L. and Harrison, C. (eds.) (2004) *Systemic Functional Linguistics and Critical Discourse Analysis: Studies in Social Change* (London: Continuum).

Power (only books published after 2000)

Bakker, I. and Gill, S. (2003) *Power, Production, and Social Reproduction: Human In/security in the Global Political Economy* (Basingstoke: Palgrave Macmillan).

Barnett, M. N. and Duvall, R. (2004) *Power in Global Governance* (New York: Cambridge University Press).

Chowdhry, G. and Nair, S. (2002) *Power, Postcolonialism, and International Relations: Reading Race, Gender, and Class* (London and New York: Routledge).

Clough, P. and Mitchell, J. P. (eds.) (2001) *Powers of Good and Evil: Moralities, Commodities and Popular Belief* (New York: Berghahn Books).

Dye, T. R. and Harrison, B. C. (2005) *Power and Society* (Belmont, CA: Thomson/Wadsworth).

Egan, D. and Chorbajian, L. (eds.) (2005) *Power: A Critical Reader* (Upper Saddle River, NJ: Pearson Prentice Hall).

Foucault, M. (2000) *Power* (New York: New Press). Distributed by W. W. Norton.

Goverde, H. (2000) *Power in Contemporary Politics: Theories, Practices, Globalizations* (London Thousand Oaks, CA: Sage.

Grillo, E. (ed.) (2005) *Power without Domination: Dialogism and the Empowering Property of Communication* (Amsterdam and Philadelphia: John Benjamins).

Haugaard, M. (ed.) (2002) *Power: A Reader* (Manchester, UK and New York: Manchester University Press). Distributed exclusively in the USA by Palgrave.

Lentner, H. H. (ed.) (2000) *Power in Contemporary Politics: Theories, Practices, Globalizations* (London: Sage).

Lukes, S. (2004) *Power: A Radical View* (Houndmills, UK and New York: Palgrave Macmillan).

Nye, J. S. (2004) *Power in the Global Information Age: From Realism to Globalization* (London and New York: Routledge).

Øterud, Ø. and Engelstad, F. (2004) *Power and Democracy: Critical Interventions* (Aldershot, UK and Burlington, VT: Ashgate).

Russell, B. (2004) *Power: A New Social Analysis* (London and New York: Routledge).

Scott, J. (2001) *Power* (Malden, MA: Blackwell).

Suri, J. (2003) *Power and Protest: Global Revolution and the Rise of Detente* (Cambridge, MA: Harvard University Press).

Westwood, S. (2002) *Power and the Social* (London and New York: Routledge).

Legitimacy

Barker, R. S. (1990) *Political Legitimacy and the State* (Oxford: Clarendon Press and New York: Oxford University Press).

Beetham, D. (1991) *The Legitimation of Power* (Basingstoke: Macmillan).

Clark, I. (2005) *Legitimacy in International Society* (Oxford: Oxford University Press).

Coicaud, J. M. and Curtis, D. A. (ed.) (2002) Legitimacy and Politics: A Contribution to the Study of Political Right and Political Responsibility (Cambridge, UK and New York: Cambridge University Press).

Coicaud, J. M. and Heiskanen, V. (eds.) (2001) *The Legitimacy of International Organizations* (Tokyo and New York: United Nations University Press).

Connolly, W. E. (ed.) (1984) *Legitimacy and the State* (Oxford: Blackwell).

Franck, T. M. (1990) *The Power of Legitimacy among Nations* (New York: Oxford University Press).

Freedman, J. O. (1978) *Crisis and Legitimacy: The Administrative Process and American Government* (Cambridge, UK and New York: Cambridge University Press).

Habermas, J. (1975) *Legitimation Crisis* (Boston, MA: Beacon Press).

Jost, J. T. and Major, B. (eds.) (2001) *The Psychology of Legitimacy: Emerging Perspectives on Ideology, Justice, and Intergroup Relations* (Cambridge and New York: Cambridge University Press).

Mueller, C. (1973) *The Politics of Communication:. A Study in the Political Sociology of Language, Socialization, and Legitimation* (New York: Oxford University Press).

Raz, J. (ed.) (1990) *Authority* (New York: New York University Press).

Schmitt, C. and Seitzer, J. (ed.) (2004) *Legality and Legitimacy* (Durham, NC: Duke University Press).

Simmons, A. J. (2001) *Justification and Legitimacy: Essays on Rights and Obligations* (Cambridge New York: Cambridge University Press).

Sniderman, P. M. (1996) *The Clash of Rights: Liberty, Equality, and Legitimacy in Pluralist Democracy* (New Haven, CN: Yale University Press).

Discourse and power

Aronowitz, S. (1988) *Science as Power: Discourse and Ideology in Modern Society* (Houndmills, Basingstoke: Macmillan).

Barsamian, D. (1992) *Stenographers to Power: Media and Propaganda: Interviews with Noam Chomsky et al.* (Monroe, Maine: Common Courage Press).

Blackledge, A. (2005) *Discourse and Power in a Multilingual World* (Amsterdam Philadelphia: John Benjamins).

Bourdieu, P., Passeron, J. C. and De Saint Martin, M. (1994) *Academic Discourse: Linguistic Misunderstanding and Professorial Power* (Stanford, CA: Stanford University Press).

Corson, D. (1995) *Discourse and Power in Educational Organizations* (Cresskill, NJ: Hampton Press).

Daudi, P. (1986) *Power in the Organisation: The Discourse of Power in Managerial Praxis* (Oxford, UK and New York: Blackwell).

Diamond, J. (1996) *Status and Power in Verbal Interaction: A Study of Discourse in a Close-Knit Social Network* (Amsterdam and Philadelphia: John Benjamins).

Fairclough, N. (1989) *Language and Power* (Harlow: Longman).

Fisher, S. and Todd, A. D. (eds.) (1988) *Gender and Discourse: The Power of Talk* (Norwood, NJ: Ablex).

Fraser, N. (1989) *Unruly Practices: Power, Discourse, and Gender in Contemporary Social Theory* (Minneapolis: University of Minnesota Press).

Kedar, L. (ed.) (1987) *Power through Discourse* (Norwood, NJ: Ablex).

Mumby, D. K. (1988) *Communication and Power in Organizations: Discourse, Ideology, and Domination* (Norwood, NJ: Ablex).

Pujolar, J. (2001) *Gender, Heteroglossia, and Power: A Sociolinguistic Study of Youth Culture* (Berlin and New York: Mouton de Gruyter).

Smith, D. E. (1990) *The Conceptual Practices of Power: A Feminist Sociology of Knowledge* (Boston, MA: Northeastern University Press).

Thornborrow, J. (2002) *Power Talk: Language ad Interaction in Institutional Discourse* (London: Longman).

Wodak, R. (1989) *Language, Power, and Ideology: Studies in Political Discourse* (Amsterdam and Philadelphia: J. Benjamins).

Young, L. (2006) *The Power of Language: How Discourse Influences Society* (London Oakville, CT: Equinox).

Discourse and cognition

Britton, B. K. and Black, J. B. (eds.) (1985) *Understanding Expository Text: A Theoretical and Practical Handbook for Analyzing Explanatory Text* (Hillsdale, NJ: Lawrence Erlbaum Associates).

Edwards, D. (1997) *Discourse and Cognition* (London: Sage).

Flower, L. (1989) *Planning in Writing: The Cognition of a Constructive Process* (Berkeley, CA: University of California Press; Pittsburgh, PA: Carnegie Mellon University).

Garnham, A. (1987) *Mental Models as Representations of Discourse and Text* (Chichester and New York: E. Horwood Halsted Press).

Gernsbacher, M. A. and Givon, T. (eds.) (1995) *Coherence in Spontaneous Text* (Amsterdam, The Netherlands: John Benjamins).

Goldman, S. R., Van den Broek, P. W. and Graesser, A. C. (eds.) (1999) *Narrative Comprehension, Causality, and Coherence. Essays in Honor of Tom Trabasso* (Mahwah, NJ: Lawrence Erlbaum Associates).

Graesser, A. C., Gernsbacher, M. A. and Goldman, S. R. (eds.) (2003) *Handbook of Discourse Processes* (Mahwah, NJ: Lawrence Erlbaum).

Herman, D. (ed.) (2003) *Narrative Theory and the Cognitive Sciences* (Stanford, CA: CSLI).

Johnson-Laird, P. N. (1983) *Mental Models: Towards a Cognitive Science of Language, Inference and Consciousness* (Cambridge and New York: Cambridge University Press).

Kasher, A. (ed.) (1989) *Cognitive Aspects of Language Use* (Elsevier Science).

Kintsch, W. (1998) *Comprehension: A Paradigm for Cognition* (New York: Cambridge University Press).

Koenig, J. P. (ed.) (1998) *Discourse and Cognition: Bridging the Gap* (Stanford, CA: CSLI).

Liebert, W. A., Redeker, G. and Waugh, L. R. (eds.) (1997) *Discourse and Perspective in Cognitive Linguistics* (Amsterdam and Philadelphia: John Benjamins).

Malrieu, J. P. (1999) *Evaluative Semantics: Cognition, Language, and Ideology* (London and New York: Routledge).

Molder, H. and Potter, J. (eds.) (2005) *Conversation and Cognition* (Cambridge, UK and New York: Cambridge University Press).

Oakhill, J. and Garnham, A. (eds.) (1992) *Discourse Representation and Text Processing* (Hove: Psychology Press).

Semino, E. and Culpeper, J. (eds.) (2002) *Cognitive Stylistics: Language and Cognition in Text Analysis* (Amsterdam and Philadelphia: John Benjamins).

Singer, M. (1990) Psychology of Language: *An Introduction to Sentence and Discourse Processes* (Hillsdale, NJ: Lawrence Erlbaum).

van Dijk, T. A. and Kintsch, W. (1983) *Strategies of Discourse Comprehension* (New York and London: Academic Press).

van Oostendorp, H. and Goldman, S. R. (eds.) (1999) *The Construction of Mental Representations during Reading* (Mahwah, NJ: Lawrence Erlbaum).

van Oostendorp, H. and Zwaan, R. A. (eds.) (1994) *Naturalistic Text Comprehension* (Norwood, NJ: Ablex).

Weaver, C. A., Mannes, S. and Fletcher, C. R. (eds.) (1995) *Discourse Comprehension: Essays in Honor of Walter Kintsch* (Hillsdale, NJ: Lawrence Erlbaum).

Name Index

Subject Index

racist reporting, 20–1, 24; _see also_ racism and the press
racist talk, 44–6; _see also_ conversation, and discourse
radical media, 37, 58
relevance, 249, 238
reproduction of social power, 9ff.
research, and racism, 76
resolution 144
reversal, of accusation of racism, 128, 151–2
rhetoric, 105
rhetoric, political discourse, 182
rhetoric, war, 185–210
rhetorical question, 252
Rushdie, Salman, 77, 158

schemas,
    discourse, 105
    political discourse, 179
scope,
    of access, 69–70
    power, 40
scripts, knowledge, 160
security, 203–7
security council, 194, 234
self-disclosure, 52
semantic memory, 159ff.
setting, and access, 69
short-term memory, manipulation, 217–19
situation, 238
    defining the, 191ff., 240
    discourse analysis as, 12ff.
    and power, 66
    ideology as, 34
    manipulating, 221
social
    inequality, 8
    influence on discourse, 16
    power, 29
    problems, 6, 7
    representations, 222
    structure, 4, 16
social–political functions of racism denial, 128–32
society, and manipulation, 213ff.
sounds, 104
speech acts, 105
    and power, 37, 90
speech style, 45
state terrorism, 225

stereotypes, in textbooks, 115
Stokes, Sir John, 157ff.
stories, and racism, 110, 132–3
strikes, and news, 61
style,
    and racism, 133
    political discourse, 182
Sun, The, 139ff.
symbolic elites, 14, 32, 36, 37, 38
symbolic power, 12, 14, 32, 33
syntax, 104
systemic linguistics, 237

talk,
    classroom, 49
    courtroom, 98
talk, racist, 44–6; _see also_ discourse; racism
teaching CDS, 24
terrorism, 205f.
textbooks, 12, 61–2
    and ideology, 36–7
    and racism, 114–16
    and stereotypes, 115
    and Third World, 62, 115
texts, institutional, 54
    topics of conversation, 109
Third World,
    and news, 57
    in textbooks, 62, 115
topics
    of conversation, racist, 109
    and power, 91
    and racism, 112, 132
    news, 60
    of political discourse, 179
topoi, 198–9
    in parliamentary discourse, 117
triangle, discourse–cognition–society, 16, 213
turn-taking, 43

UNESCO, 57

values, 225
verbal derogation, 45
violation of human rights, 19

war rhetoric, 185–210
written discourse, 54

Zapatero, José Luís Rodríguez, 254ff.